I0753986

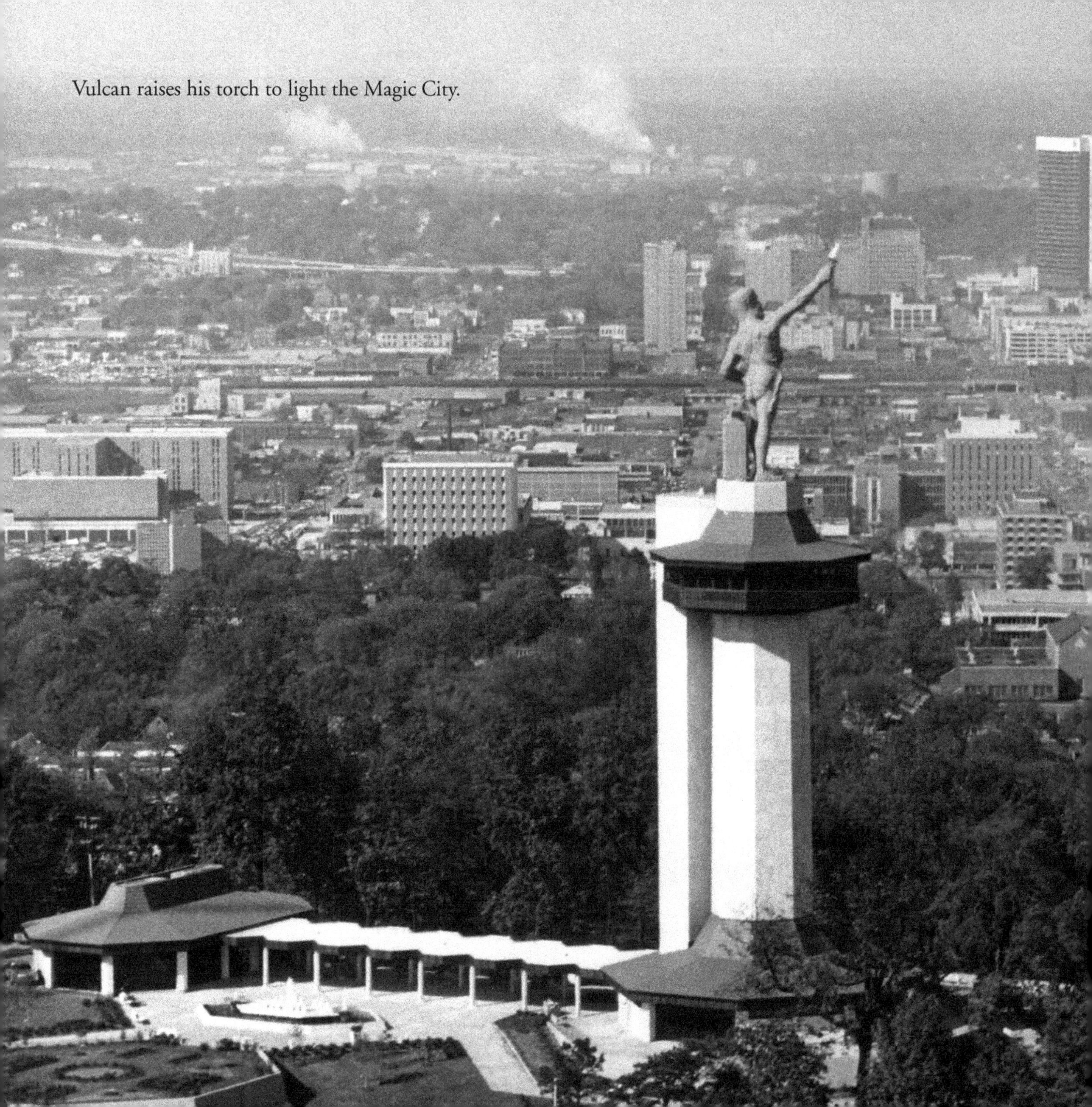

Vulcan raises his torch to light the Magic City.

HISTORIC PHOTOS OF BIRMINGHAM IN THE 50s, 60s, AND 70s

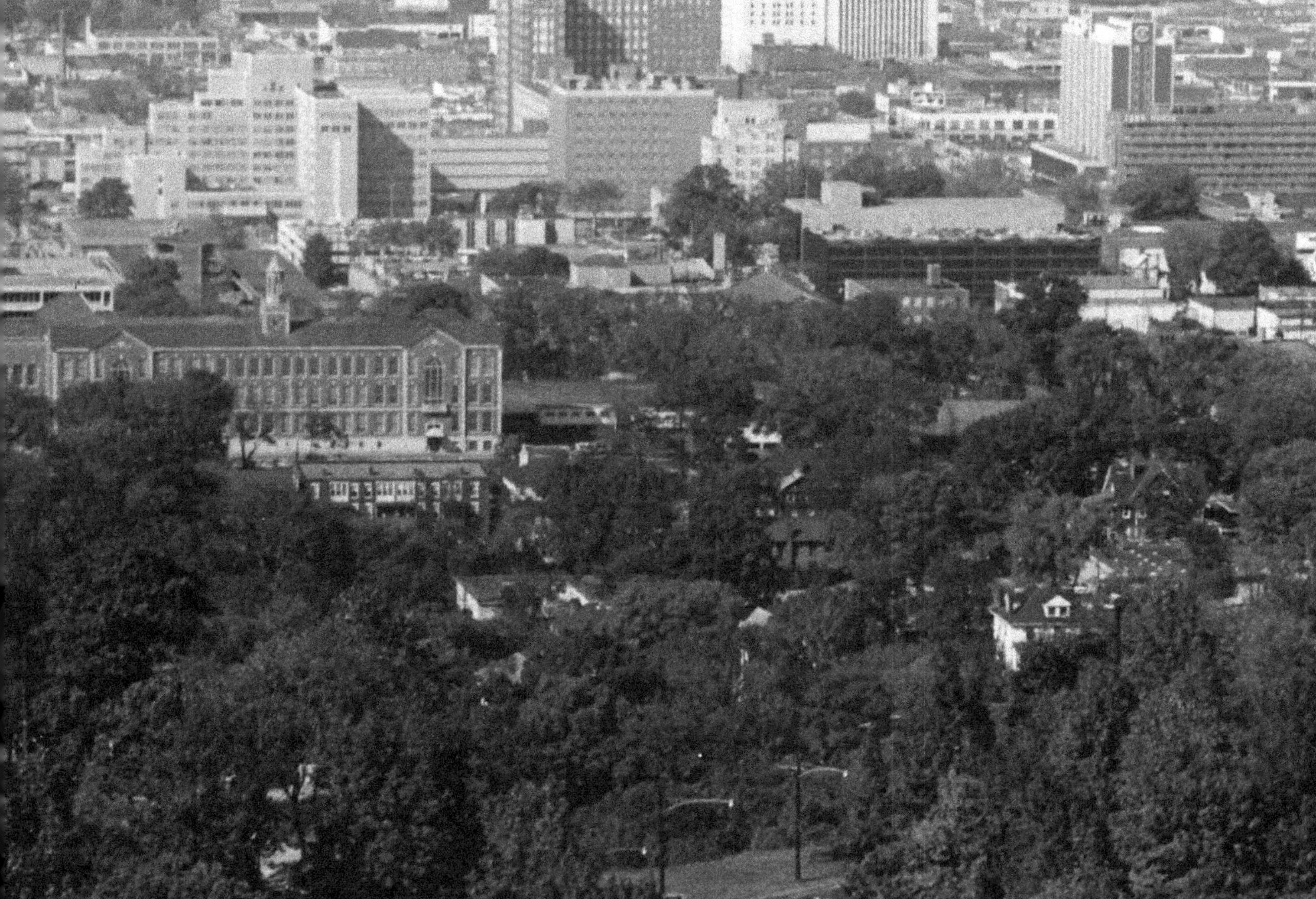

Turner Publishing Company
www.turnerpublishing.com

Historic Photos of Birmingham in the 50s, 60s, and 70s

Library of Congress Control Number: 2010932272

ISBN: 978-1-59652-752-2

Printed in the United States of America

ISBN 978-1-68442-129-9 (hc)

Contents

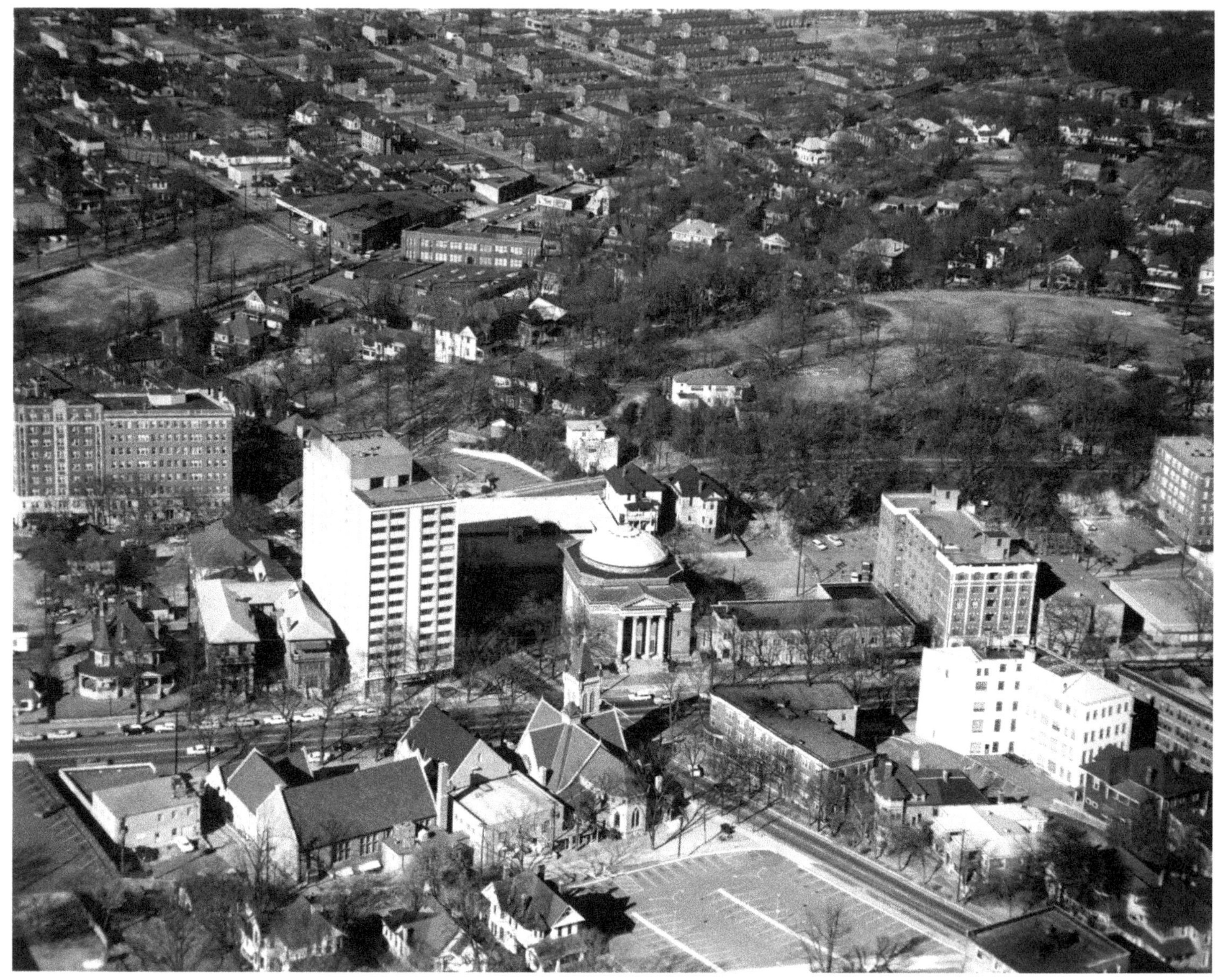

From a good vantage point on Red Mountain, the rear of South Highlands Presbyterian Church, 21 Restaurant, Temple Emanu-El, and some apartment buildings and a few houses are visible.

Acknowledgments

This volume, *Historic Photos of Birmingham in the 50s, 60s, and 70s,* is the result of the cooperation and efforts of many individuals and organizations. It is with great thanks that we acknowledge the valuable contribution of the Birmingham Public Library and the University of Alabama at Birmingham for their generous support, along with the following individuals:

James Baggett, Birmingham Public Library Archives
Don Veasey, Birmingham Public Library Archives
Yolanda Valentin, Birmingham Public Library Archives
Gigi Gowdy, Birmingham Public Library Archives
Jason Kirby, Birmingham Public Library
Elizabeth Willauer, Birmingham Public Library
Ben Petersen, Birmingham Public Library
Timothy L. Pennycuff, University of Alabama at Birmingham Archives
Jennifer L. Beck, University of Alabama at Birmingham Archives

We also wish to acknowledge the continued support of the Birmingham Public Library Board:

Gwendolyn B. Guster Welch, President
Shanta' Craig Owens, Vice-President
Samuel A. Ruemore, Jr., Parliamentarian
E. Bryding Adams
Thomas J. Adams, Jr.
Nell Allen
Gwendolyn R. Amamoo
Georgia Morgan Blair
Anthony Alann Johnson
Dora Sims

And special thanks to William A. Bell, Mayor of Birmingham

PREFACE

Look at a photograph. Is it just a pretty picture to accompany an interesting story or can it be something more? Could it be that a simple snap of a camera can capture more than what the photographer originally intended? Indeed, photographs often contain a vast amount of insight into the past, preserving far more than the original photographer may have been conscious of when he recorded the image. Jim Baggett, head archivist at the Birmingham Public Library Department of Archives and Manuscripts, agrees: "Photographs are not just illustrations but historical documents that can be read for historical information."

The snapshots presented in this book contain a vast amount of knowledge about Birmingham, Alabama, during the prosperous 1950s, turbulent 1960s, and changing 1970s. With pictures, one of the most important senses, sight, is engaged. As a result, photographs can sometimes give a more complete view of history than a simple written document. The structure of society, organization of government, the reactions of people to the events happening around them, evolution of fashion trends, the marketing tactics of advertisers, the impact of entertainment, and the importance of religious observations are just a small fraction of what can be gleaned from a photograph.

Much thought was given to selecting the images that appear in this book. Historic events, famous visitors to Birmingham, average citizens, prominent Birmingham architecture, and memorable landmarks are just some of the subjects that were chosen. These photographs will introduce the reader to yesteryear of the recent past and broaden his knowledge of how Birmingham today came to be.

The book is divided into three sections. Chapter 1 covers Birmingham during the 1950s and includes billowing Sloss Furnaces, a visit with beautiful Miss Alabama, the public's race to sales at Birmingham department stores, and blockbuster movies hitting downtown theaters. Chapter 2 highlights the transformational events of the 1960s, for better or worse, such as the construction of new buildings that altered the landscape, youngsters racing in the Soap

Box Derby, Birmingham honoring its veterans during Veteran's Day parades, and the turbulent protests of the civil rights movement. Chapter 3 is dedicated to the 1970s, when medical research and educational institutions emerged as key players in the city's economy, new roadways were carved into the local terrain, and the demographic move to the suburbs went mainstream.

The Birmingham Public Library Department of Archives and Manuscripts houses most of the historic photographs seen in this book. In partnership with Turner Publishing Company and the University of Alabama at Birmingham Archives, it is a great honor to present these pictures to the general public. It is our hope and desire that this book will not only entertain readers but add to their knowledge of recent city history and reinforce recognition of the vital role they play in the future of the community. The old truism still applies: those who do not learn from the past are doomed to repeat it. The history of Birmingham is not closed; it is still being written, and those who call the city home are its writers. So delve deep into each photograph, learn from them, and enjoy looking at these windows into the past.

—Jessica L. Barton

A man points to the construction of Birmingham City Hall. Completed in December 1950, by May 1951 it needed to be remodeled and repaired owing to faulty roofing. In the cornerstone is a time capsule that will be opened in 2050.

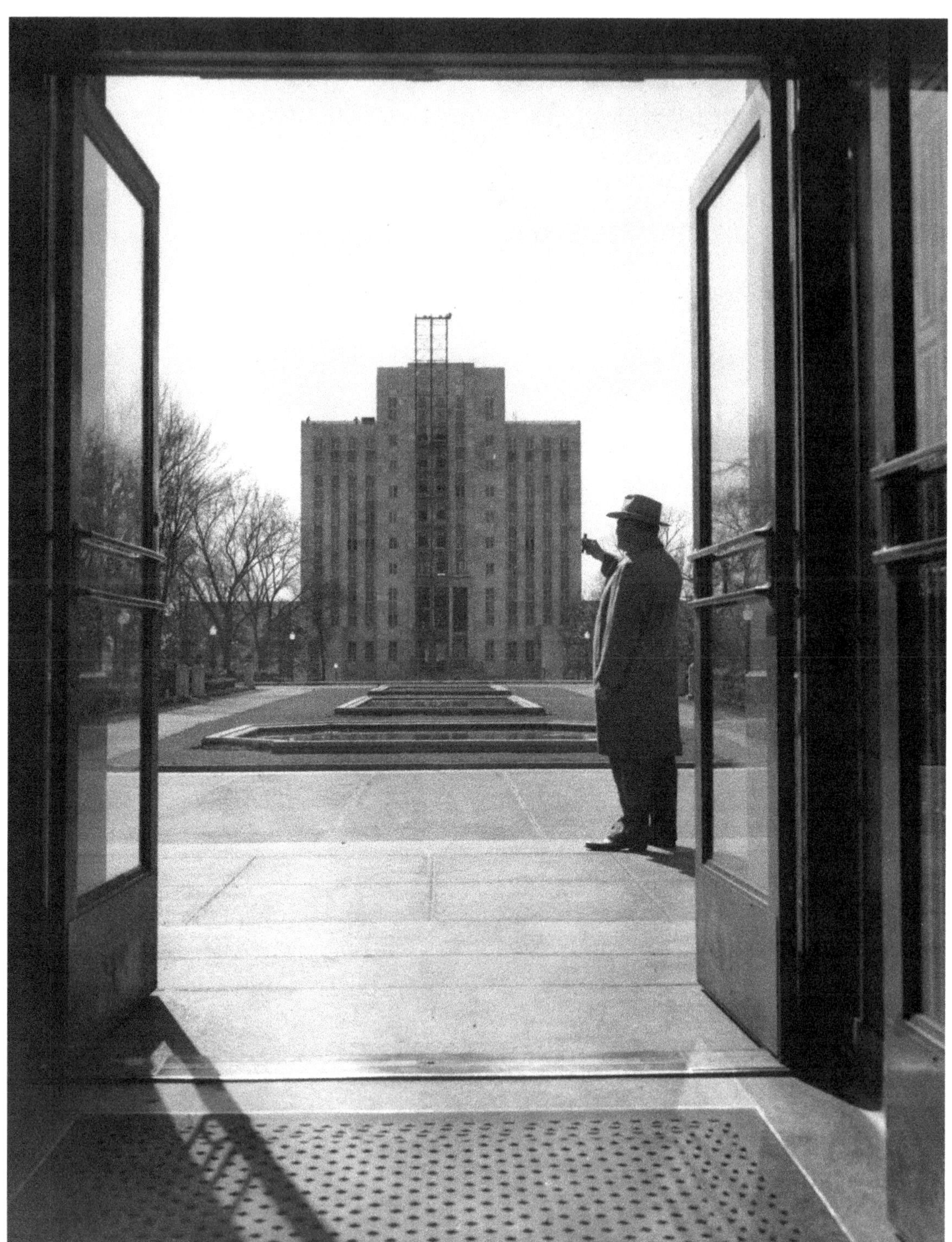

Steel Giant with a Glass Jaw

(1950–1959)

After the Great Depression of the 1930s and the war-torn years of the 1940s, Birmingham was more than ready for peace and prosperity. World War II had helped resuscitate the local economy, which by the 1950s was booming, nevermind the fact that Birmingham's continued dependence on the coal and steel industry, and the refusal of some city leaders to take industrial risks, created a "steel giant with a glass jaw," as Irving Beiman described it in the *Birmingham News*. The photographs in this section portray the excitement of shoppers as they visit downtown shops, activities for youngsters like racing in the Shell Oil Soap Box Derby, fashion shows on early WAFM-TV for the woman about town, and football games at Legion Field for football fans.

After the war, city leaders were also able to focus on cultural improvements. The revival of the Birmingham Symphony, the founding of the Birmingham Zoo, and the establishment of the Birmingham Museum of Art were all key cultural accomplishments undertaken during the 1950s. In addition to being the native home of famous actors, Birmingham also helped launch the careers of country singers. The city was visited by celebrities like Fess Parker, one of Walt Disney's best-liked movie stars, and Eddie Rickenbacker, the World War I flying ace and race car driver.

The poorly diversified economy did not go unheeded, and business helped lead the way in making improvements. Insurance companies along with banking became staples of the downtown Birmingham business district. Department stores, like Pizitz, Loveman's, and Woolworth's, though not economic powerhouses, helped keep the economy on a steady footing. Nothing, however, would revolutionize Birmingham like the Medical Center. Its impact had been felt for years, but it was during the 1950s that it began to become a key component in the fabric of the economy.

Segregation remained an axiom of truth unquestioned and understood during the decade, despite a growing undercurrent of discontent. *Brown v. Board of Education,* a 1954 landmark ruling that deemed as unconstitutional separate schools for blacks and whites, and the 1955 Montgomery Bus Boycott would ignite the Birmingham civil rights movement of the 1960s, but in the current decade the city breathed with relief and brimmed with promise. The photographs included here represent a Birmingham enjoying a period of contented growth and development.

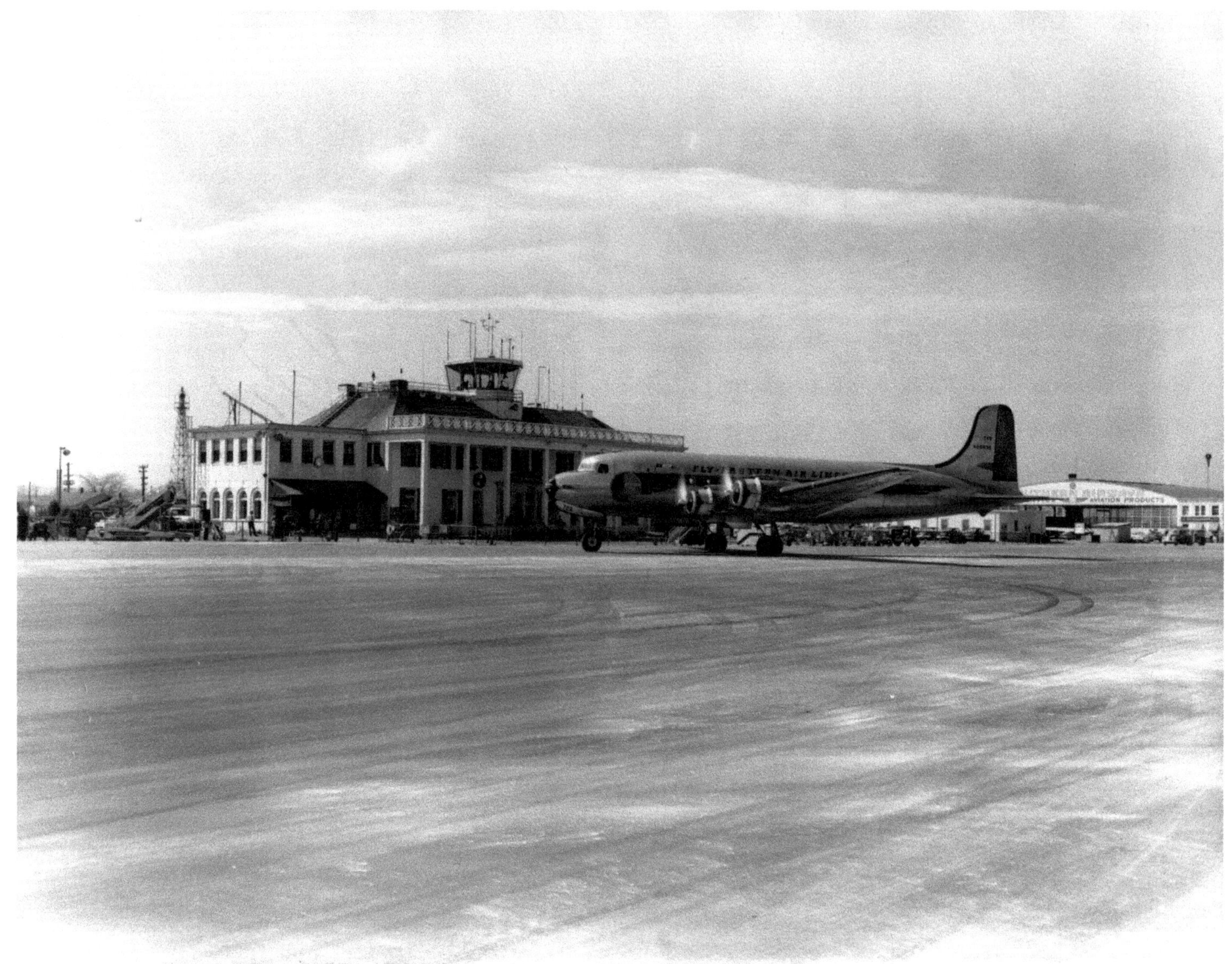

An Eastern Air Lines four-engine propeller plane is ready for takeoff at the Birmingham Municipal Airport. The age of commercial jet travel was coming, but propeller-driven aircraft provided the flying public its wings throughout much of the 1950s.

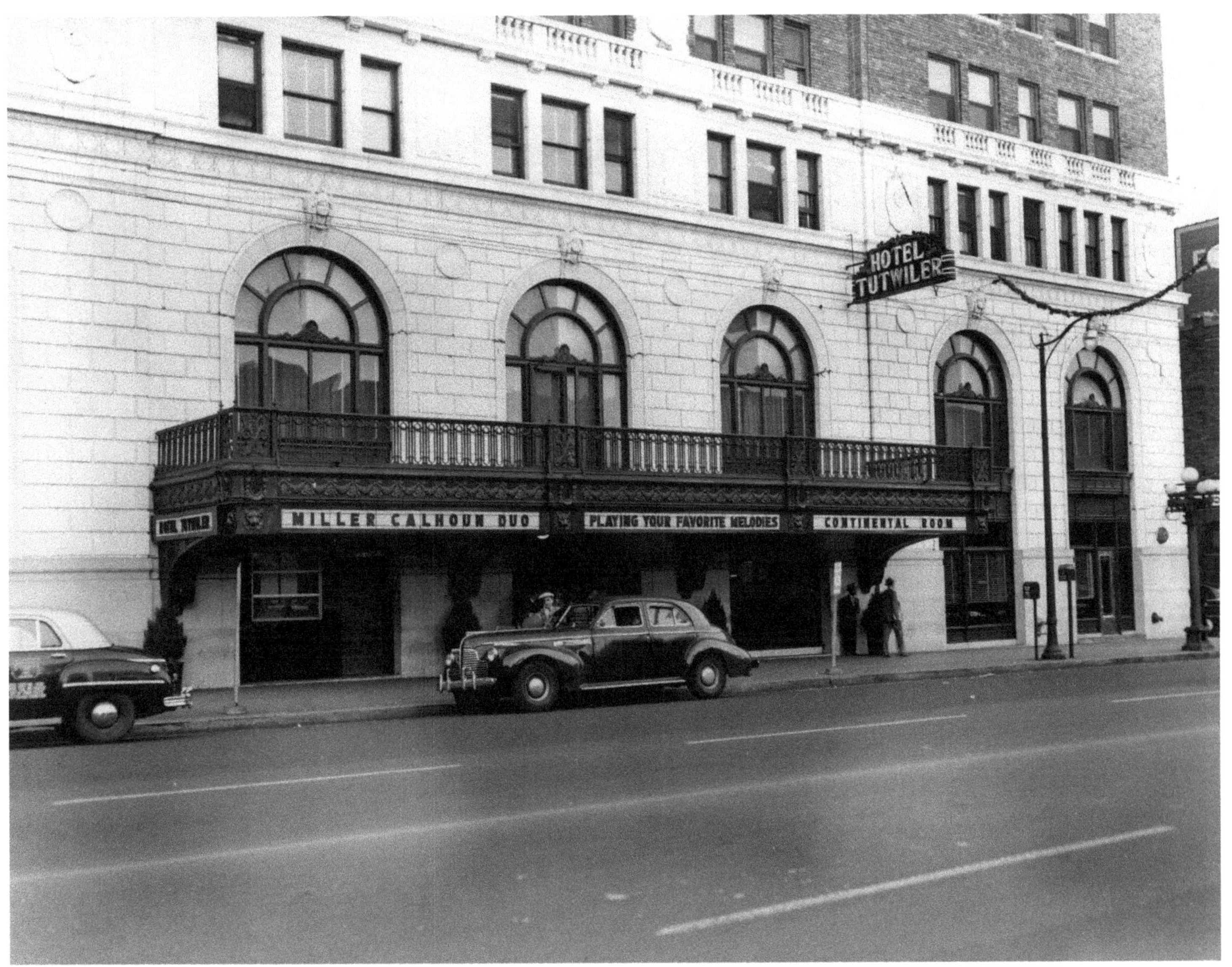

Named after the principal stockholder, Major Edward M. Tutwiler, the Tutwiler Hotel opened in 1914. Urged by the president of the Tennessee Coal, Iron and Railroad Company to build a hotel that would attract representatives of the nation's iron and steel industry, Robert Jemison, Jr., developed the luxurious hotel to cater to these and other prominent visitors to the city.

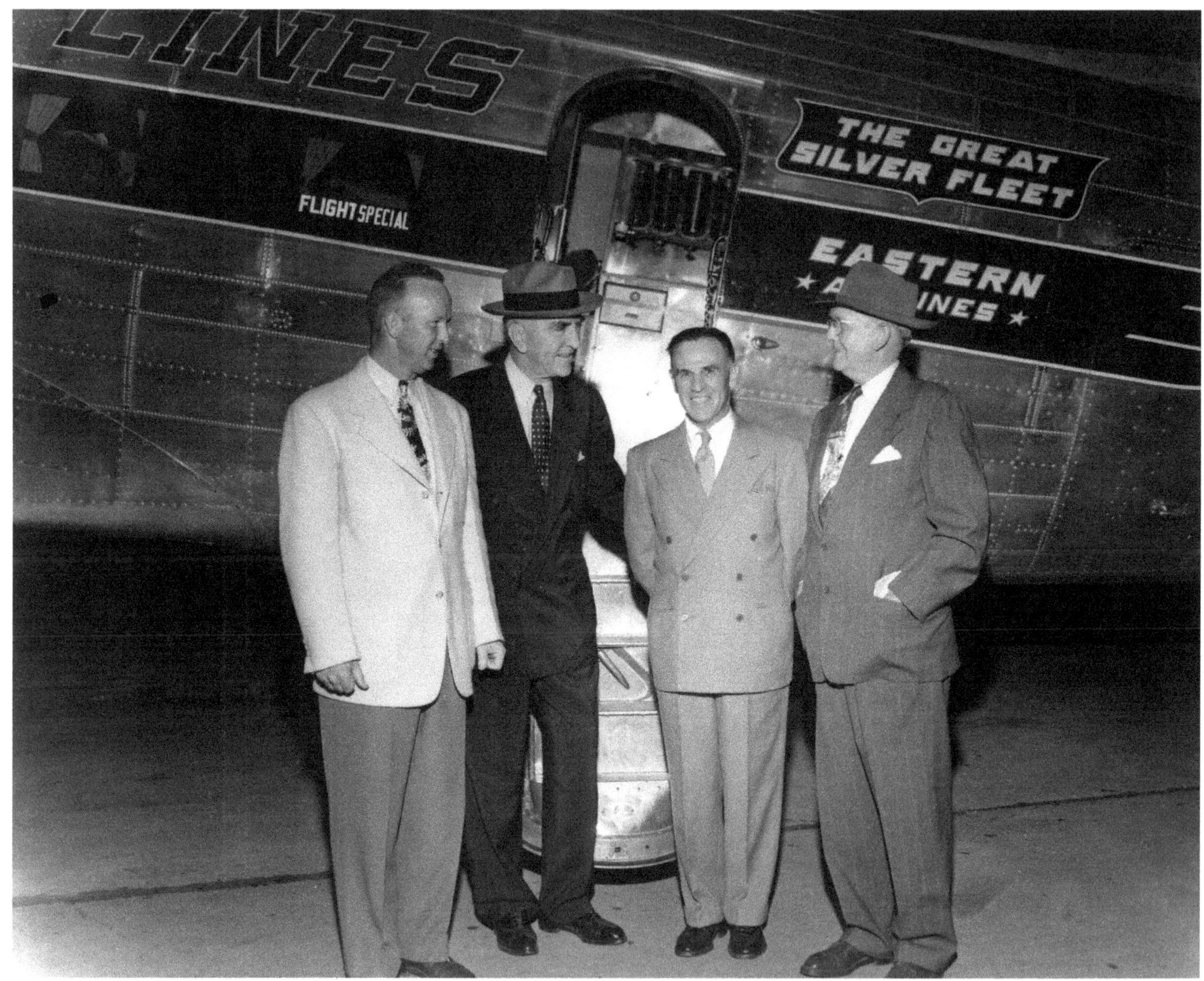

Eddie Rickenbacker, renowned World War I ace, race-car driver, and Eastern Airlines CEO, visited Birmingham in the 1950s. During the Great War, Rickenbacker had become good friends with James Meissner, who later organized the flight industry in Birmingham.

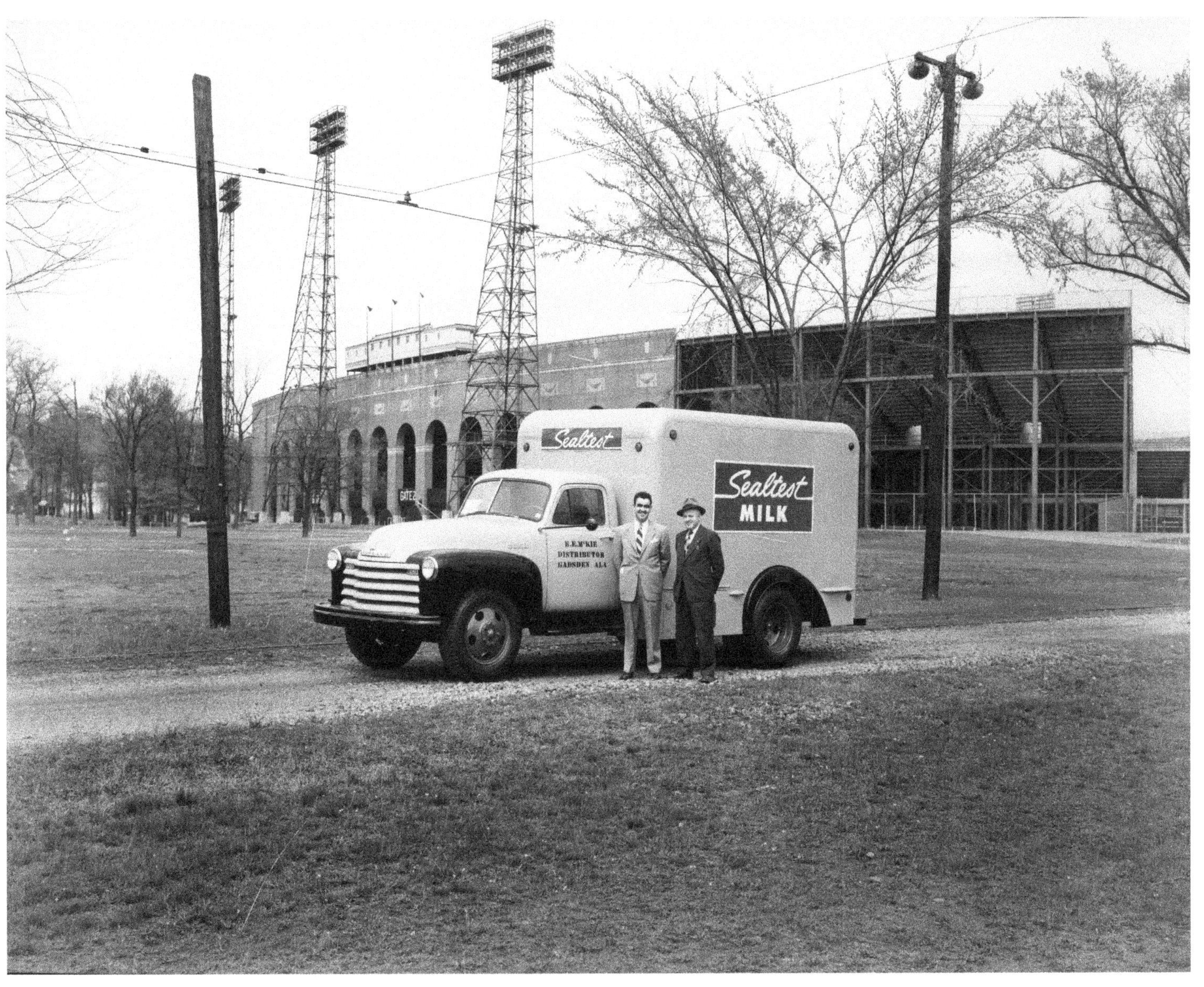

A Sealtest delivery truck filled with Southern Dairies products and crew pose for a publicity shot. Visible in the background is Legion Field, the venue for many sporting events in Birmingham.

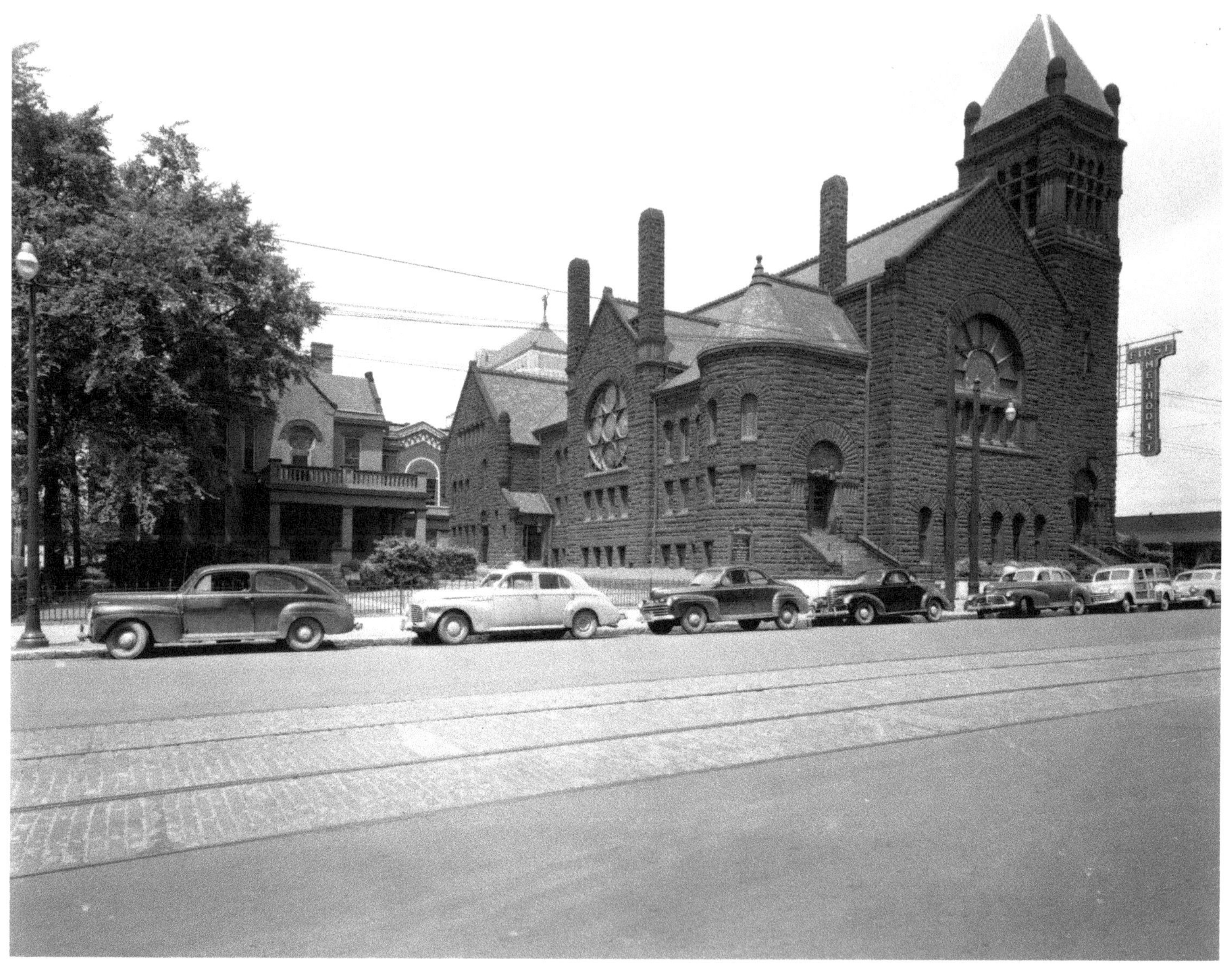

First Methodist Church holds the distinction of being the first Methodist congregation to be organized in Birmingham. Its first building was constructed on land donated by James Withers Sloss, one of the founders of Birmingham and Sloss Furnace creator. The building shown, made of Ohio Brownstone and featuring Romanesque architecture, is located at 530 19th North.

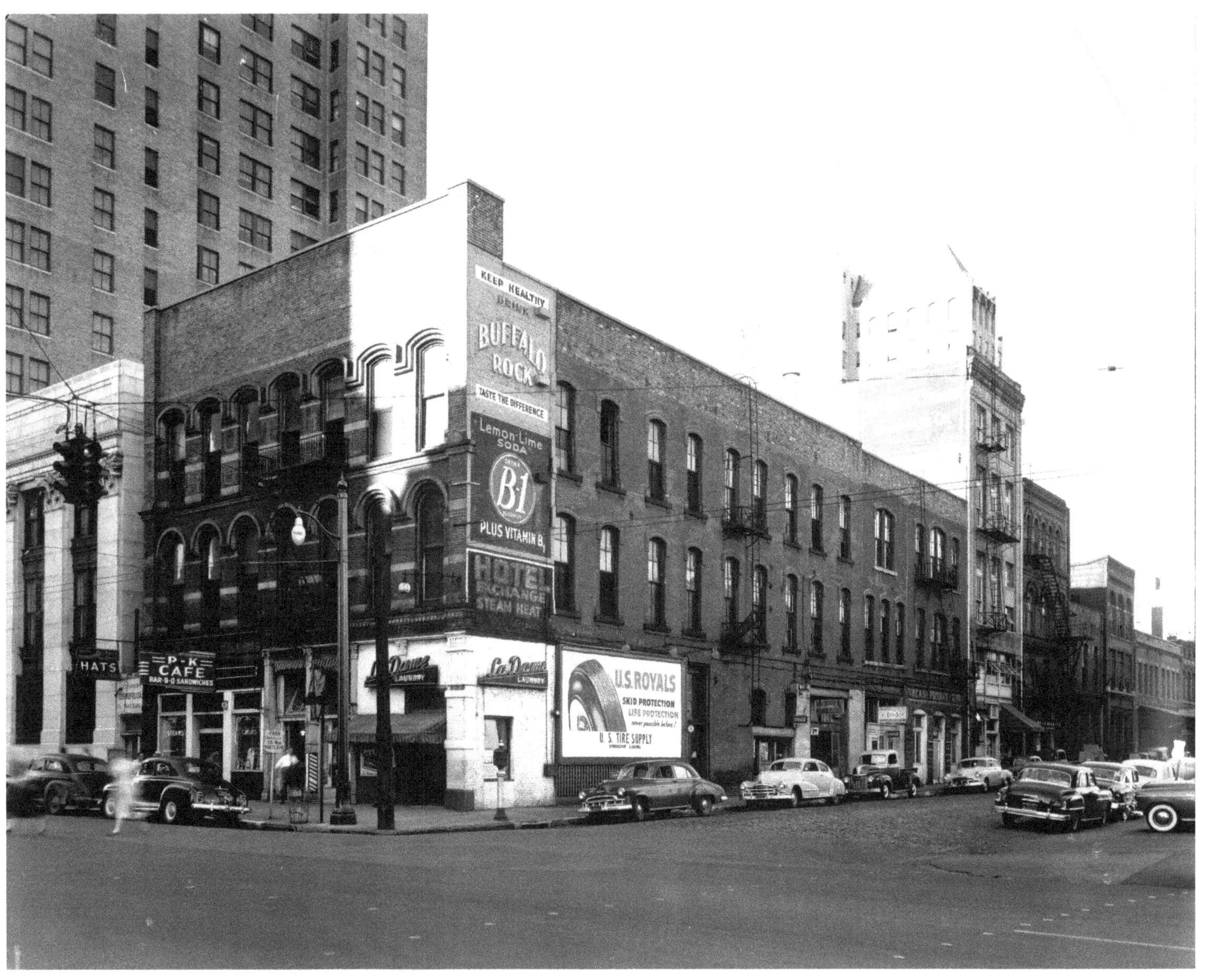

LaDame Laundry Cleaners and the Gilbert Hotel along with other businesses stand at the intersection of Morris Avenue and 20th Street North. This building was originally the offices of Elyton Land Company, the company responsible for the founding of Birmingham in 1871.

Located in midtown, the Watts Building is an example of 1920s Art Deco. In 1927, Thomas Haynes Watts III commissioned its construction to replace the original four-story Watts Building. The new building, with its terra cotta gables, dormer windows, and high mansard roof, cost $1,000,000.

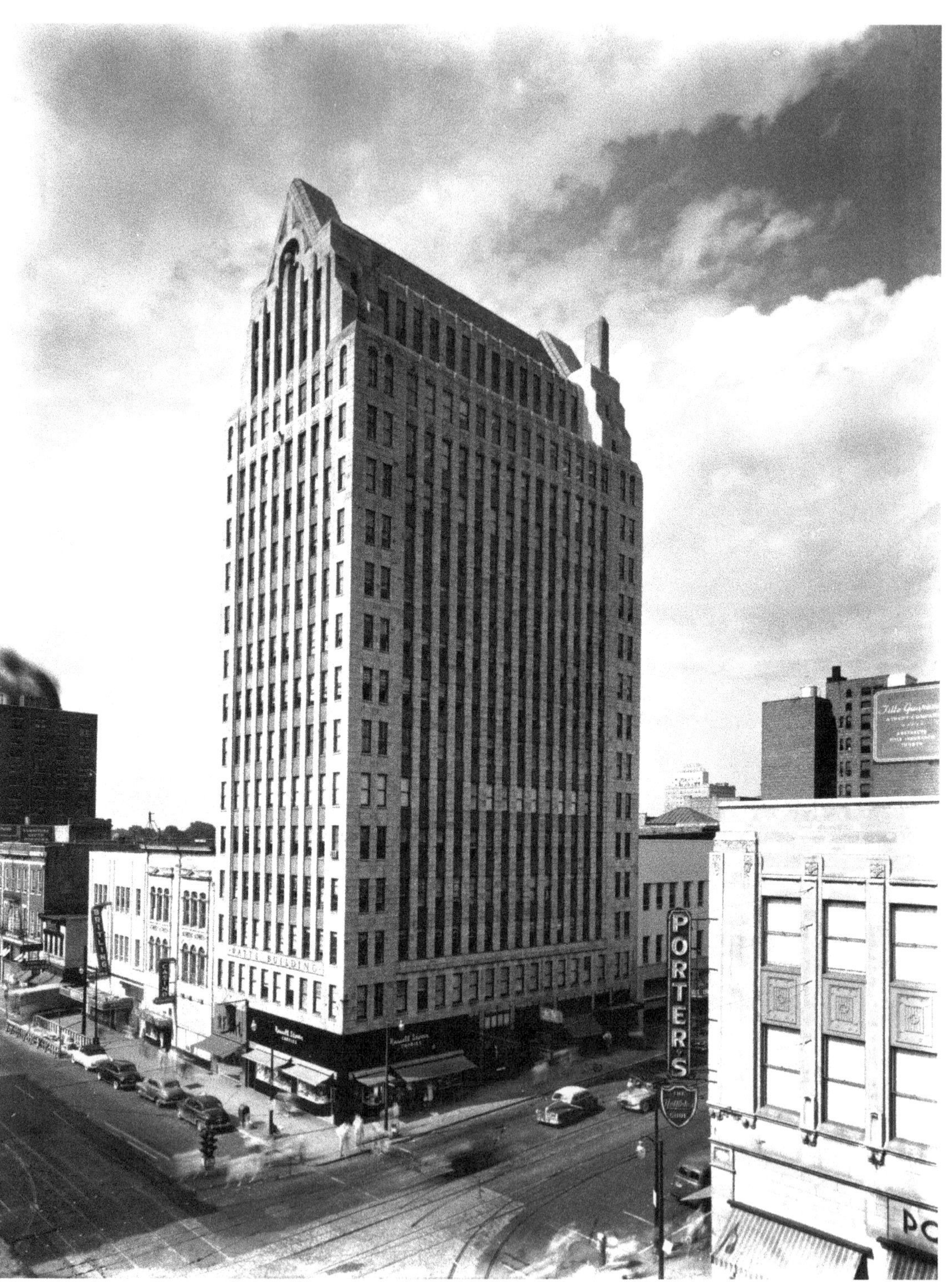

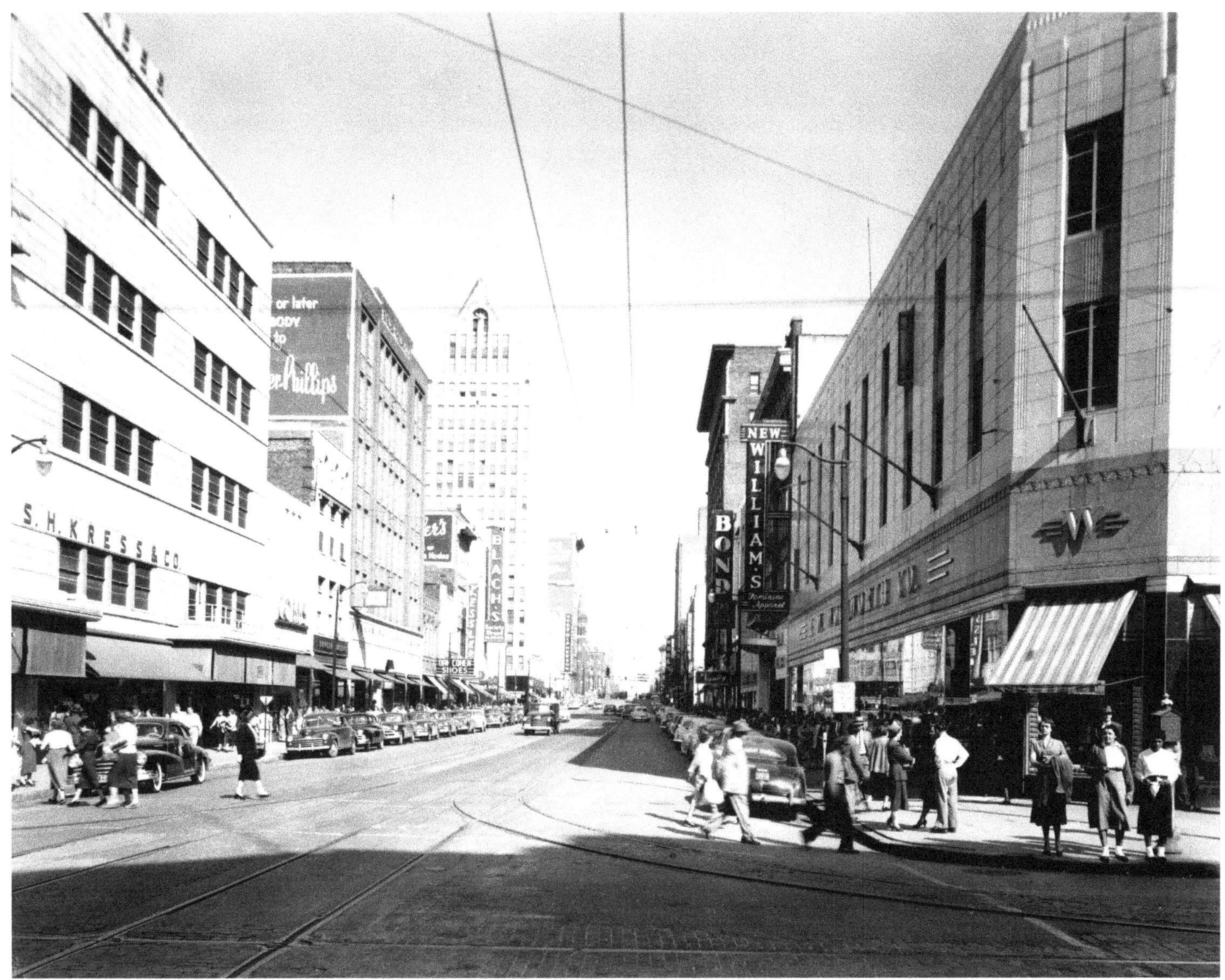

The busyness of the street signifies the importance of 3rd Avenue North. Woolworth's five-and-dime store, S. H. Kress & Company, another nationwide chain popular during the 1950s, and Cobb's, a women's clothing store, were some of the businesses located on this street.

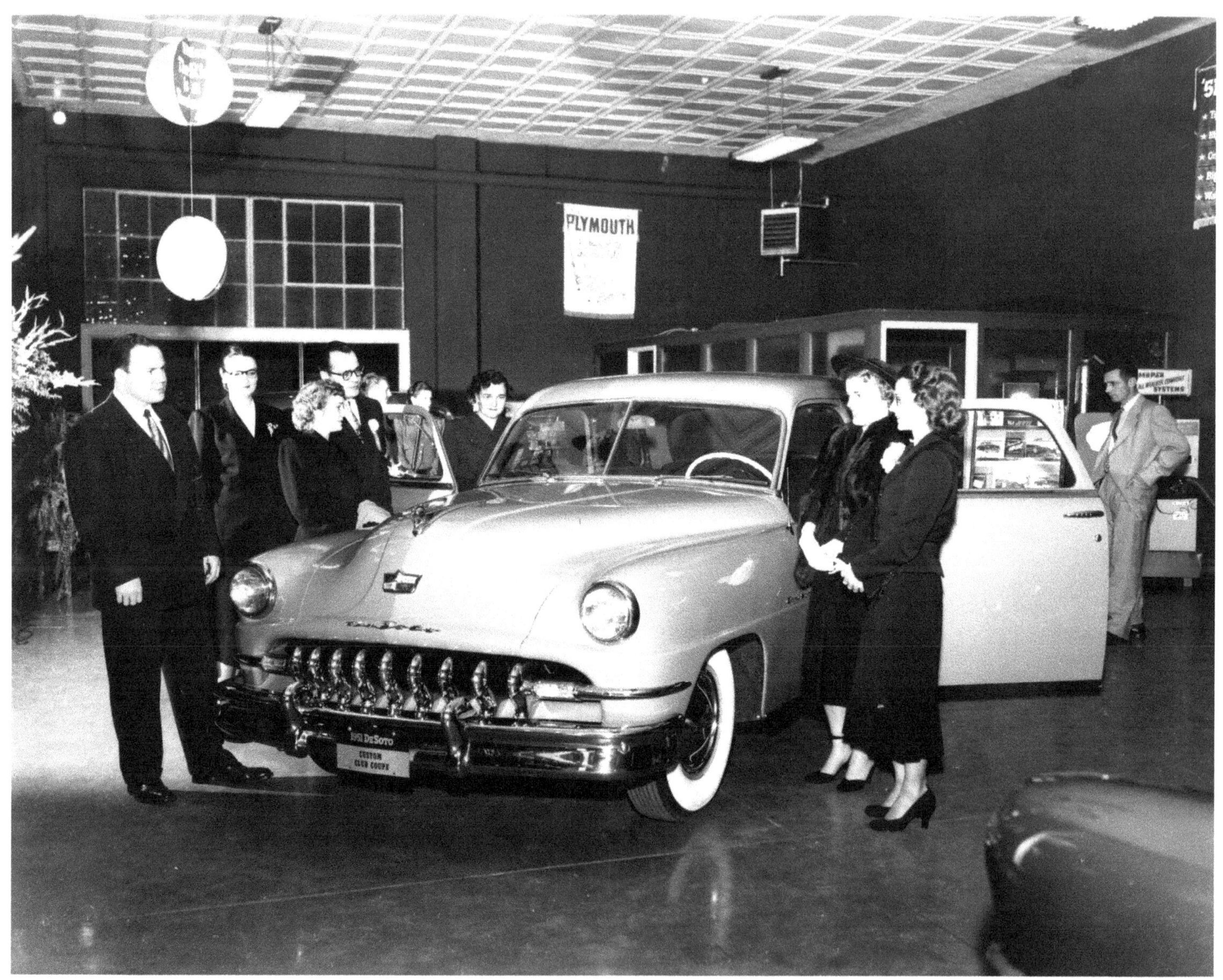

Like the rest of America, Birmingham residents were eager to participate in the booming 1950s economy. One way to take part was in purchasing a new automobile. Kirksey Motors' showroom displays the 1951 DeSoto, a popular car manufactured by Chrysler.

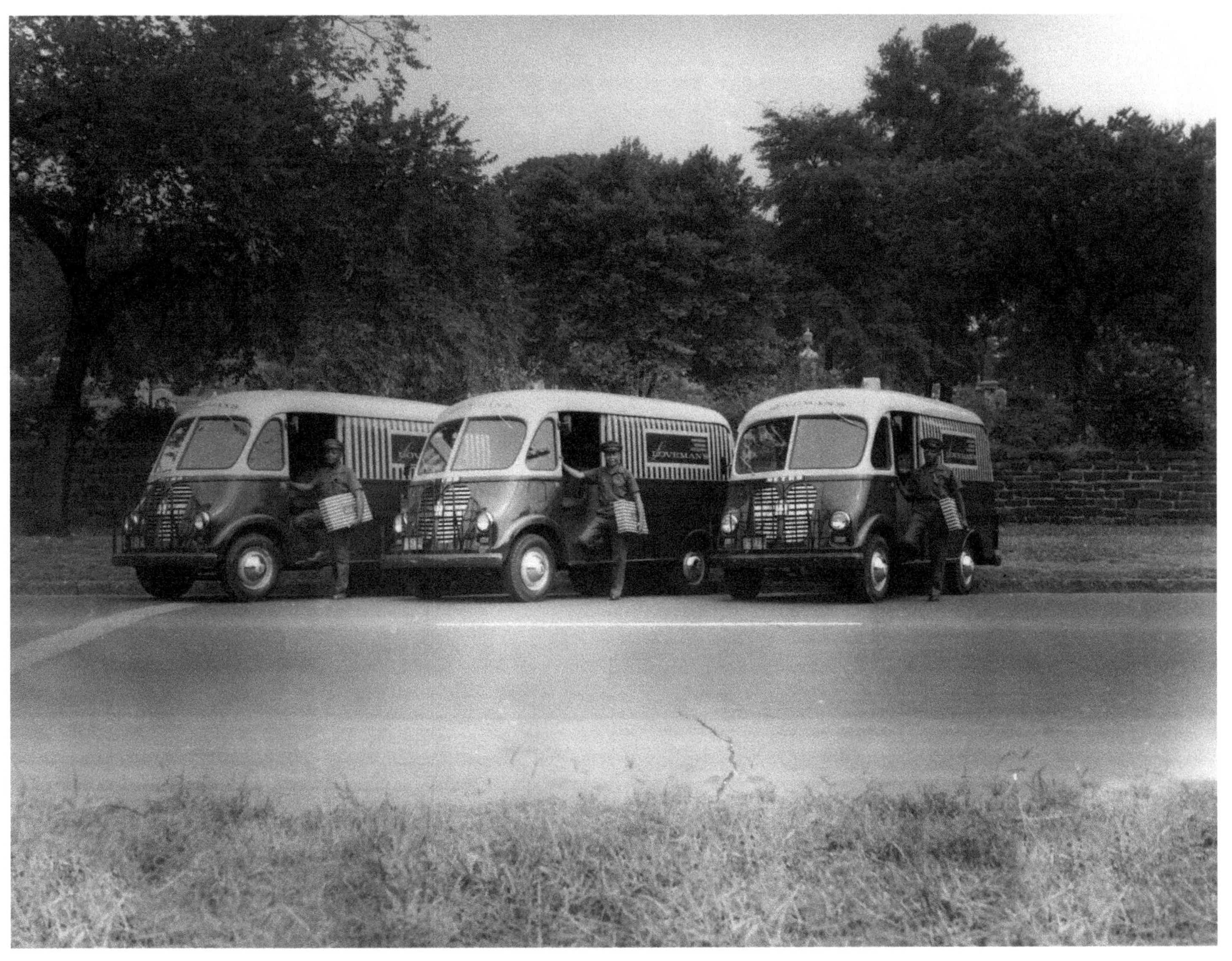

Drivers for Loveman Joseph & Loeb department store are ready to embark on their daily round. The delivery vans are parked outside Oak Hill Cemetery.

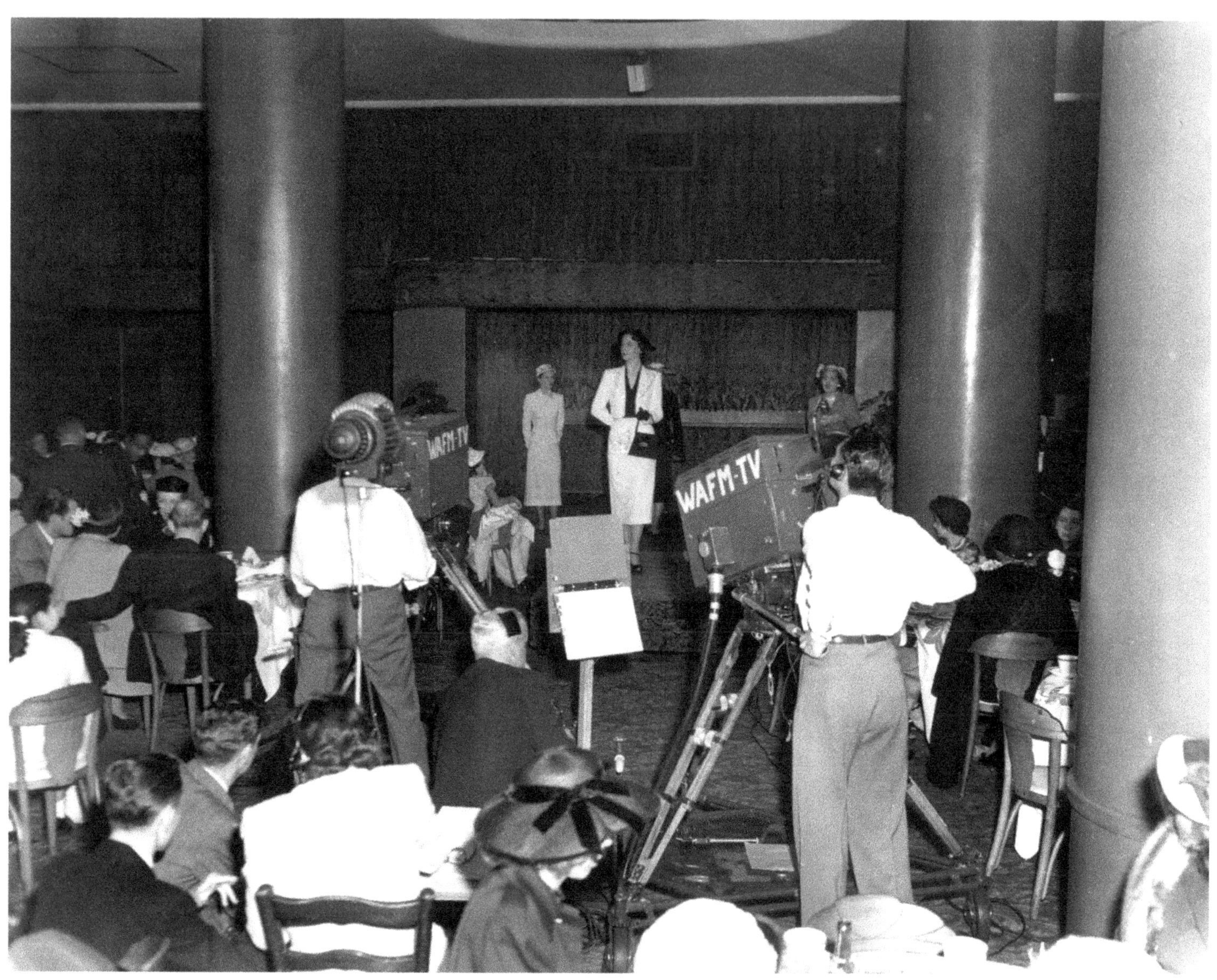

In time for the Easter weekend, a fashion show flaunts the latest spring styles at the Tutwiler Hotel. WAFM-TV cameras were on hand to televise the local event, one of a number of popular themes in the early days of local television programming.

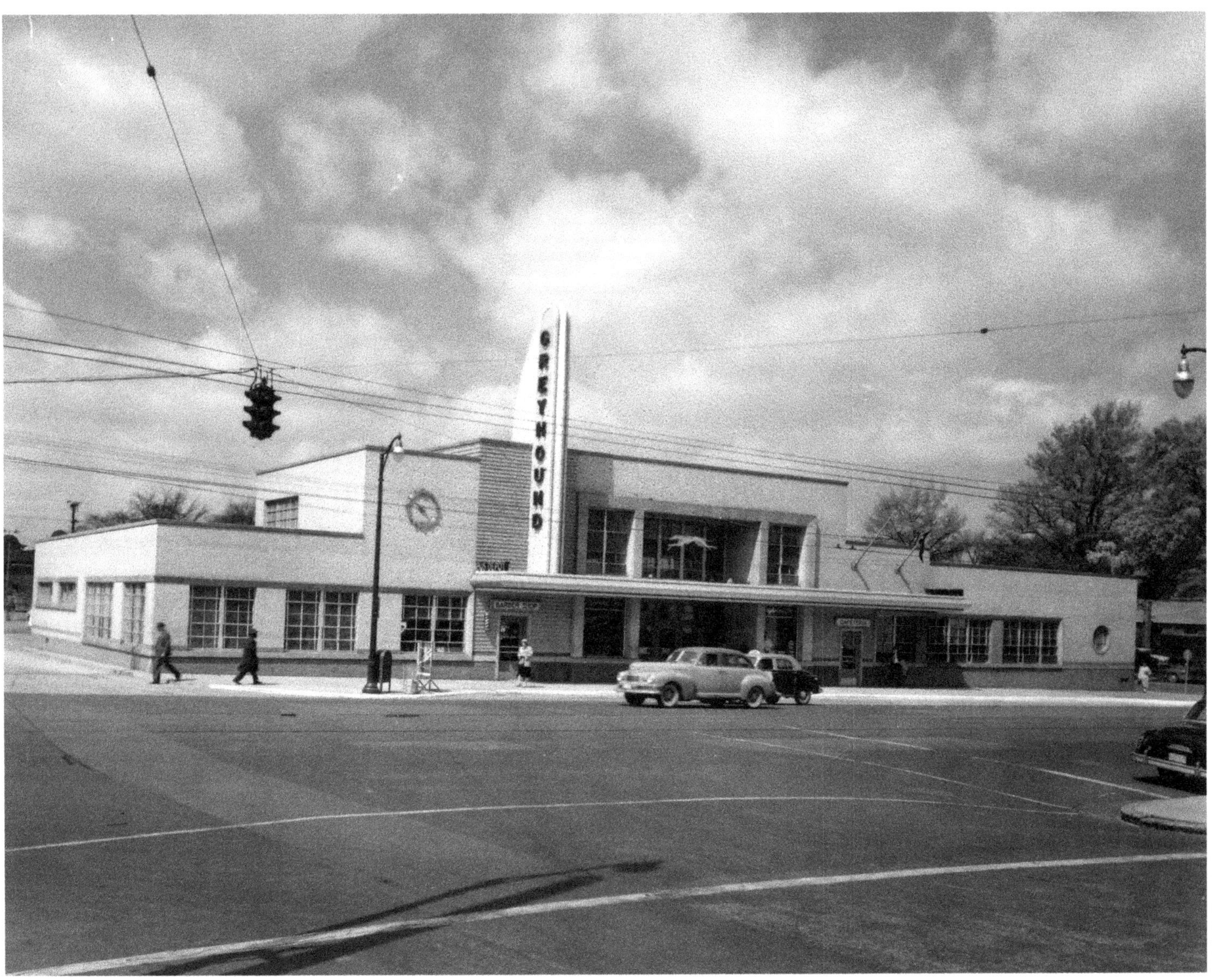

Constructed by Southeastern Greyhound Lines in 1950, Birmingham Greyhound Station was the city's main bus terminal. At a cost of $750,000, the station could accommodate 30 buses. It was worth the price because the high volume of traffic made it a necessity, according to Southeastern Greyhound Lines president Guy A. Huguelet.

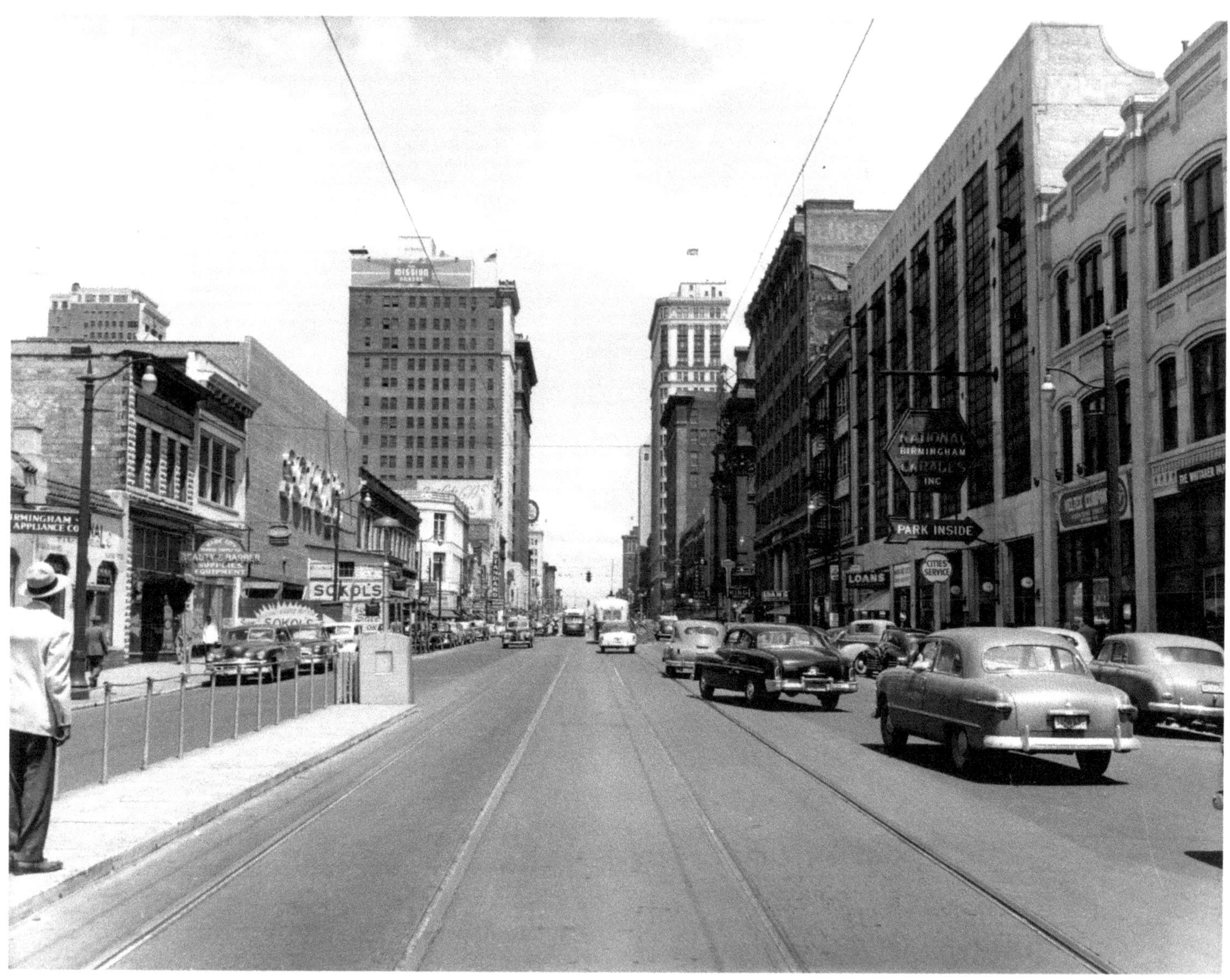

In the early 1950s, streamlined streetcars, seen here in the distance, were still serving the transportation needs of local commuters, but bus service was coming. The Birmingham Transit Company, which had ordered 47 of the streetcars from Pullman Standard in 1947 at a cost of $25,000 each, would replace them with buses only six years later.

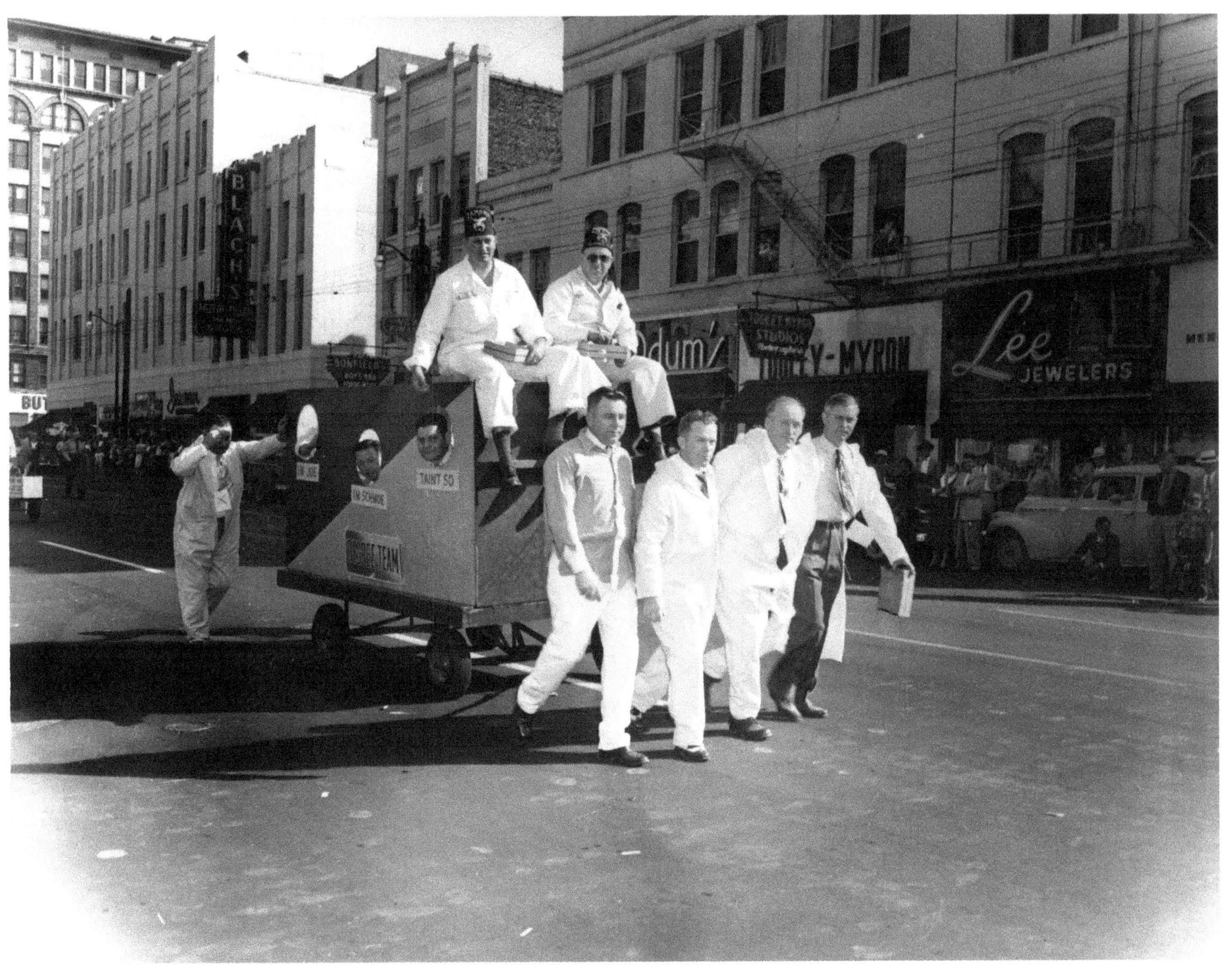

The Shriners of Birmingham march along 20th Street North during a 1950s parade. The makeshift float quips, "I'm Joe, I'm Schmoe. Taint So."

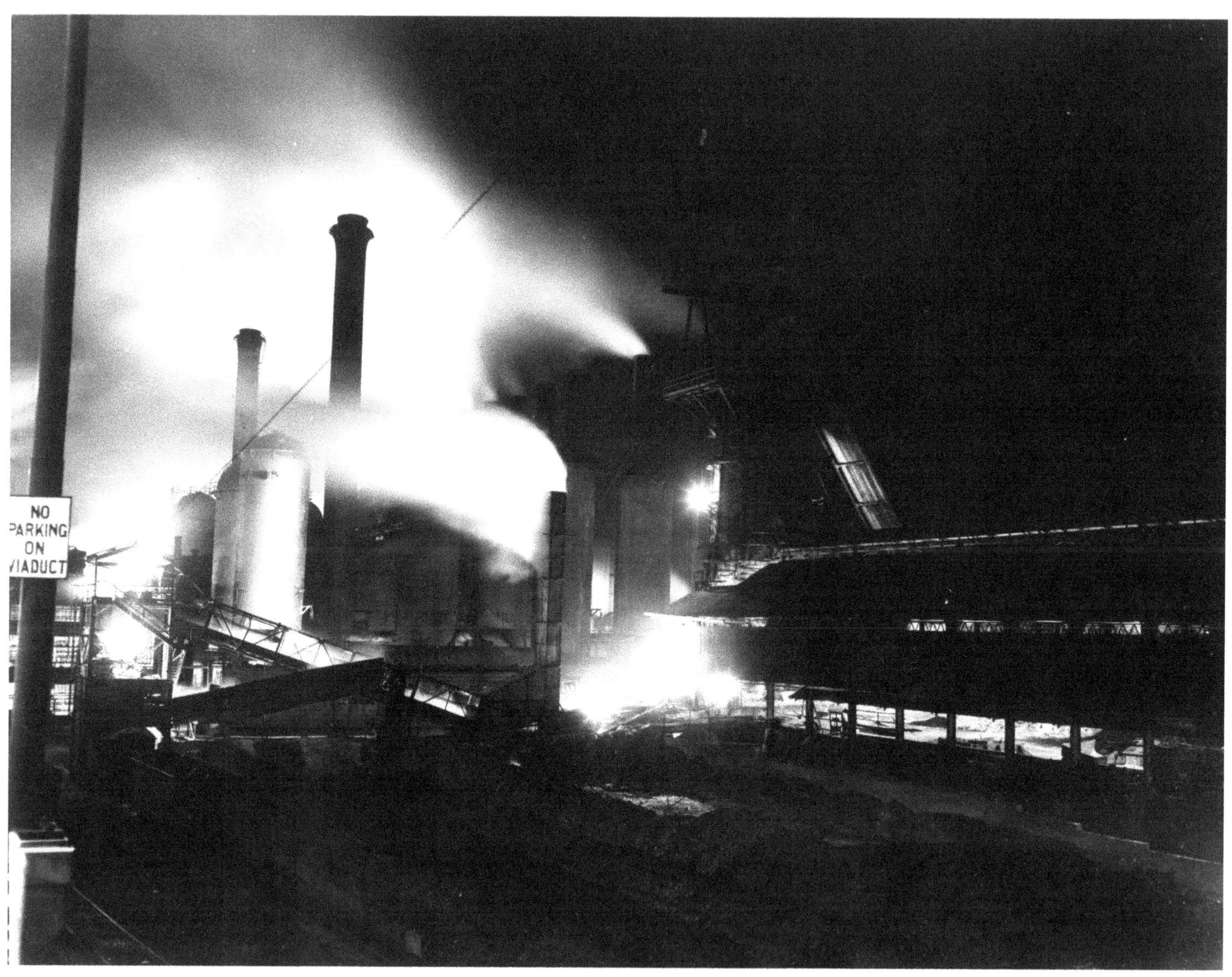

Sloss Furnaces, one of the oldest blast furnaces where iron ore was smelted, burns through the night. Built in 1881, Sloss Furnaces was a main part of James Withers Sloss's dream of developing Birmingham's iron industry.

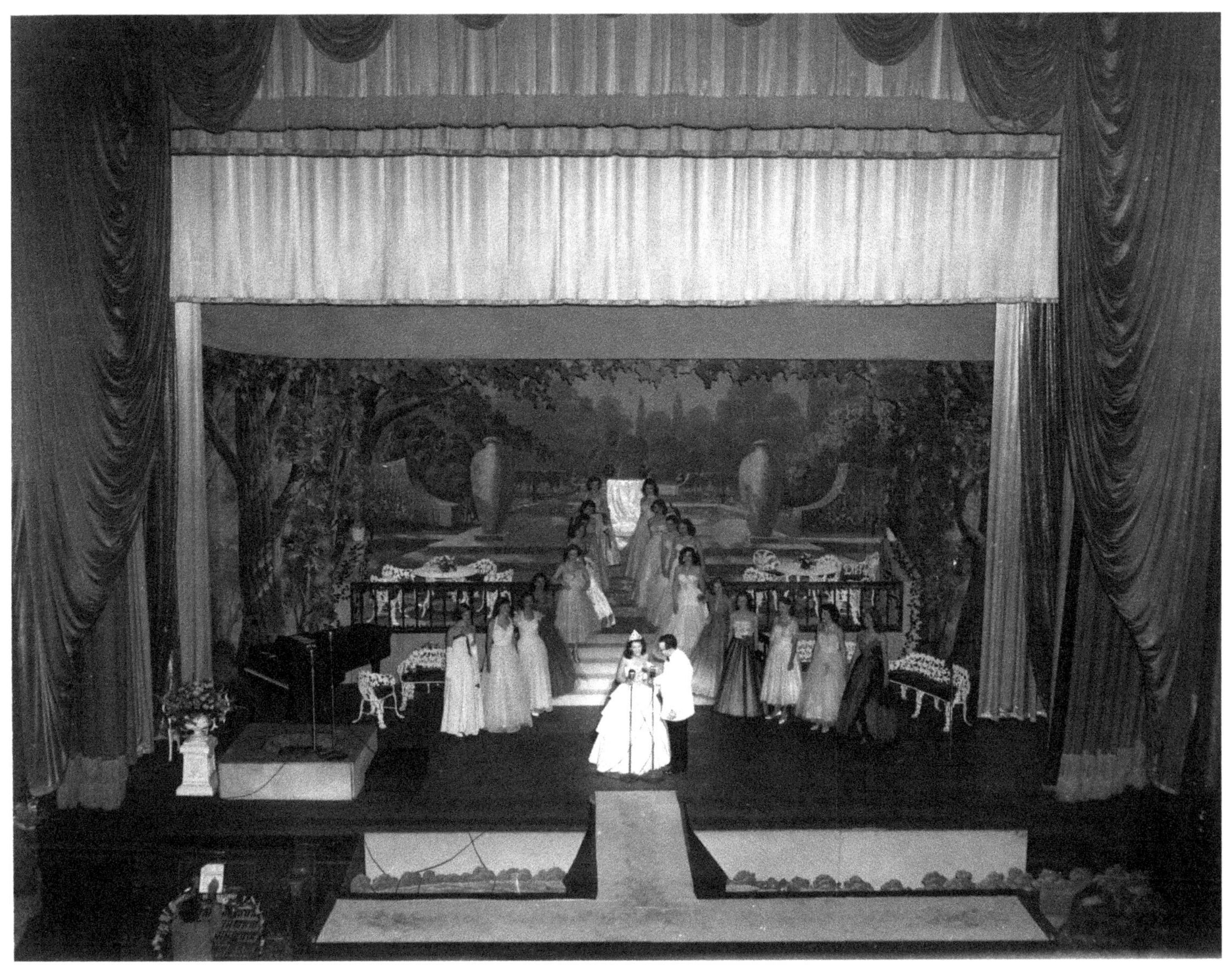

The Alabama Theater hosts the 1951 Miss Alabama pageant. The winner, Jeanne Moody, had been a music, drama, and dance student in New York for three years before participating in the pageant.

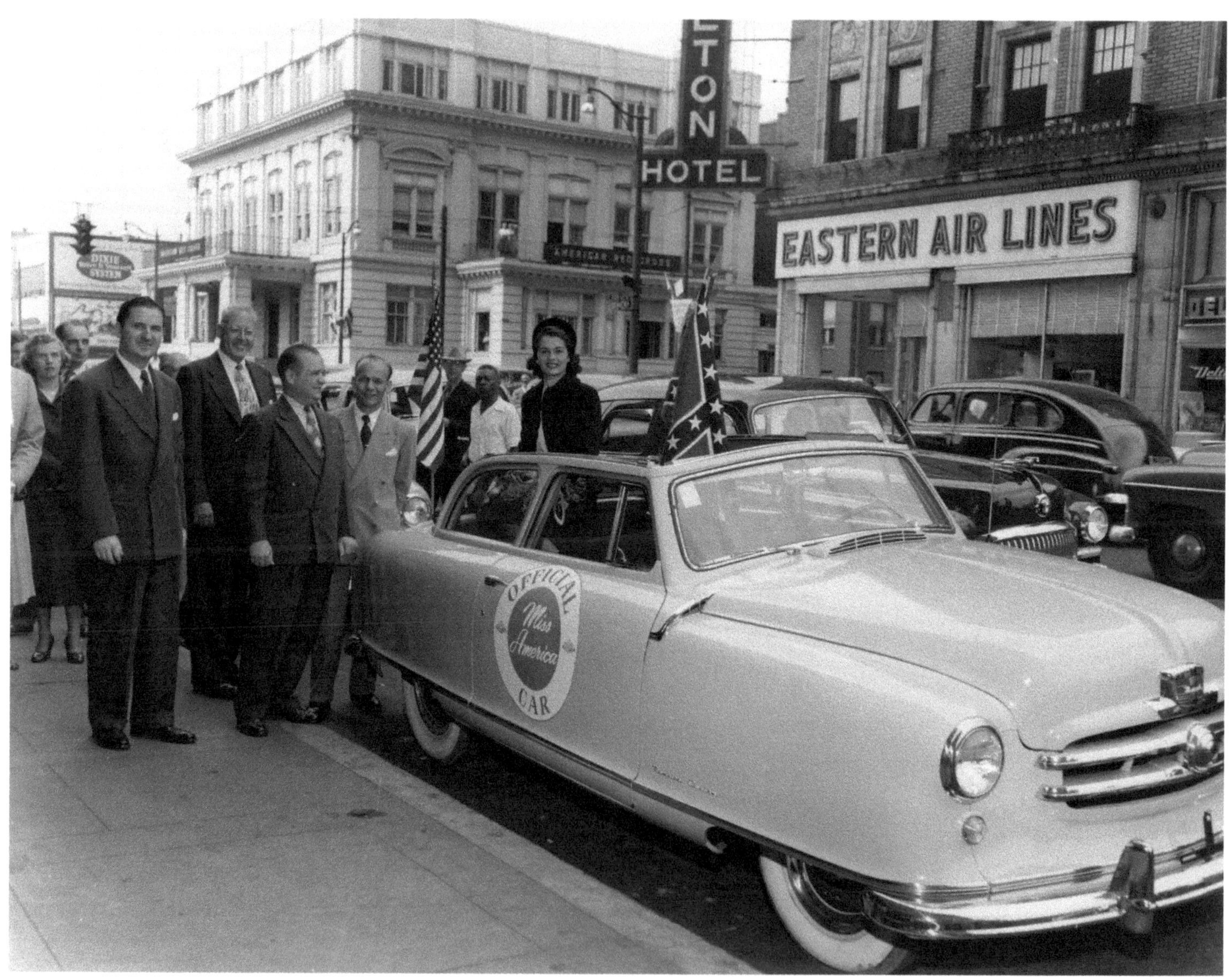

Miss America Yolanda Betbeze, an Alabamian, stands in an open-top Nash automobile outside the Tutwiler Hotel. Betbeze would go on to create mischief for the annual pageant by refusing to don bathing suits and focusing the pageant on its scholarship programs. This led sponsors to create rival pageants Miss USA and Miss Universe. Betbeze later participated in a feminist demonstration in Atlantic City in opposition to the pageant.

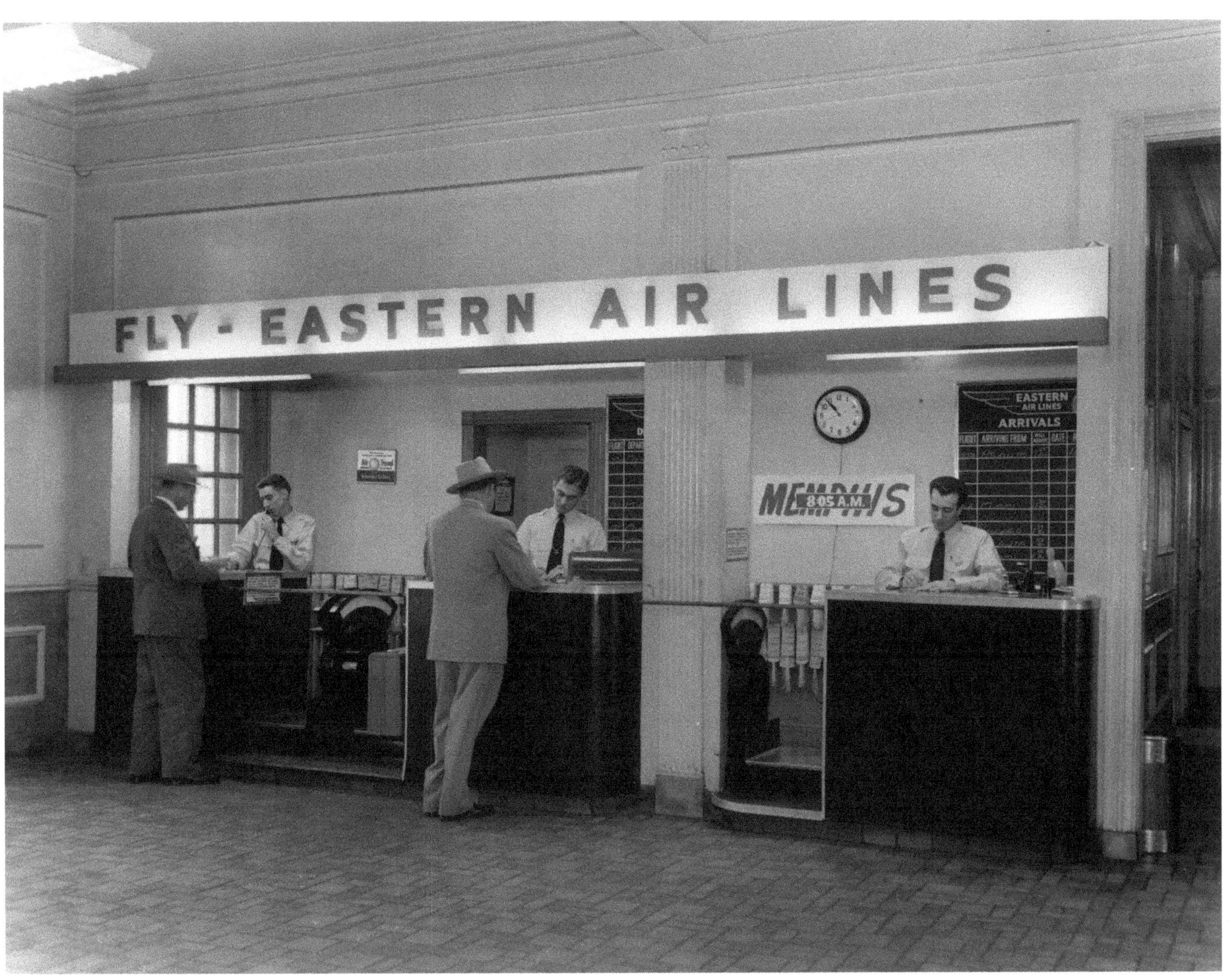

Travelers purchase tickets at the offices of Eastern Air Lines, a staple of the flight industry in Birmingham. Flying had become a wonder of the modern world and was well on its way to being taken for granted, but departures and arrivals—posted on blackboards with chalk—look almost primitive in today's age of the computer.

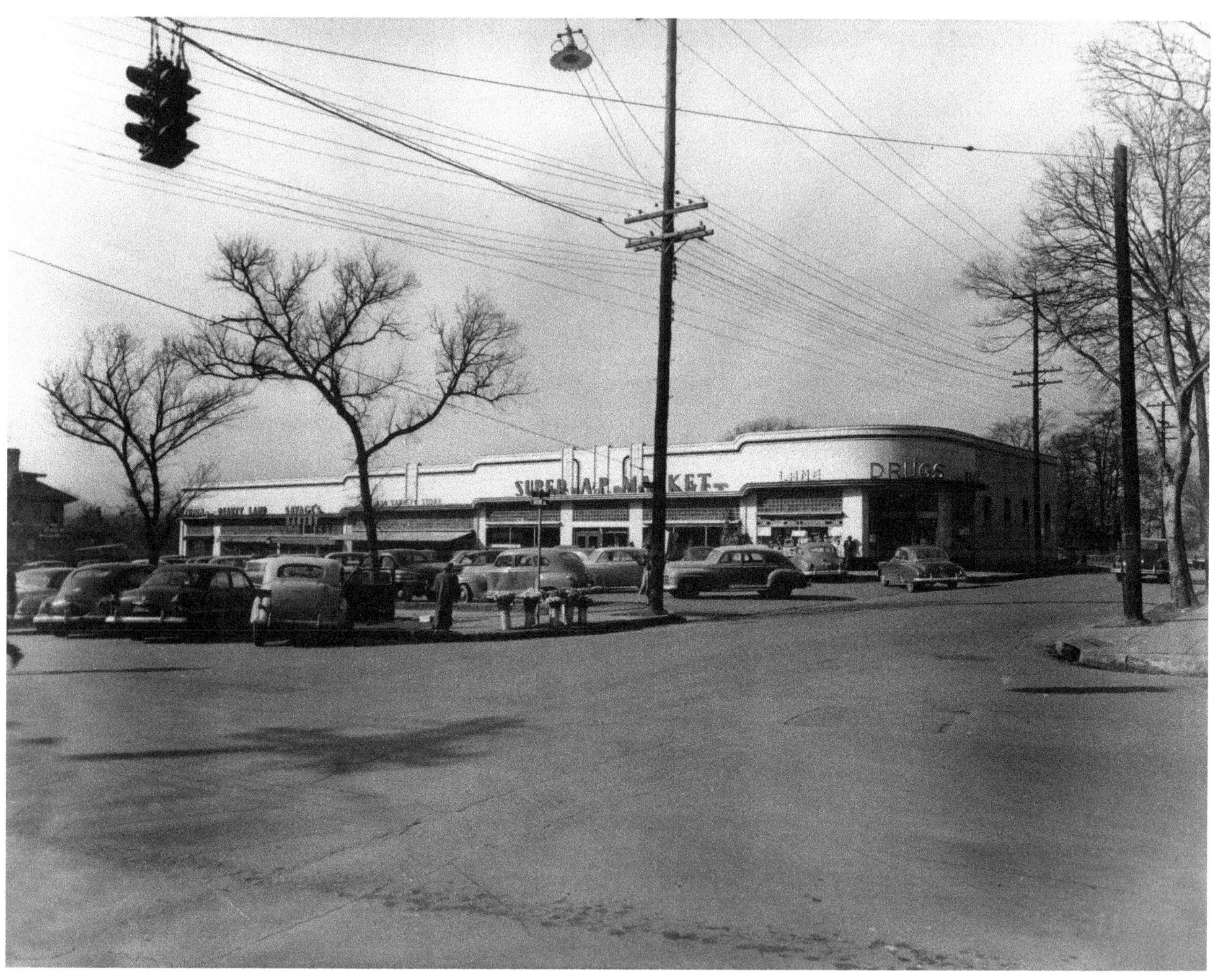

Highland Avenue Shopping Center on Highland Avenue between 11th Way South and 22nd Street South seems to be enjoying brisk business on this day in the 1950s. A curbside flower vendor displays a row of fancy petals at center in this image.

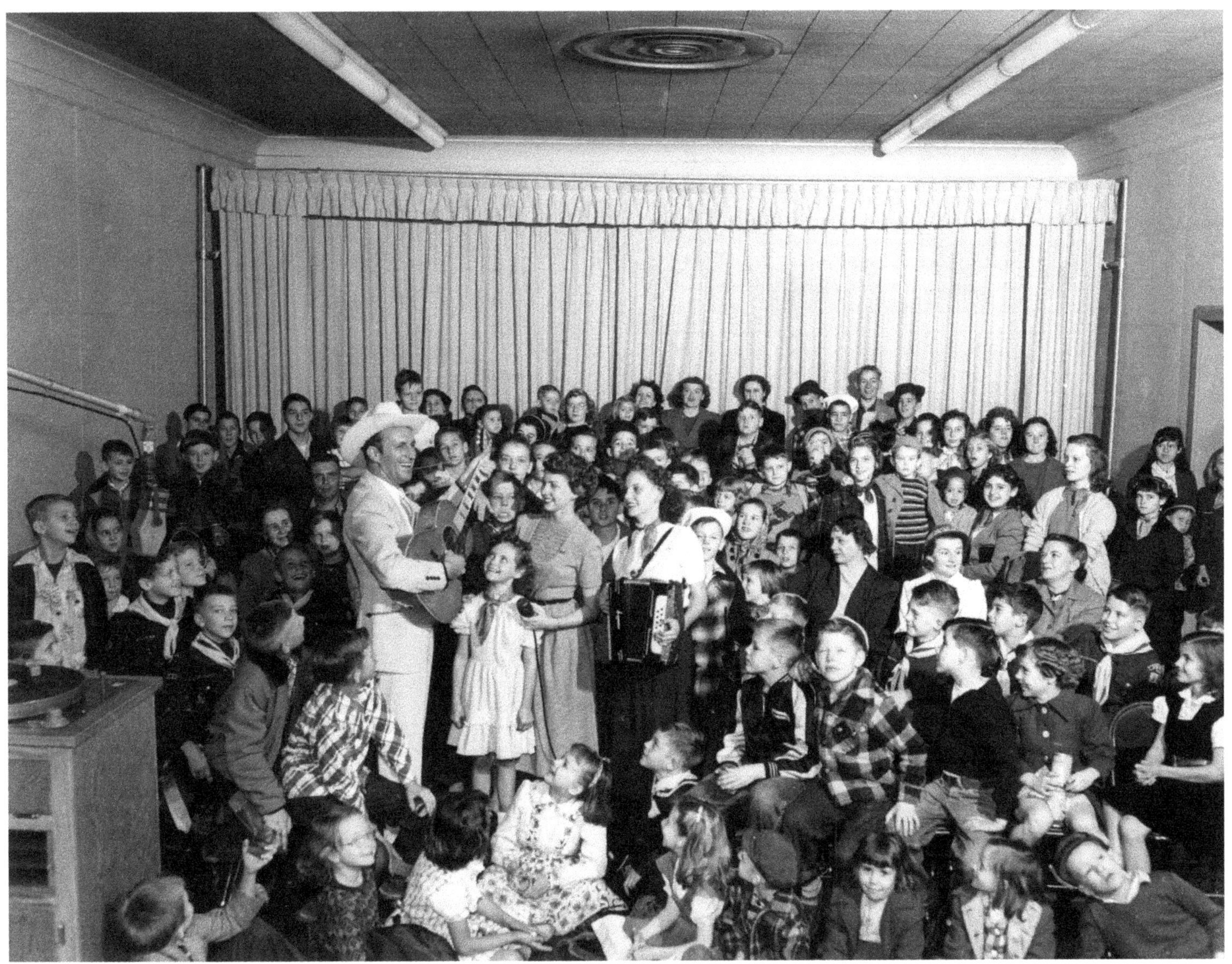

Happy Hal Burns entertains a group of children at the WBRC studio. Burns worked in radio, television, theater, rodeo, and motion pictures. In addition to working as a manager and promoter, Burns was also a songwriter, composing more than 100 songs.

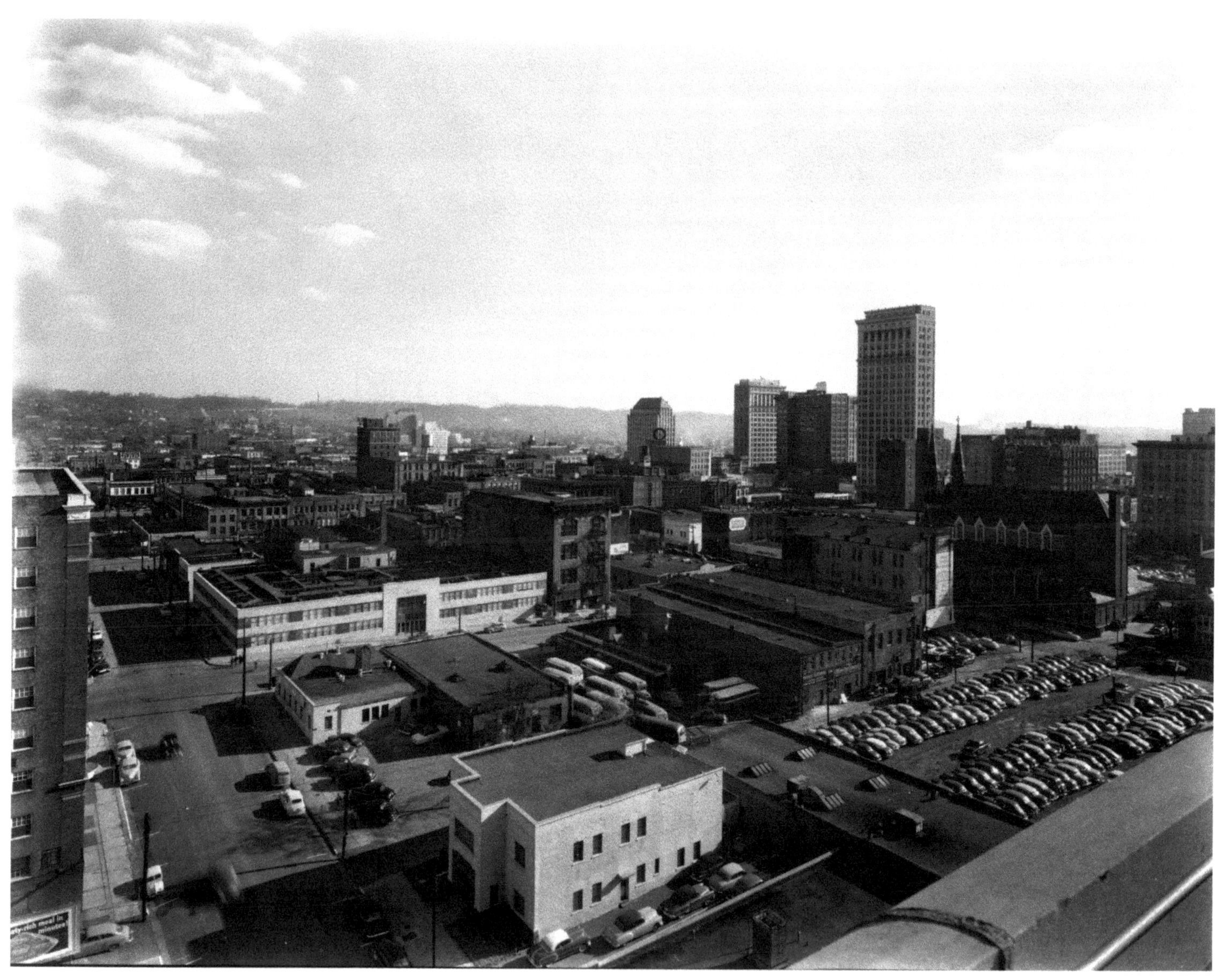

A view of the Birmingham skyline from the American Life Insurance Building at 2306 Fourth Avenue North. The Martin Building housed the Municipal Court.

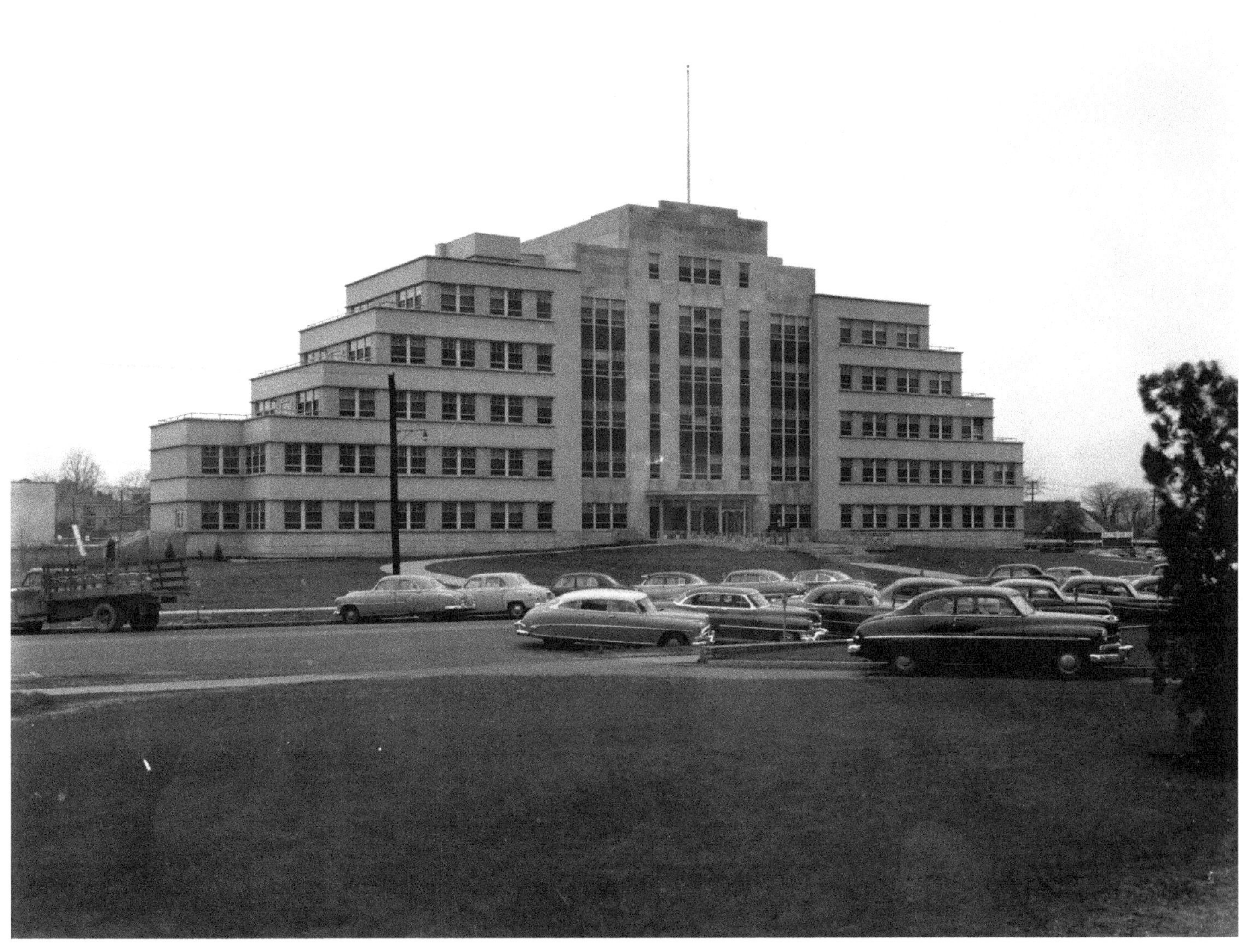

The Crippled Children's Clinic and Hospital, located at 620 19th South, was across from the Jefferson-Hillman Hospital. Most of the patients at the clinic had been stricken with polio, leaving them paralyzed or severely handicapped. Jonas Salk's polio vaccine was first tested in 1952 and would be acclaimed as miraculous for its ability to prevent the disease.

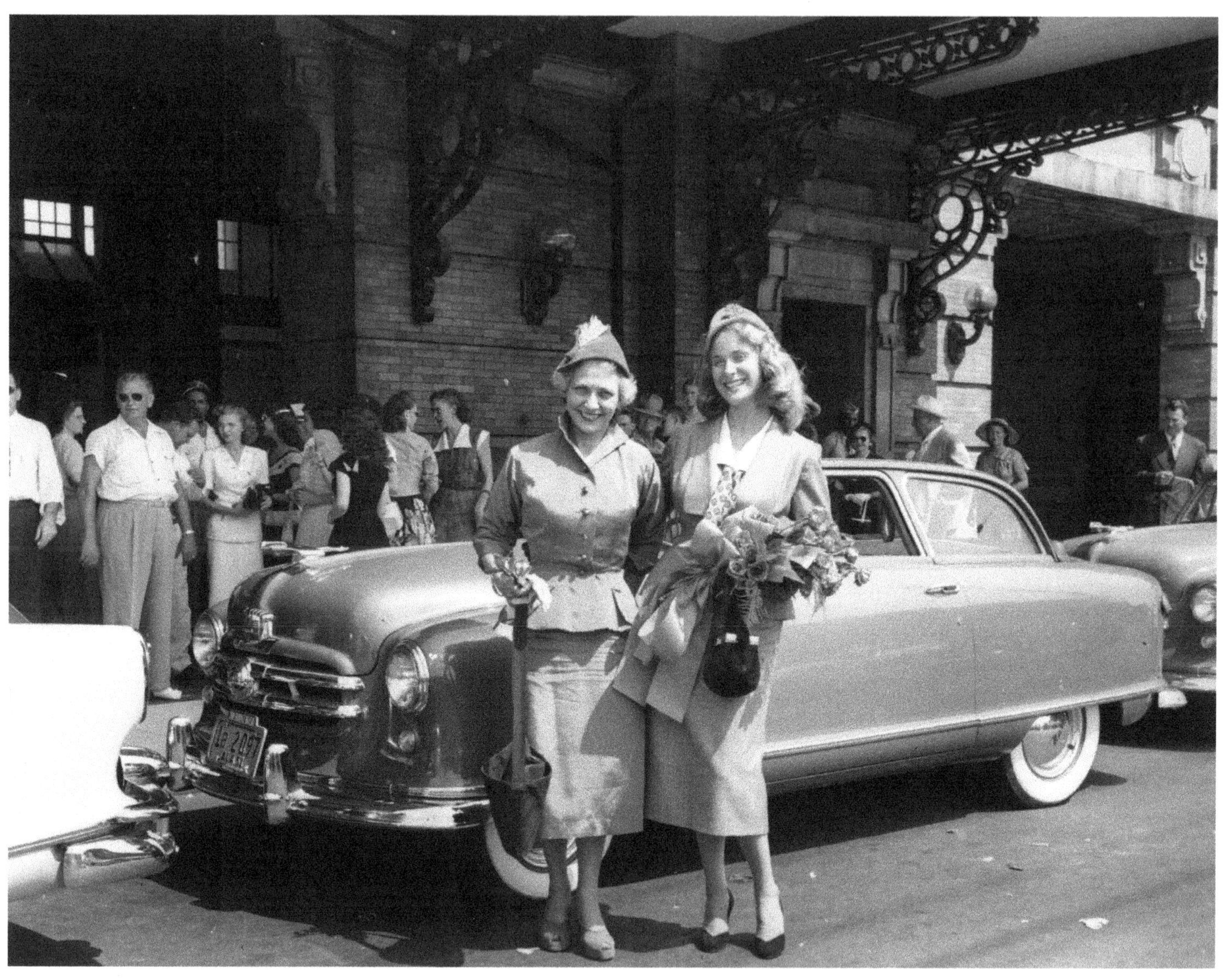

At the Terminal Station, Birmingham residents wave good-bye to Miss Alabama Jeanne Moody. Built in 1909, the Terminal Station required two years and $2 million to complete. For 60 years, the "temple of travel" greeted travelers with a sign welcoming them to "Birmingham, the Magic City."

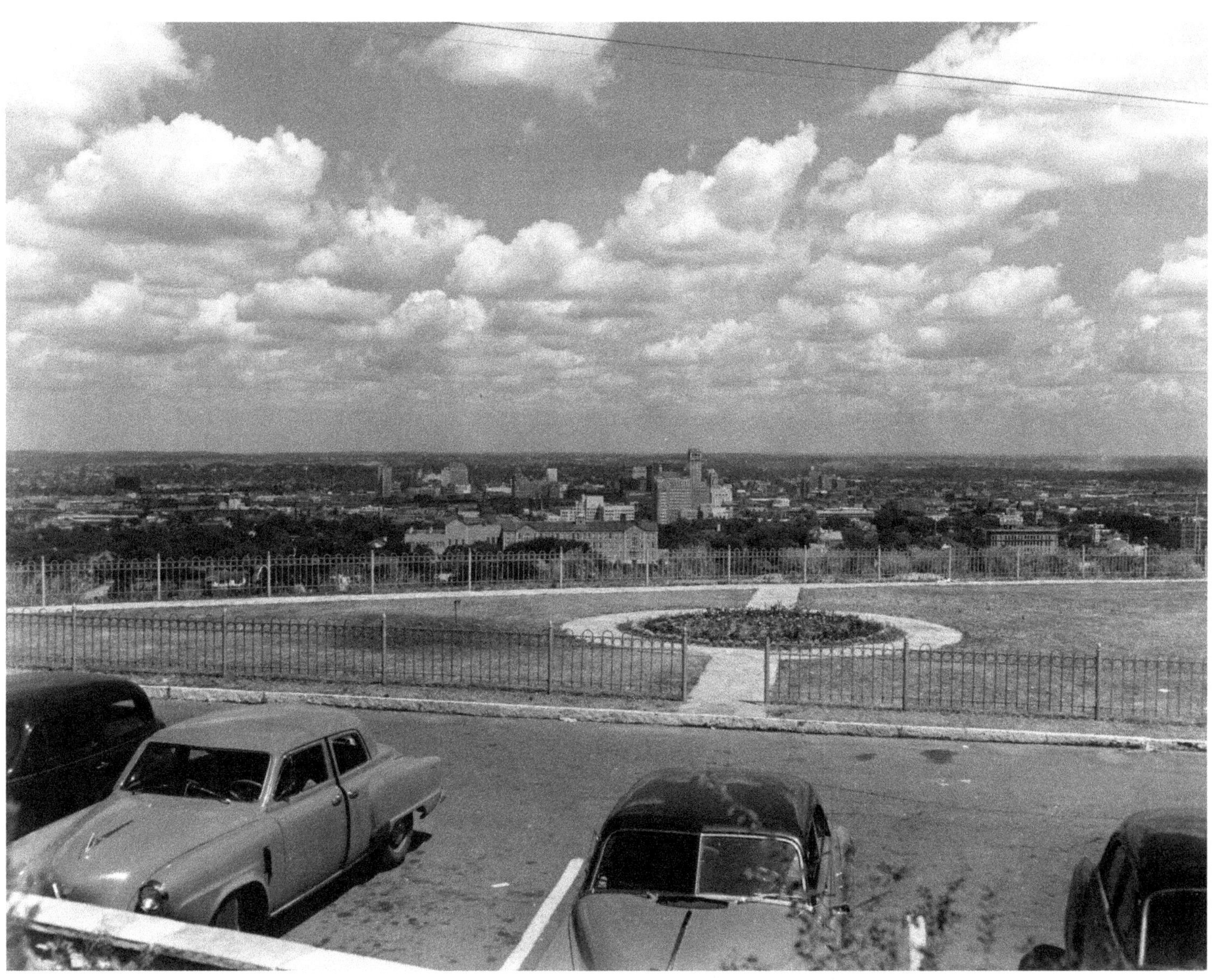

A skyline view of Birmingham from the parking area below the giant statue of Vulcan on Red Mountain.

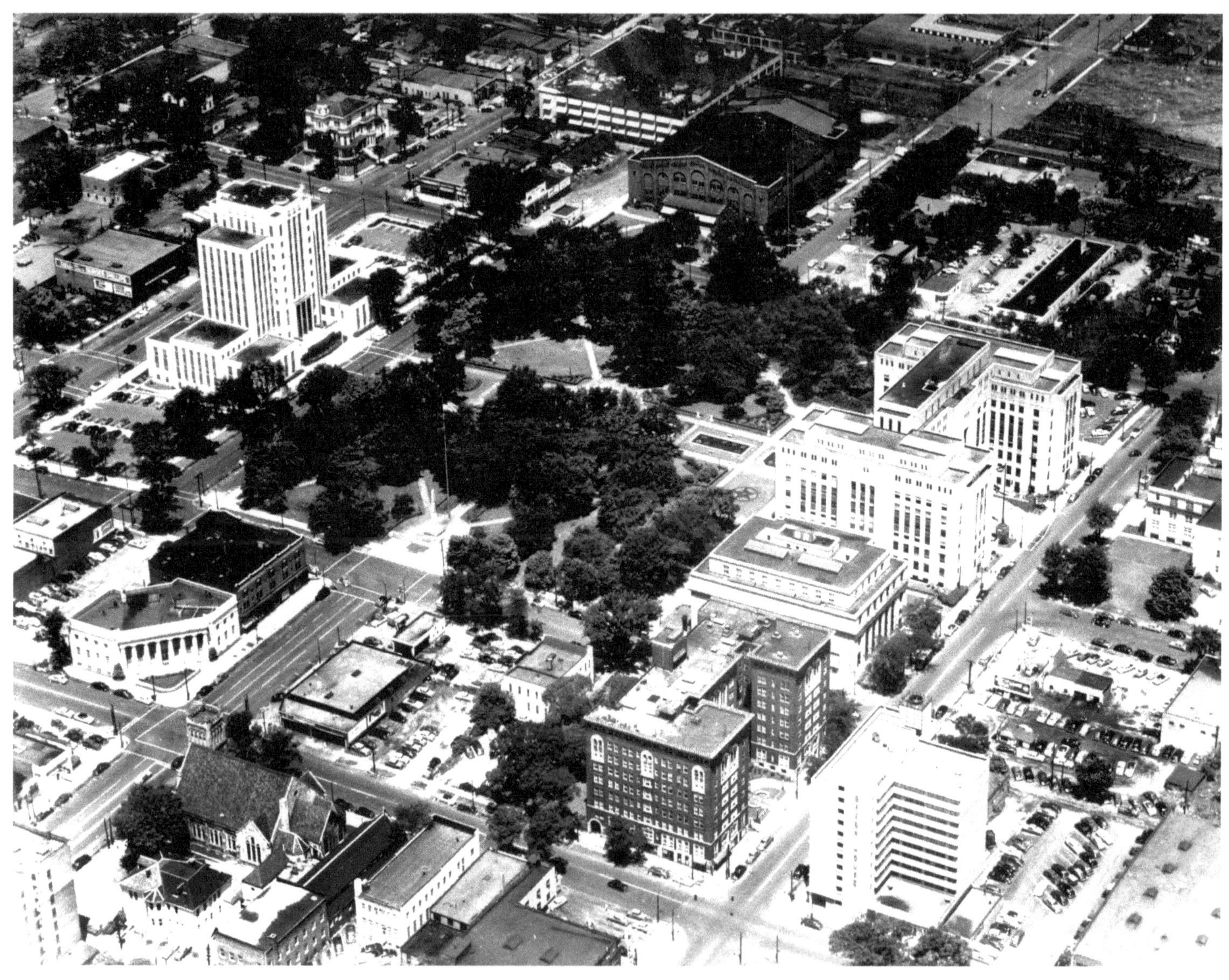

This bird's-eye view shows the Birmingham City Hall (at left), Municipal Auditorium, Jefferson County Courthouse (the white building directly across from City Hall), and Birmingham Public Library (the large building beside the Courthouse).

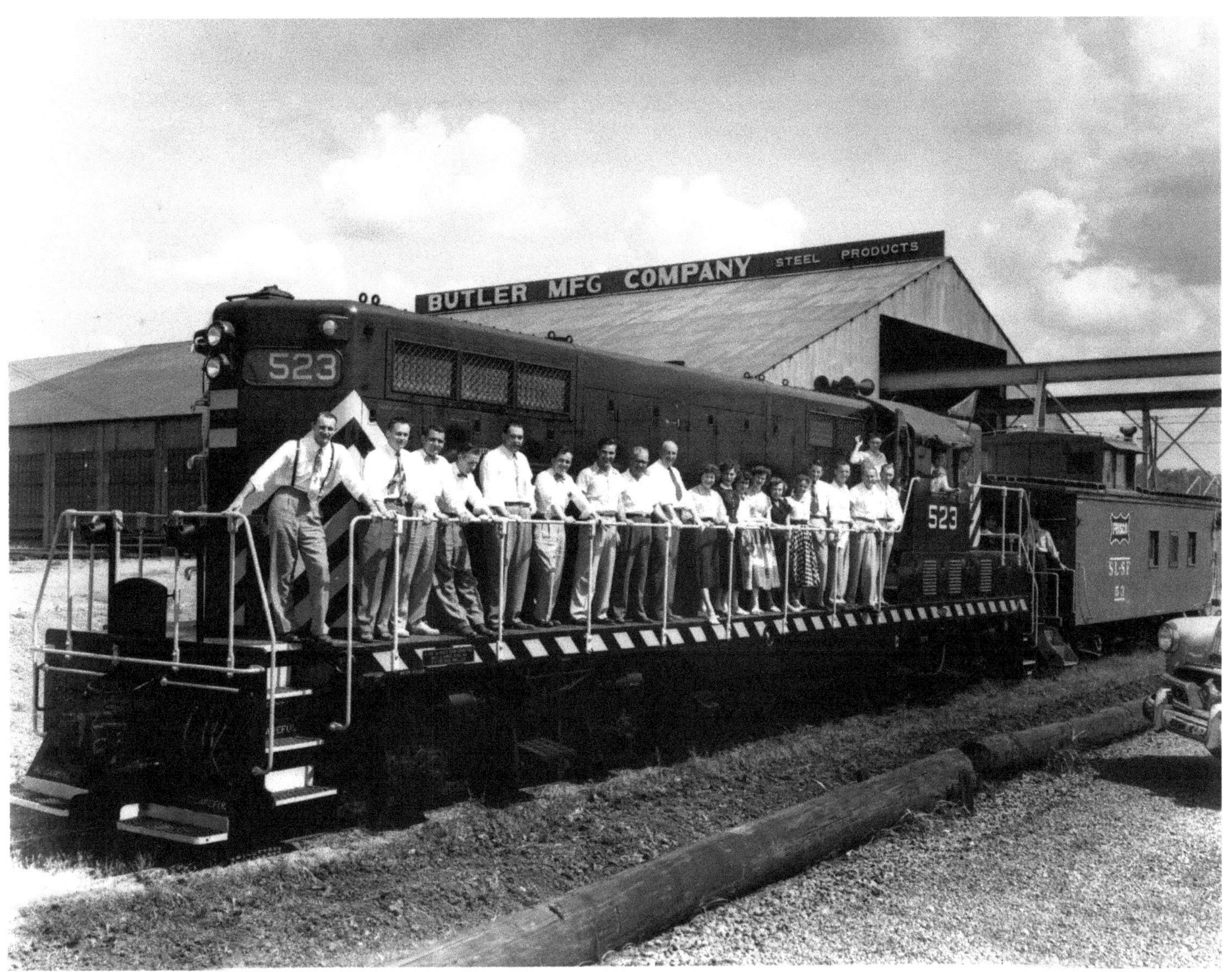

Butler Manufacturing Company employees pose on a diesel railroad engine outside the factory. Companies like Butler Manufacturing located in Ensley that specialized in "all types of special steel products, steel buildings, and welded tanks" benefited from the high demand for metal products created by World War II and the postwar booming economy.

Established in 1872, First Presbyterian Church of Birmingham has played an important role in the city from its founding. The congregation constructed this building on 4th Avenue North in 1888. When this photograph was taken, the church had just installed stained-glass windows to depict the life of Christ and God's covenant with His people.

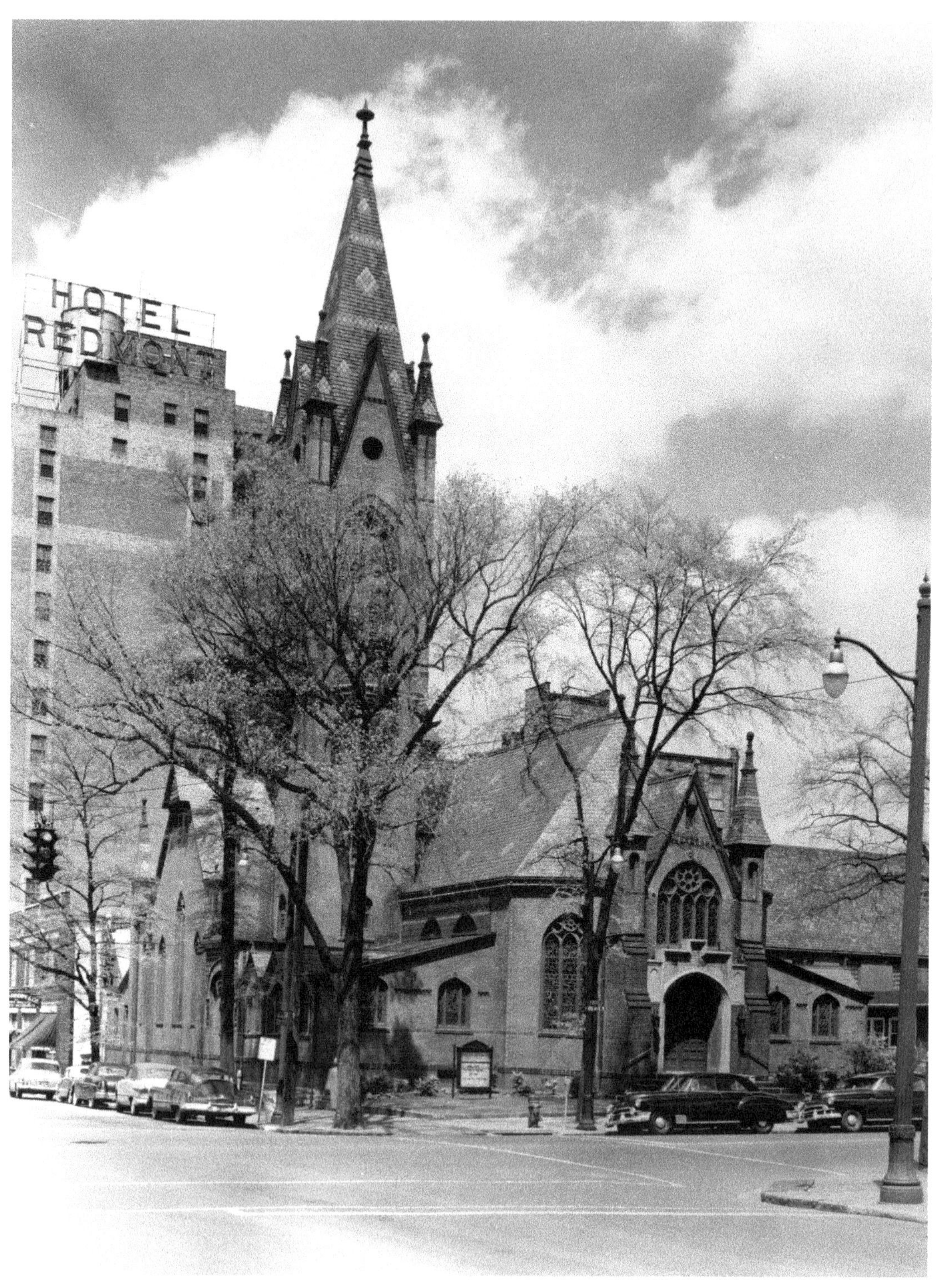

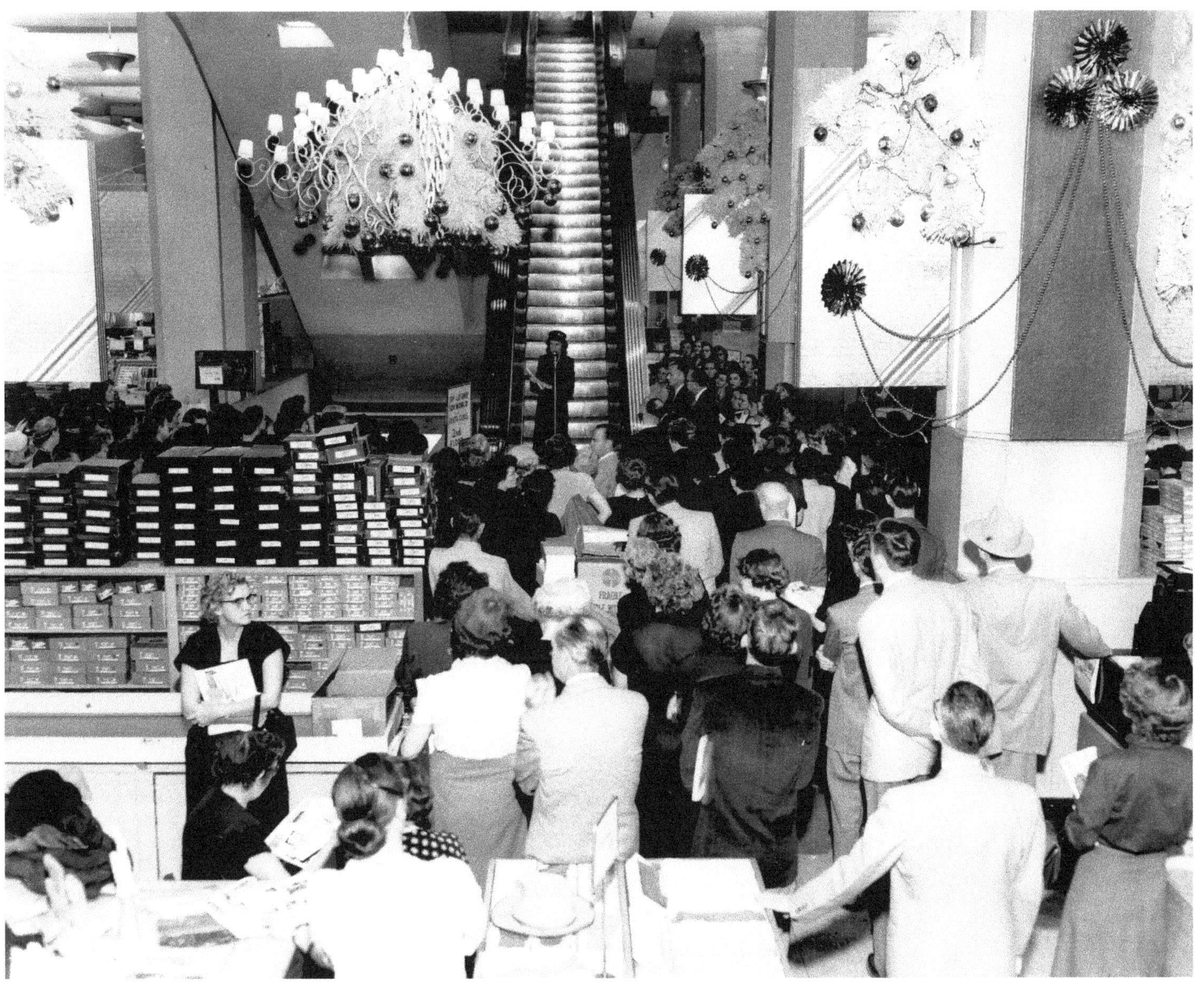

This interior shot shows some of the Christmas decorations in Pizitz Department Store located at 1821 2nd Avenue North. Louis Pizitz started a chain of Birmingham department stores in 1898 and the name soon became synonymous with shopping.

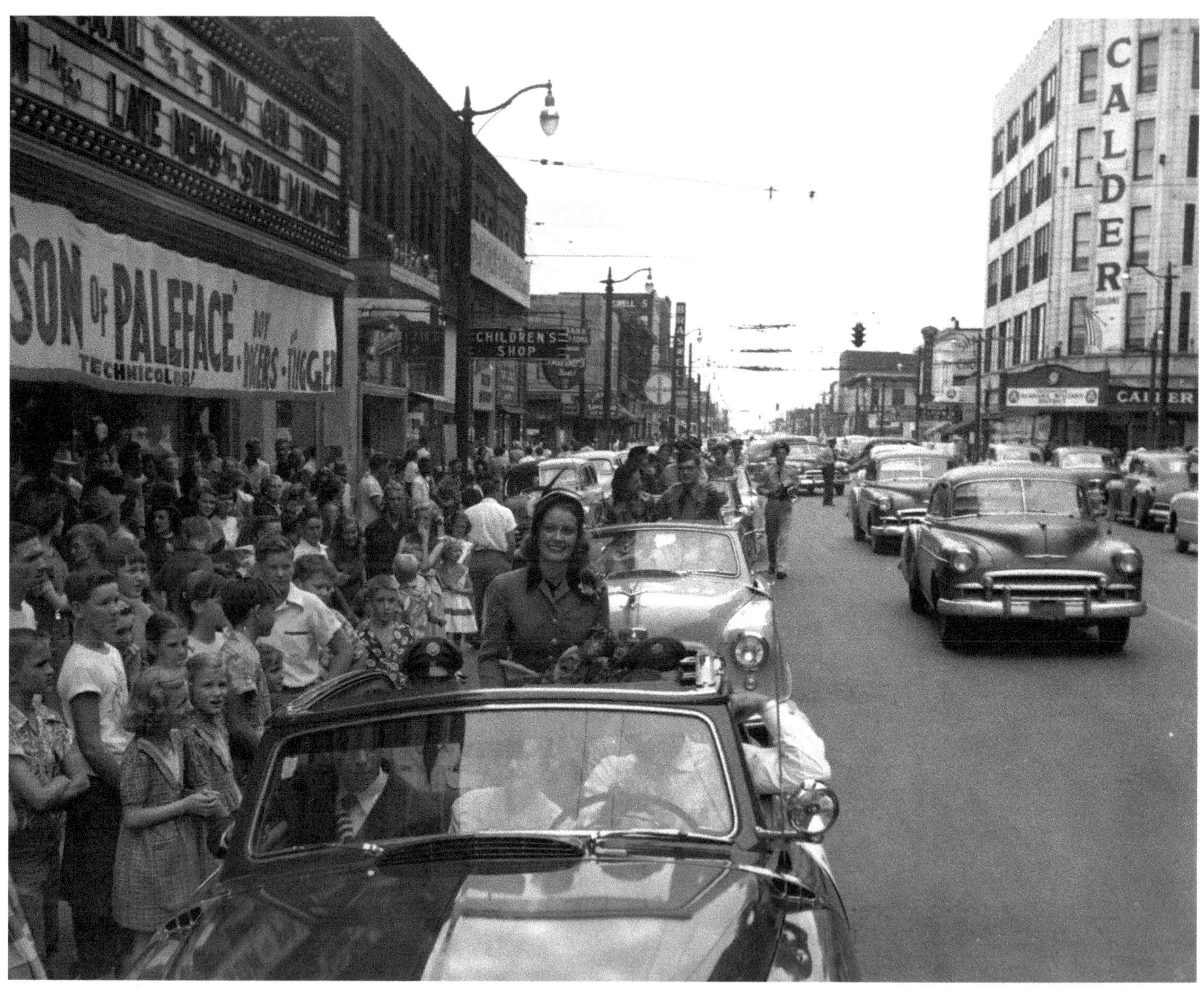

Miss Alabama 1952, Gwen Harmon, stops in front of the Alabama Theater to greet well-wishers. Birmingham customarily hosted a parade that led to the Terminal Station, where Miss Alabama would board an Atlantic City–bound train to participate in the Miss America pageant.

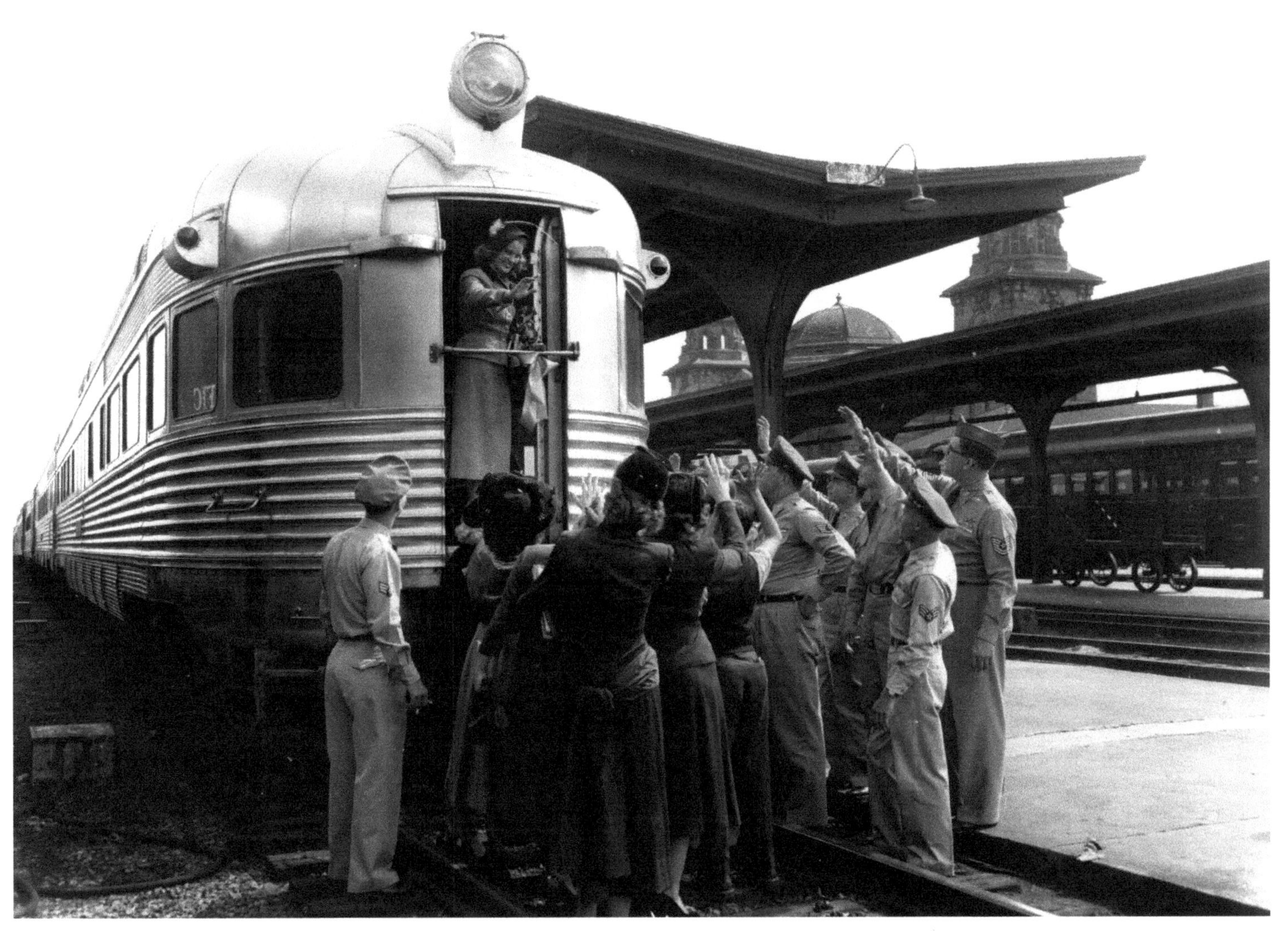

A group gathers to wish Miss Alabama Gwen Harmon good luck as she embarks from Terminal Station on her journey to participate in the Miss America pageant in Atlantic City, New Jersey.

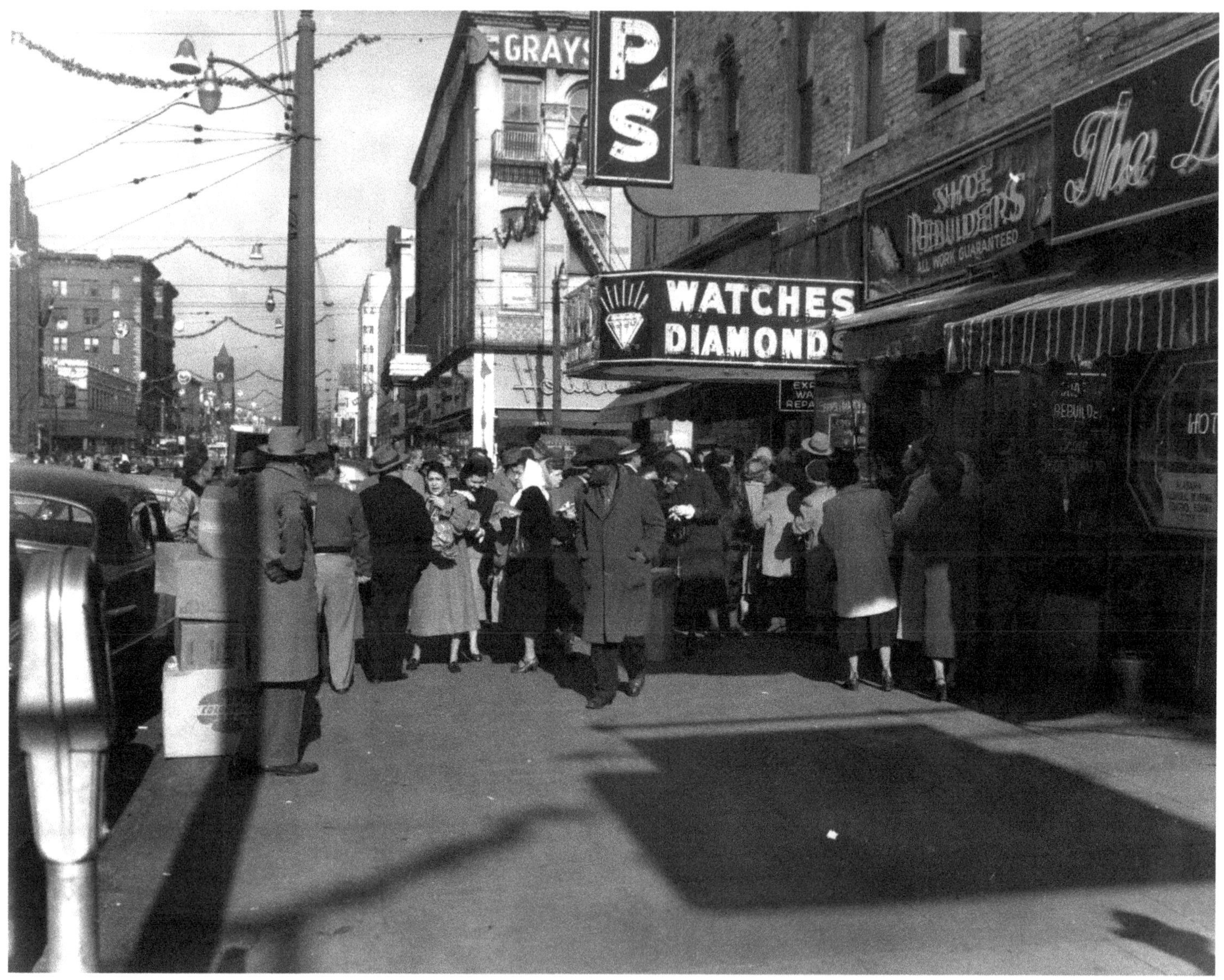

People gather at the grand opening of another Epp's jewelry store on 19th Street at 2nd Avenue North.

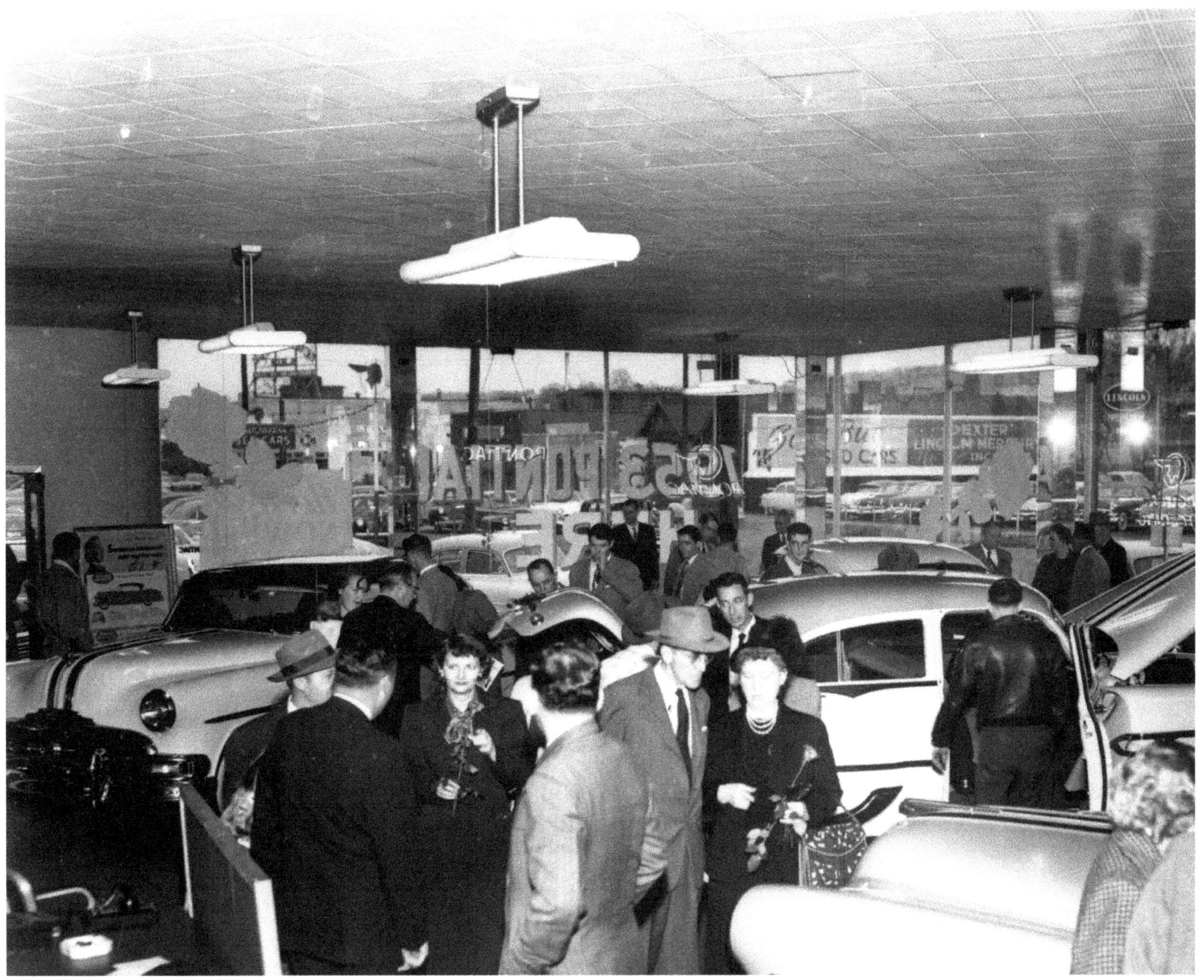

Customers check out the displayed cars in the showroom at Shaver Pontiac on 6th Avenue South. Though some Birmingham residents could afford brand-new cars, others could not. Shaver Pontiac was just one of Birmingham's many used-car dealerships that offered affordable automobiles.

Title Guarantee and Trust Company Building, the second skyscraper in Birmingham, was built in 1903. Its brown brick exterior reflects a turn-of-the century Commercial architectural style, with Renaissance Revival detailing in the windows and building base.

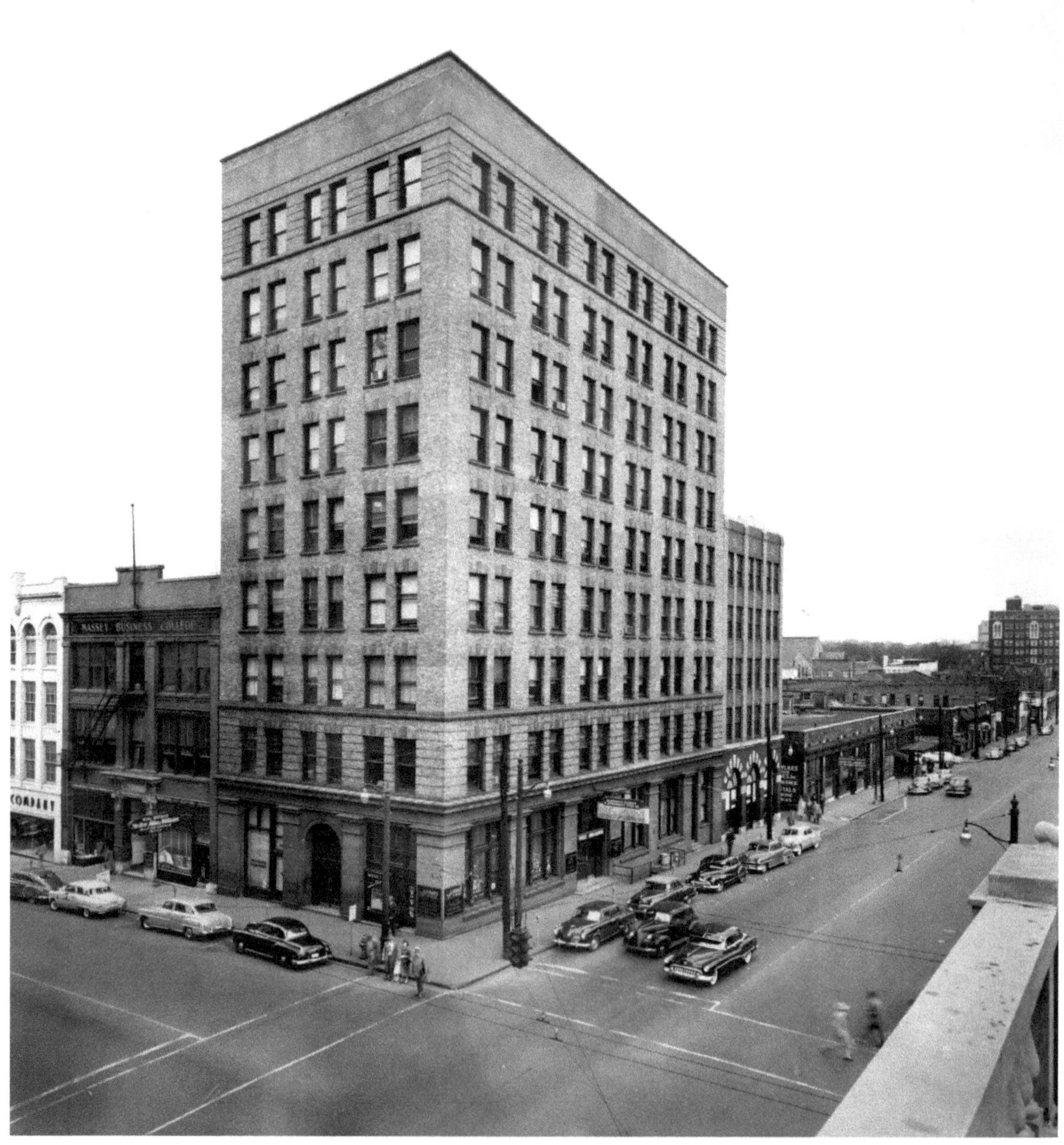

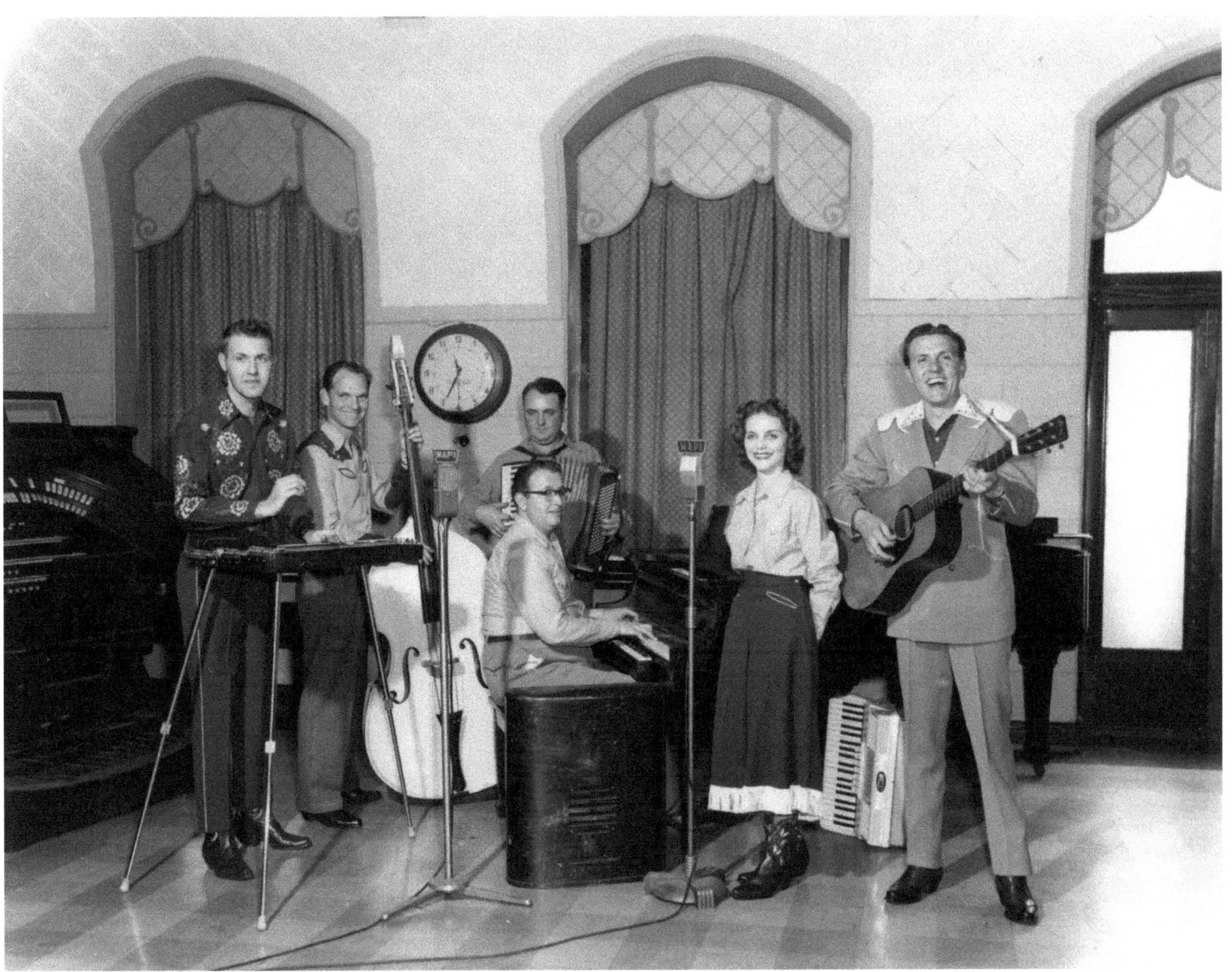

"Happy" Wilson (with guitar) and the "Golden River Boys" perform their radio broadcast for Birmingham's WAPI. A native of Wilson County, Alabama, Eugene "Happy" Wilson entertained Birmingham residents with his down-home tunes. Wilson was also a composer and radio station manager in Alabama and Tennessee.

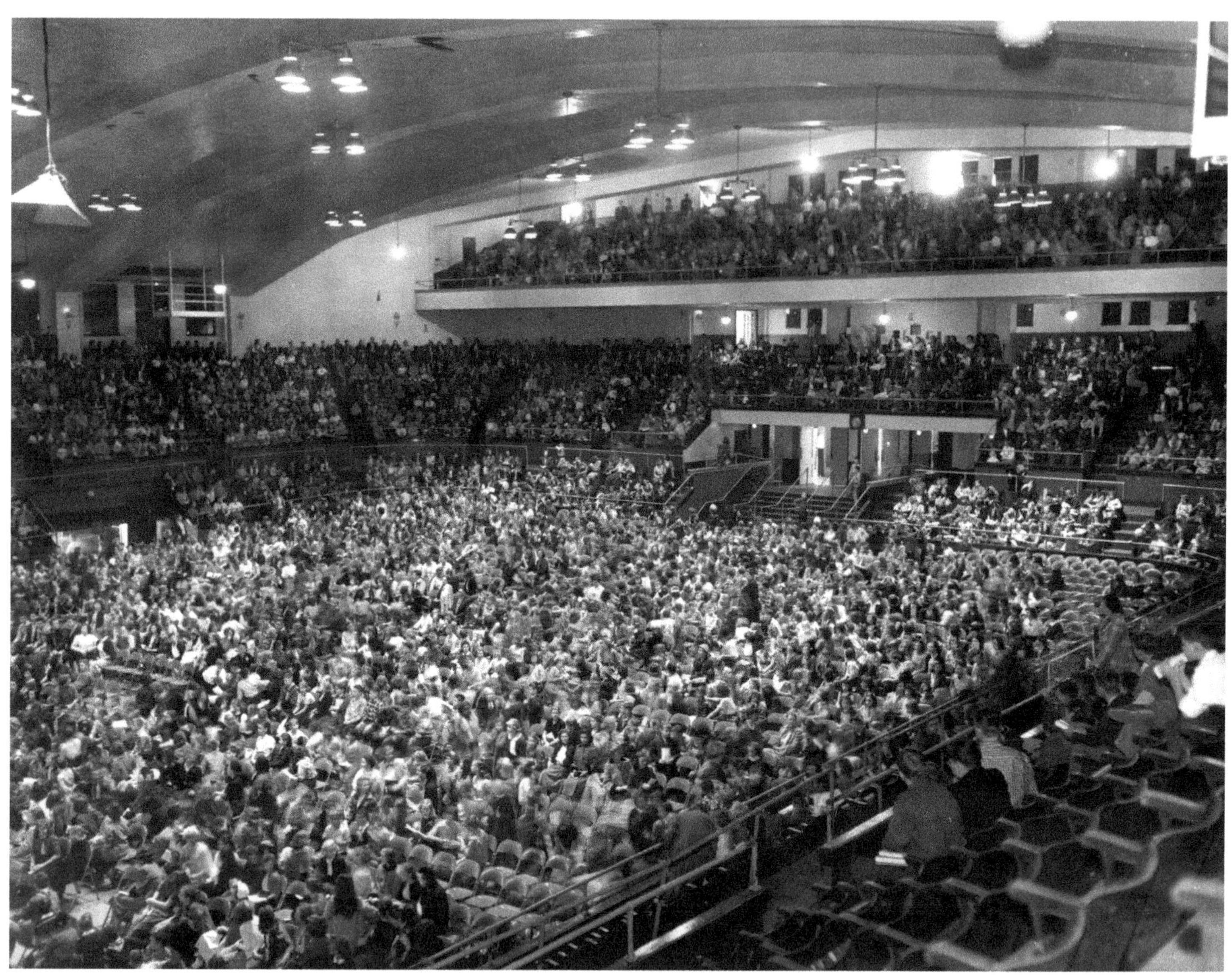

A crowd gathers to hear the Birmingham Symphony perform. Though created during the Great Depression in 1933, the symphony's performances were halted by World War II. By the 1950s, culturally minded Birmingham residents succeeded in reestablishing the orchestra.

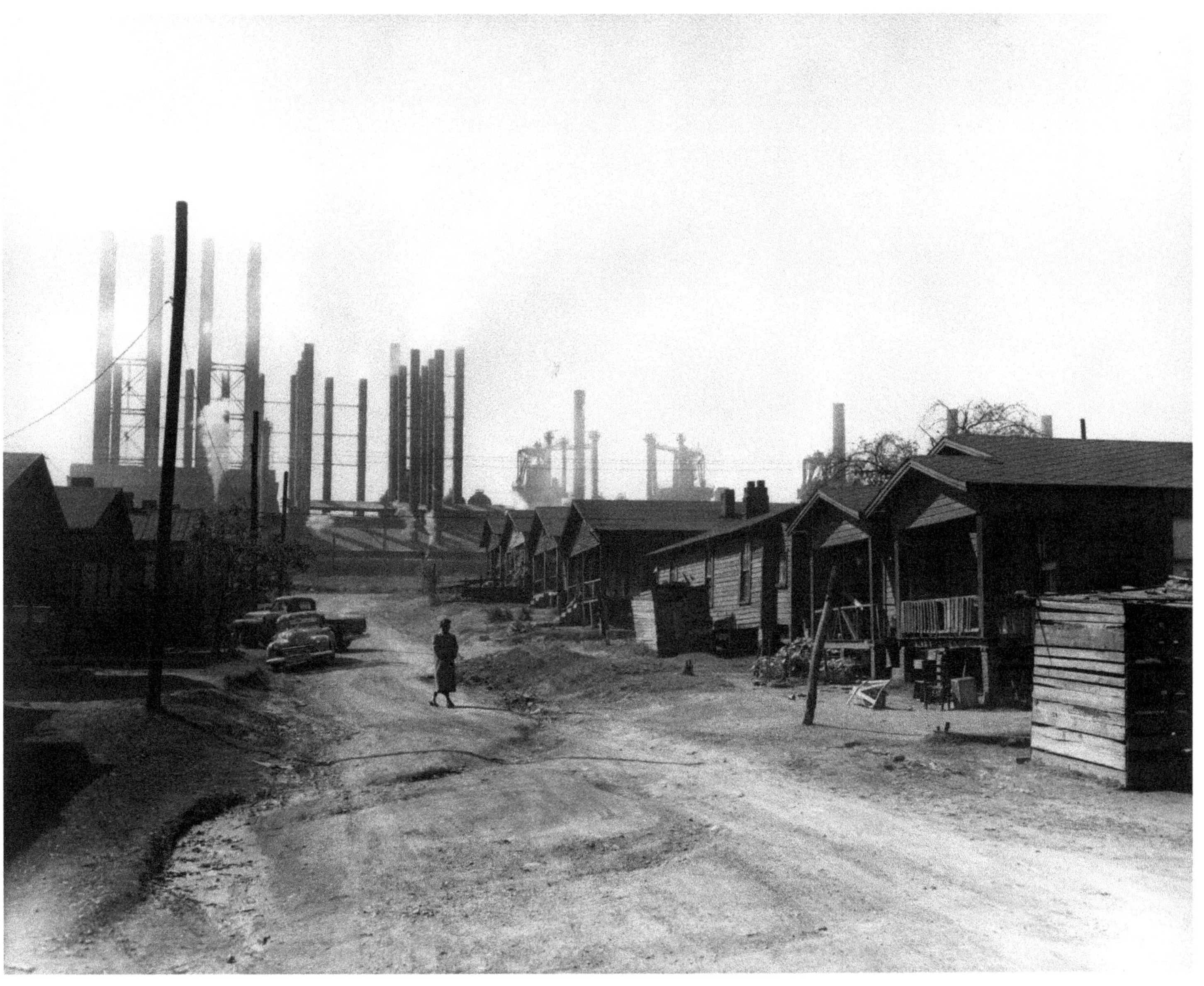

With U.S. Steel looming in the background, this solitary woman wends her way home. The coal and steel industry was the backbone of the Birmingham economy during most of the twentieth century.

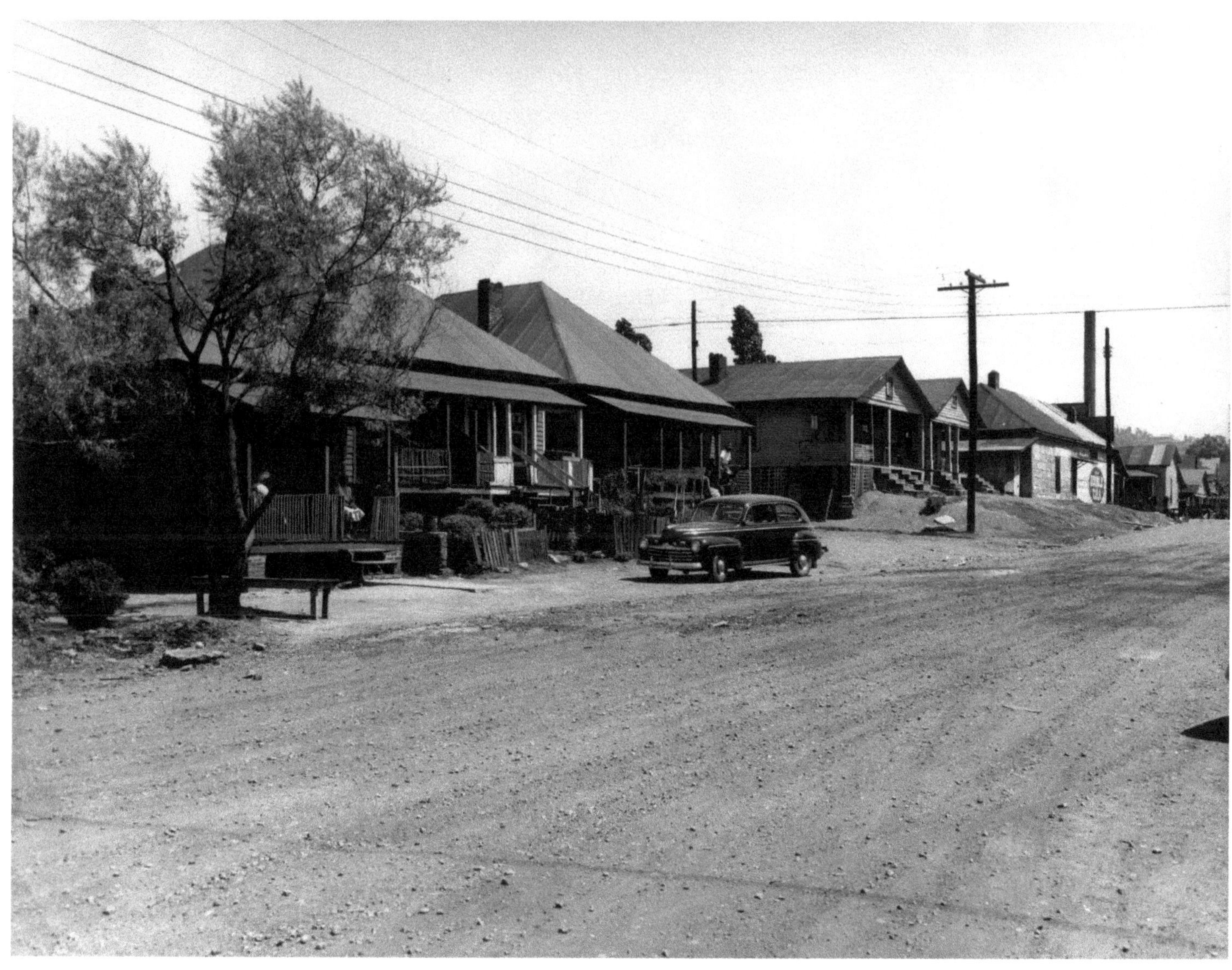

U.S. Steel housing lines a street in Ensley on the outskirts of Birmingham. Founded by Memphis millionaire Enoch Ensley, who had come to Birmingham to invest money in the booming coal industry, the town was home to Tennessee Coal Iron & Railroad Company, which was later sold to United States Steel.

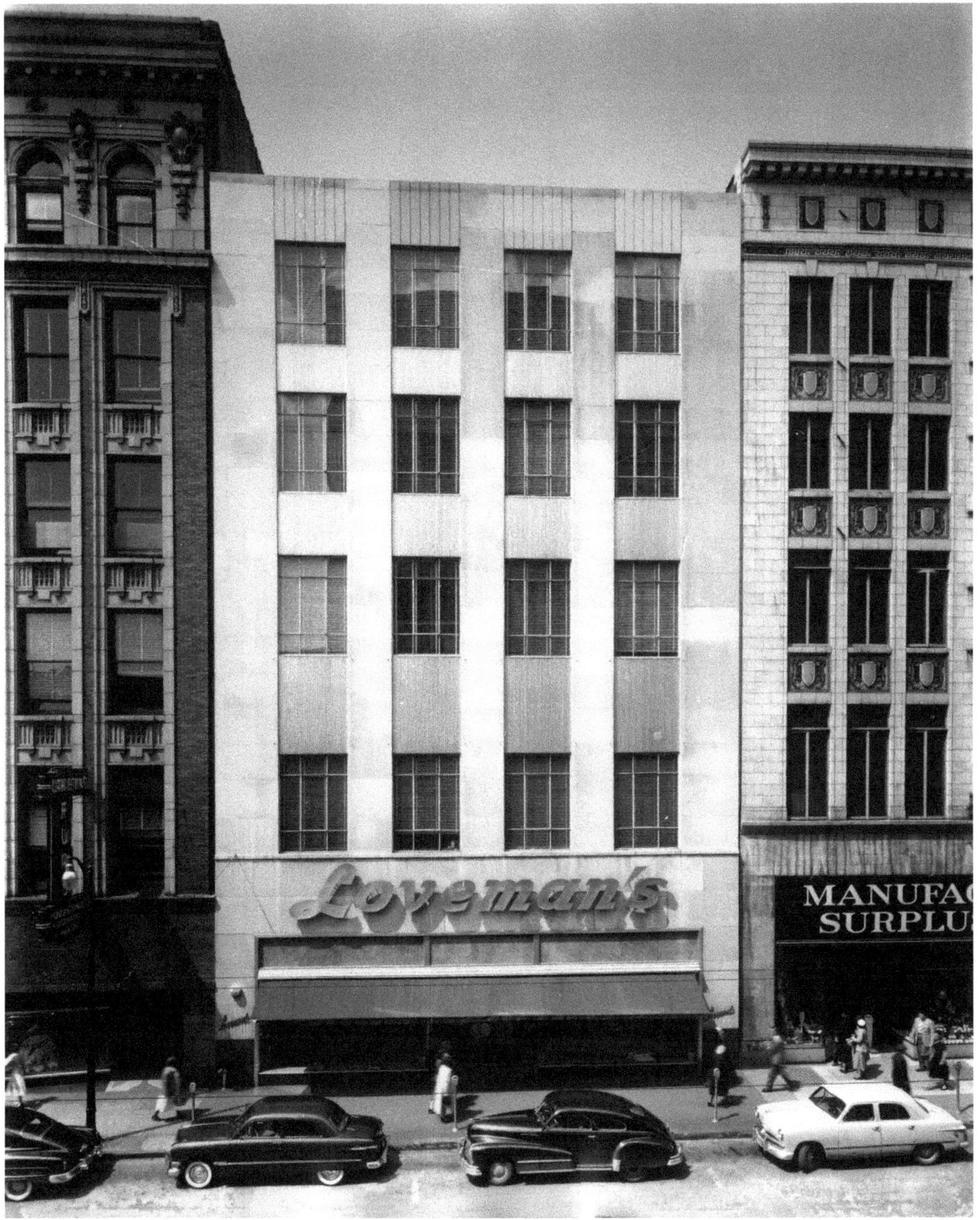

This is the annex for Loveman, Joseph & Loeb Department Store on 2nd Avenue North. Loveman's was founded in 1887 and by 1911 was billed as the South's most magnificent department store. A fire destroyed the store in 1934, but the exterior of the annex survived. Loveman's rebuilt and continued to serve the needs of Birmingham until 1980, when the chain filed for bankruptcy.

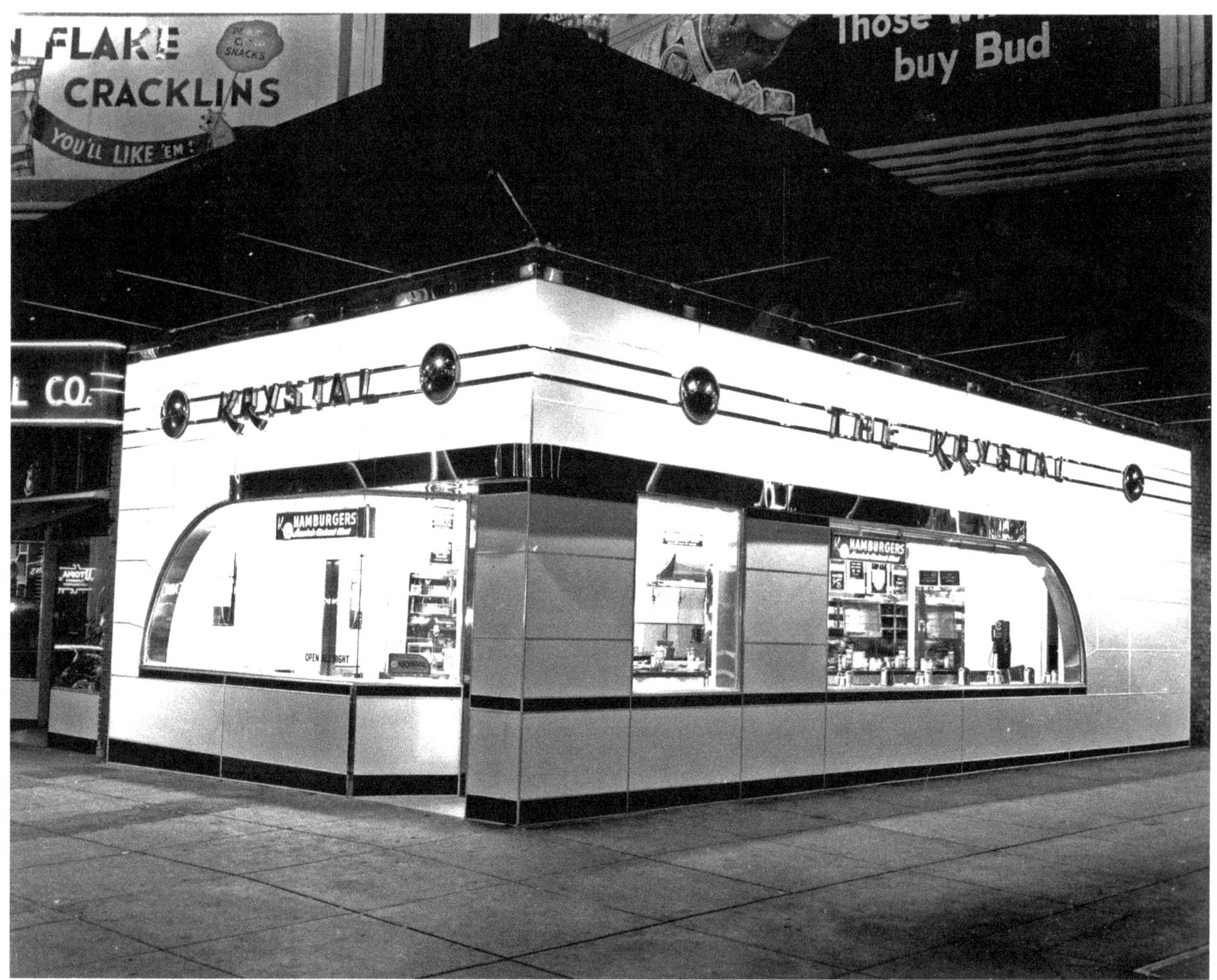

Krystal, founded in Chattanooga, Tennessee, and famous across the South for its specialty pickle-onion-and-mustard hamburger, opened its first outlet in Birmingham here at 1800 2nd Avenue North.

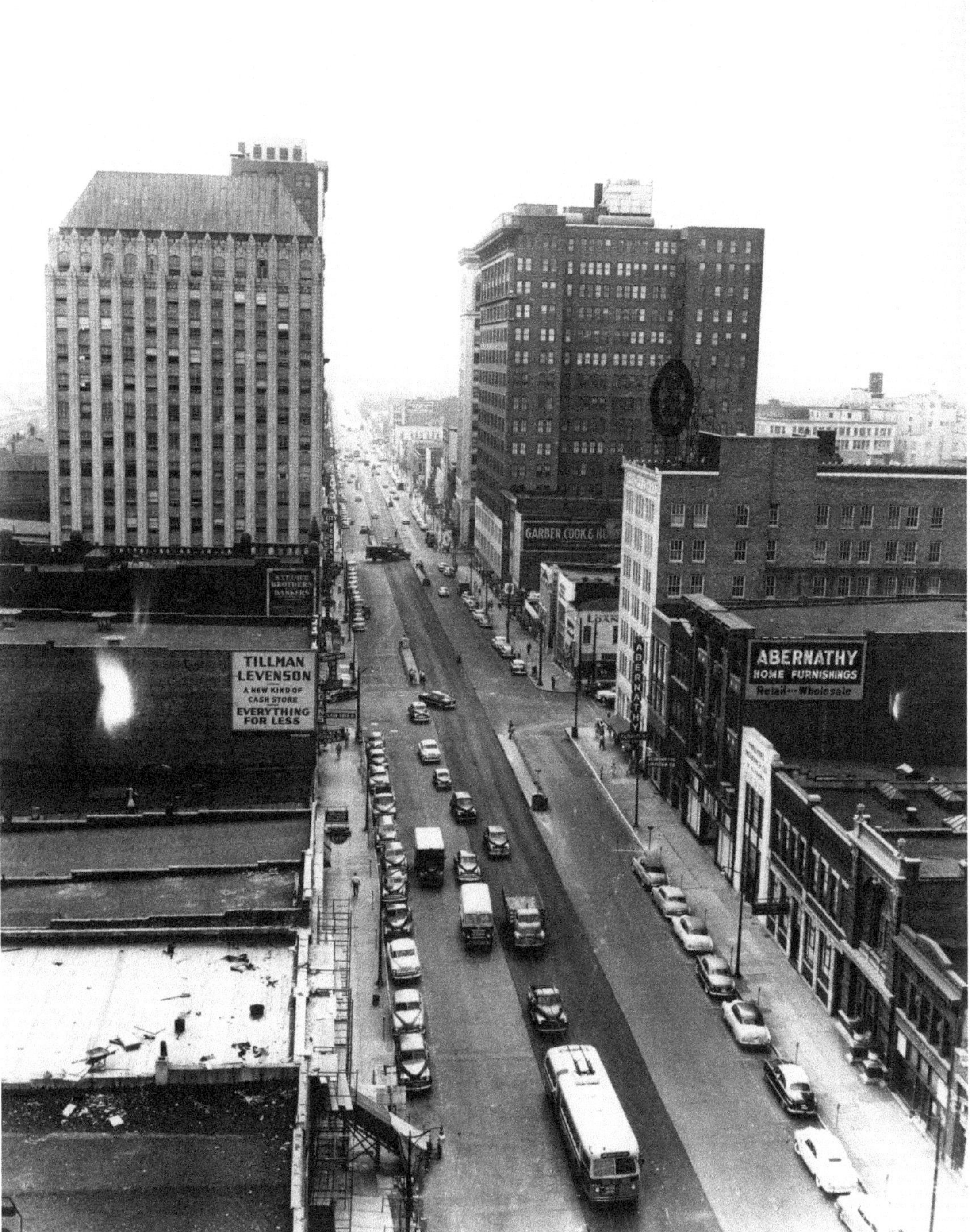

Automobile traffic on 1st Avenue North on this day in the 1950s seems to be light. Abernathy Home, Employees Insurance Company of Alabama, and the City Federal Building line the street.

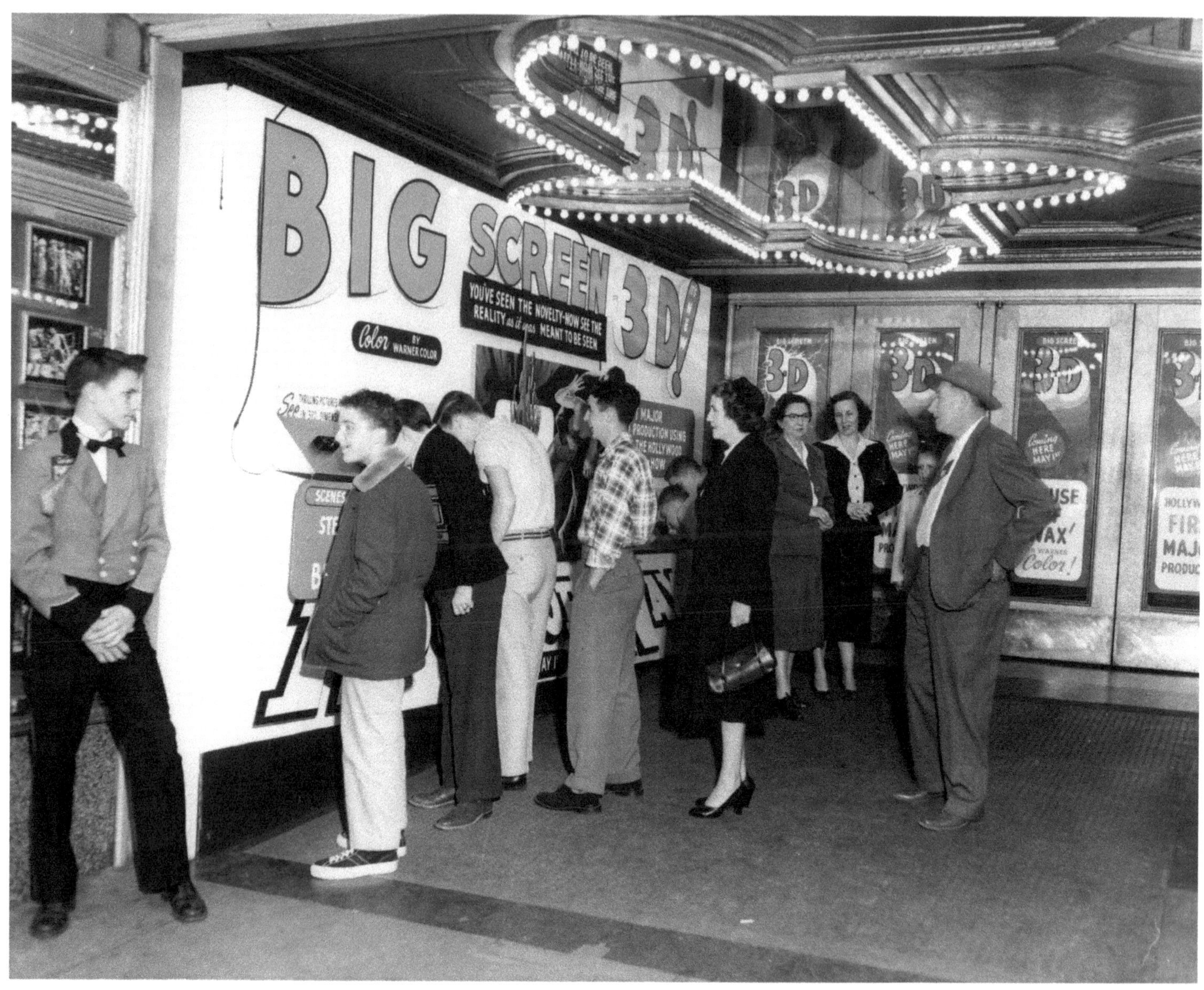

At the Alabama Theater, people view the 3-Dimensional Vision movies display. Located on 3rd Avenue North, the Alabama Theater was built in 1927 and offered not just movies but pageants, fashion shows, and other forms of entertainment.

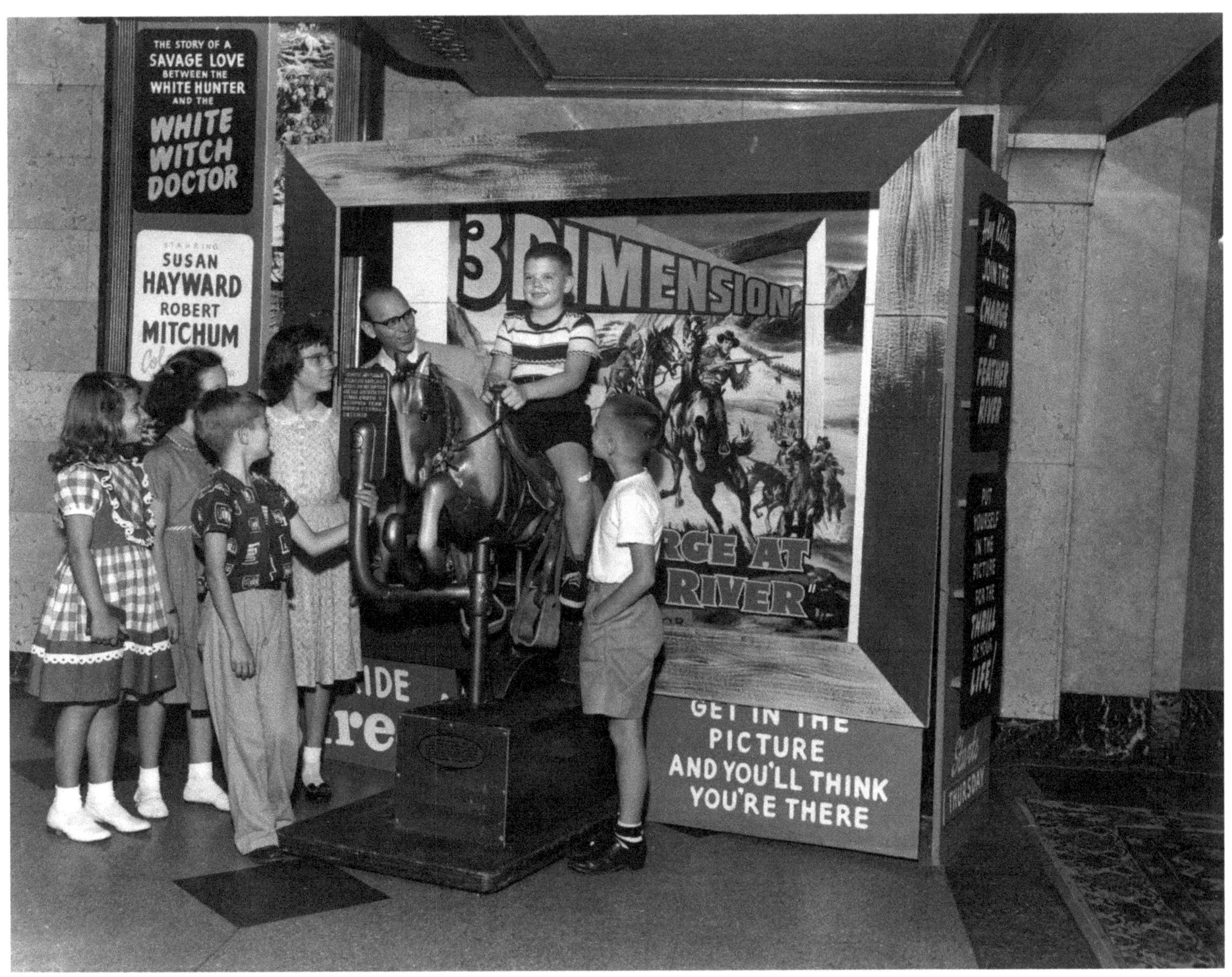

A group of children ride a mechanical horse at the Alabama Theater while an advertisement announces the up-coming 3-Dimensional Western *Charge at Feather River.* The attraction invited young cowboys to imagine themselves as part of the movie.

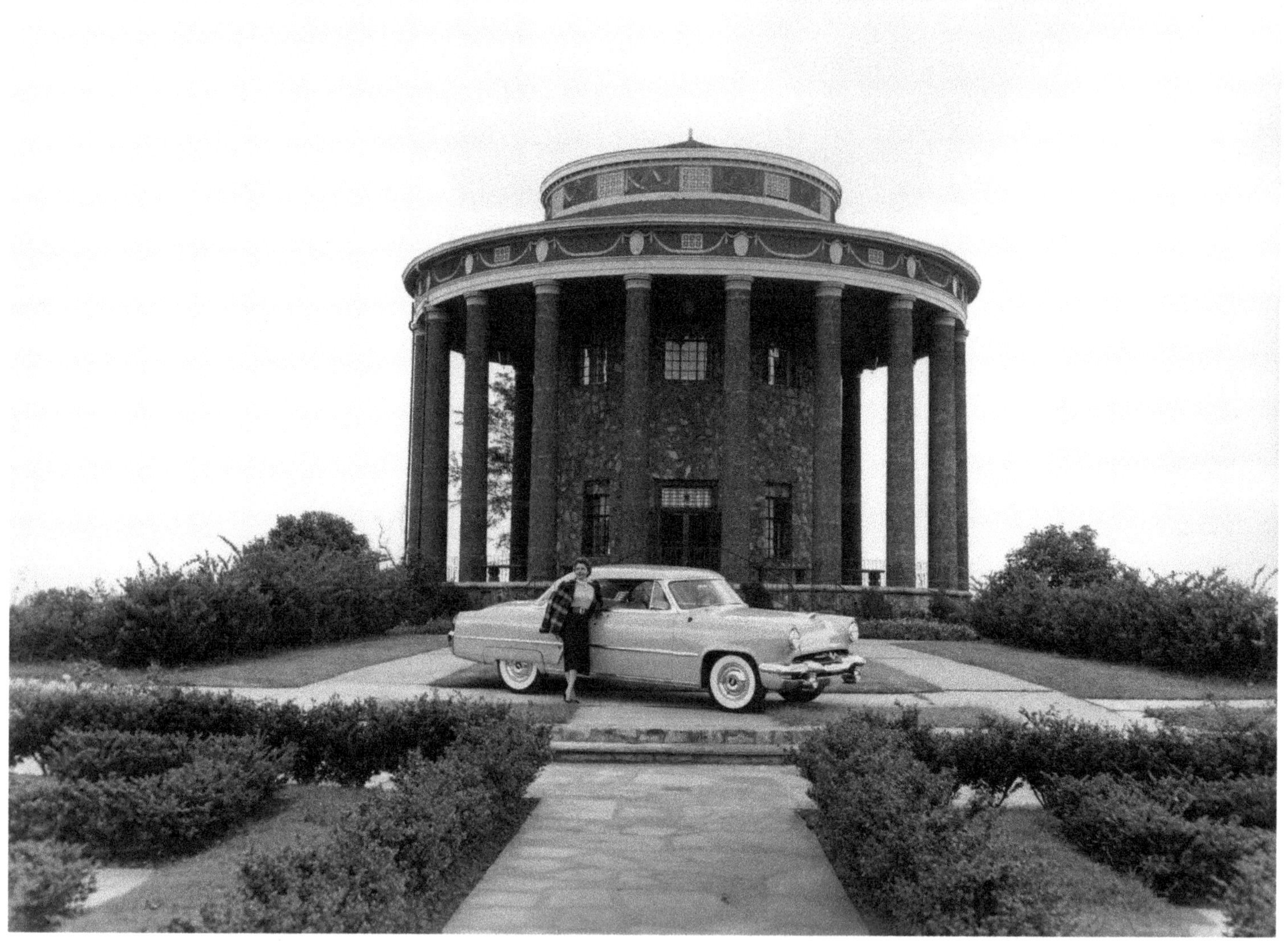

Former mayor of Birmingham George B. Ward, an admirer of ancient Greek and Roman culture, built this home on Shades Mountain's crest in 1923. Called Vestavia, a replica of the Roman Temple of the Vestal Virgins, it was the scene of rambunctious parties which featured ladies dancing, guests in togas, and servants as Roman soldiers. Vestavia Hills community was named for Ward's unique home.

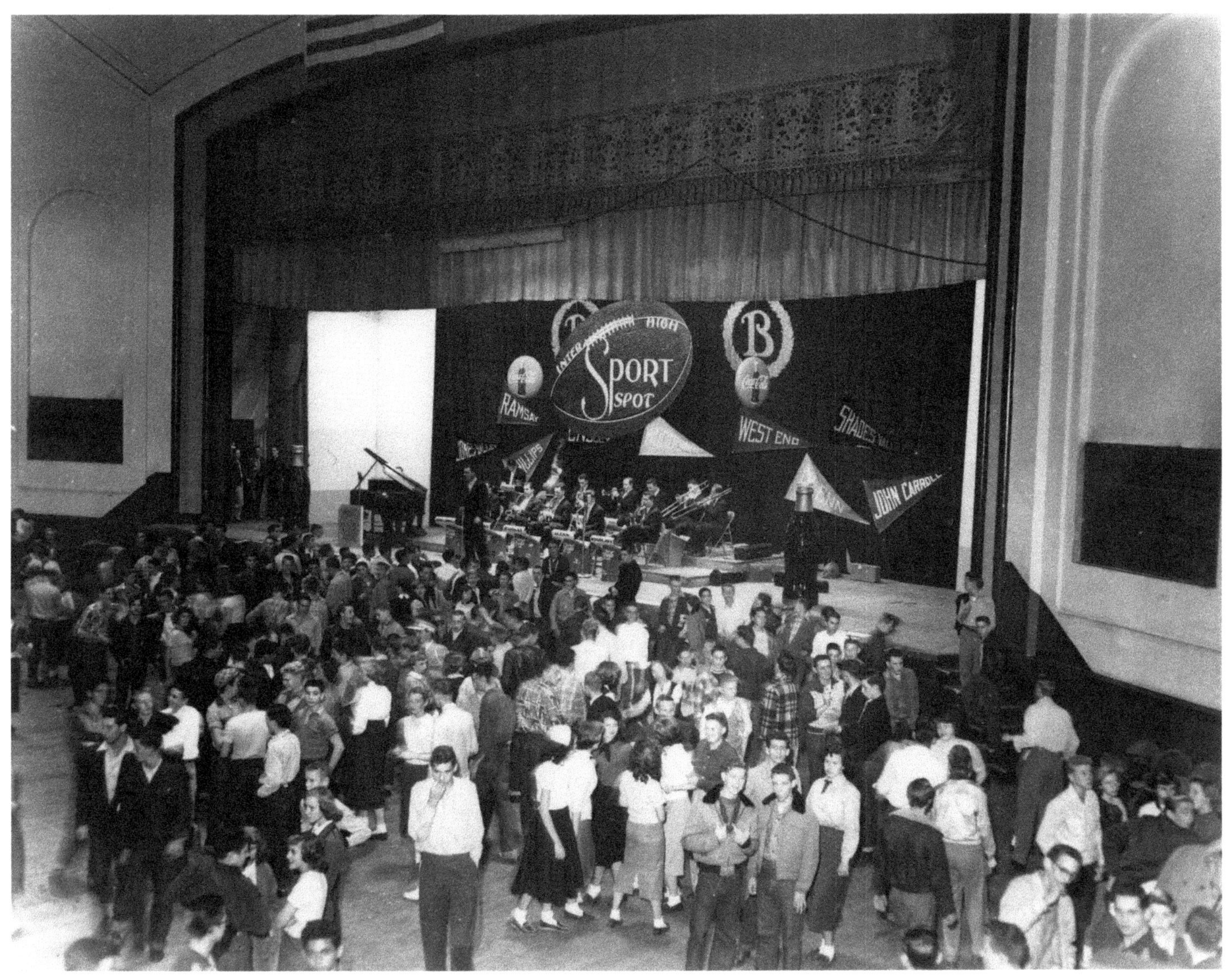

As part of its commitment to Birmingham, which had become home to a new plant, Coca-Cola hosted this dance for local high school students. A live band performed for the event.

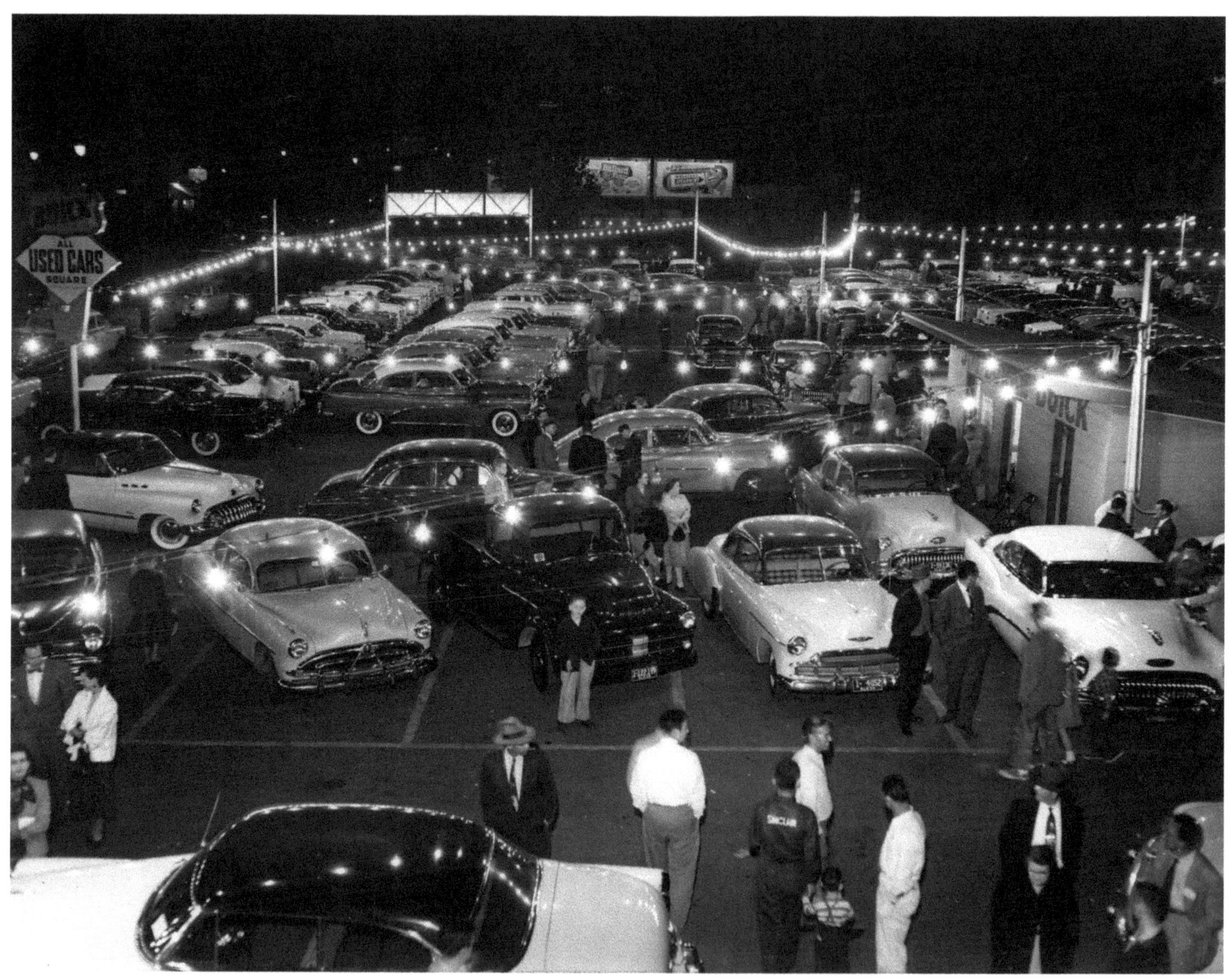

Customers search for an automobile at Jim Burke Buick Used Car Lot on 5th Avenue. White wall tires, spacious interiors, and lots of chrome created the perfect ride for the motoring public in the mid-1950s. In the distance, billboards advertise Wrigley's chewing gum and Ballard flour.

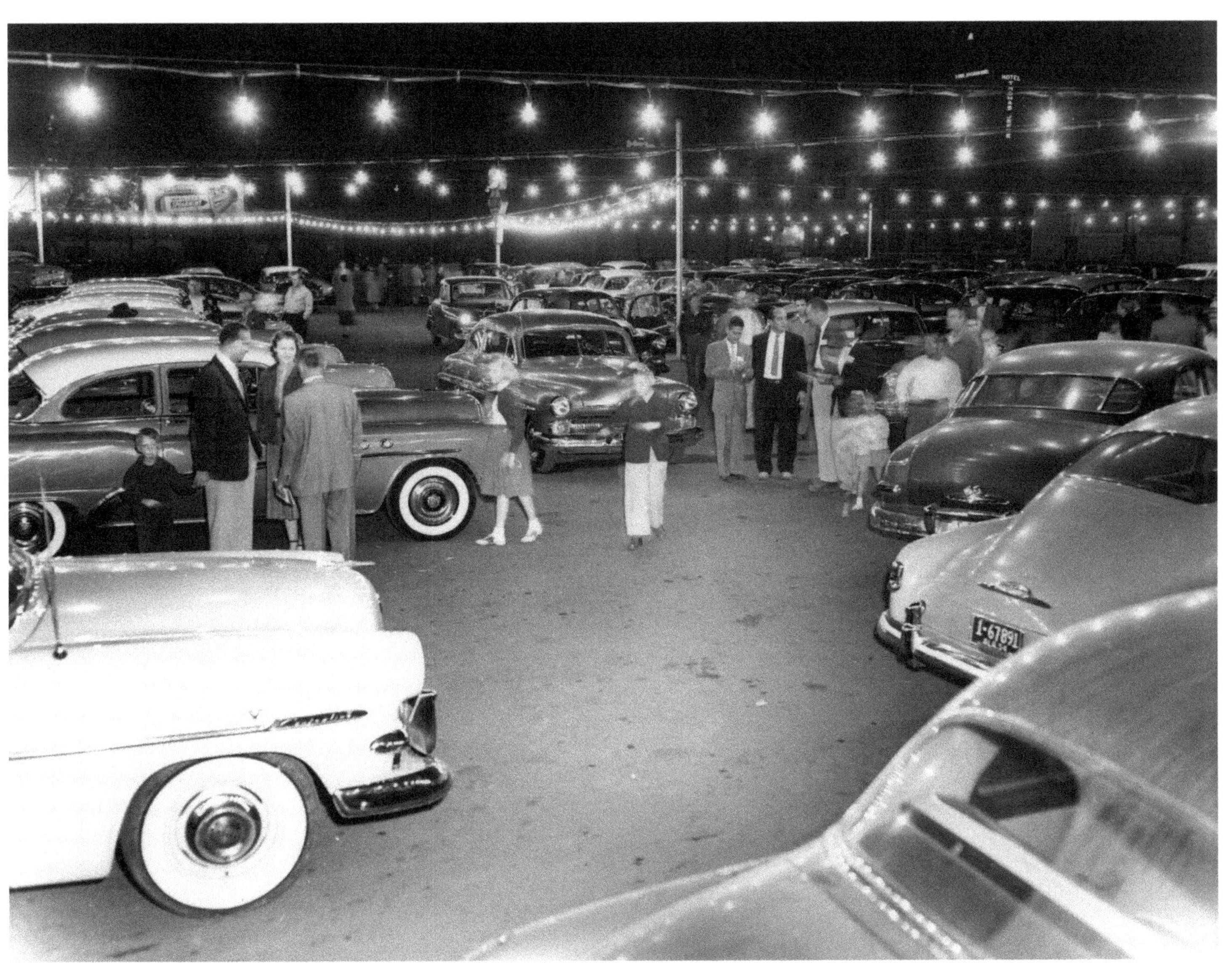

Customers peruse the lot at Jim Burke Buick here around 1954.

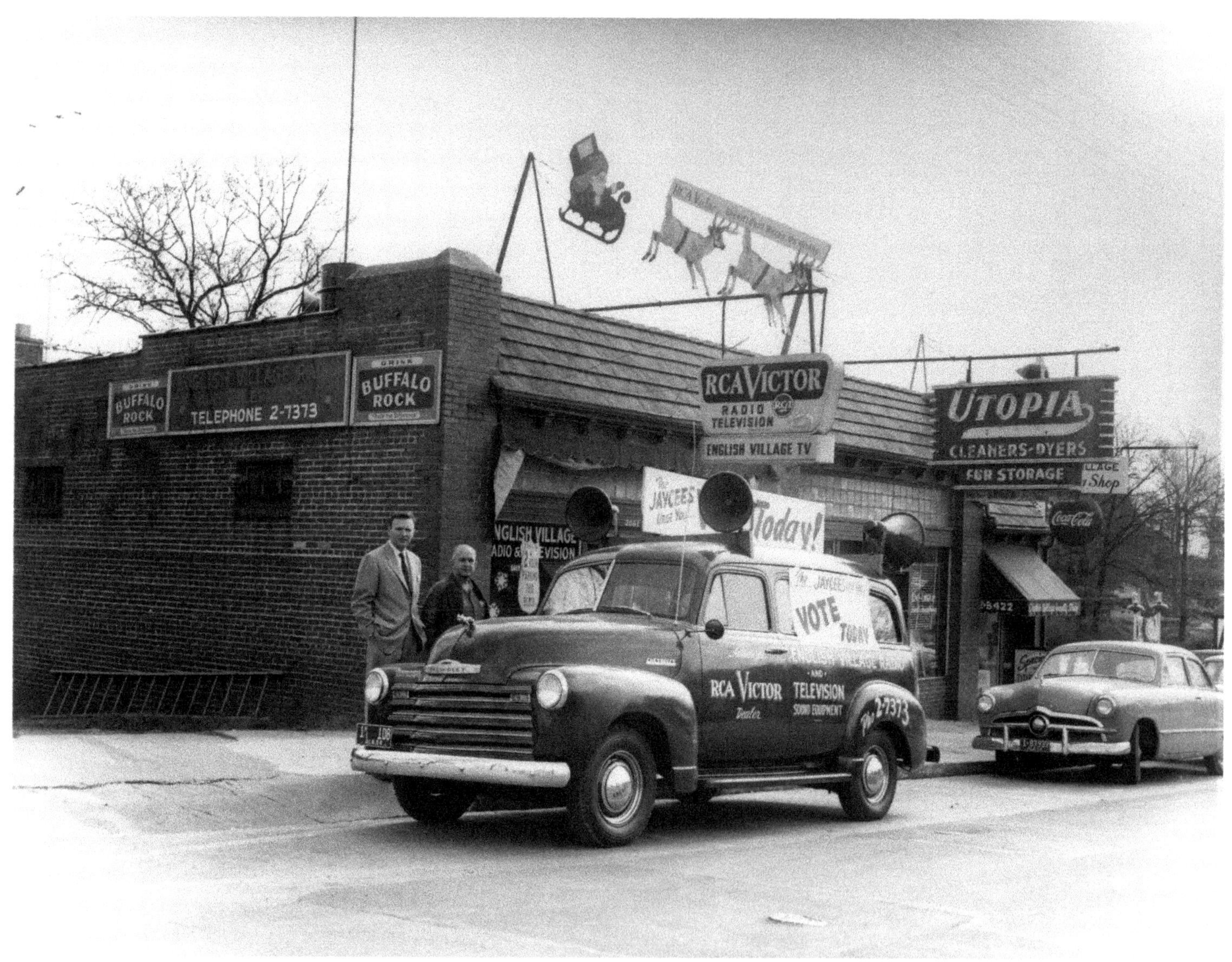

English Village, a posh Mountain Brook community built to replicate an Old World hamlet, is decorated for Christmas in 1954. The local Jaycees appear to be trying to get out the vote.

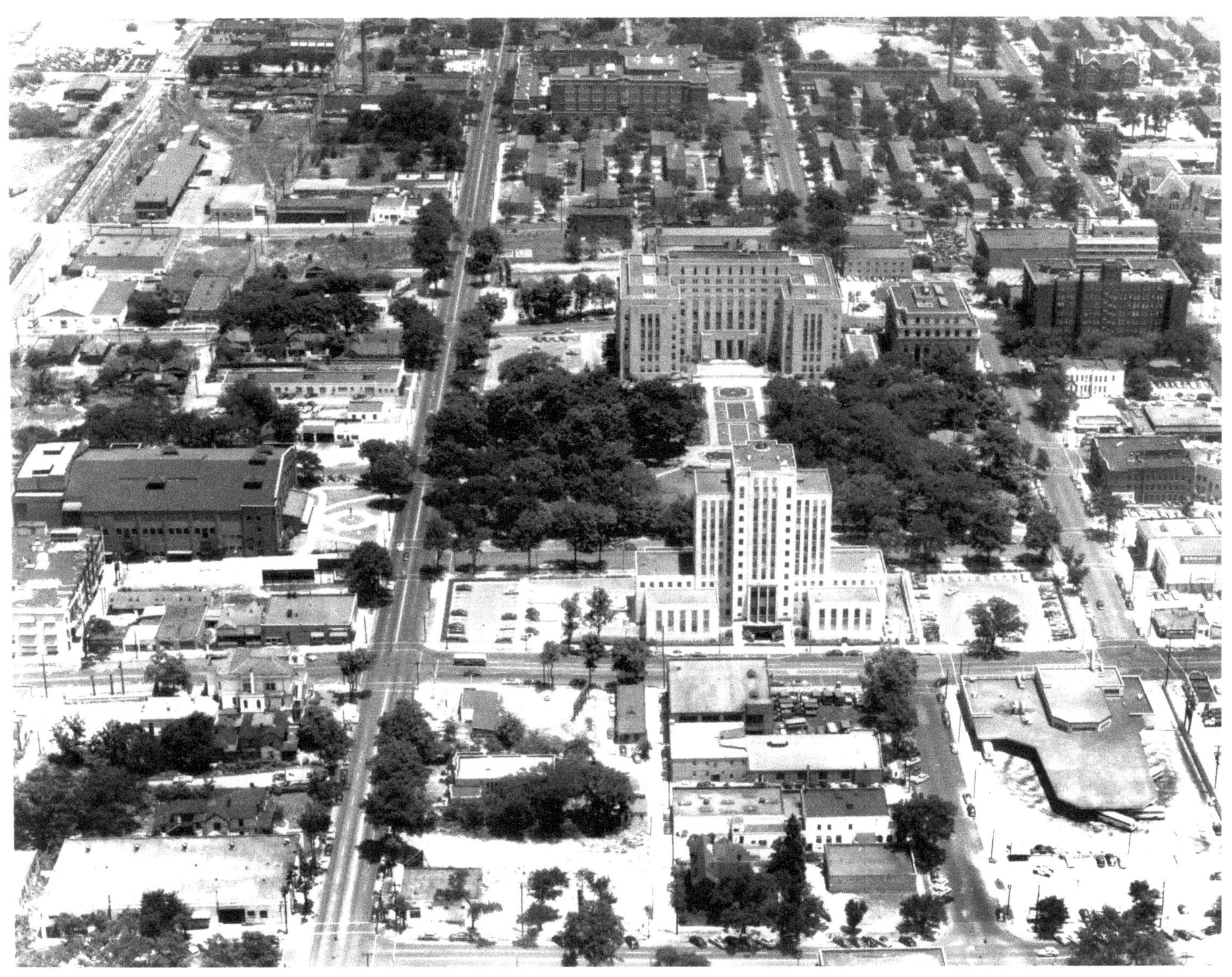

Aerial view of the Birmingham City Hall (at front, right of center), directly across from the Jefferson County Courthouse (top-center), nextdoor to which is the Birmingham Public Library (at right).

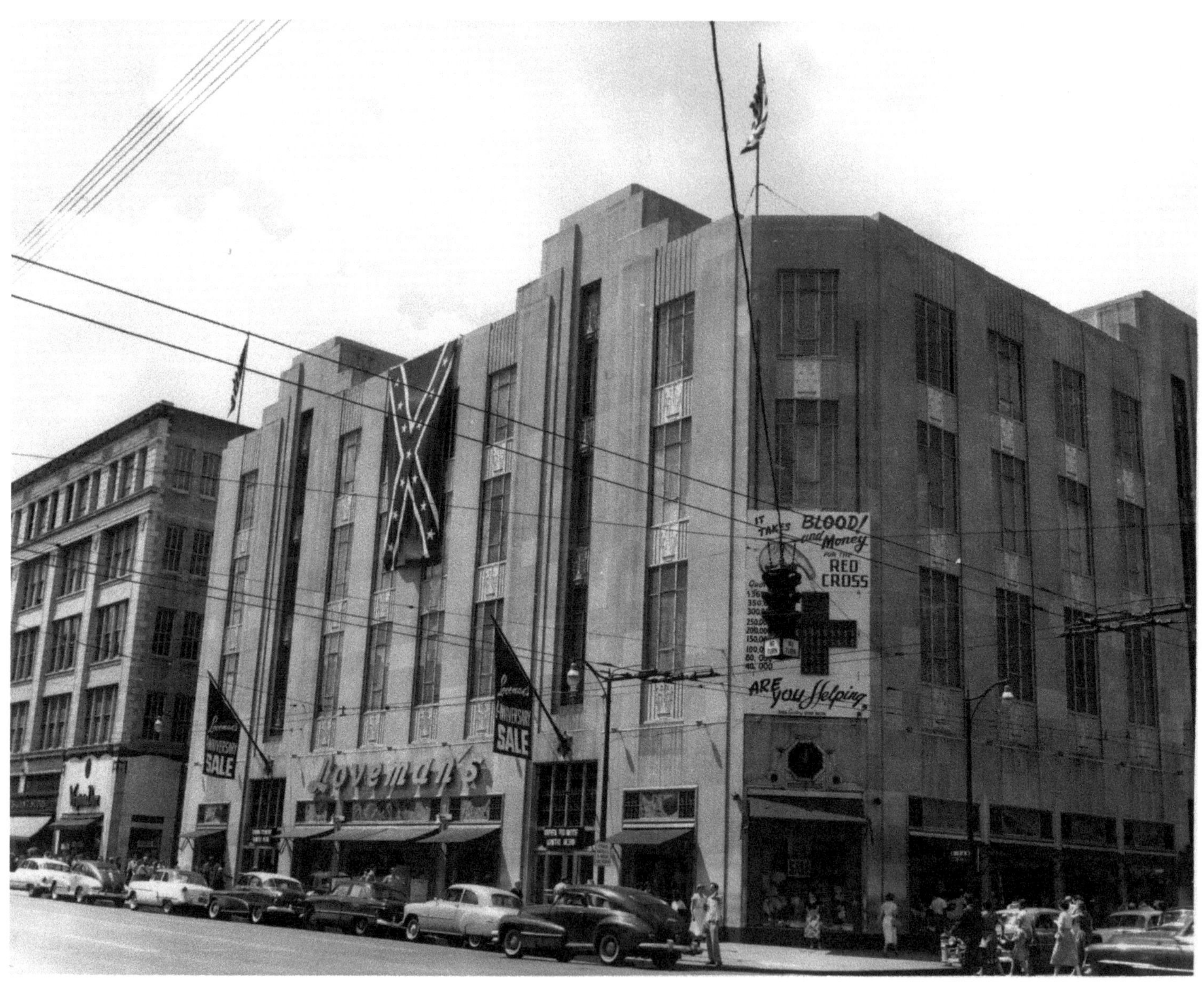

Loveman's Department store celebrates Confederate Memorial Day by draping a Confederate battle flag from the roof. In 1901, Alabama legislation declared April 26 as a day of remembrance for fallen Confederate soldiers and the end of hostilities in the South. The observance commemorates the surrender of Confederate general Joseph E. Johnston to Union general William Sherman on April 26, 1865, 17 days after General Lee's surrender to General Grant at Appomattox Court House.

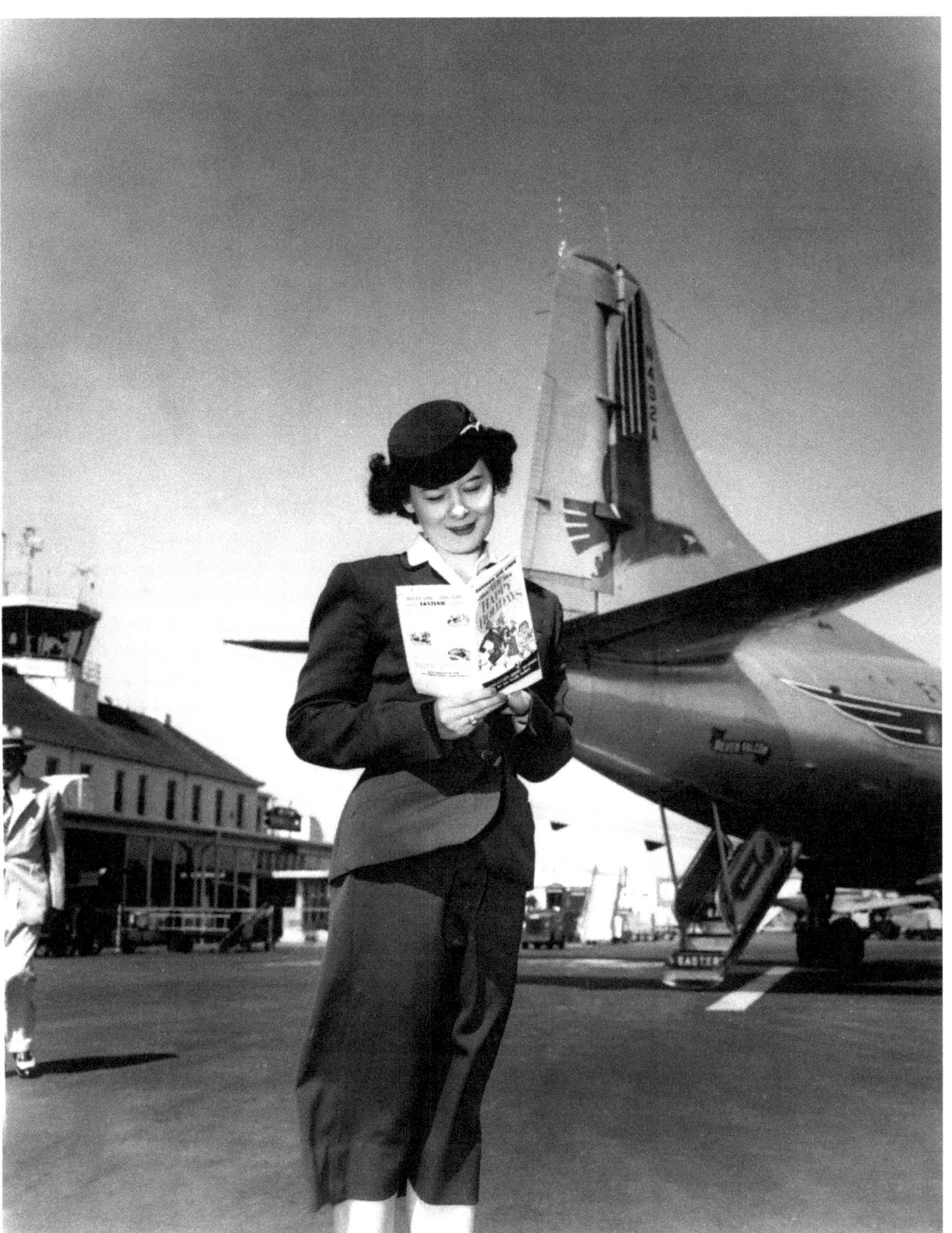

An Eastern Air Lines stewardess takes a moment on the tarmac to review a pamphlet wishing their flyers "Happy Holidays."

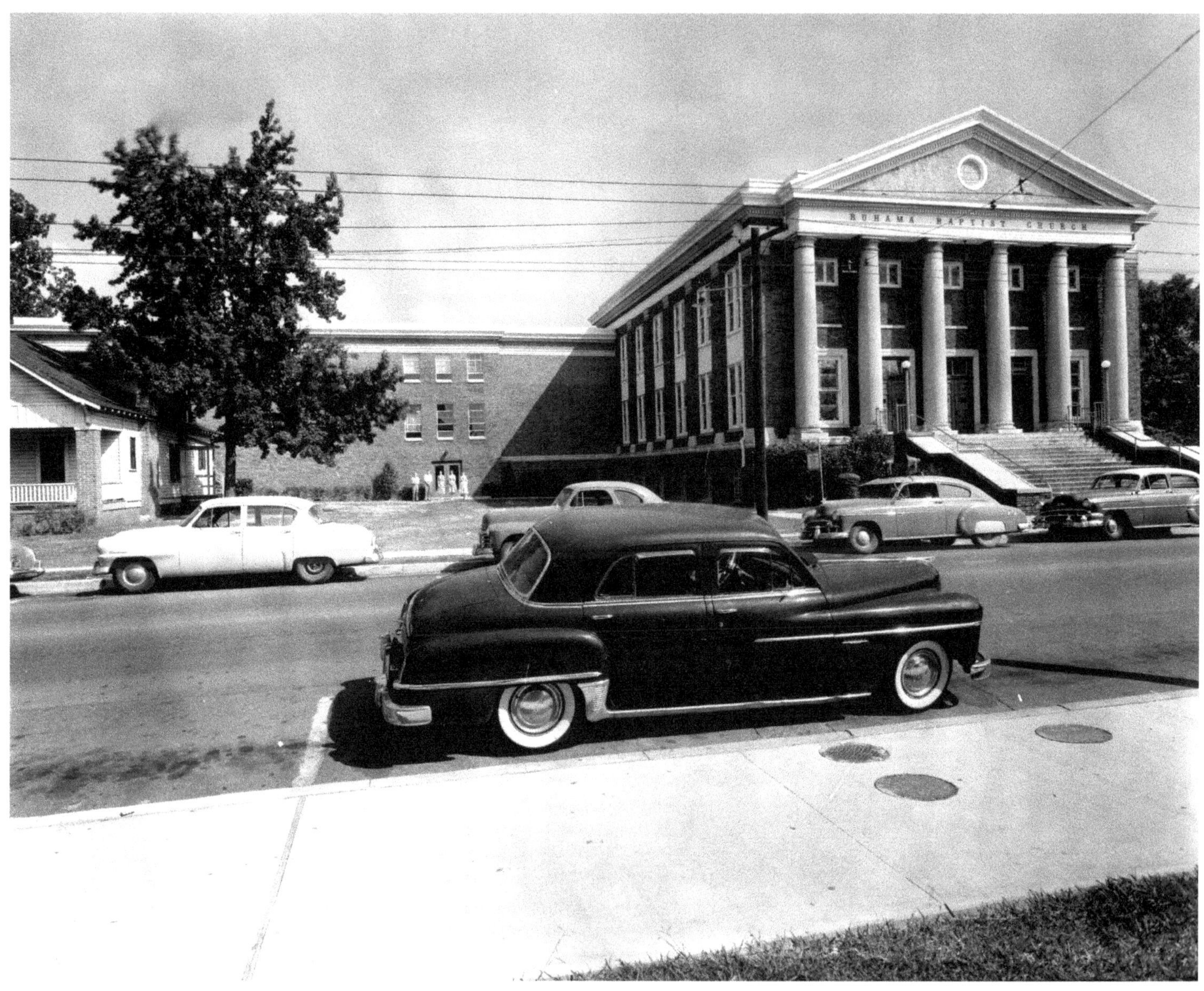

Established in 1819, Ruhama Baptist Church, located on 2nd Avenue South in East Lake here in the 1950s, was the first known Baptist church to be organized in the area that would become Birmingham. By 1954, Ruhama's membership had surpassed 3,000 in number and the congregation was becoming increasingly involved in Howard College (later Samford University).

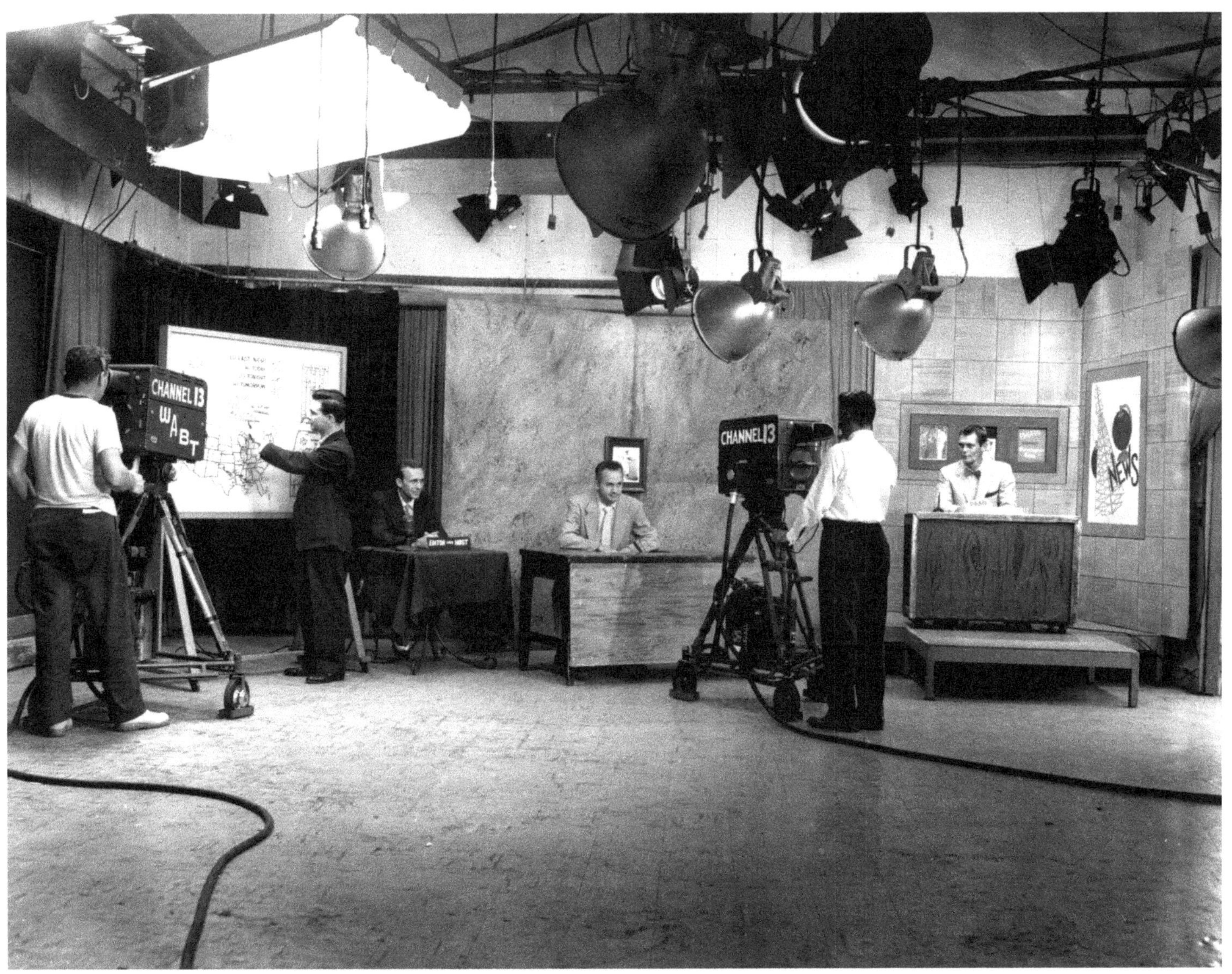

Anchors and crew of the oldest television station in Birmingham get ready for broadcast. An NBC affiliate, WABT's call letters stood for Alabama's Best Television. The station was owned by the Birmingham News during the early 1950s.

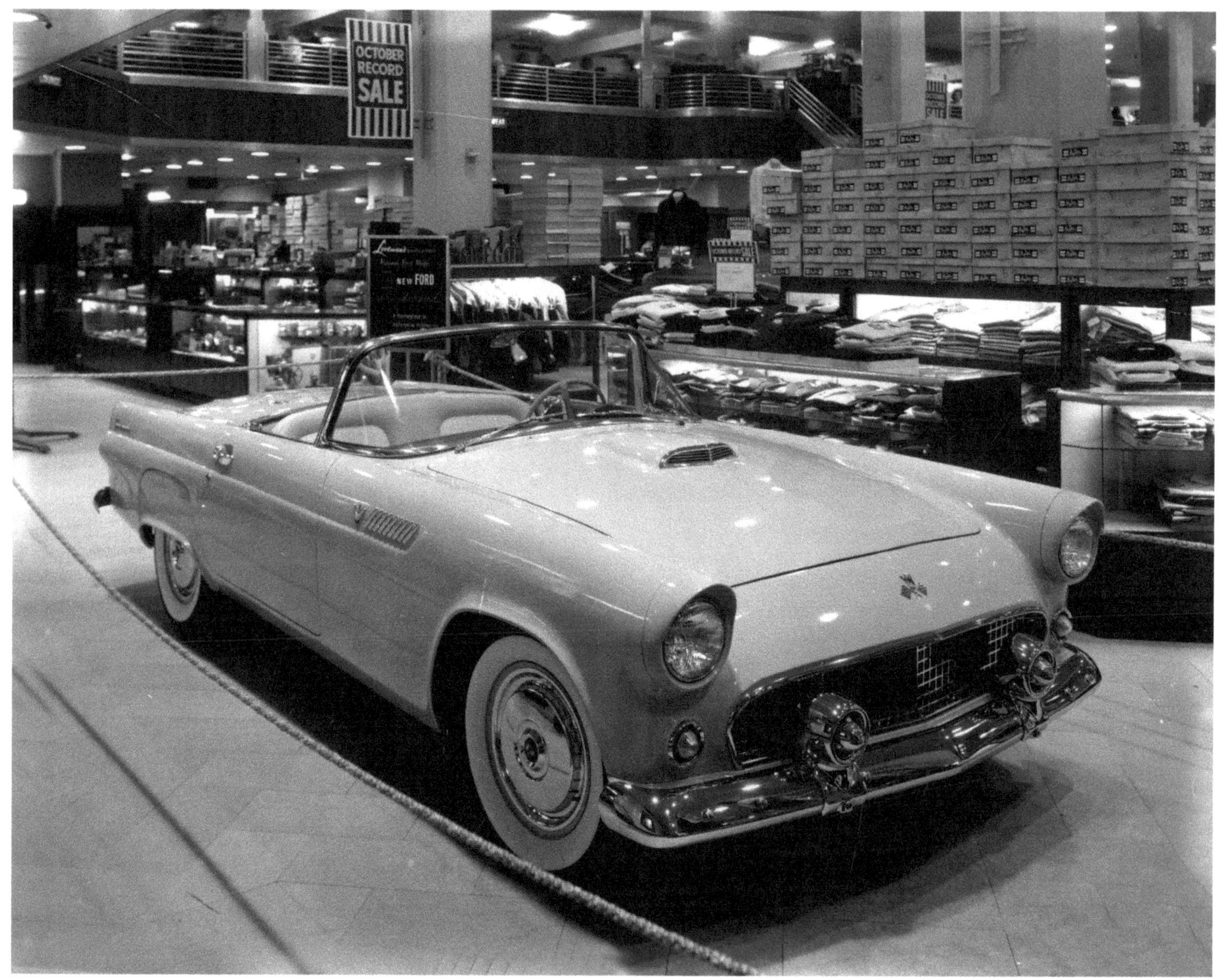

The 1955 Ford Thunderbird, a new car intended to compete with Chevrolet's Corvette, is displayed on the first floor of Loveman's Department Store. The smartly styled automobile would become legendary among car lovers across the nation.

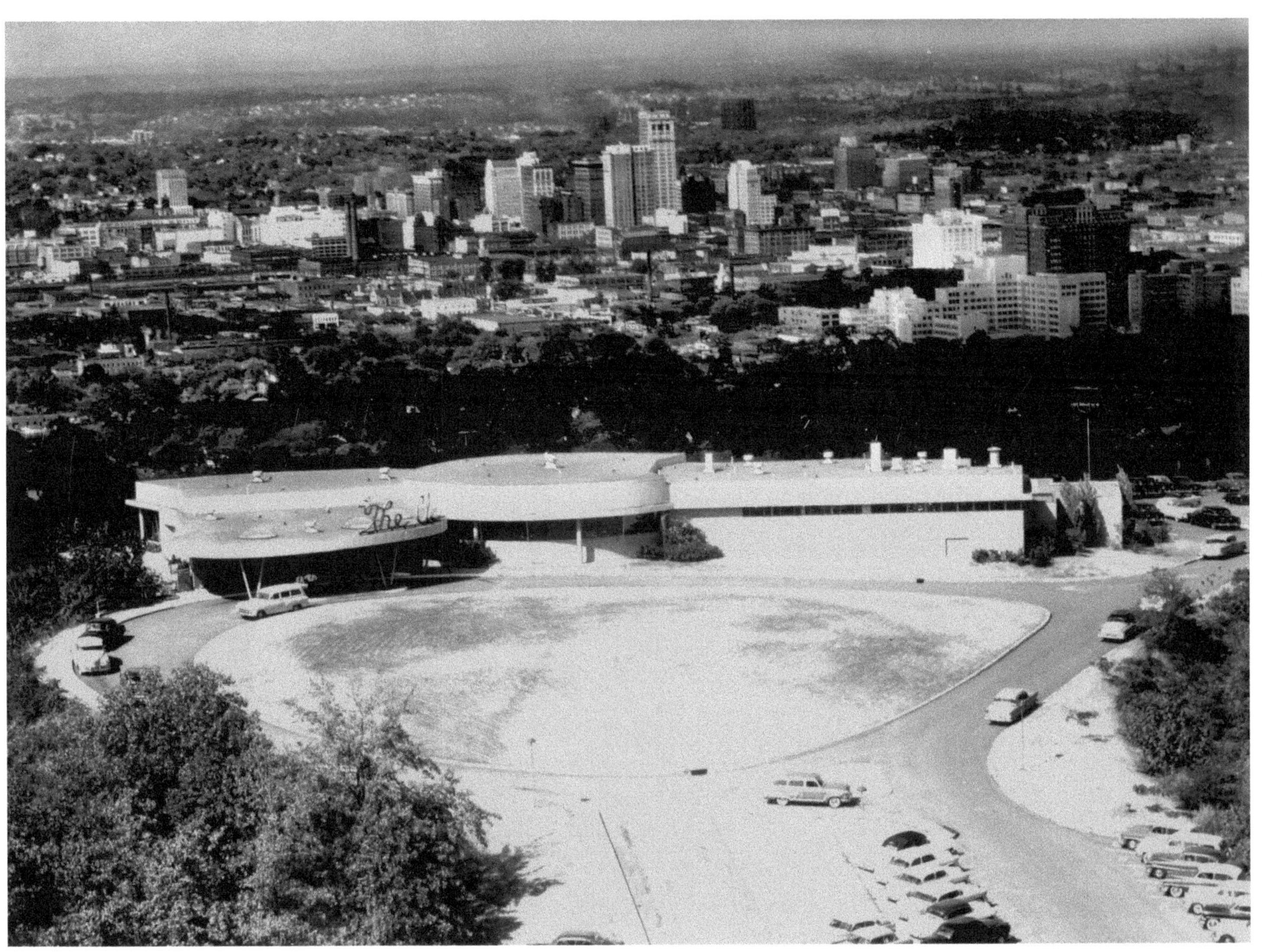

Tennessee Coal Iron Railroad Company employee Robert S. Smith wanted an elegant place to bring out-of-town colleagues. His answer was the Club. Built on what was formerly a goat farm atop Red Mountain, the Club boasted an unusual architectural design that dazzled its members and guests.

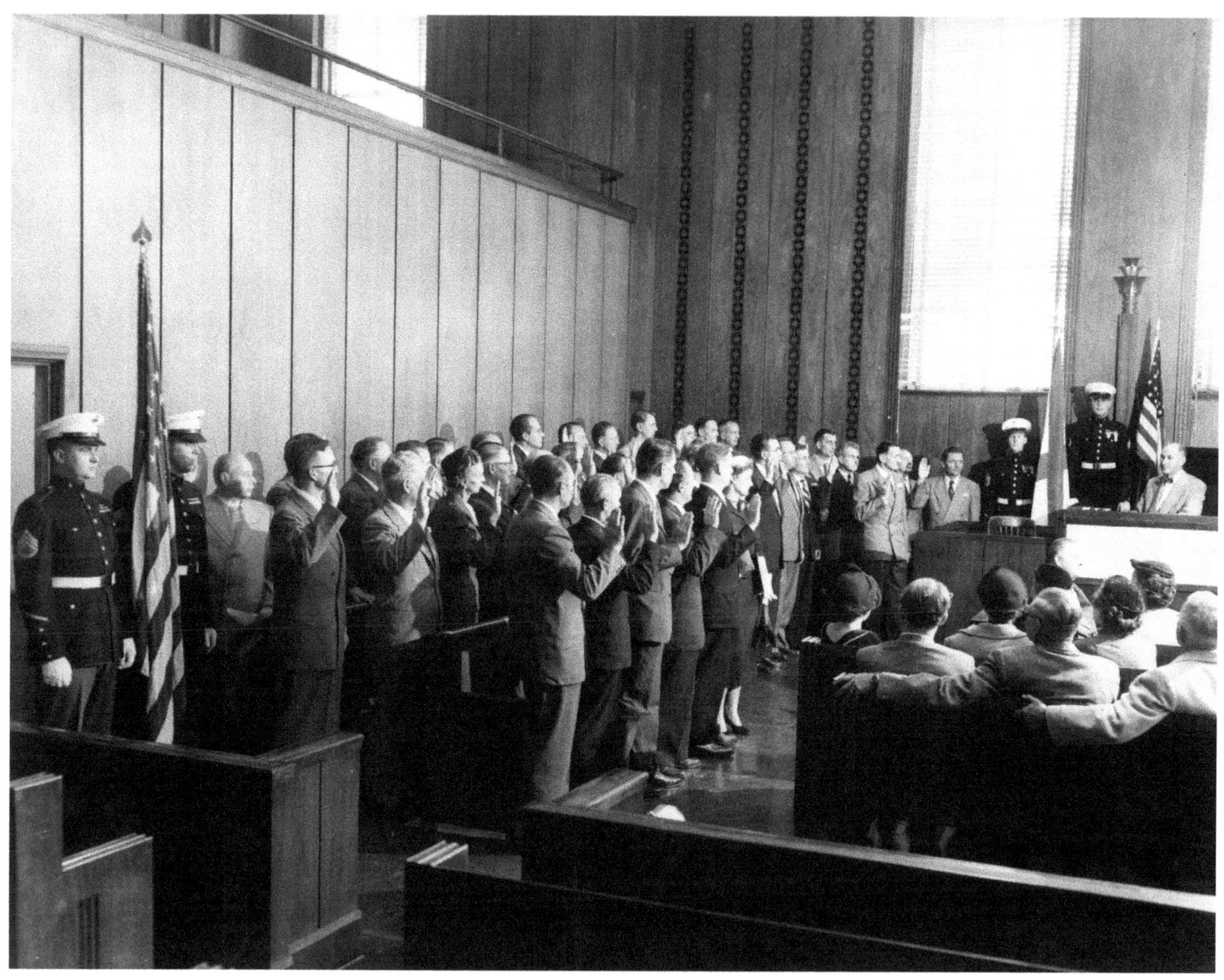

German immigrants become United States citizens at the Hugo L. Black U.S. Courthouse in Birmingham.

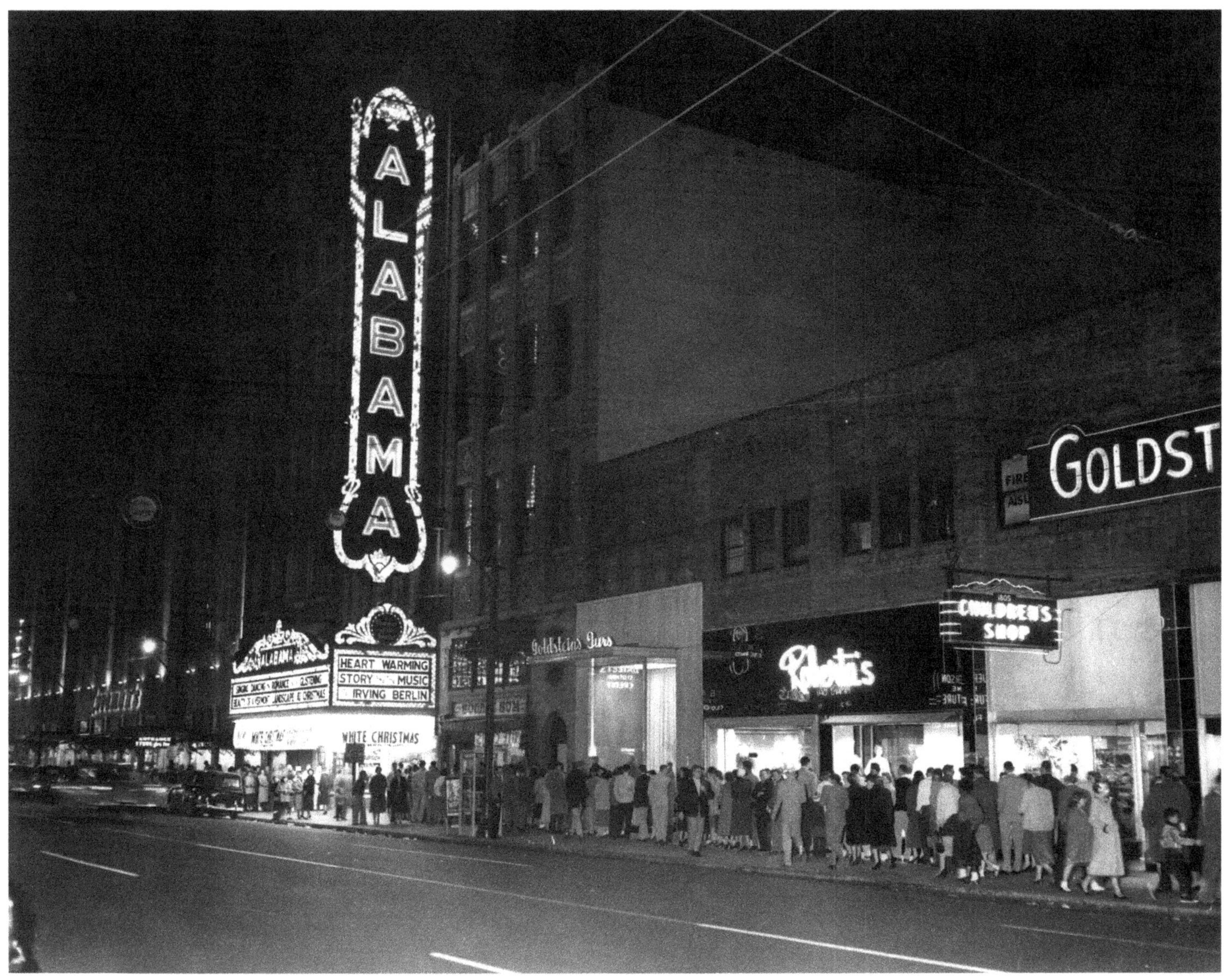

In 1954, moviegoers queue up to see *White Christmas,* starring Bing Crosby and Danny Kaye, at the Alabama Theater. Crosby's rendition of the song "White Christmas" remains one of the most popular tunes ever recorded. As to actually having a white Christmas, the city came close in 1929, when more than 5 inches covered Birmingham on December 22 (but melted away by Christmas Day), and in 1985, when flurries dusted the city on Christmas Eve and Christmas morning.

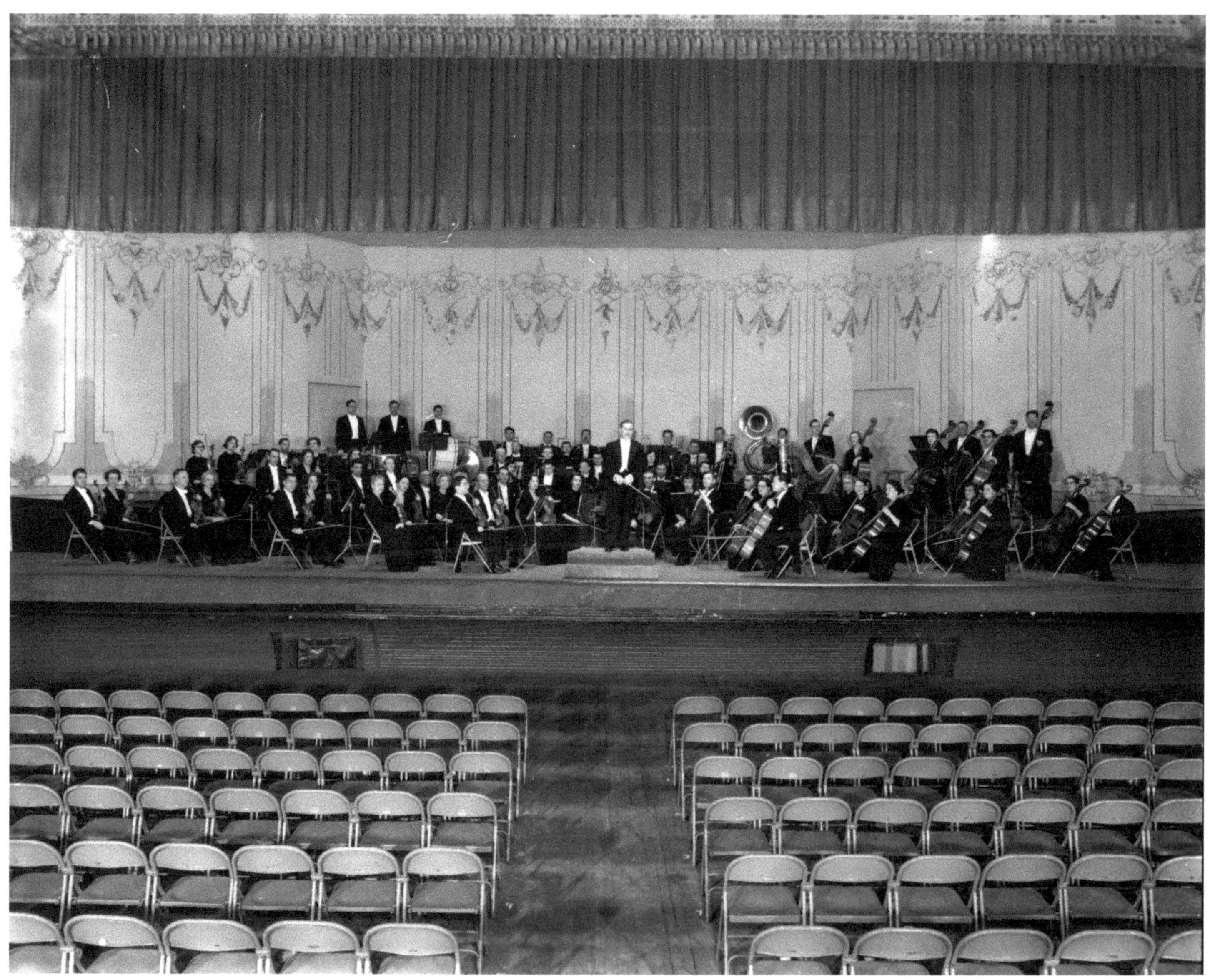

The Birmingham Symphony Orchestra rehearses for another performance.

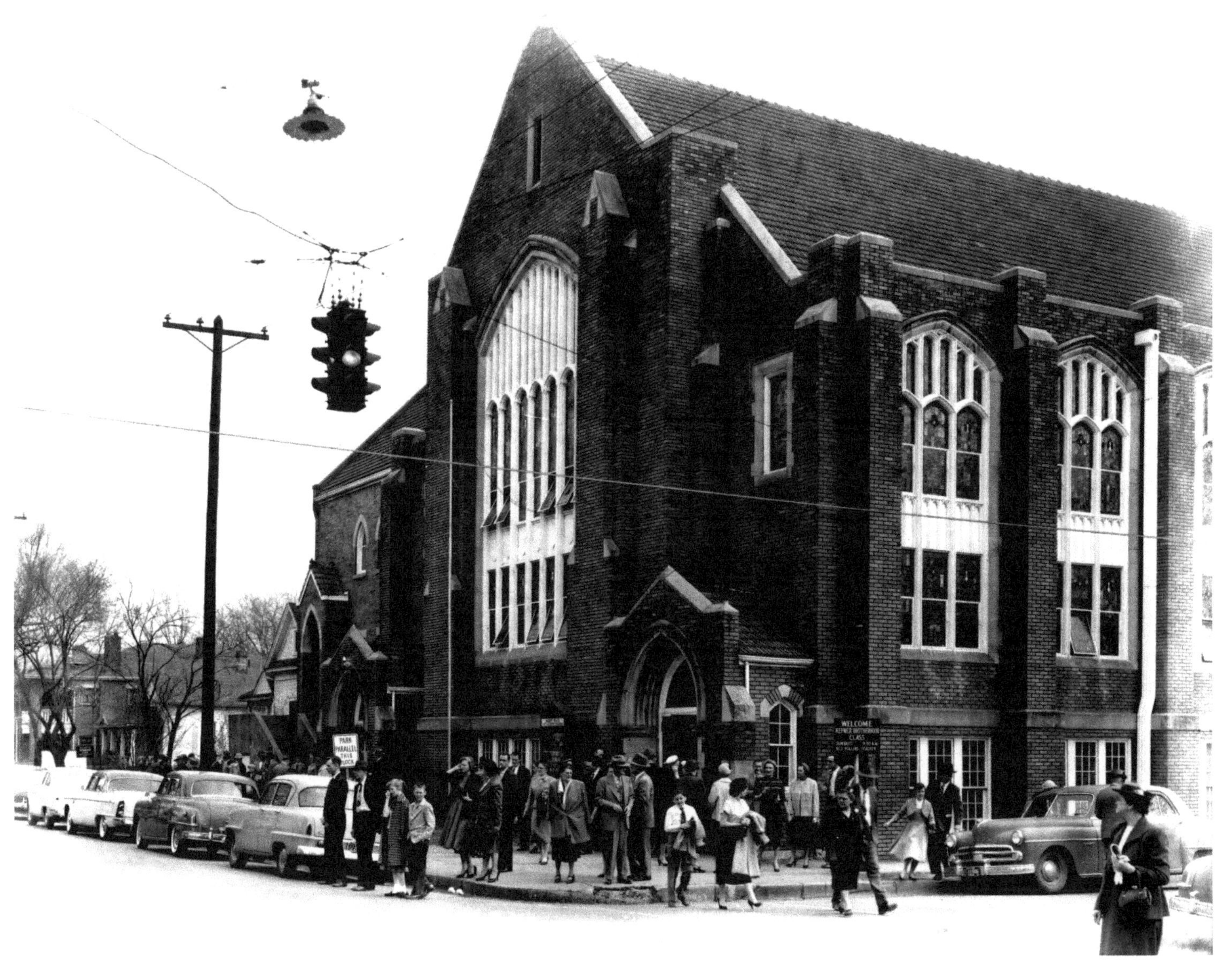

Parishioners leave the sanctuary of West End Methodist Church following services on a Sunday morning in the 1950s.

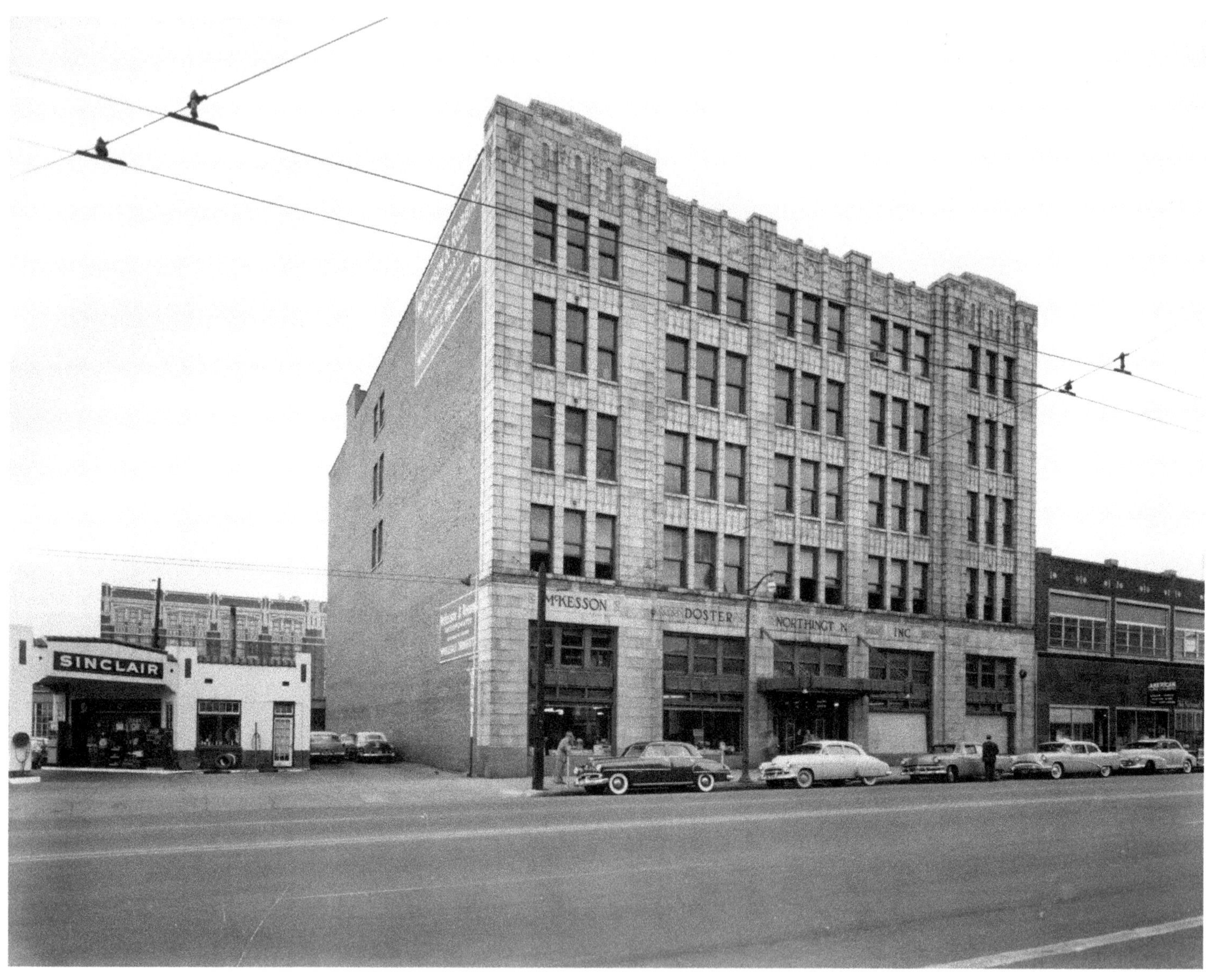

The McKesson & Robbins building, located on 1st Avenue, housed Doster and Northington Wholesale Drugs. At left, Sinclair gasoline, widely identified with its green dinosaur logo, was once a familiar brand across the United States and still operates in parts of the country today.

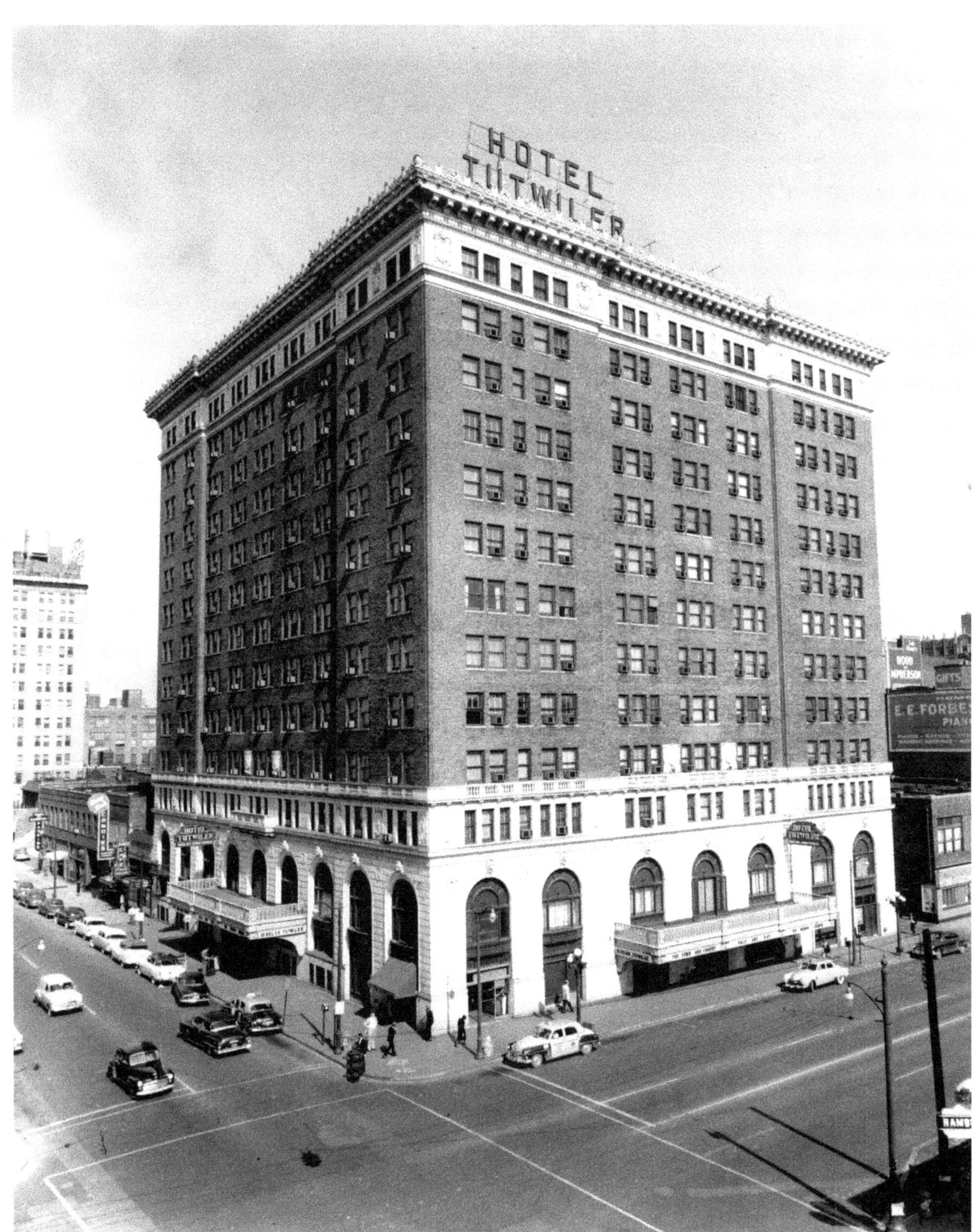

Located on 5th Avenue and designed in the Renaissance Revival style by William L. Welton, the Tutwiler Hotel offered music in the continental room for lunch and dinner along with a snack room for refreshments. Rooms were fully air-conditioned in the 1950s.

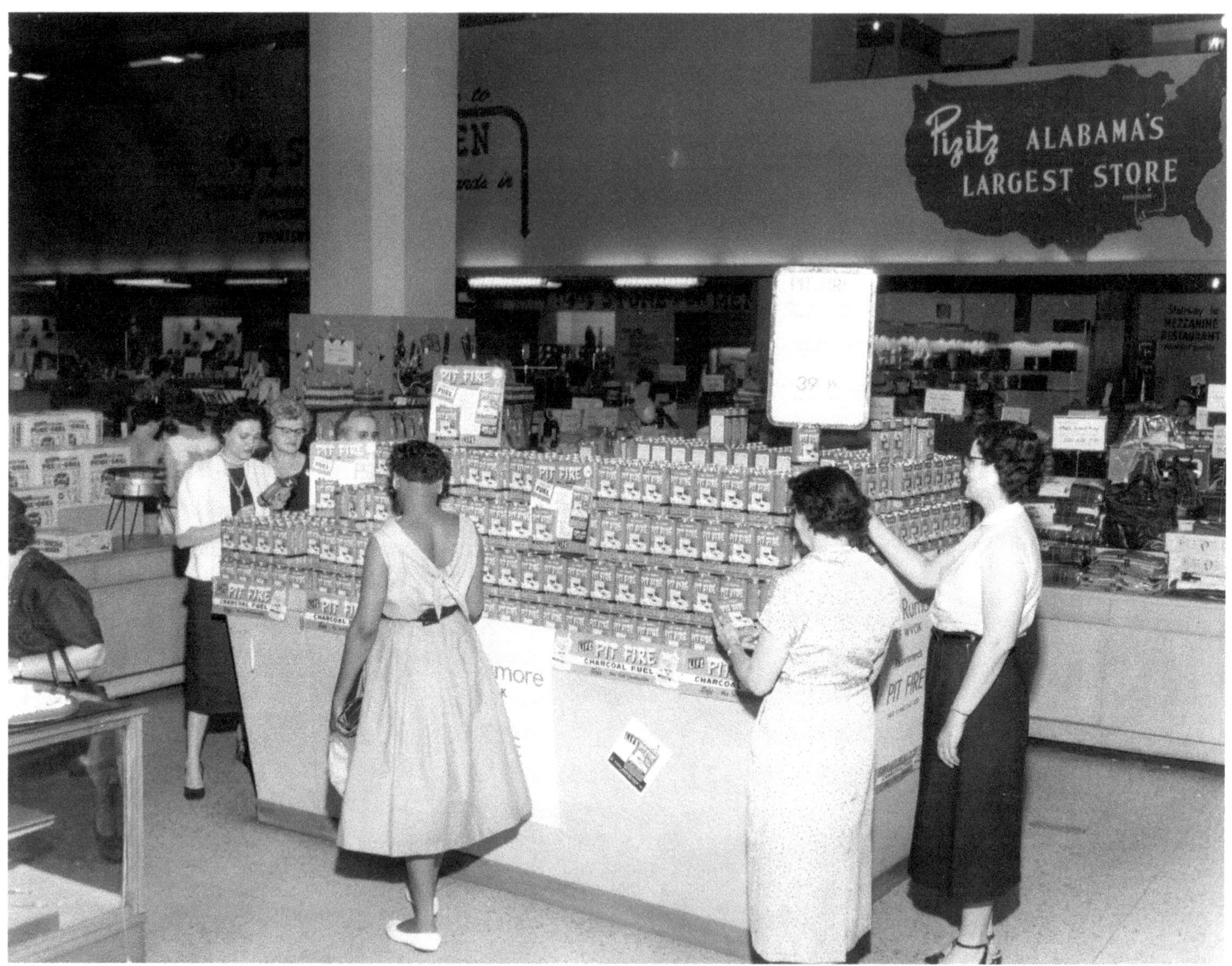

Customers examine the display of Pit Fire brand charcoal fuel and barbecue grills at Pizitz Department Store. Pizitz was founded in 1899 and expanded in the twentieth century to become a popular chain of department stores in the Birmingham area.

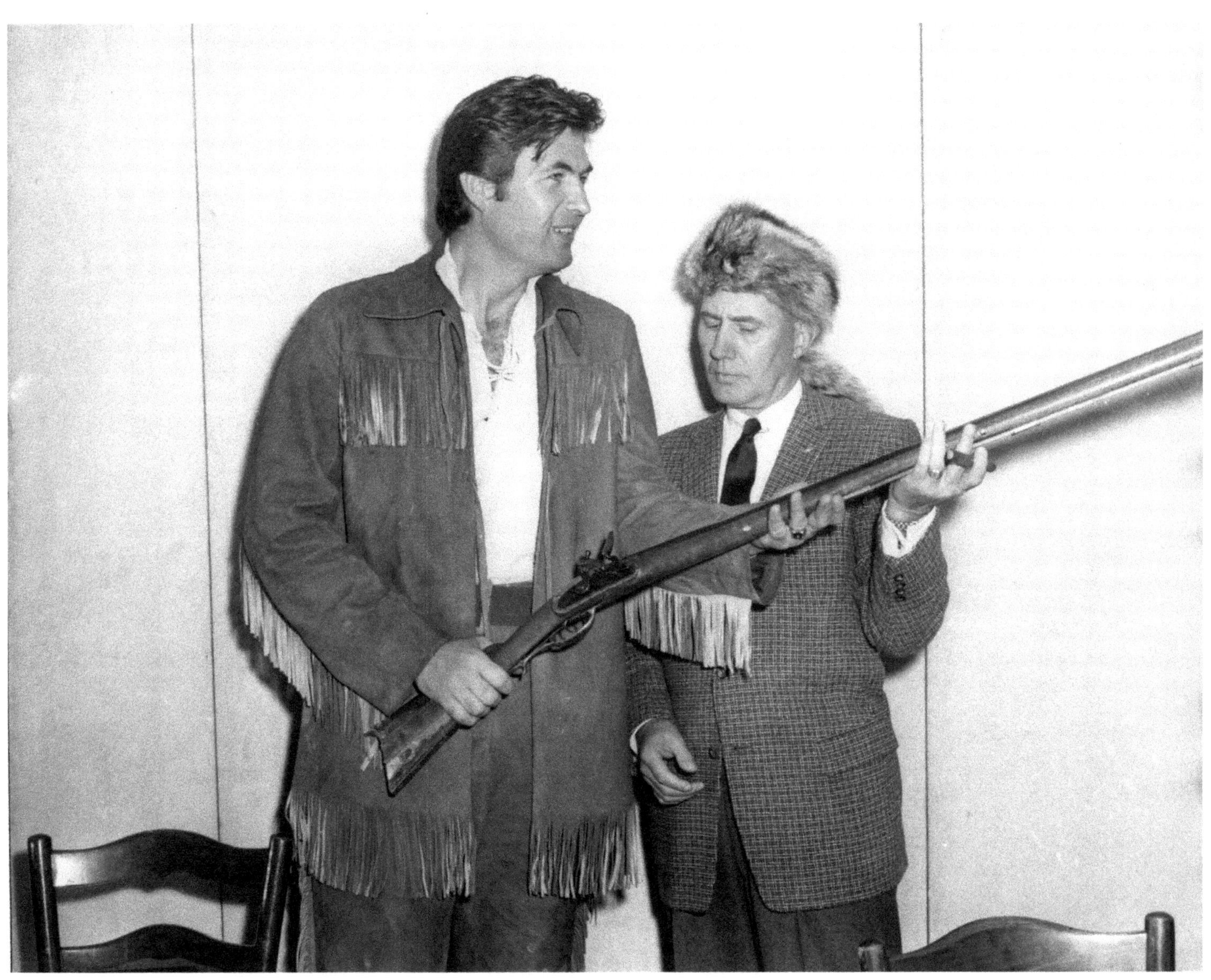

Fess Parker, who played Walt Disney's Davy Crockett, and Ira Patton, manager at the Tutwiler Hotel, take part in Birmingham's "Davy Crockett Day." Parker visited Birmingham to promote the opening of *Davy Crockett, King of the Wild Frontier,* a Disney film released to capitalize on the widely popular television program, which in the 1950s inspired Americans everywhere to don coonskin caps. Parker would team up with Ed Ames in the 1960s to play another legendary frontiersman on TV, Daniel Boone.

The American Life Insurance Company Building on the northeast corner of 23rd Street at 4th Avenue North. To its left is the Granada Hotel, and to the right, Imperial Laundry.

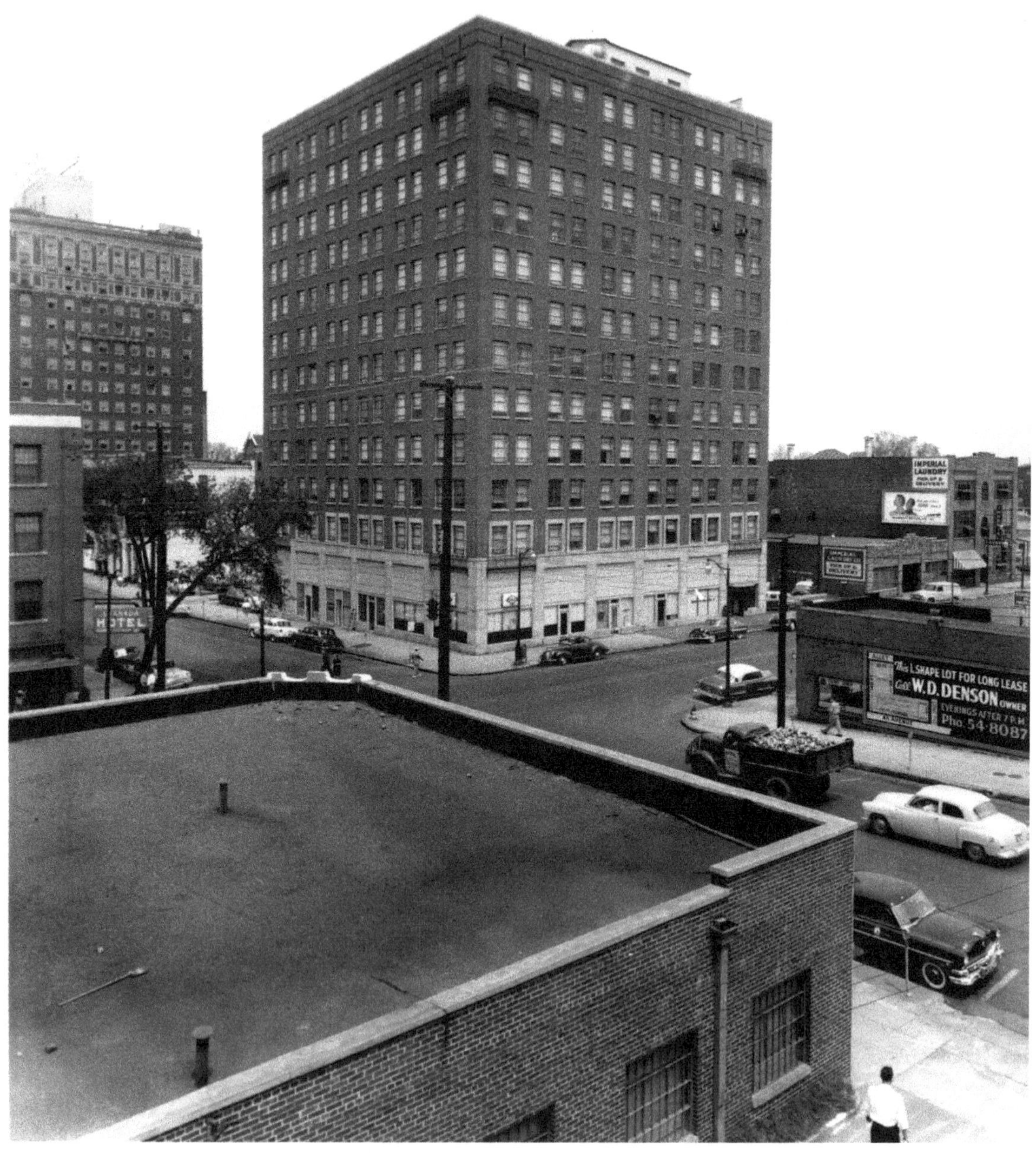

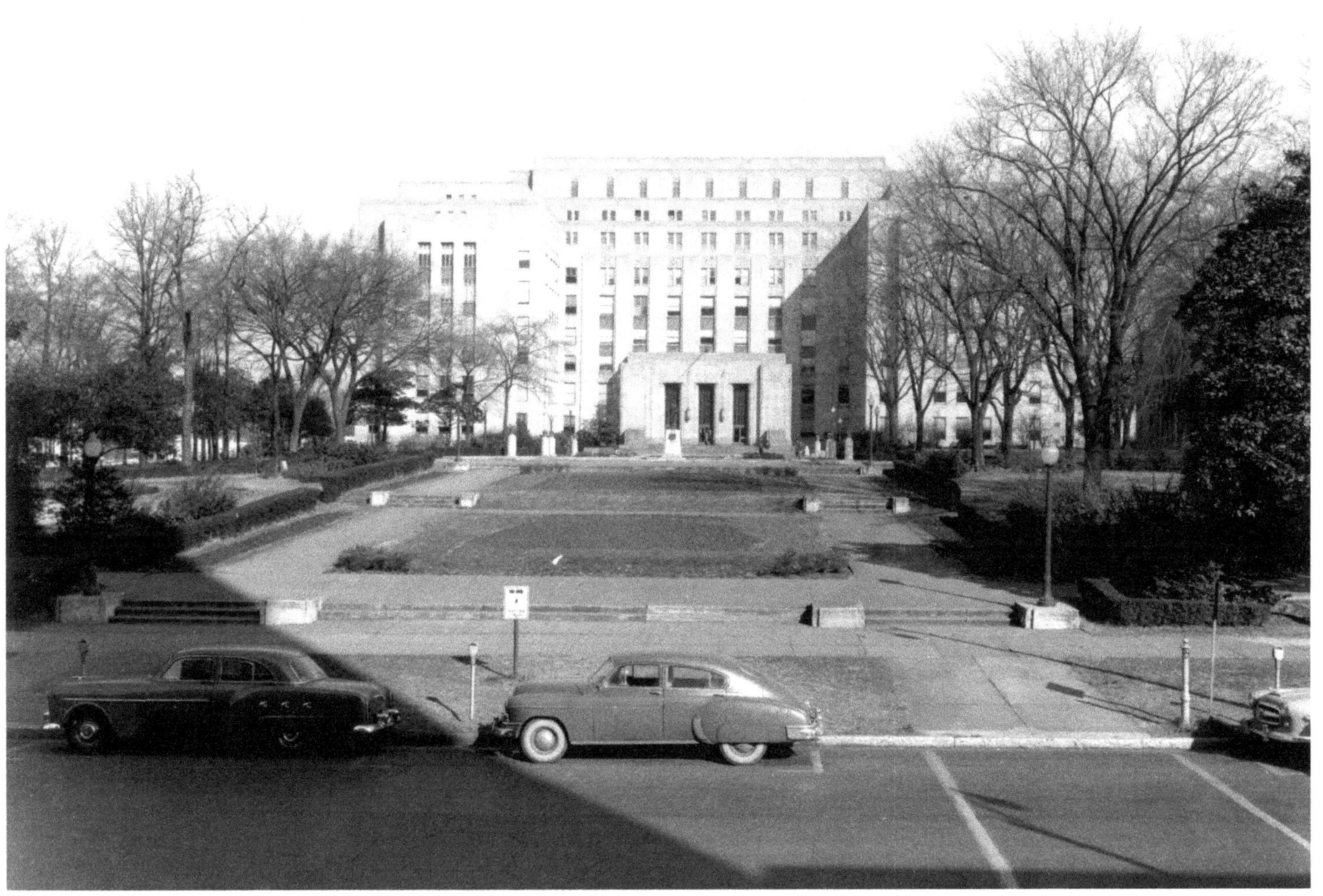

The Jefferson County Courthouse, designed by Jack B. Smith in the Modernistic style and constructed with white Indiana limestone and marble, was built in 1929. It houses the county courtrooms, commissioners' offices, and county agencies.

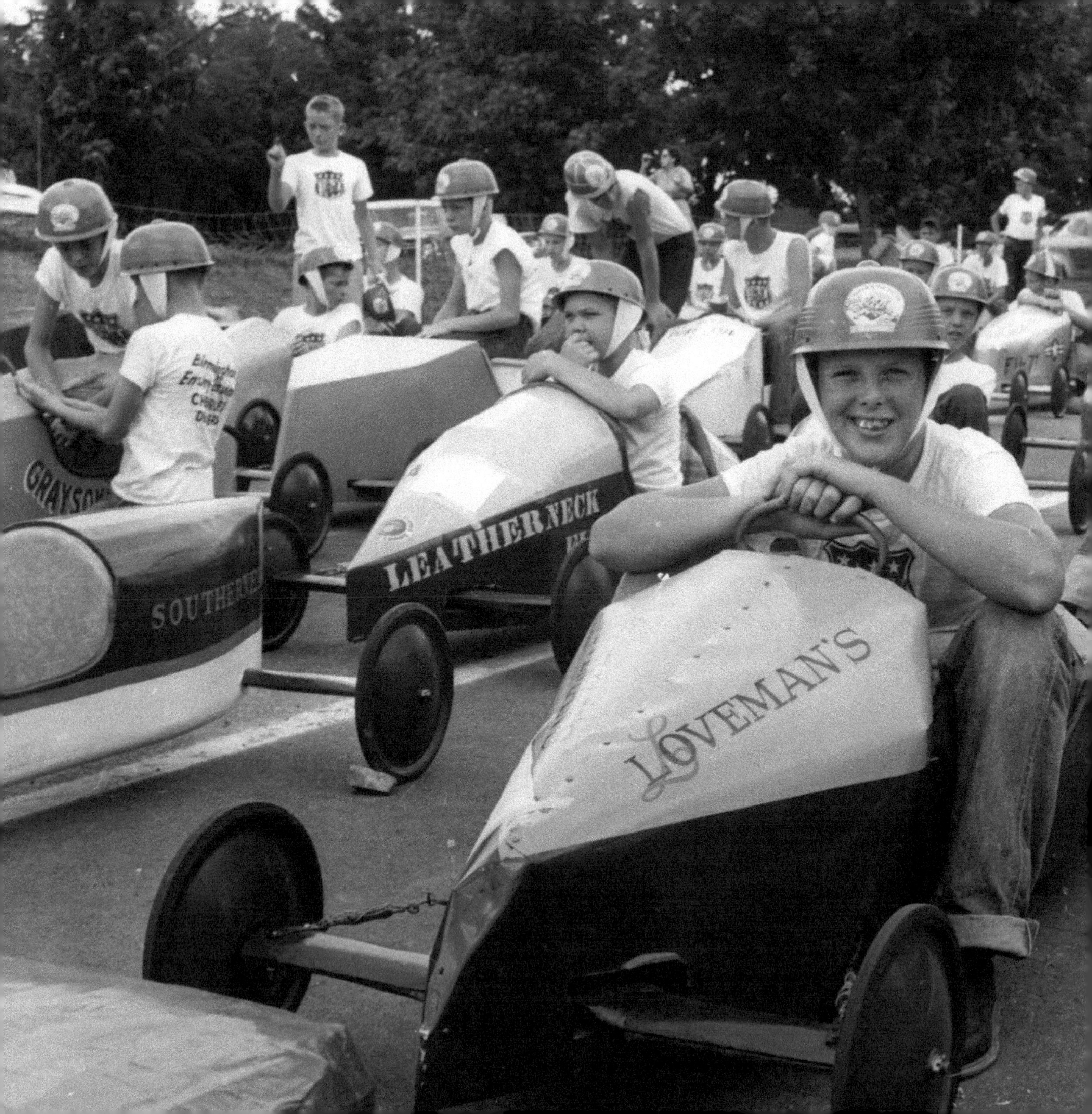
LOVEMAN'S
LEATHERNECK
SOUTHERN

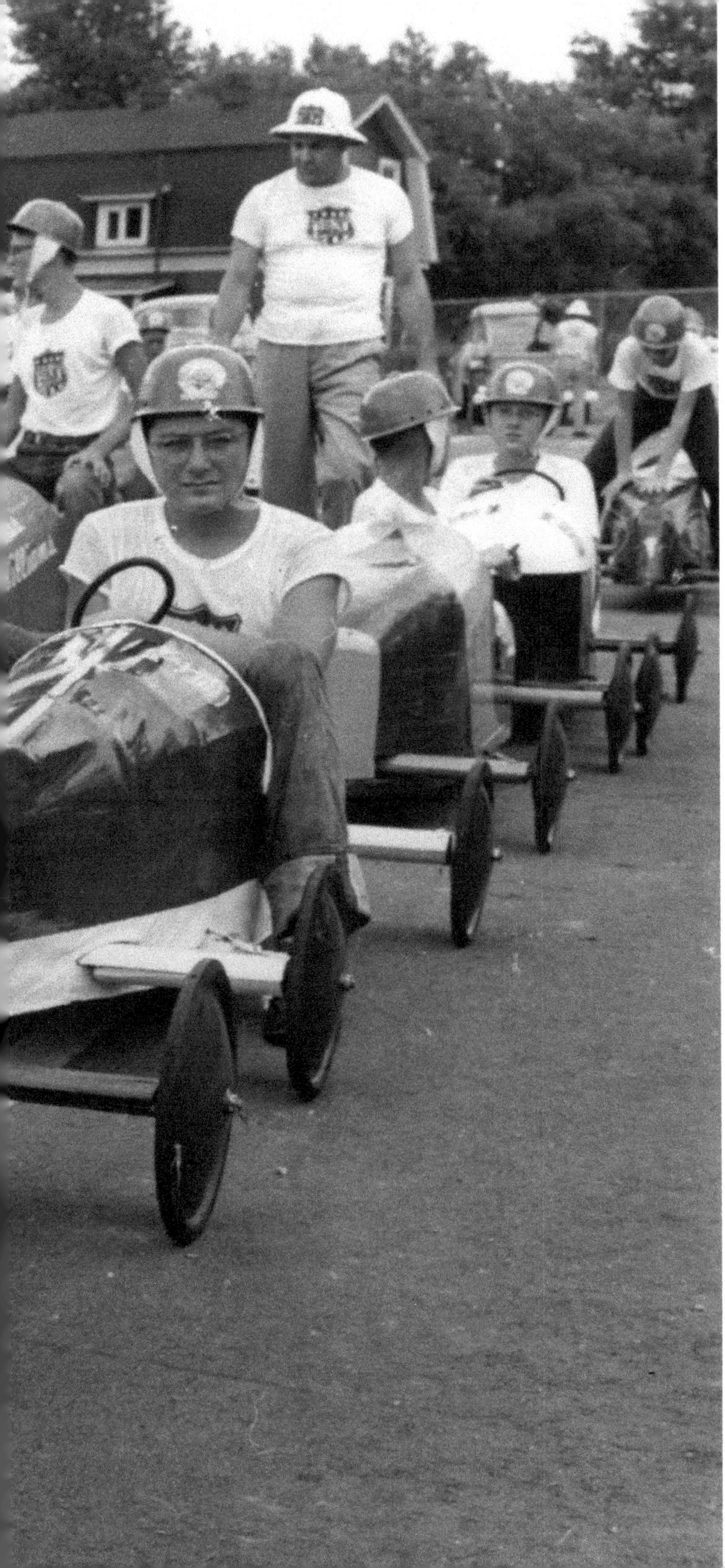

Youngsters eagerly wait for the signal to start their cars in the Shell Oil Soap Box Derby. The derby has been run each year since 1934, with championship finals held in Akron, Ohio. Each racer depends on gravity to take contestants downhill to the finish line, and, with a bit of good luck based on good engineering, to victory.

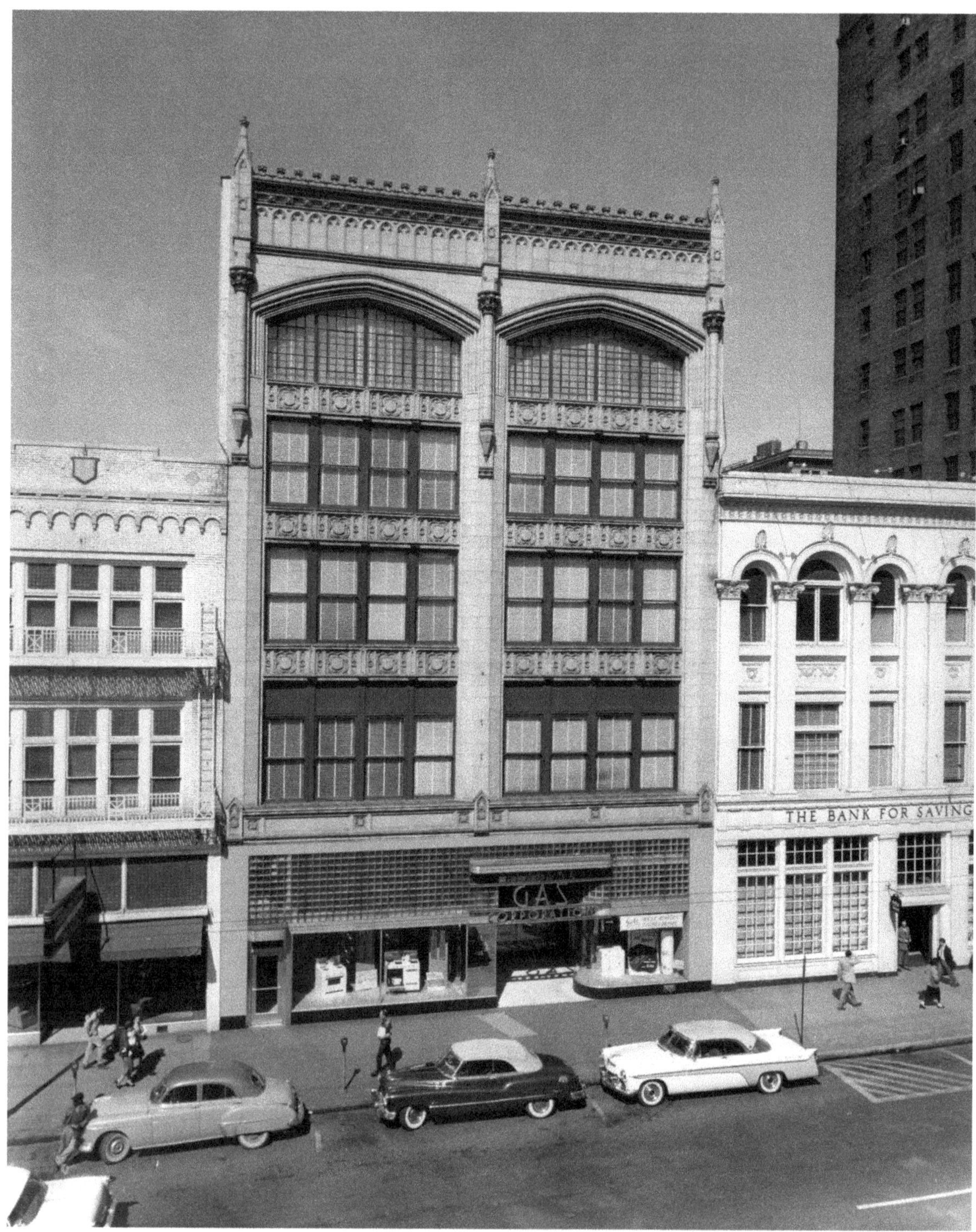

The Alabama Gas Corporation was a major supplier of natural gas for Birmingham citizens. New natural gas appliances are displayed in the building's windows in this 1950s photo.

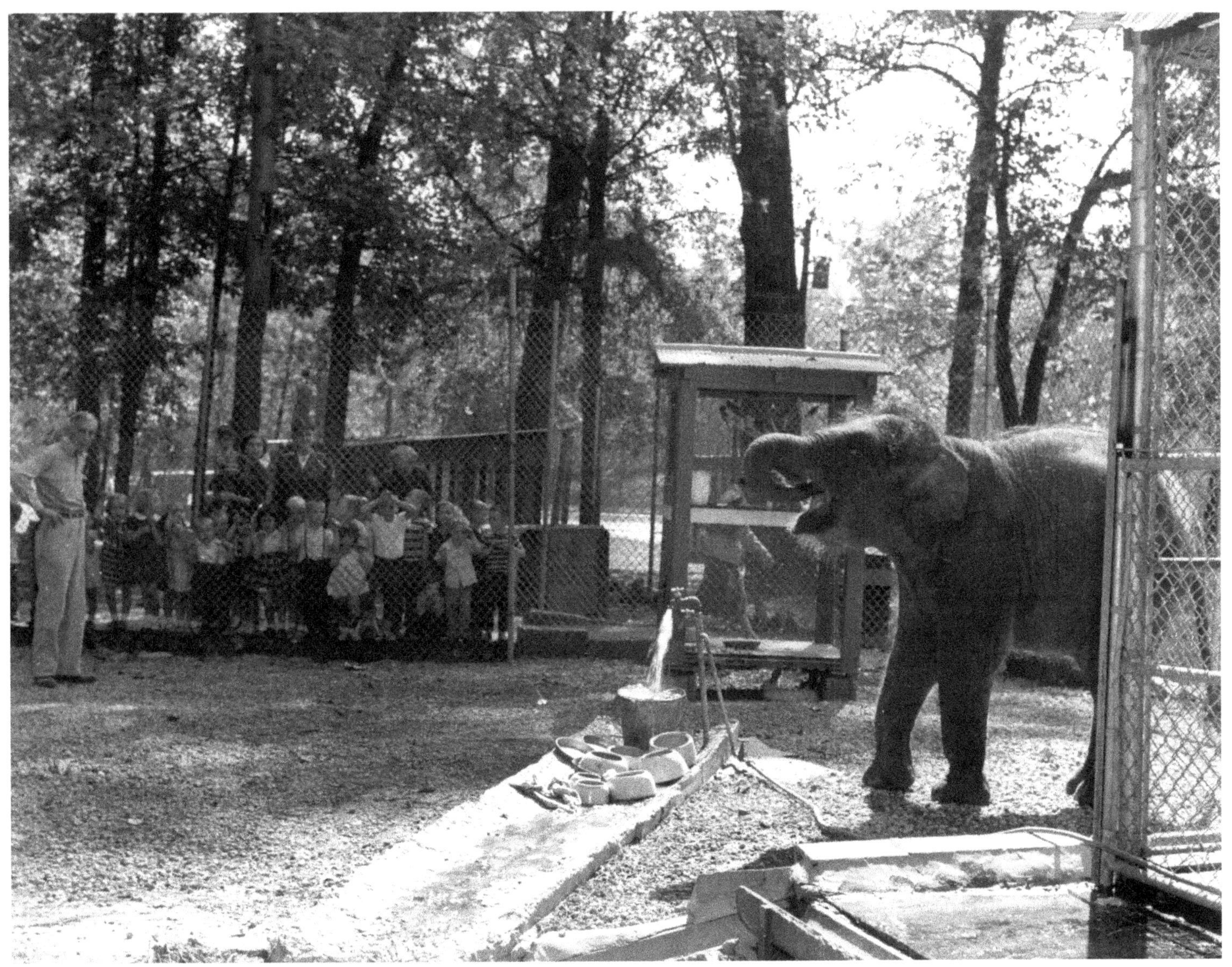

Visitors watch as an elephant at the Birmingham Zoo quaffs a refreshing drink of water. The Birmingham Zoo was the brainchild of entrepreneur and prominent citizen, Elton B. Stephens. With the support of the mayor and other members of the Junior Chamber of Commerce, the first exhibit, Monkey Island, was dedicated in 1955.

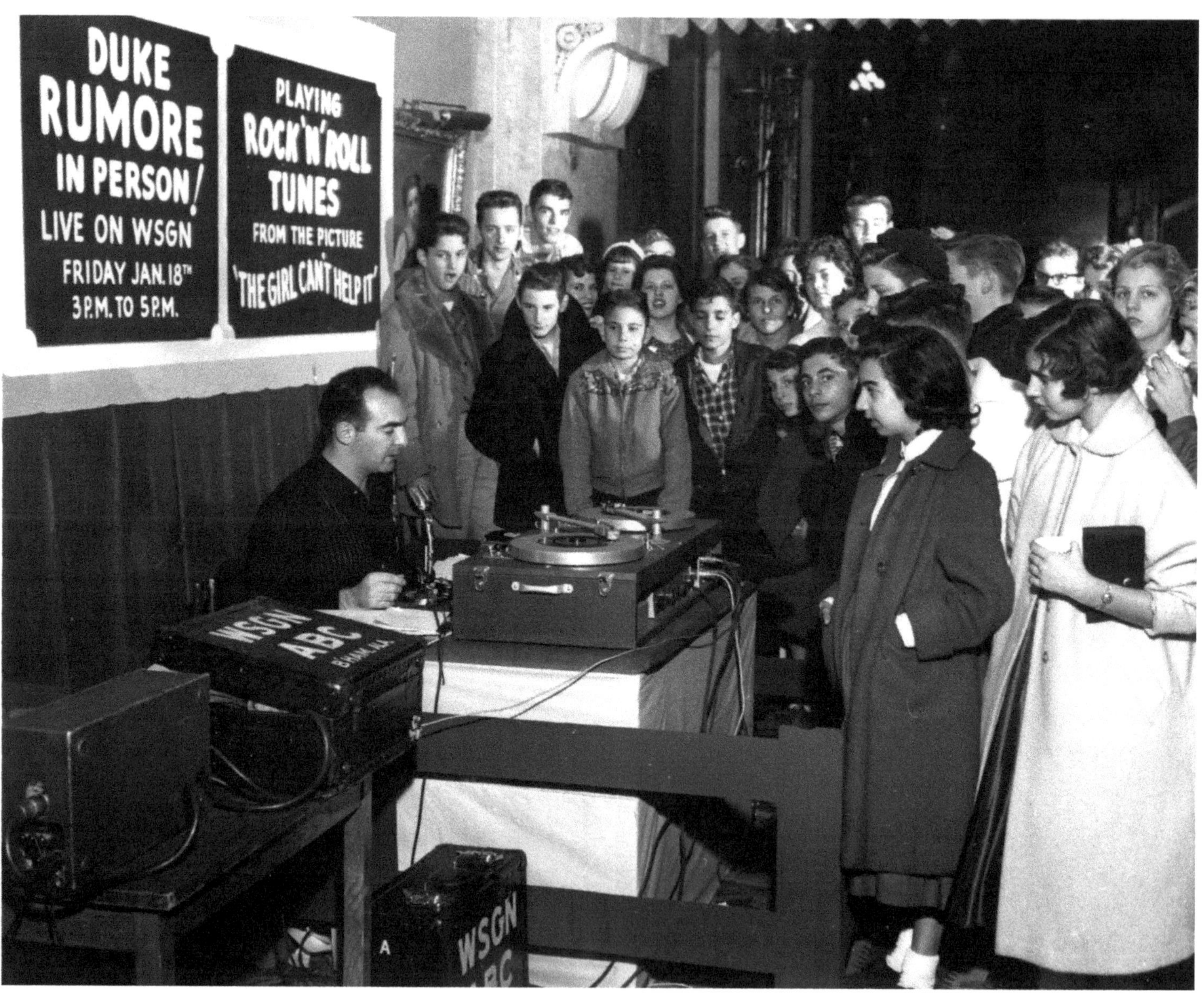

Radio personality Duke Rumore plays rock 'n' roll songs from the 1956 movie *The Girl Can't Help It,* starring Jayne Mansfield, during a live broadcast for WSGN from the lobby of the Alabama Theater. Rumore's brother, Joe, was also a local radio personality.

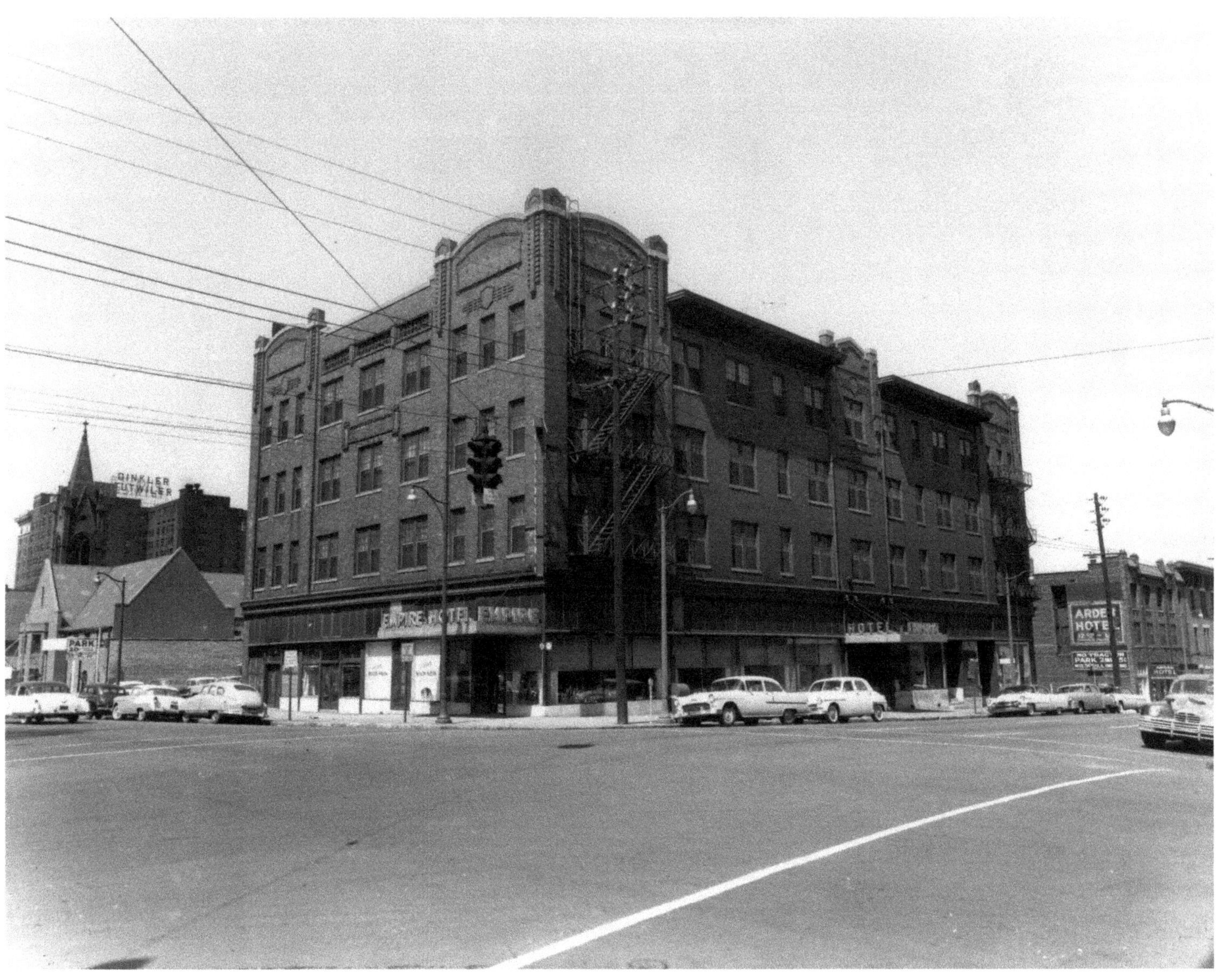

Located at 2130 4th Avenue North, the Empire Hotel was part of Birmingham's hotel district. Rooftop signage for the Tutwiler is visible in the distance at left, and a sign for the Arden at right.

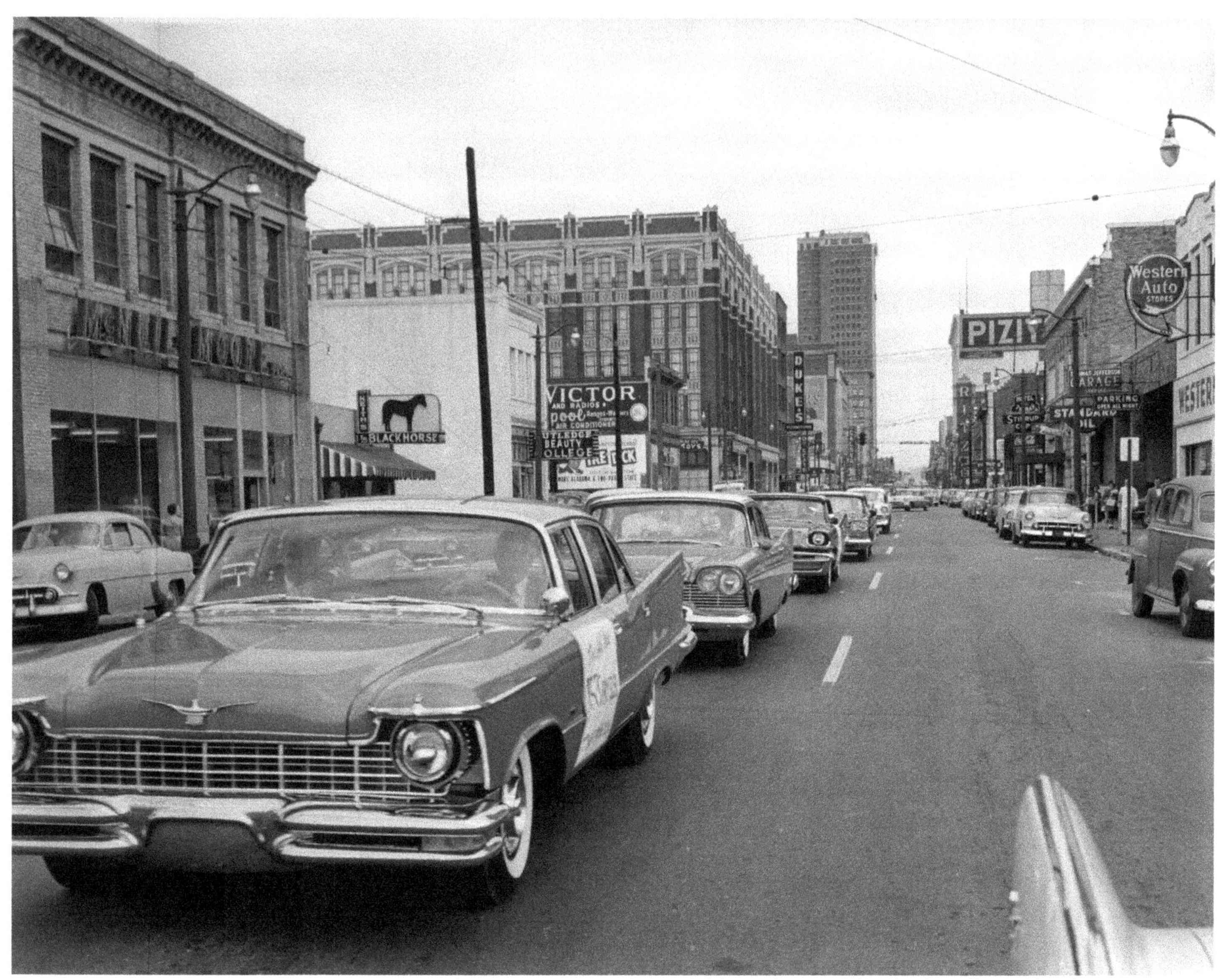

Kirksey Motors parades its new cars up the hill to Five Points South on 20th Street South.

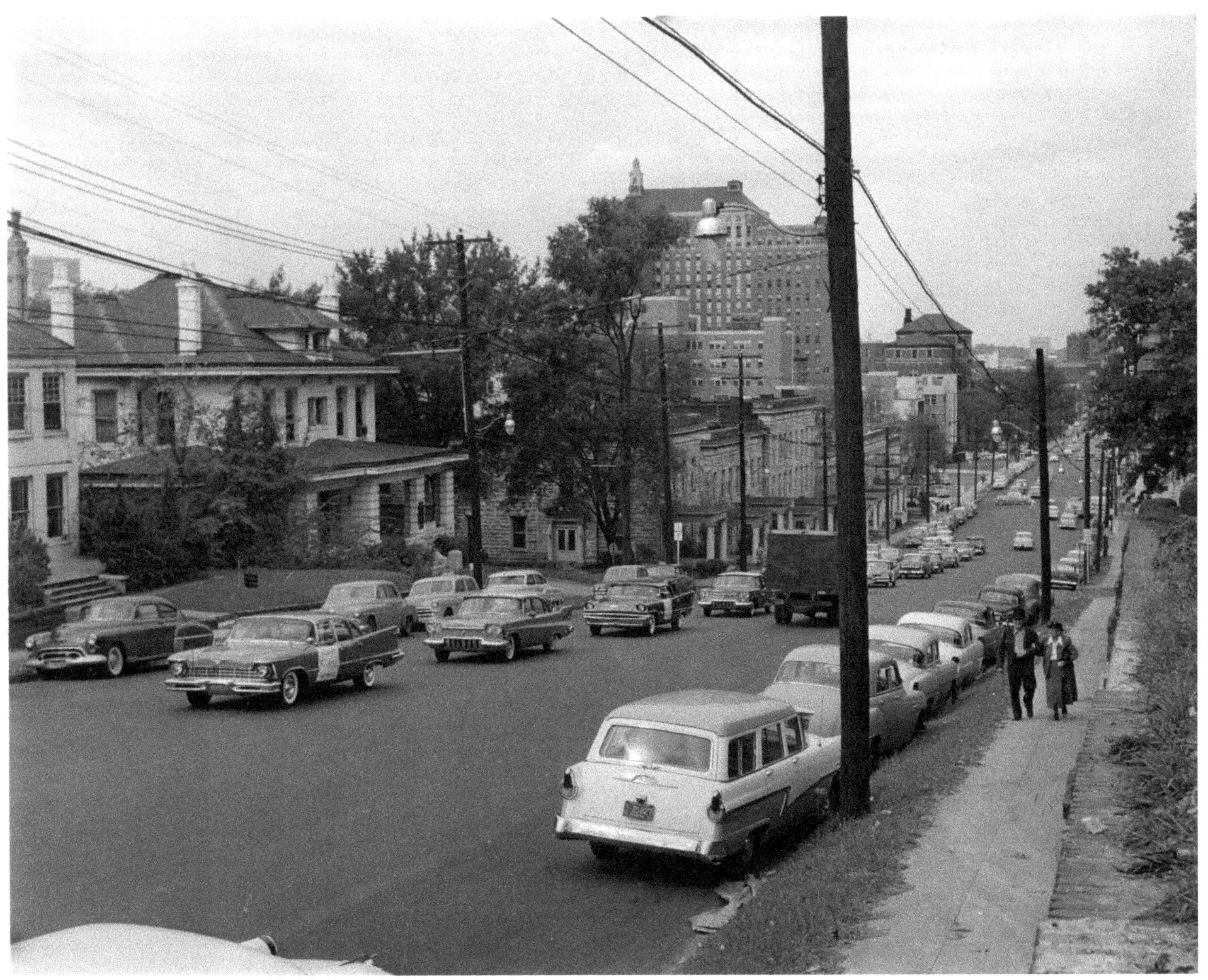

Here the Kirksey caravan travels west on 2nd Avenue North.

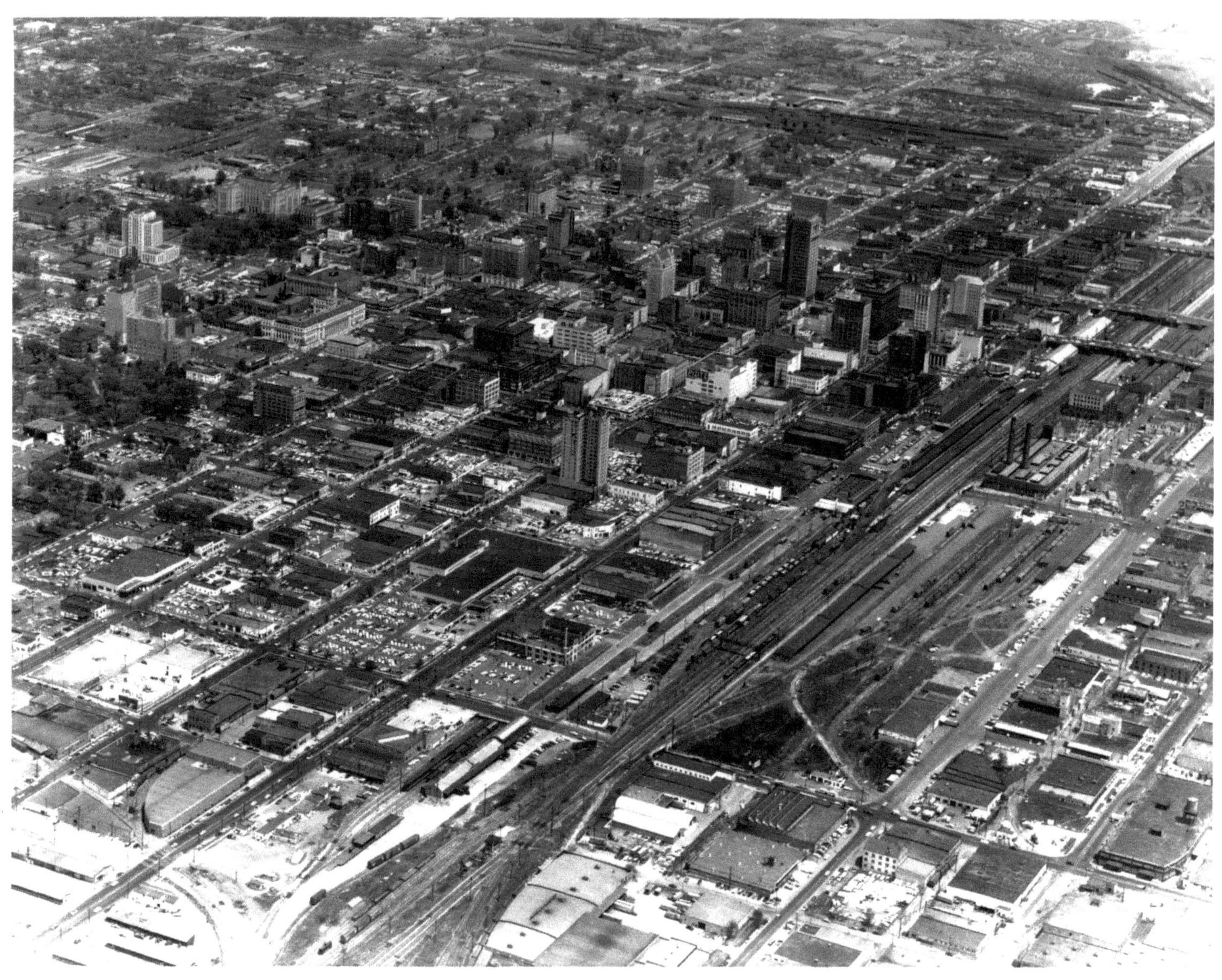

An aerial view of downtown Birmingham reveals the proliferation of parking lots to either side of the rail yards at center, a visible clue to the rise of the automobile as America's first choice in transportation.

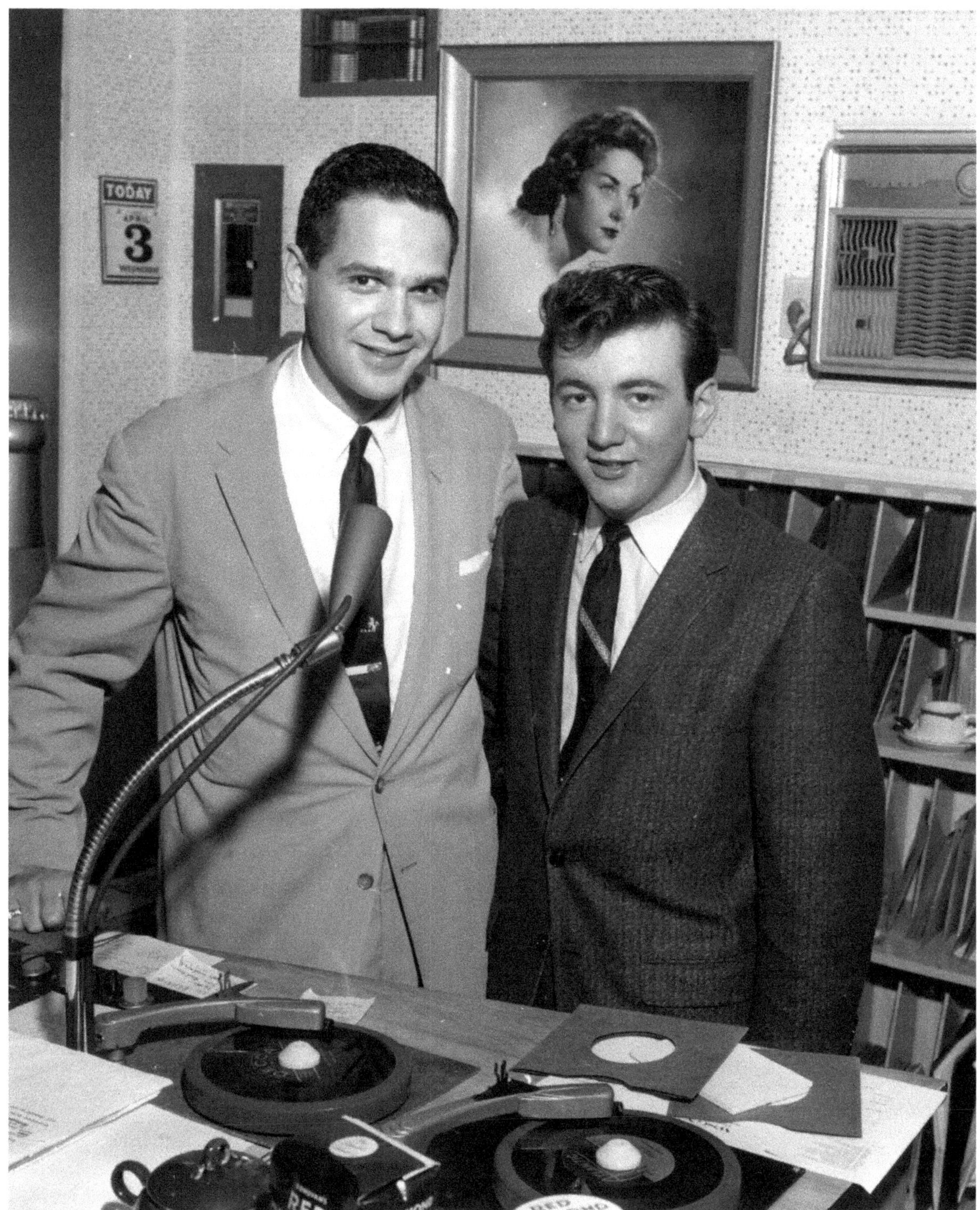

Rock 'n' roll sensation and legendary song stylist Bobby Darin (right) poses with disc jockey Jim Lucas at WSGN radio station. On the turntable are a couple of 45 r.p.m. records, holding the latest hits and ready for broadcast over the airwaves. Darin would go on to record such favorites as "Mack the Knife" and "Beyond the Sea."

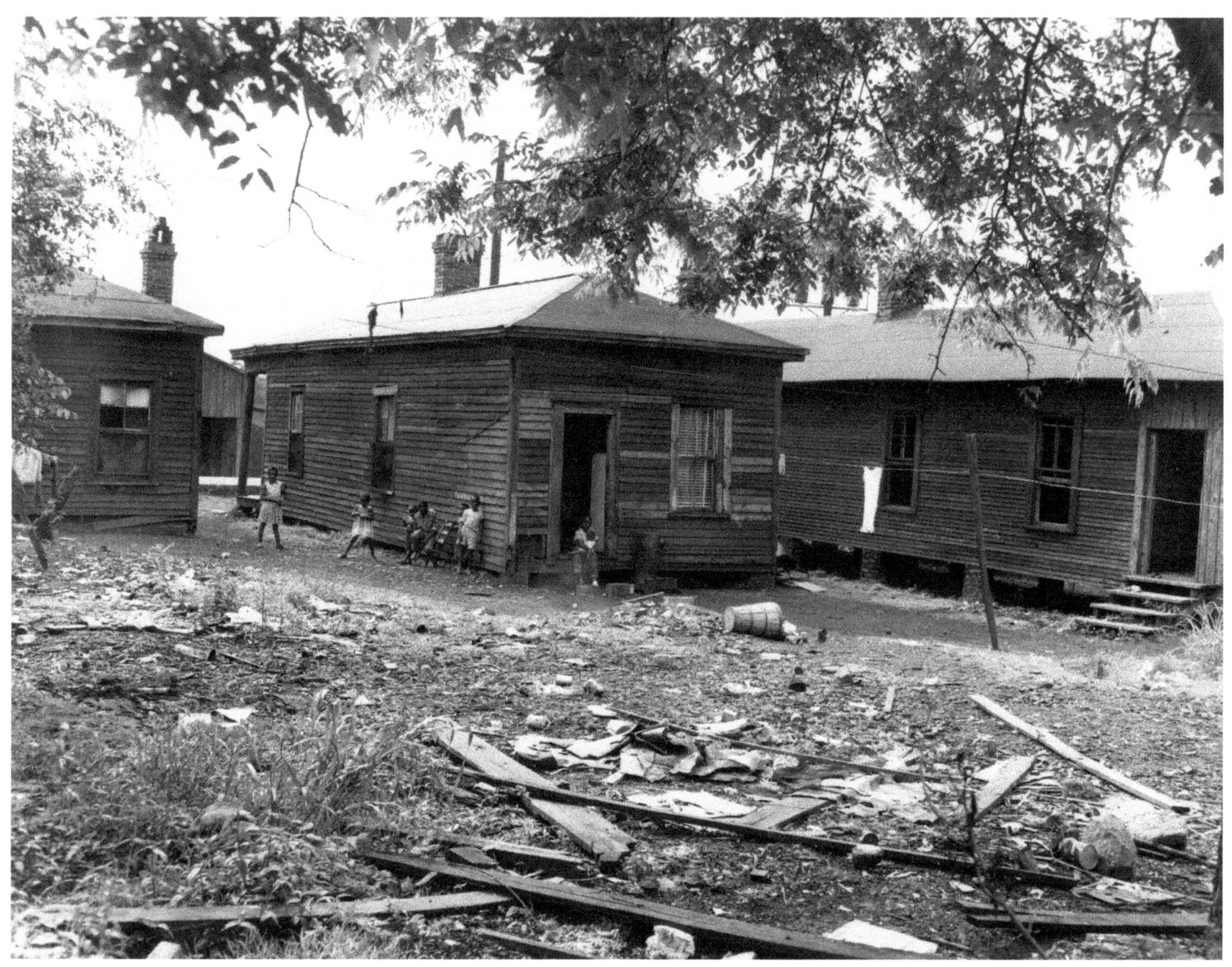

Children play outside a house that has possibly been marked for demolition. With the construction of the University of Alabama at Birmingham, city planners displaced many low-income residents from their homes with little thought given to where they would live.

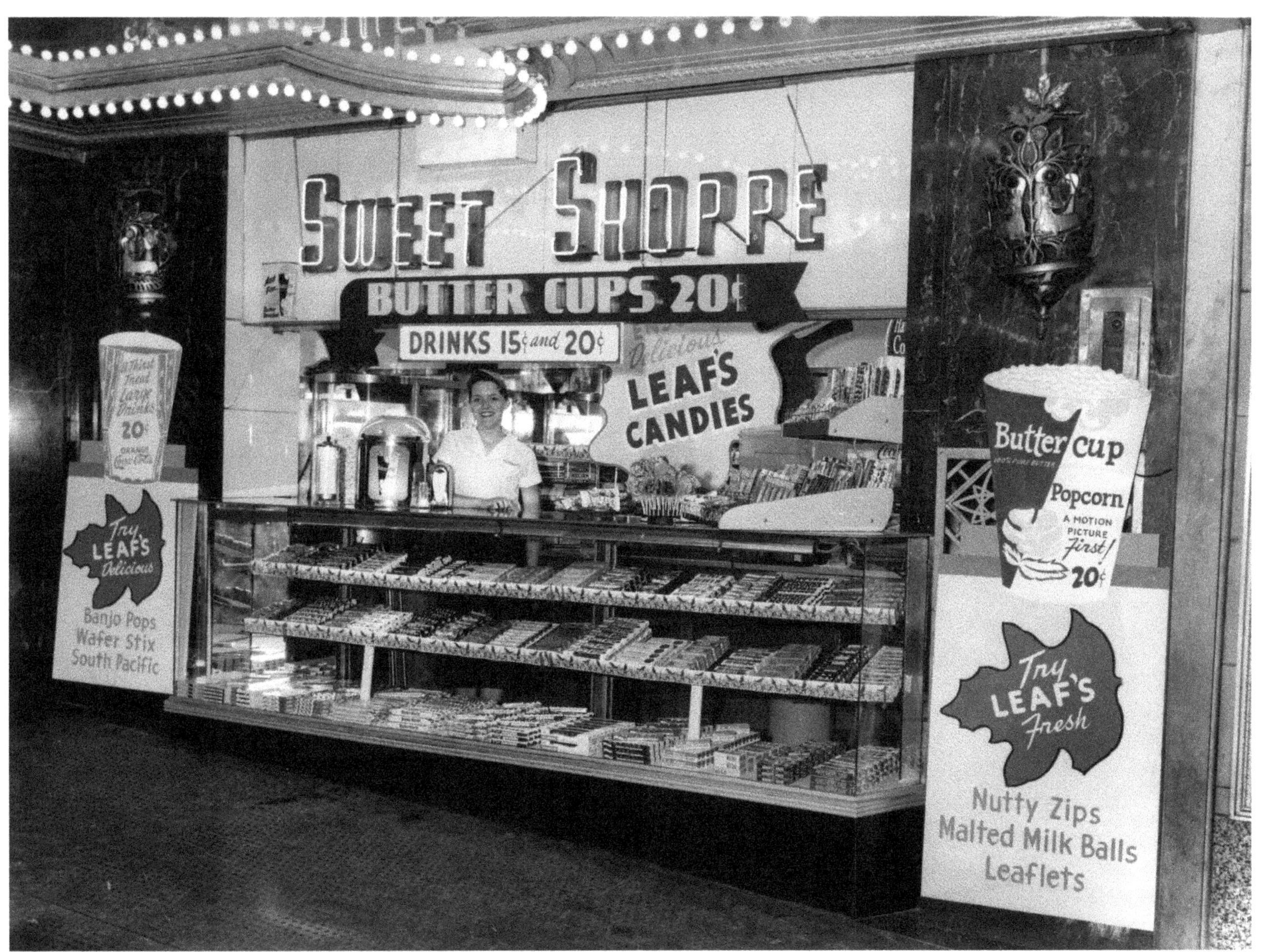

An eager candy concession clerk is ready for hungry customers at the Alabama Theater. The theater's grand lobby, near the concession counter, was lavishly decorated in terra cotta ornamentation, ornately designed chandeliers, and marble columns.

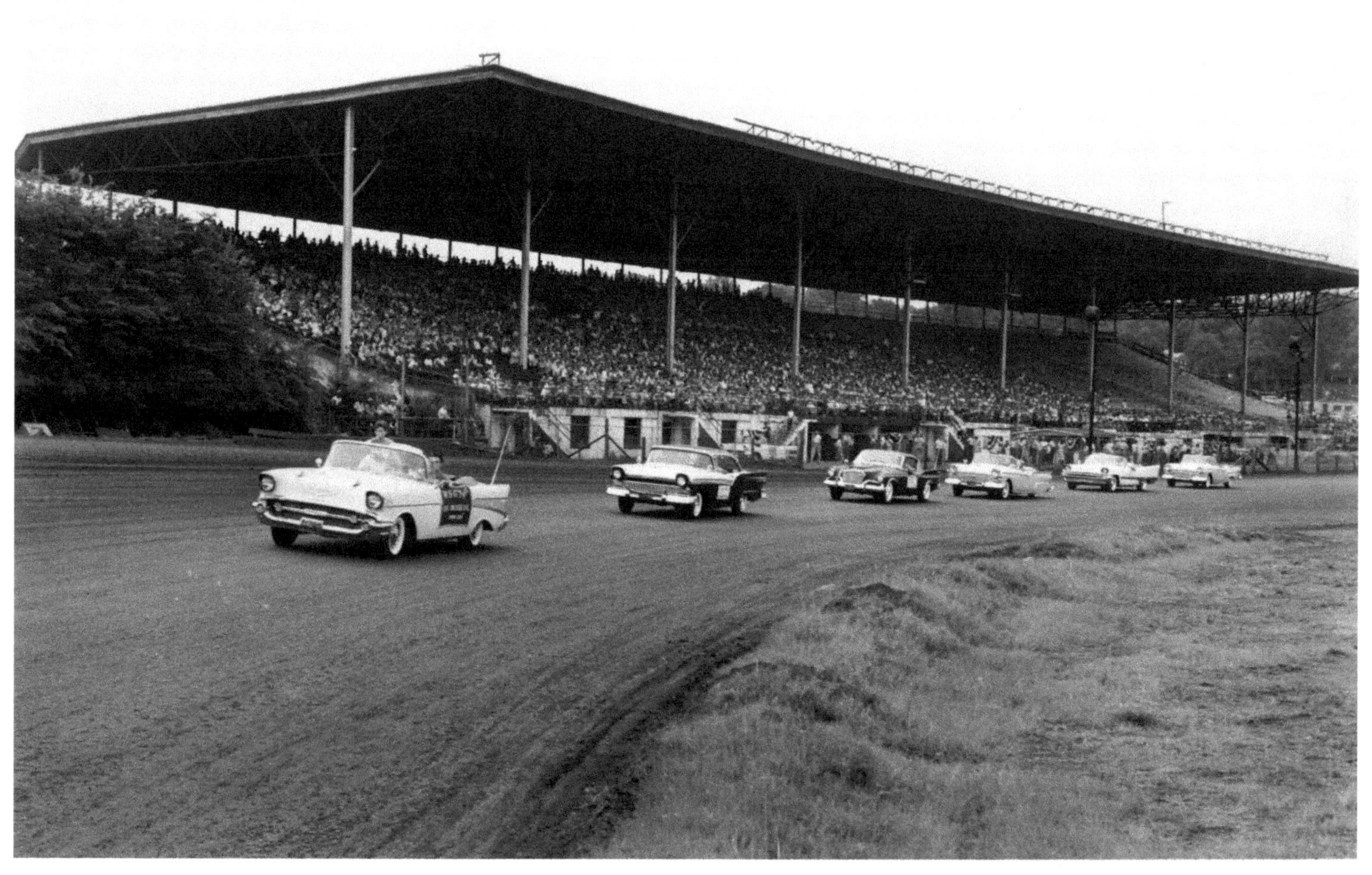

A 1957 Chevrolet Bel Air Convertible, a 1957 Ford Fairlane, and a 1957 Studebaker Hawk lead a parade of cars in front of the Grandstand at Fairground Raceway prior to the start of a race.

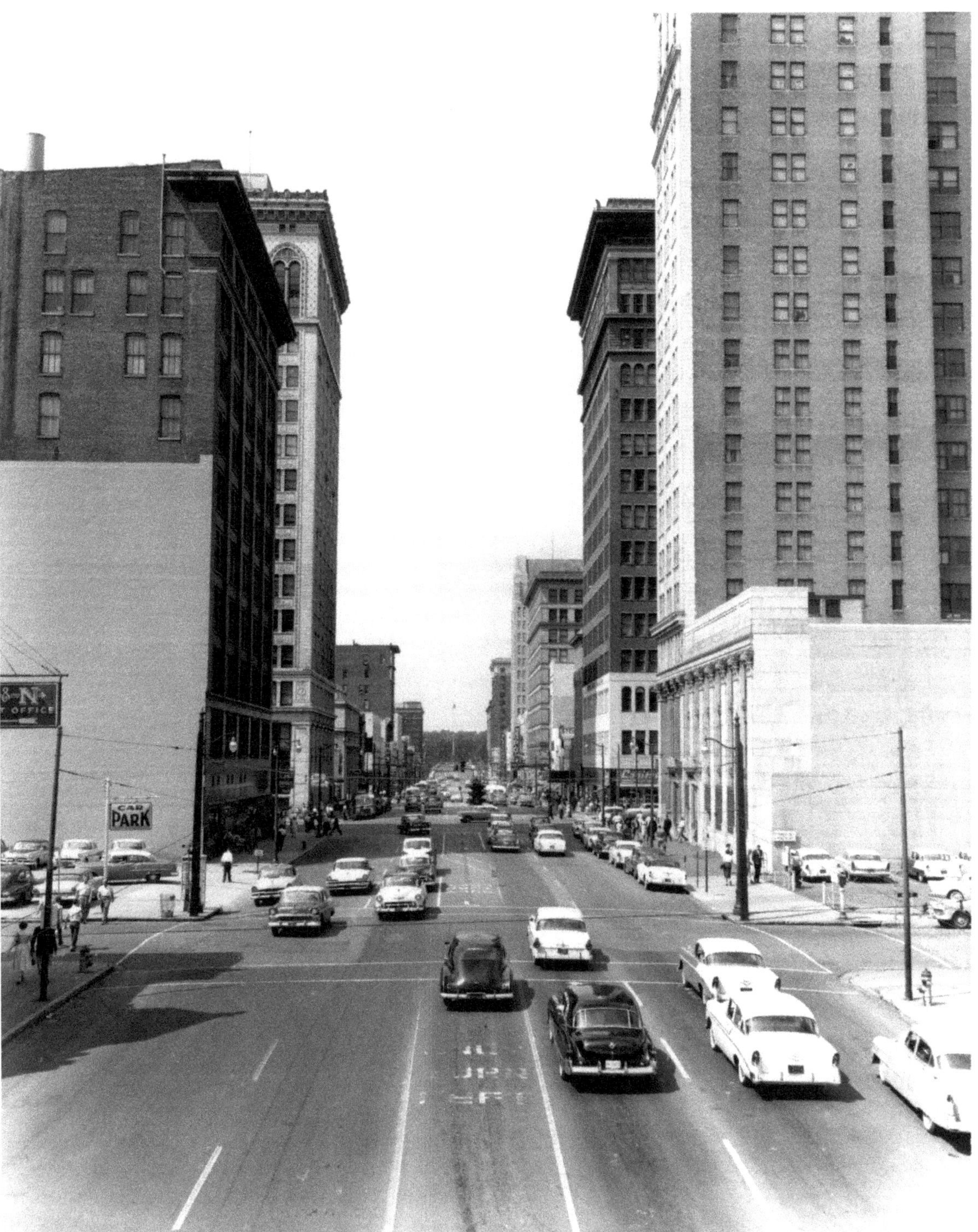

The scene on 20th Street. As seen from the railroad overpass, 20th Street served as a main thoroughfare for Birmingham.

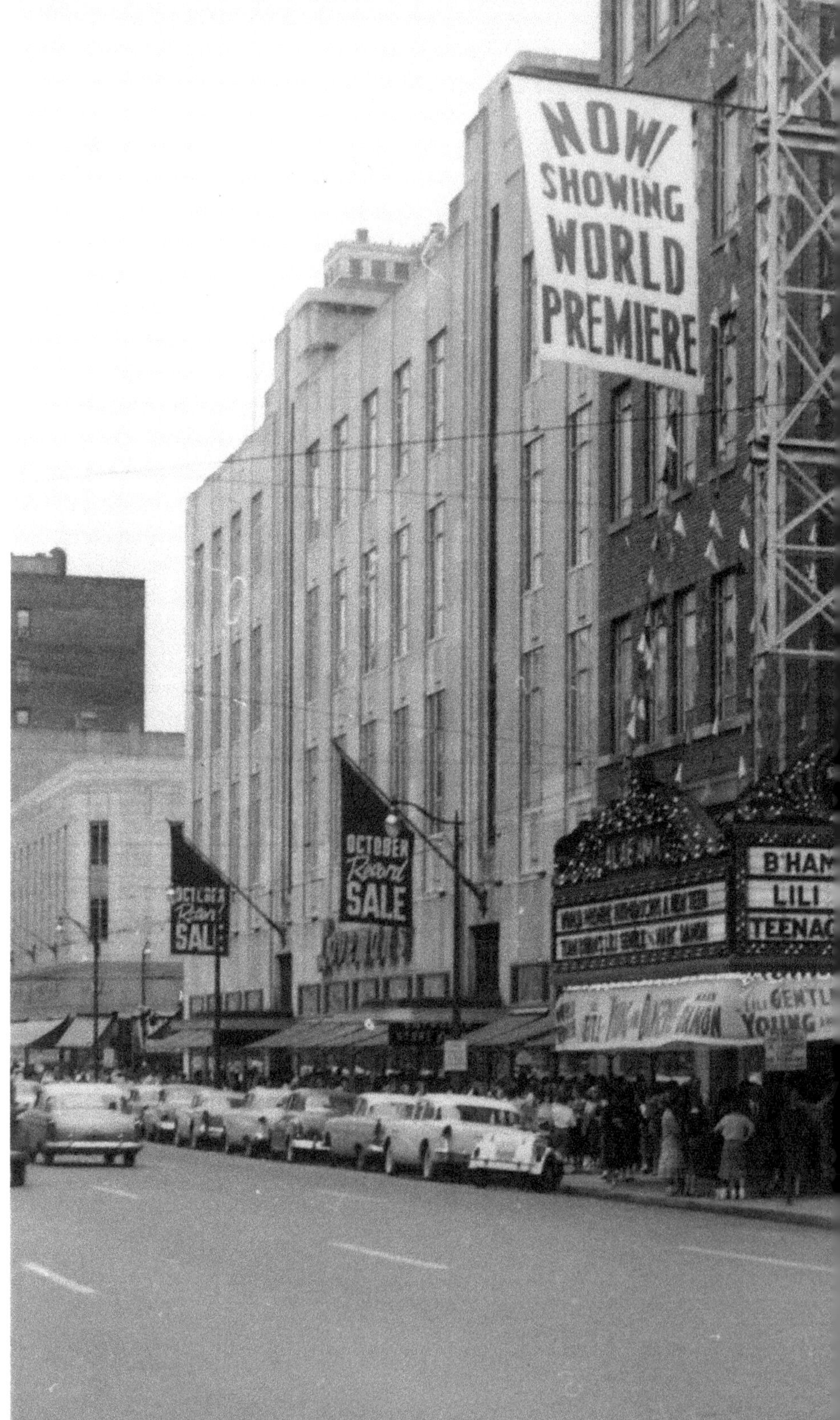

Excited moviegoers wait in long lines outside the Alabama Theater to see Birmingham native Lili Gentle star in *Young and Dangerous.* The vertical "Alabama" sign, which ordinarily advertised the theater above its marquee, had been removed for refurbishing. Next door, Loveman's was holding an "October Record Sale."

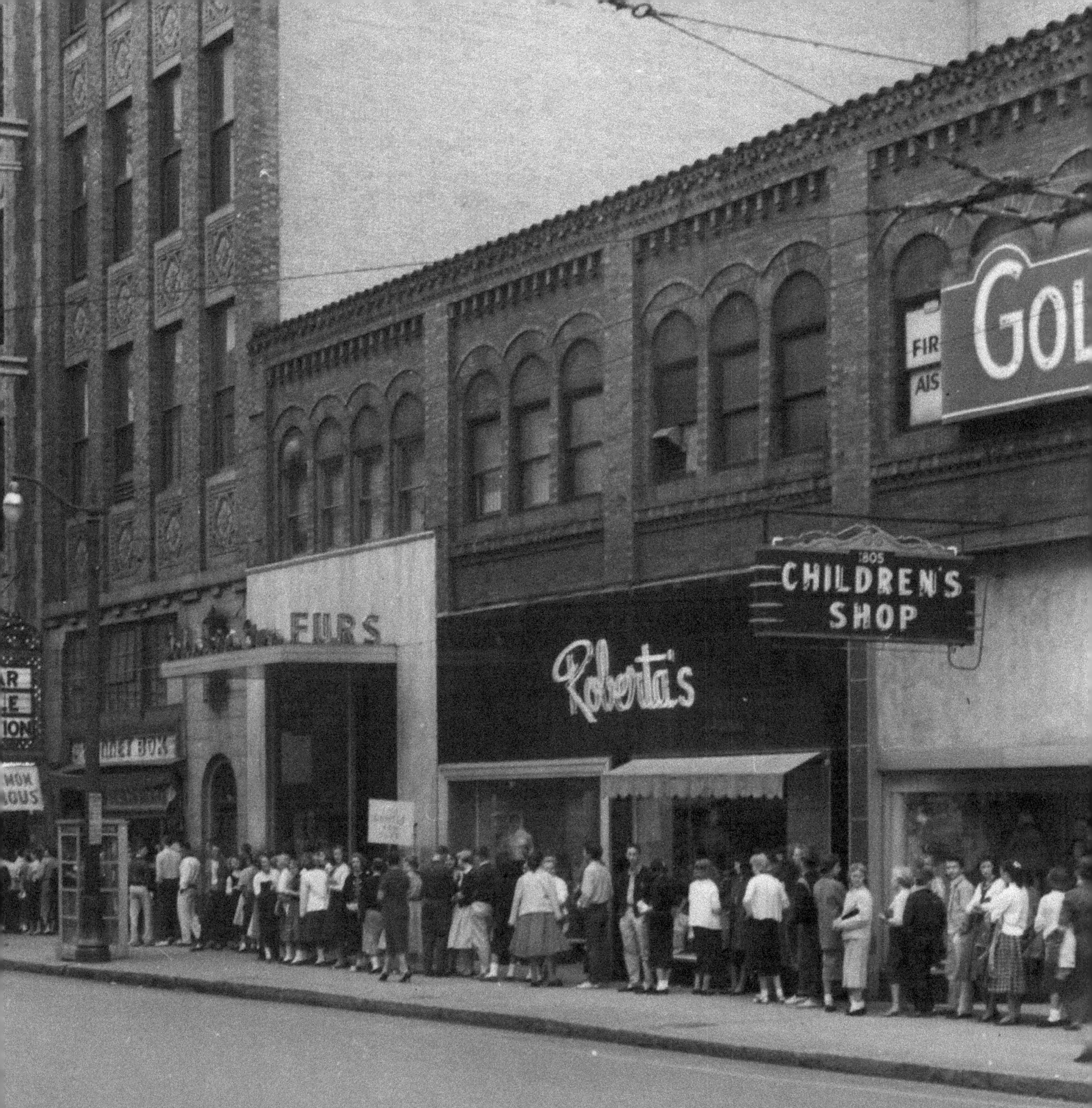
FURS
Roberta's
CHILDREN'S
SHOP

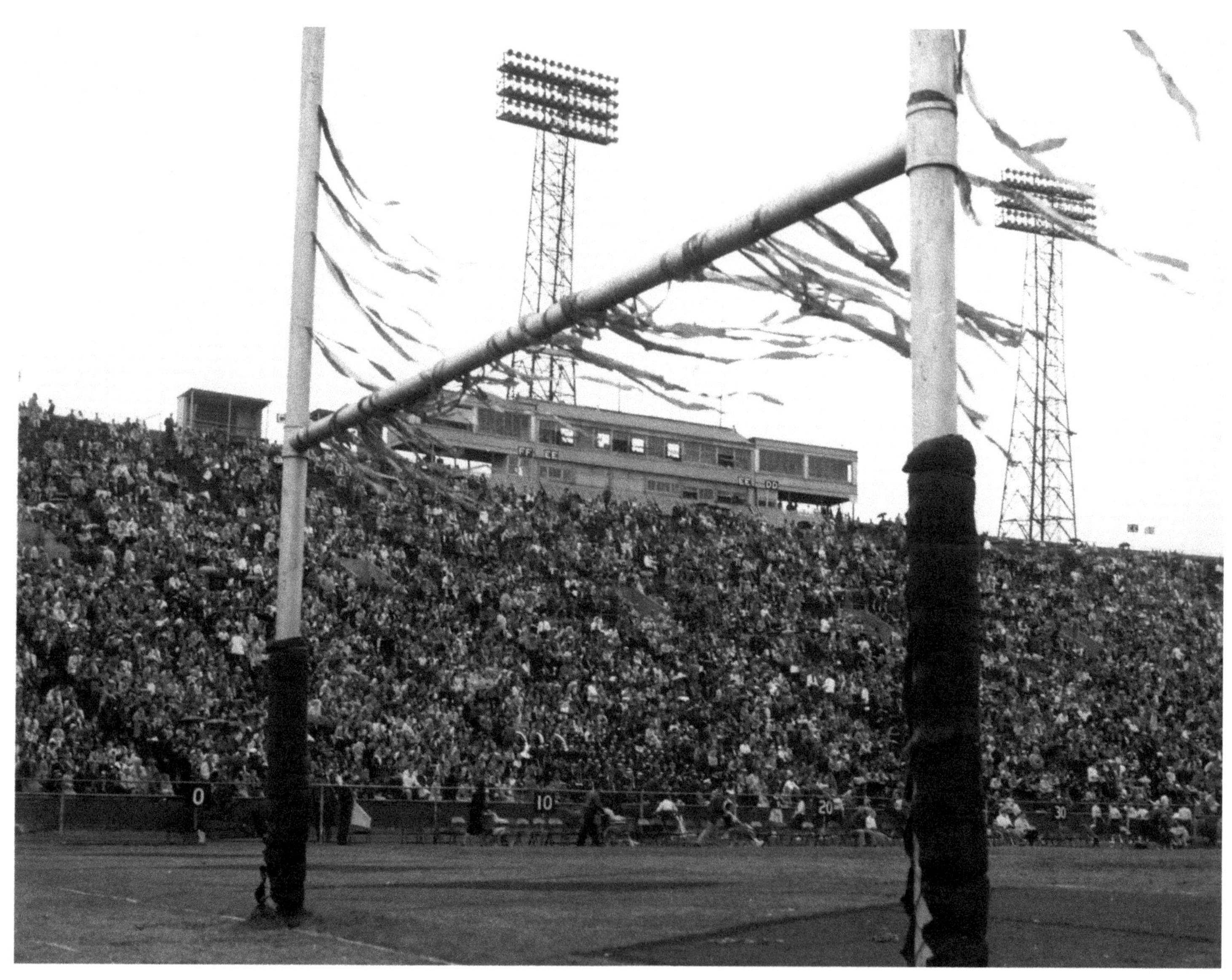

A football game is played at Legion Field for the Crippled Children's Clinic. Legion Field was built in 1927 and over the decades has hosted many exciting contests between the University of Alabama, Auburn, and other football teams.

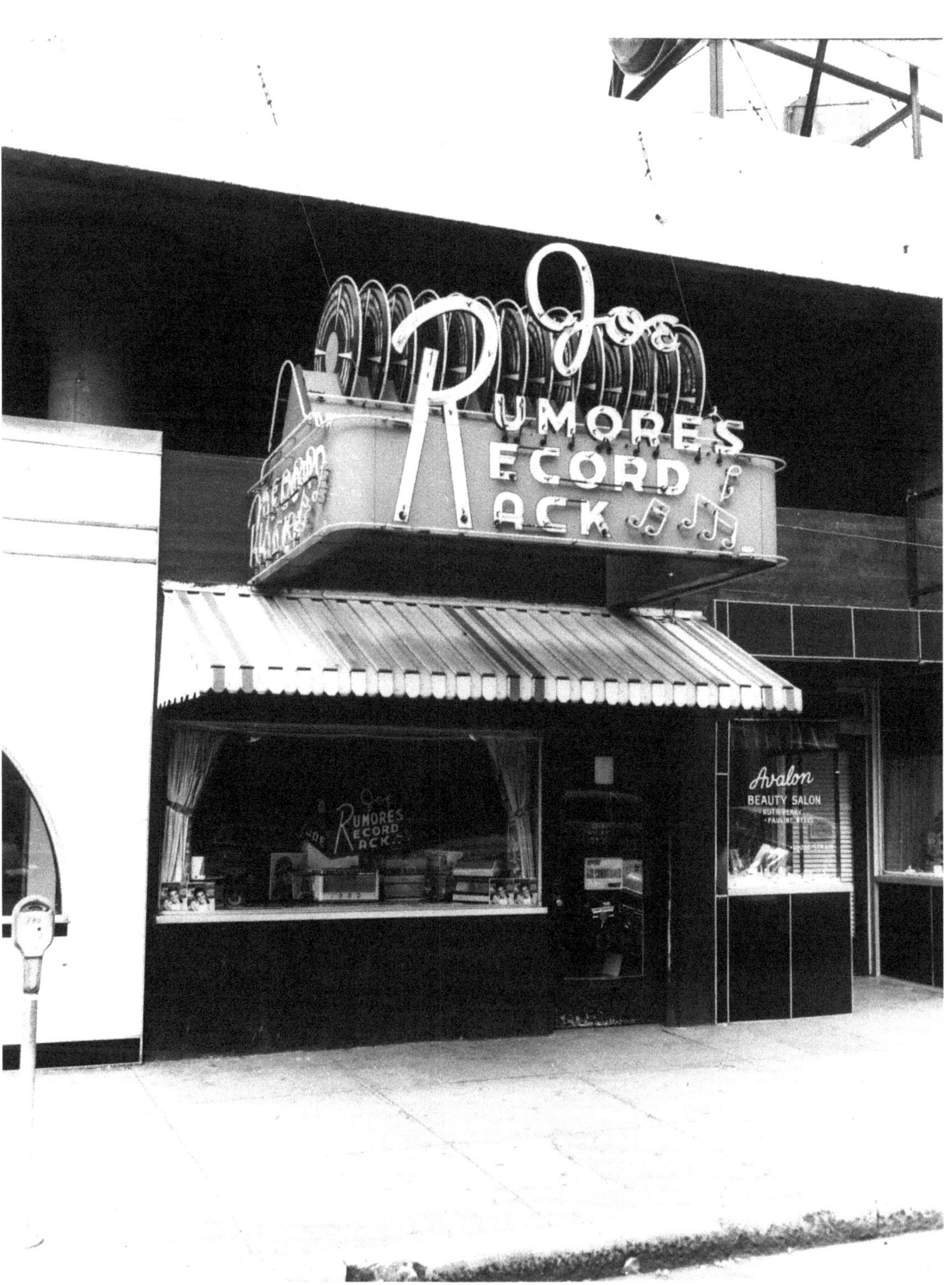

Joe Rumore, a popular radio personality, opened his Record Rack on 2nd Avenue in 1954.

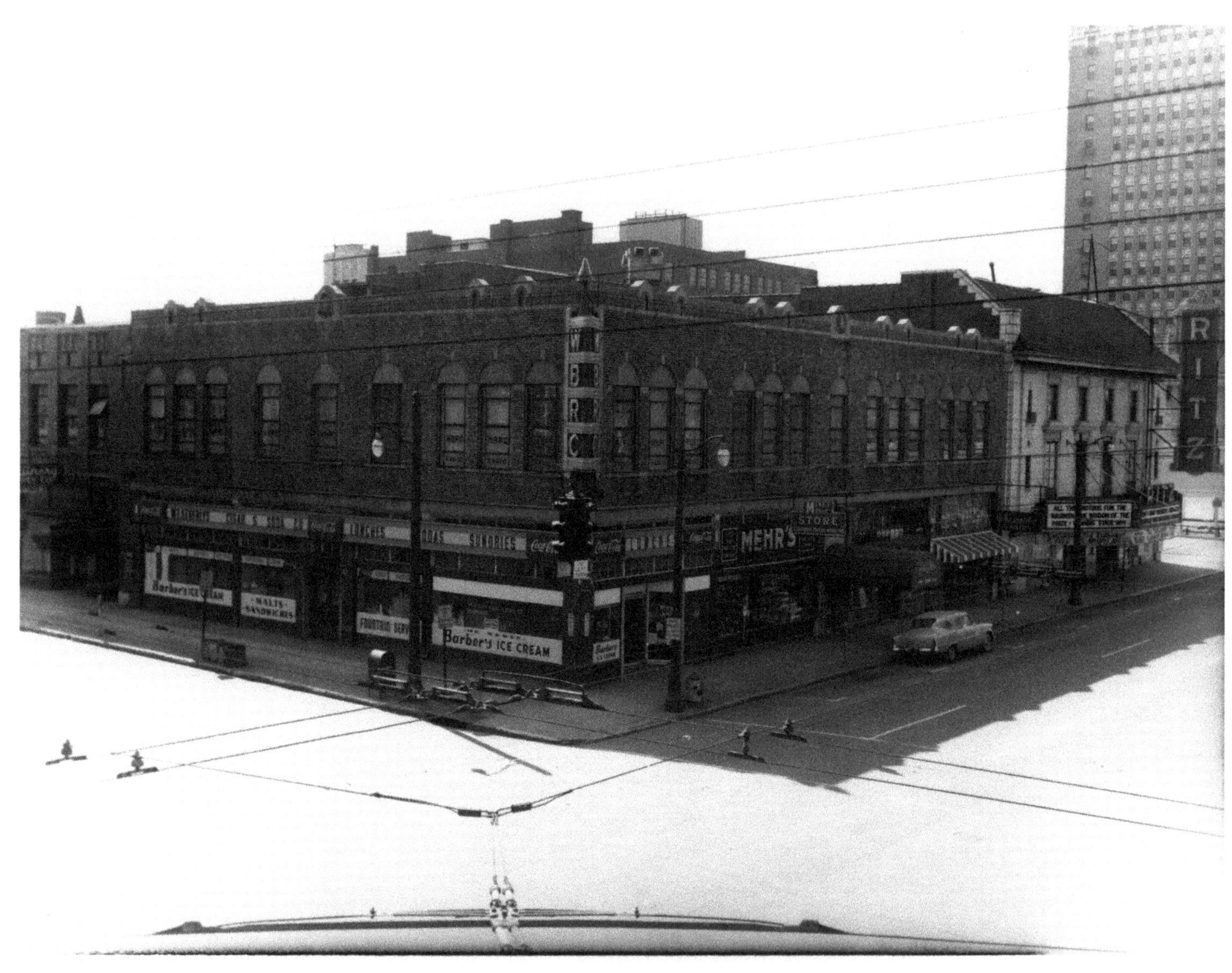

Shown here are the Ritz Theater, Mehr's Music Store, Weatherly's, and WBRC radio station.

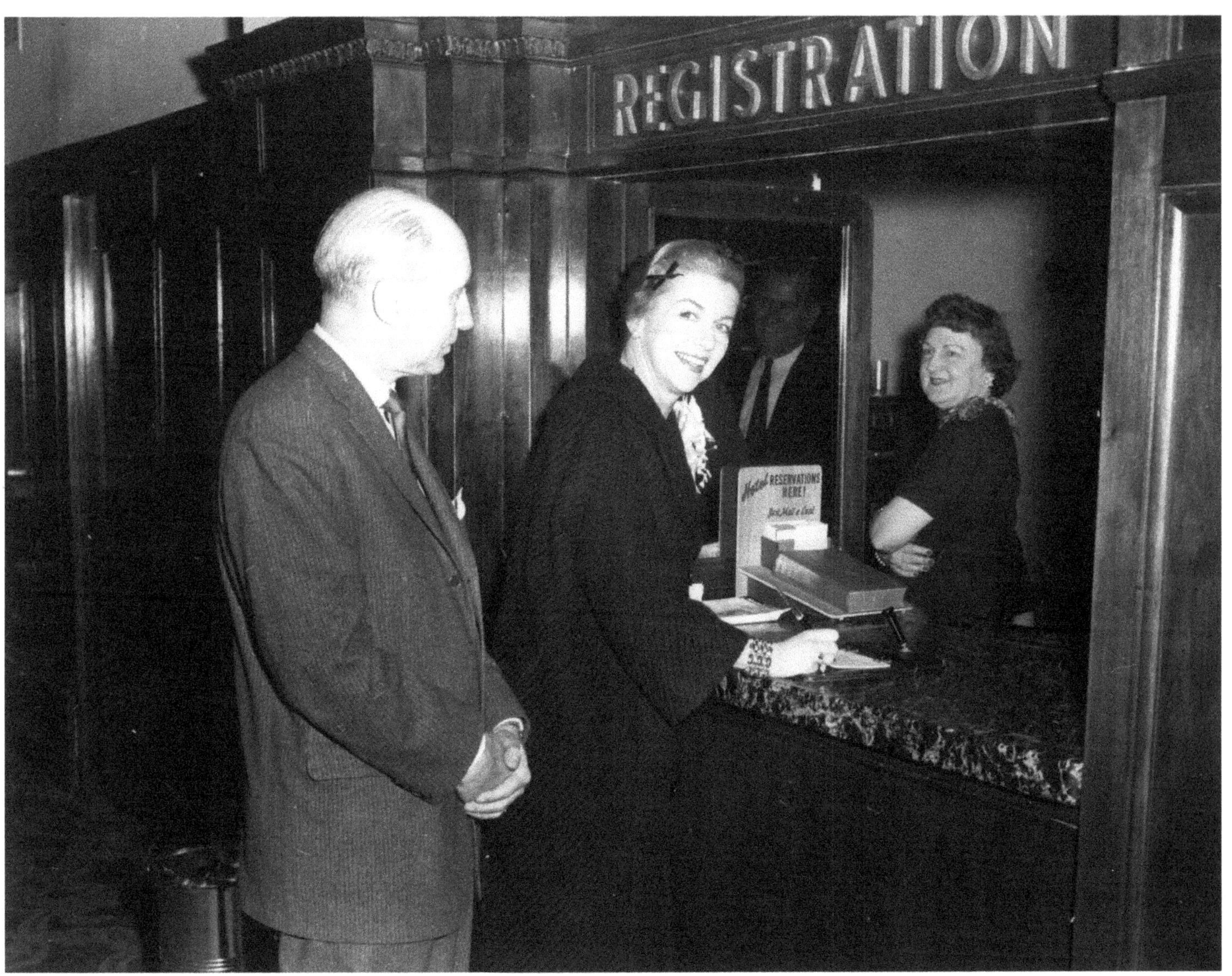

Manager Ira Patton assists actress Betty Furness with checking in at the registration desk of the Tutwiler Hotel. During the 1950s, Furness appeared on the TV program *What's My Line* and had her own show *Meet Betty Furness*. She also served as a spokesperson for Westinghouse.

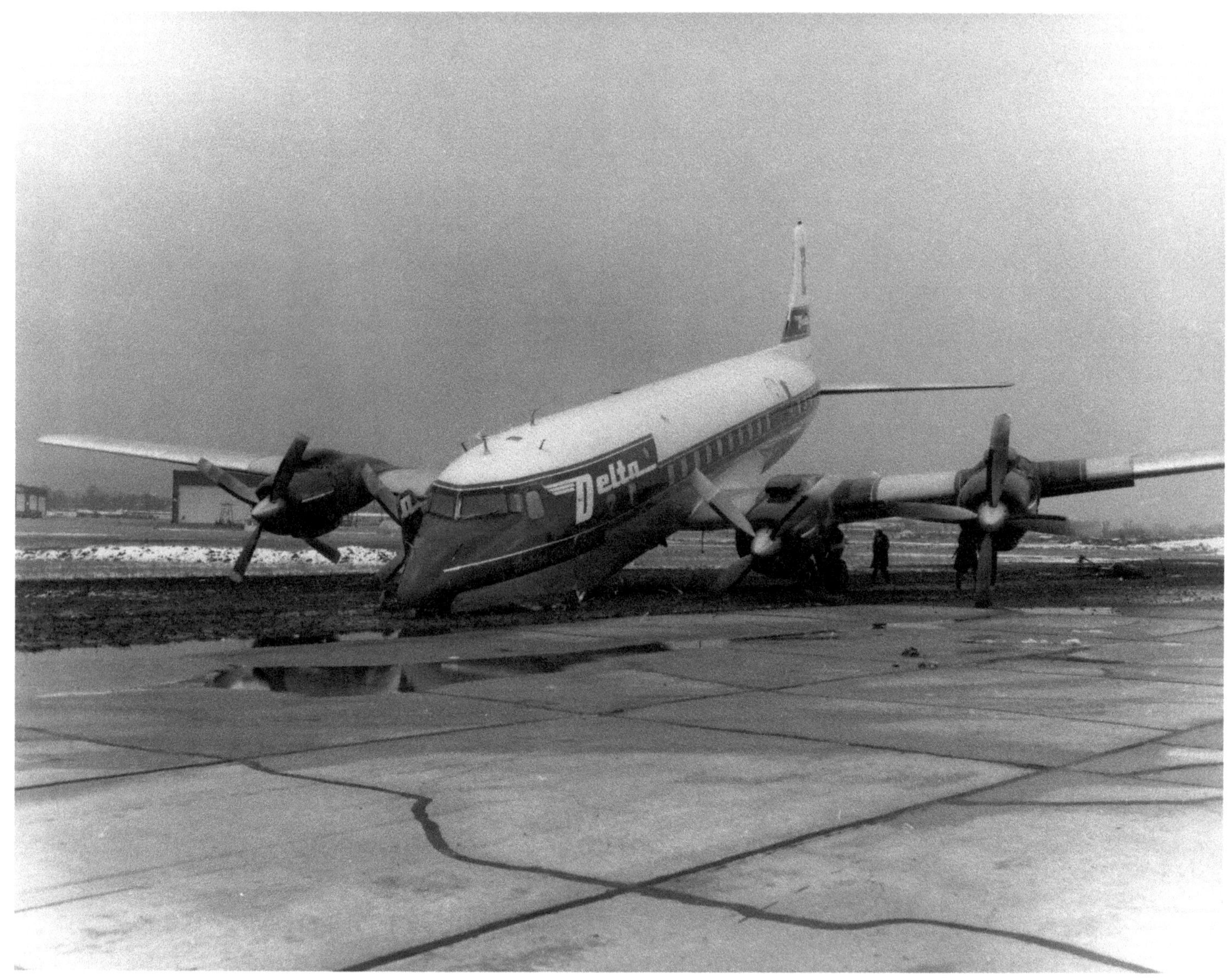

A Delta Air Lines plane crashed on the runway at the Birmingham Municipal Airport after a heavy snowfall and single-digit temperatures struck most of Alabama.

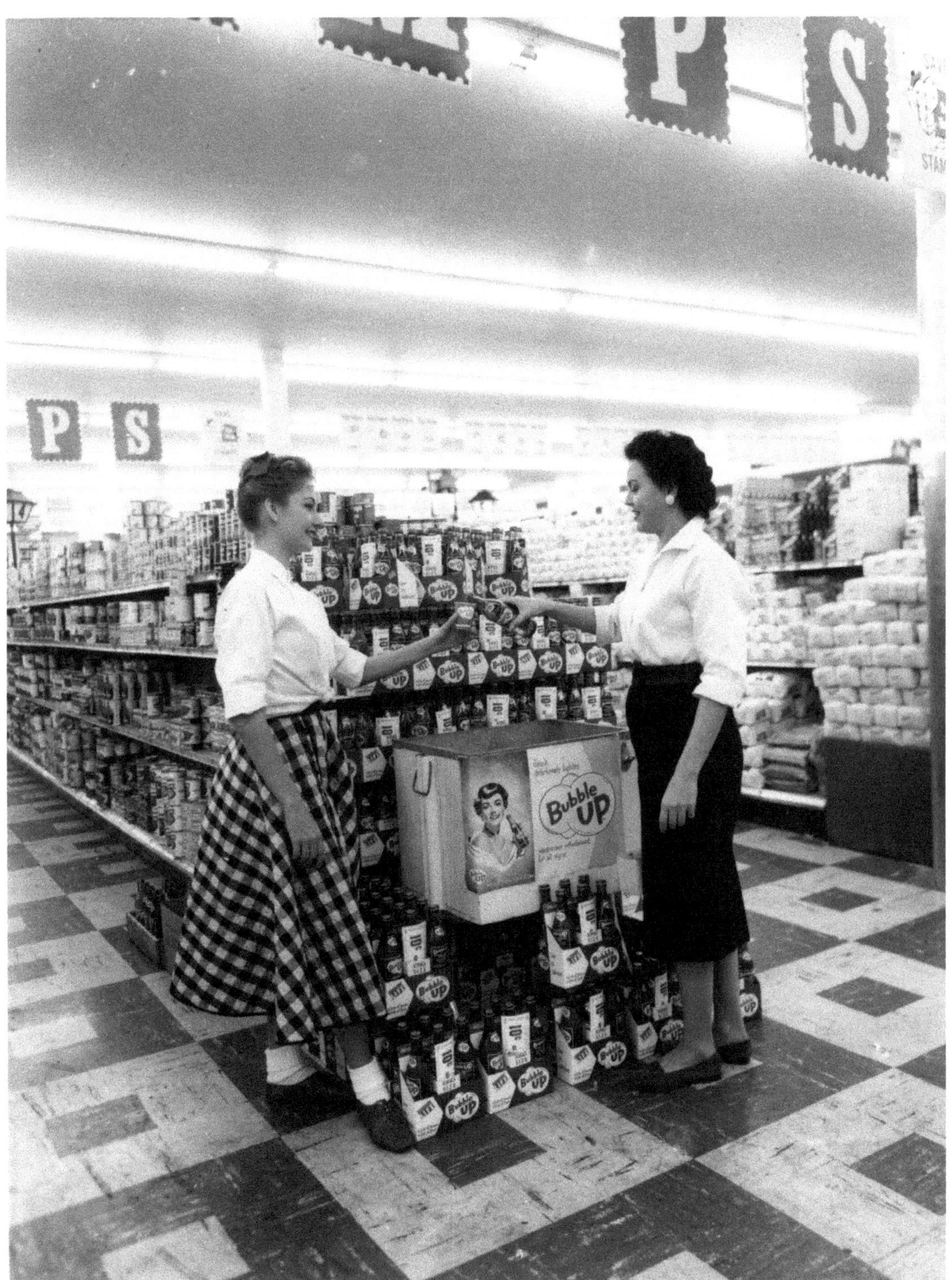

A shopper samples Coca-Cola's Bubble Up at a local grocery store.

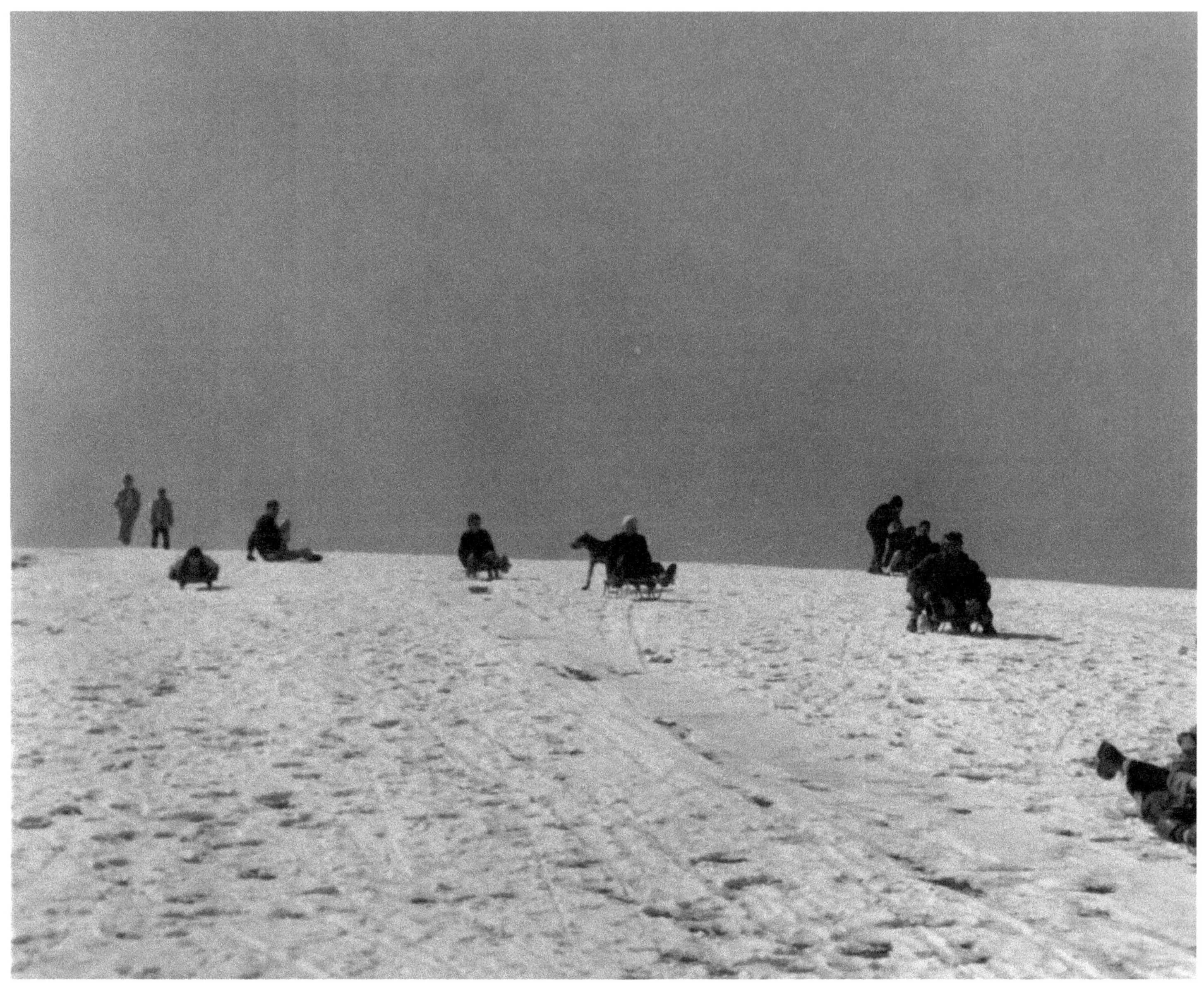

Neighborhood youth enjoy a rare day of fun in the snow. Birmingham receives an average of two inches of snowfall a year, just enough to inspire youngsters and the young at heart to look forward to all the possibilities.

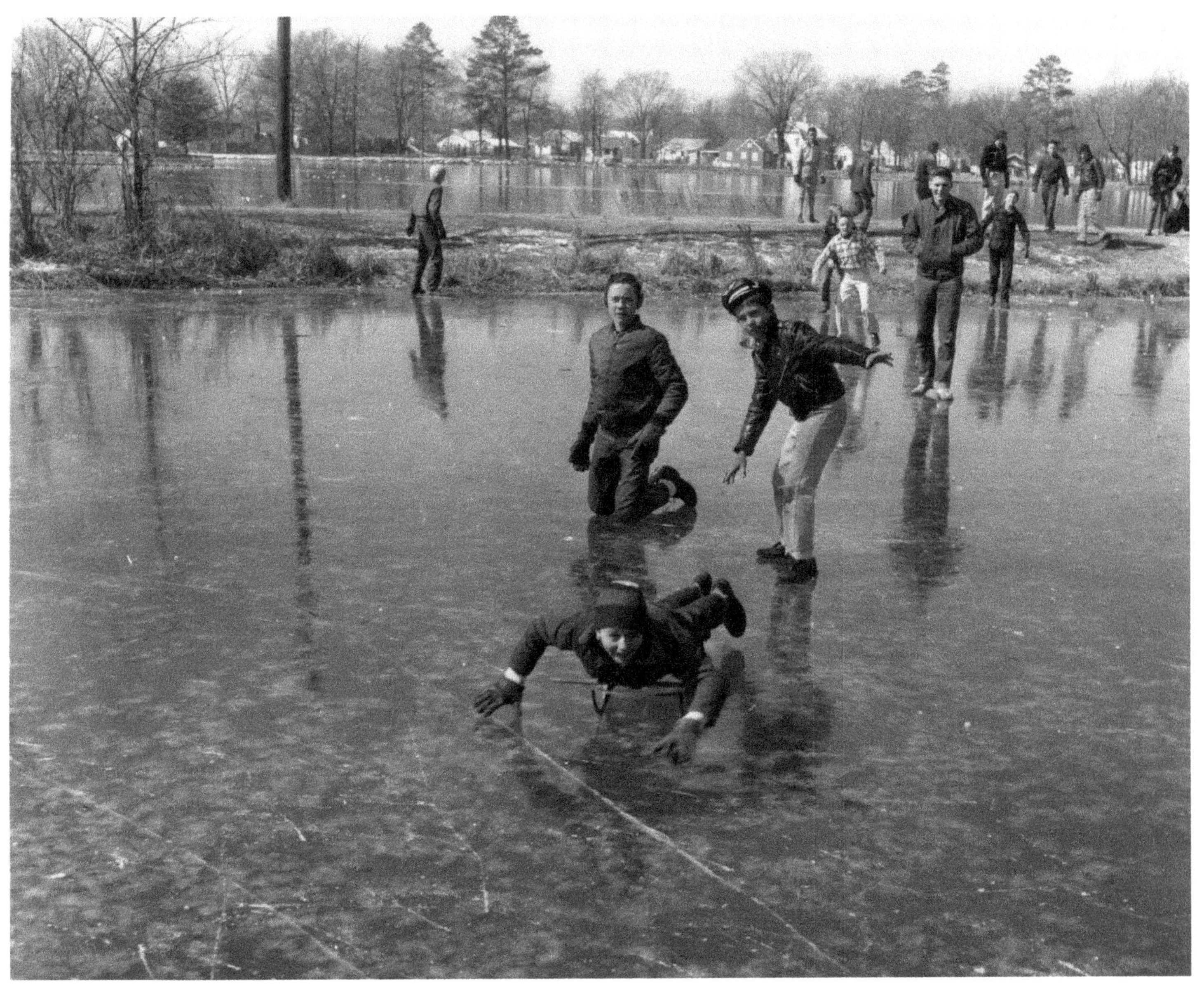

Unusually cold arctic temperatures one winter froze a Birmingham lake hard. These youth were quick to take advantage of the thick layer of solid ice.

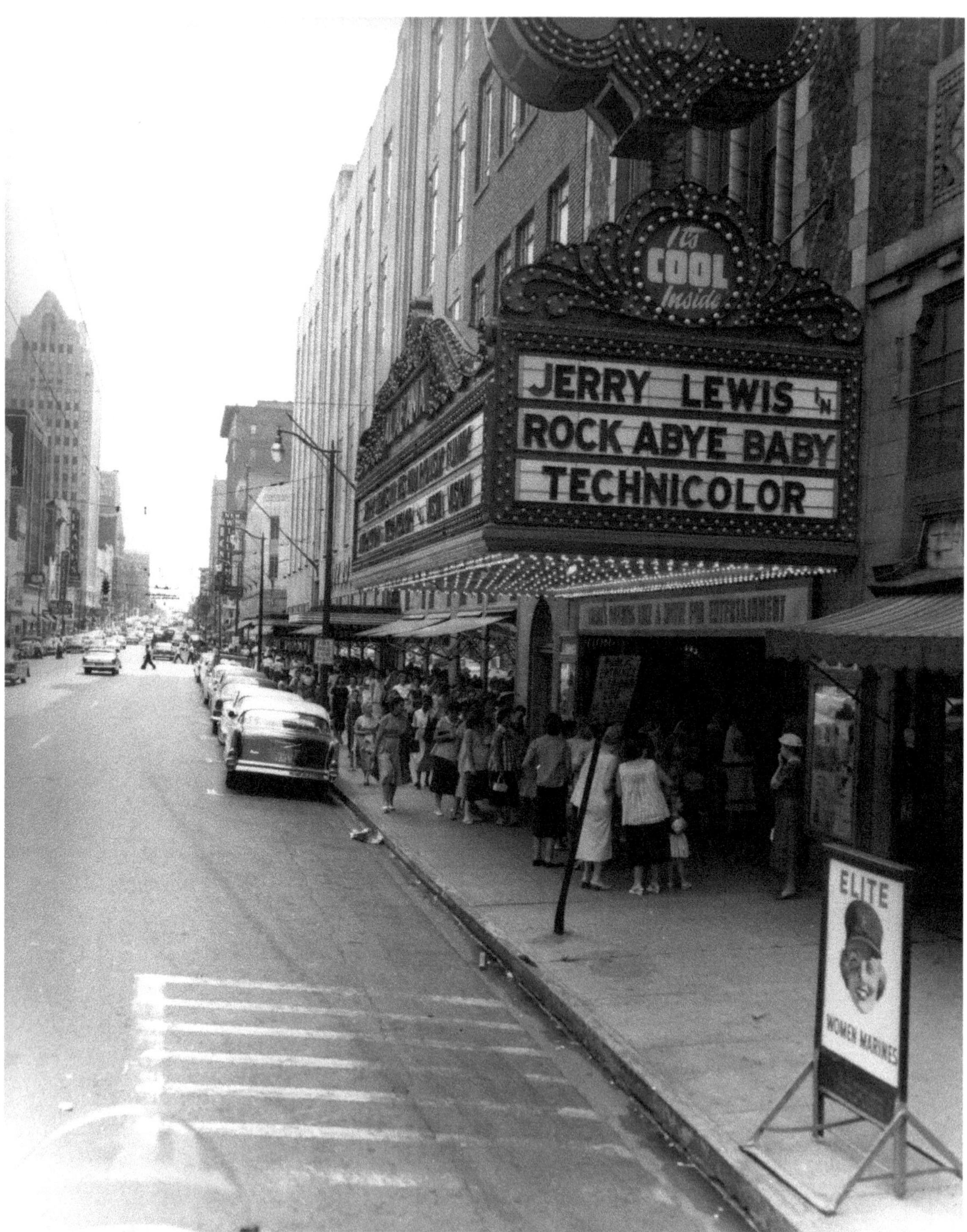

People rush inside the Alabama Theater to see Jerry Lewis in *Rock-A-Bye Baby* and to escape Alabama's humid summer heat. In a day when air-conditioning was still an expensive novelty and rare in American households, businesses able to install cool-air systems could draw more patrons. Theaters led the way with the new technology.

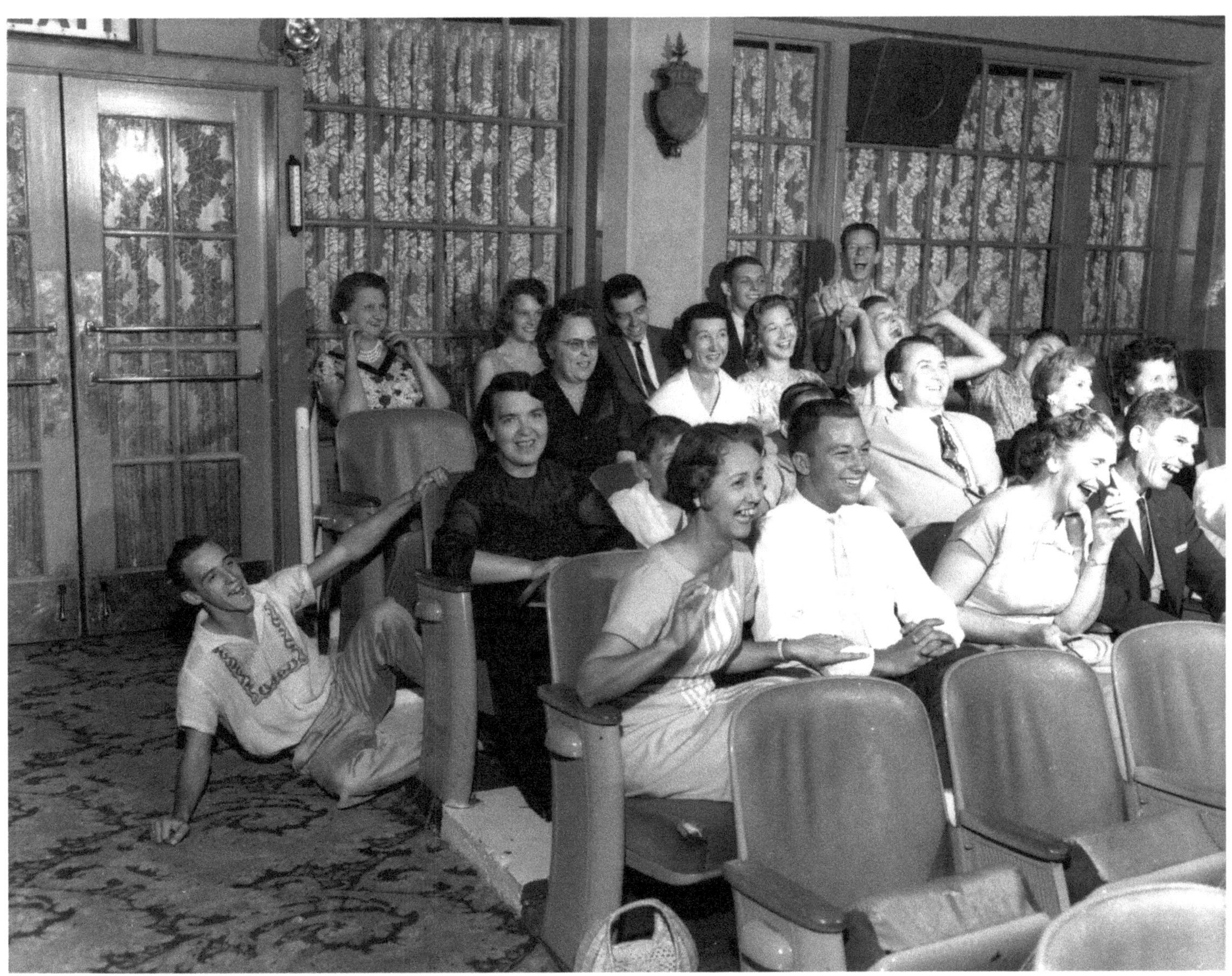

Amused viewers appreciate the humor of Andy Griffith in *No Time for Sergeants* during one of the showings at the Alabama Theater. The film was released in 1958 and starred Griffith and Don Knotts, both of whom would later star in TV's iconic *Andy Griffith Show.*

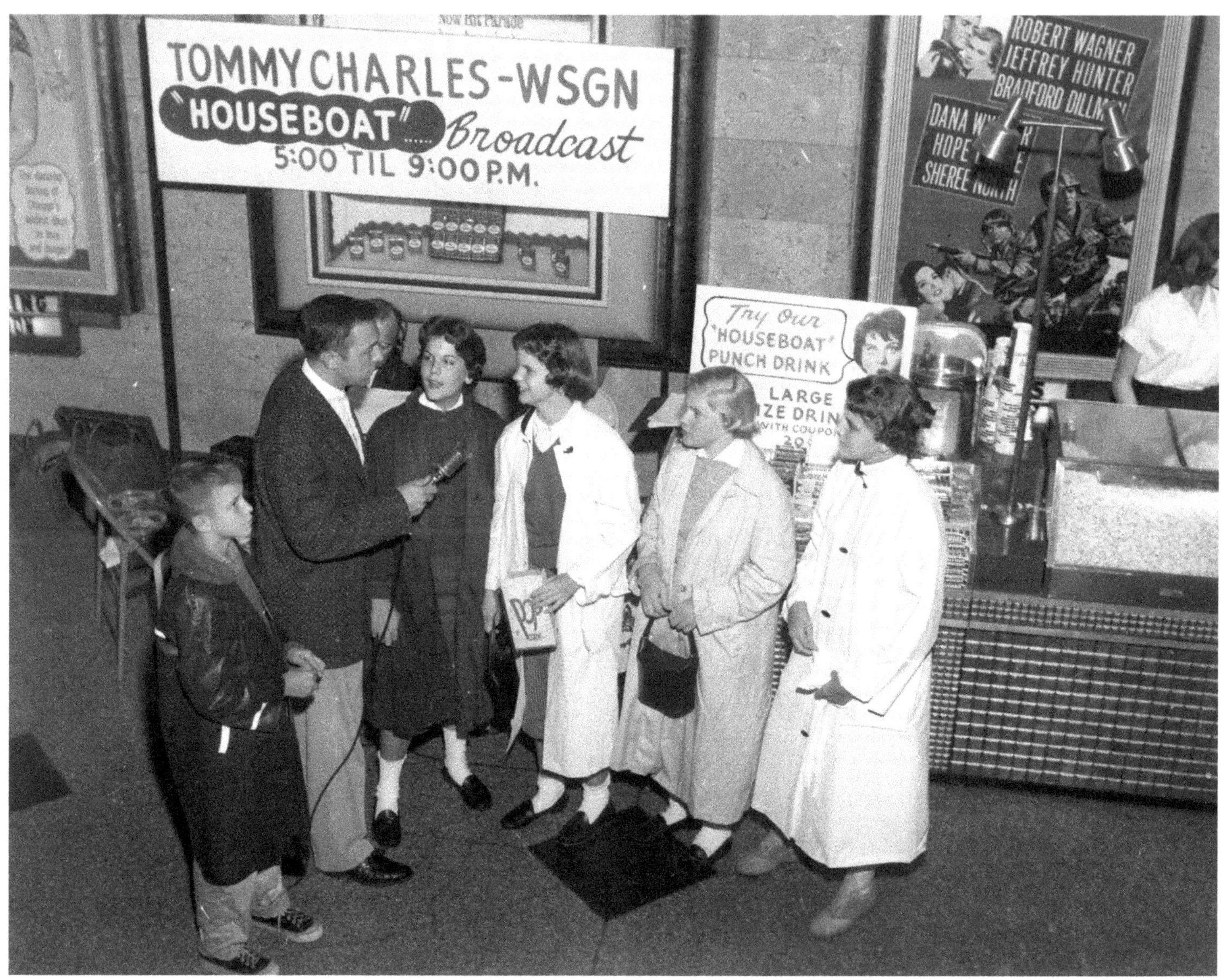

WSGN announcer Tommy Charles promotes *Houseboat* at the Alabama Theater. A prominent radio broadcaster, Charles would later lead the "Ban the Beatles" campaign at WAQY after John Lennon's infamous remark that the Beatles were "bigger than Jesus."

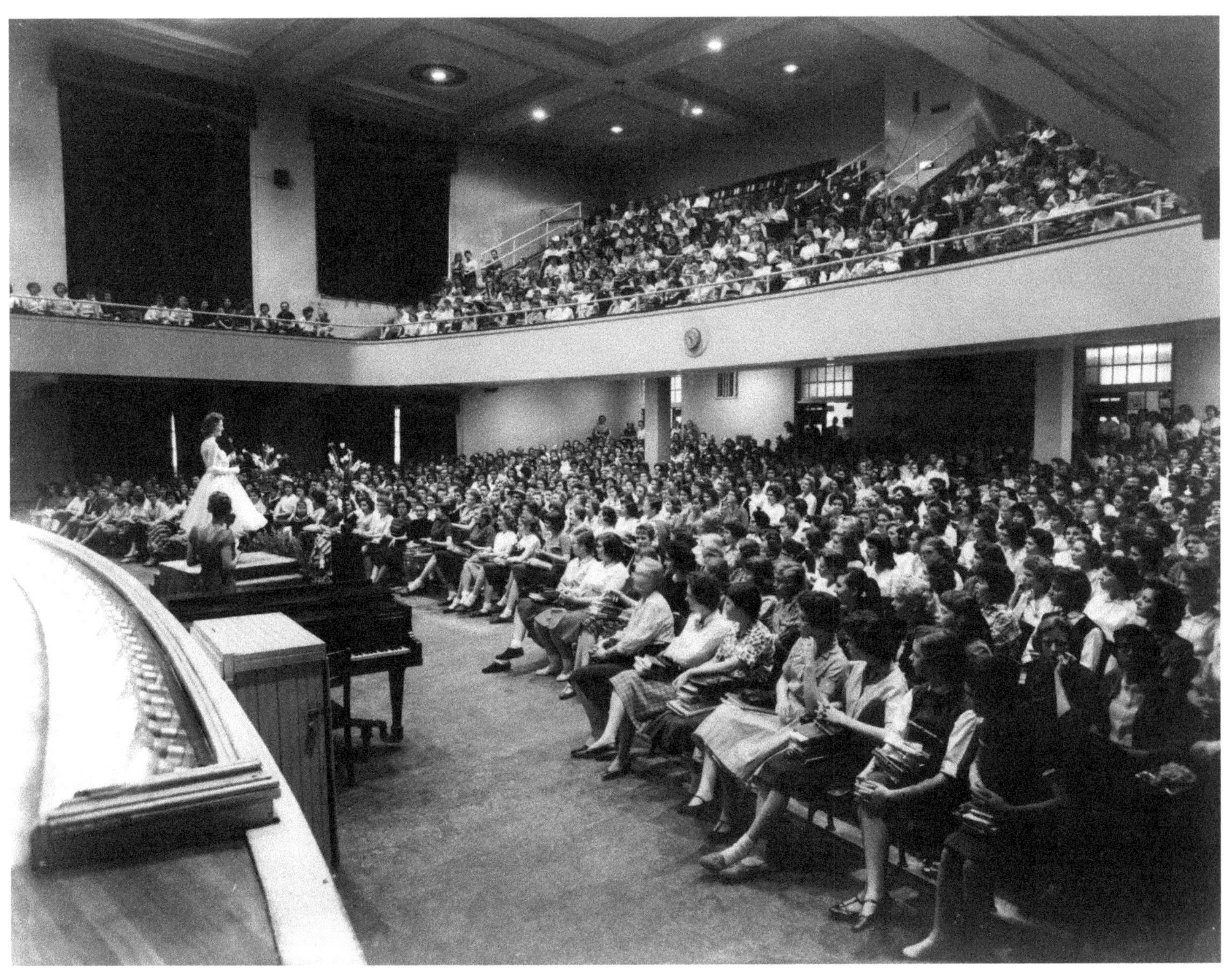

A Loveman's Department Store fashion show takes place in the auditorium at Woodlawn High School.

The Stars and Stripes flies over Birmingham City Hall.

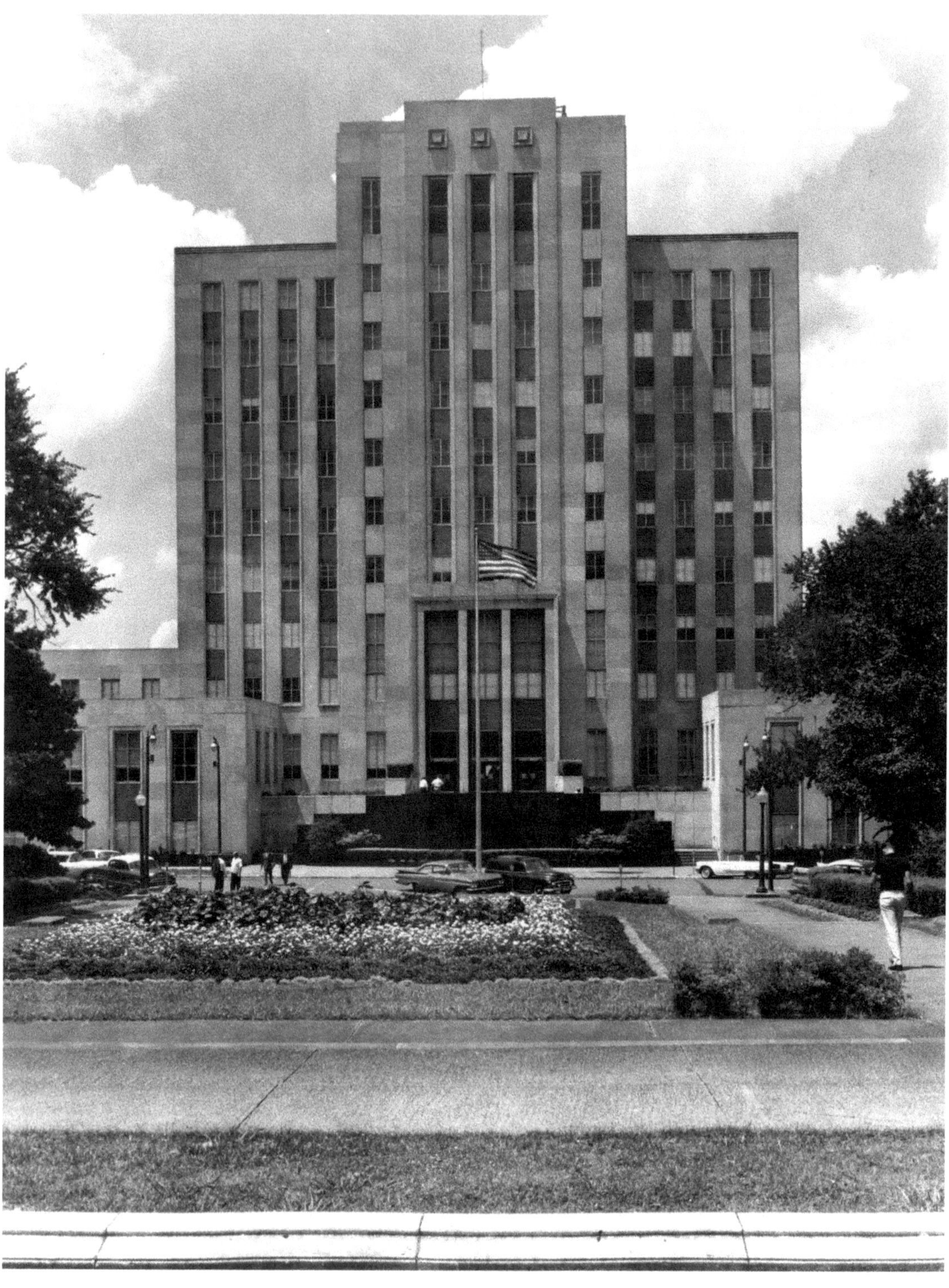

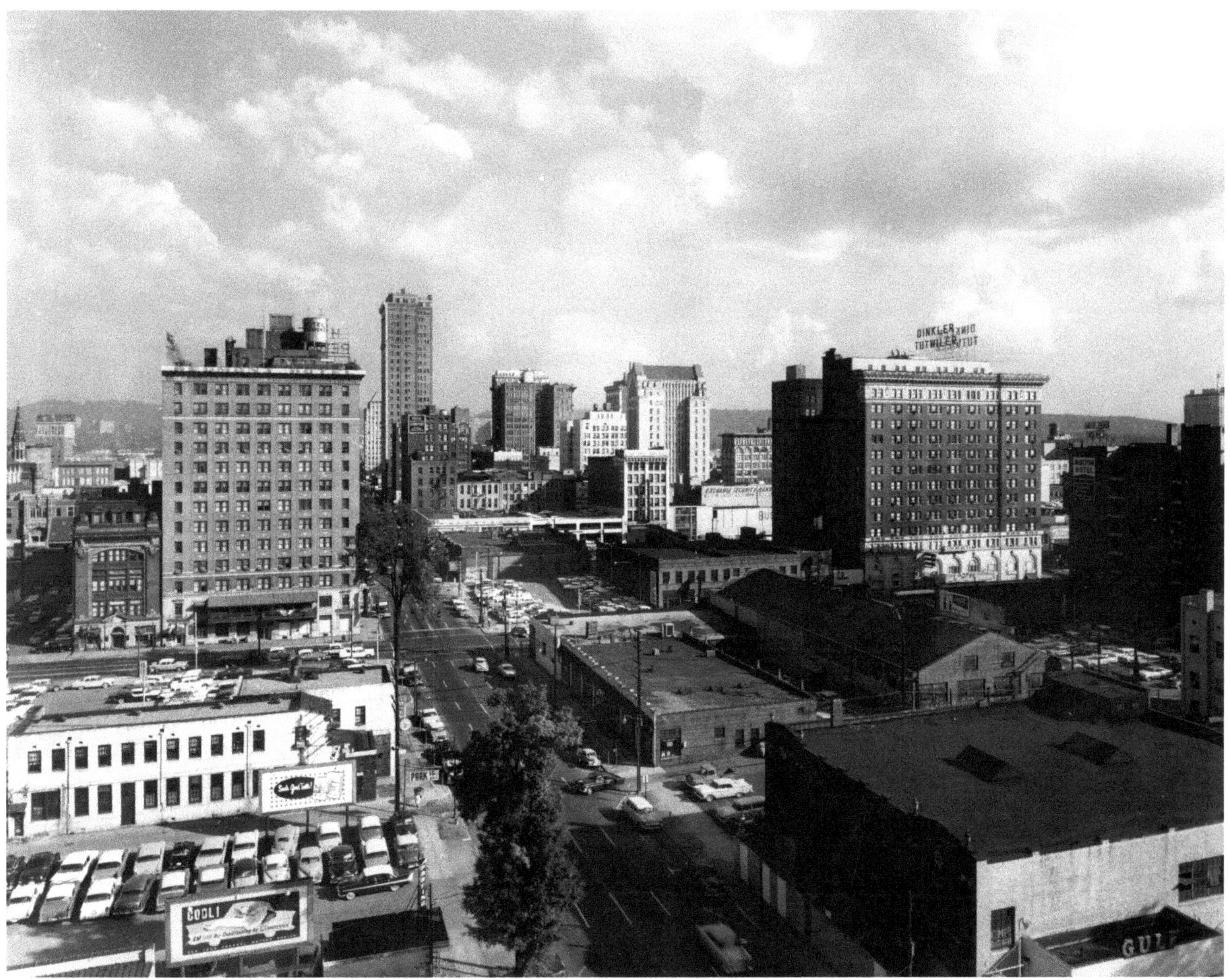

This skyline view of downtown was taken from the Essex House looking southward. The Essex House was built in the early 1950s under the 608 Program of the Federal housing authority. Its cold Industrial style contrasted with the luxurious Ridgely apartments across the street.

This northward view of 20th Street North was recorded from the vantage point of a railroad overpass. The First National Bank of Birmingham building flanks the street on the right. At left in the foreground is a ticket office for the L&N, an important rail line that began in Louisville and Nashville before the Civil War and later extended to key destinations throughout much of the South. The Hummingbird, which traveled the line through Birmingham on its way to Florida, was one of the L&N's well-known trains. Railroad passenger service was beginning to decline in the 1950s and would halt completely with the lapse of another decade.

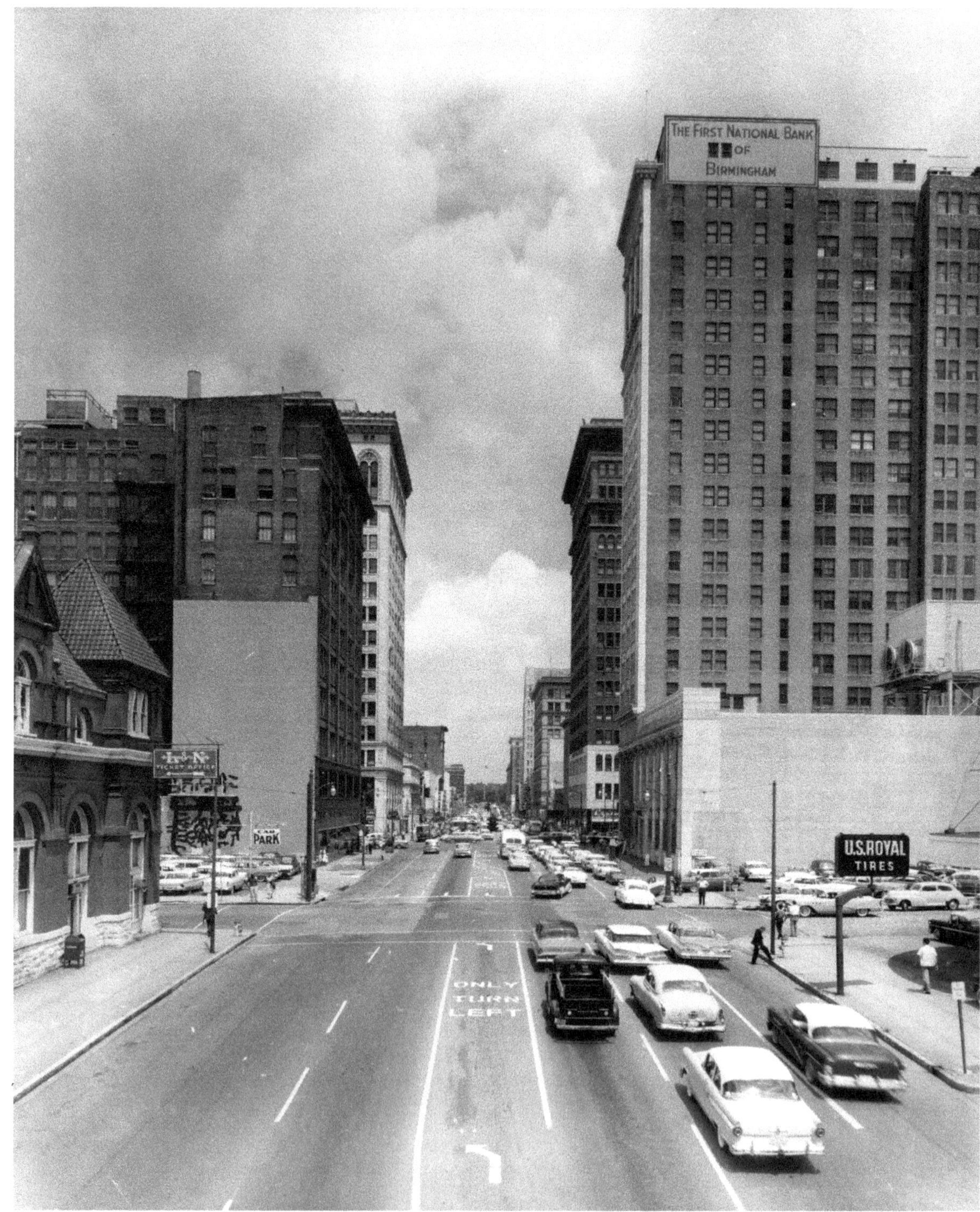

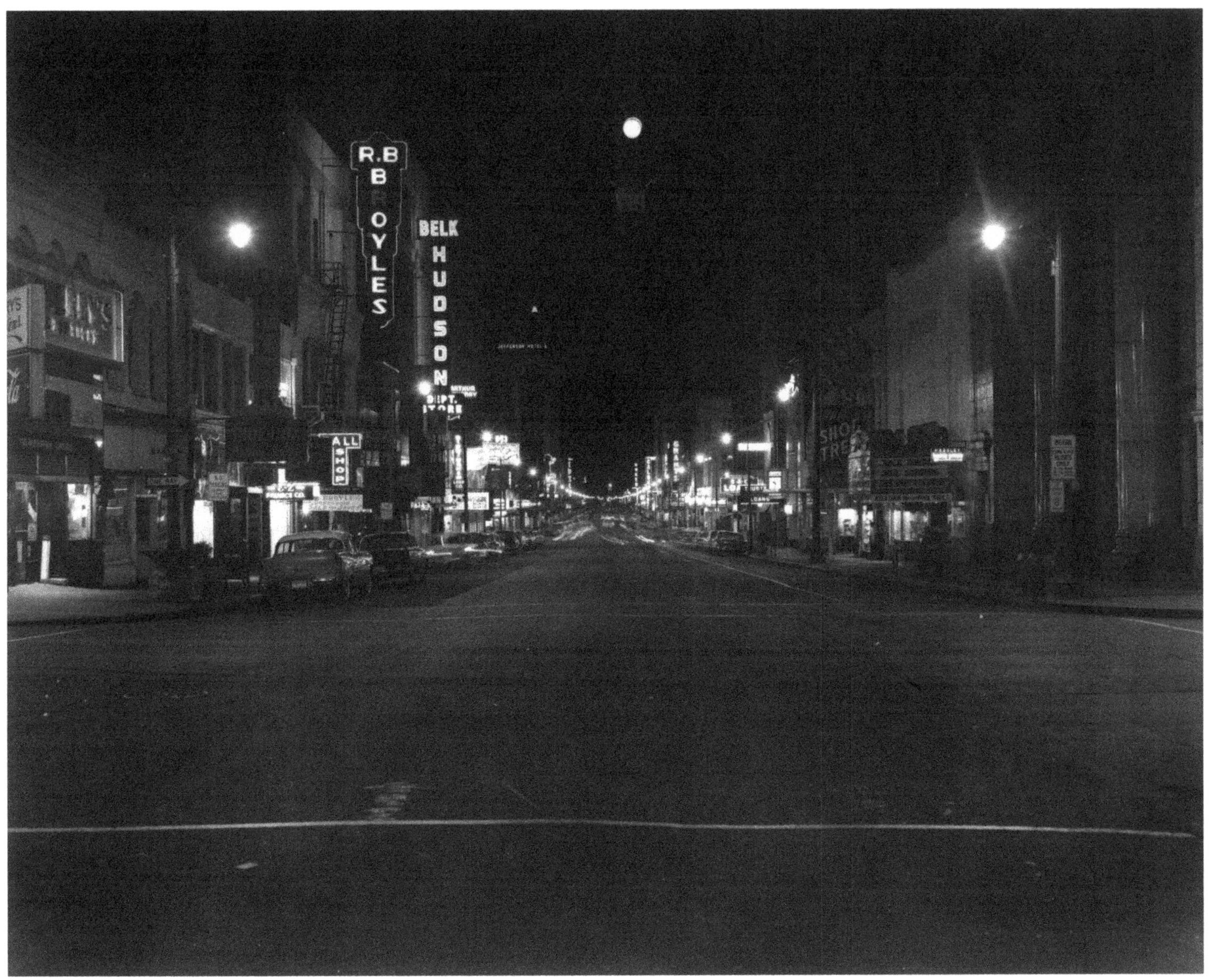

The lights of 2nd Avenue North lighten a Birmingham night sky. The Melba Theater and R. B. Broyles Furniture Store flank the foreground in this view of businesses on the street. In the 1950s, citizens still relied on downtown for shopping and entertainment, and businesses often remained open evenings.

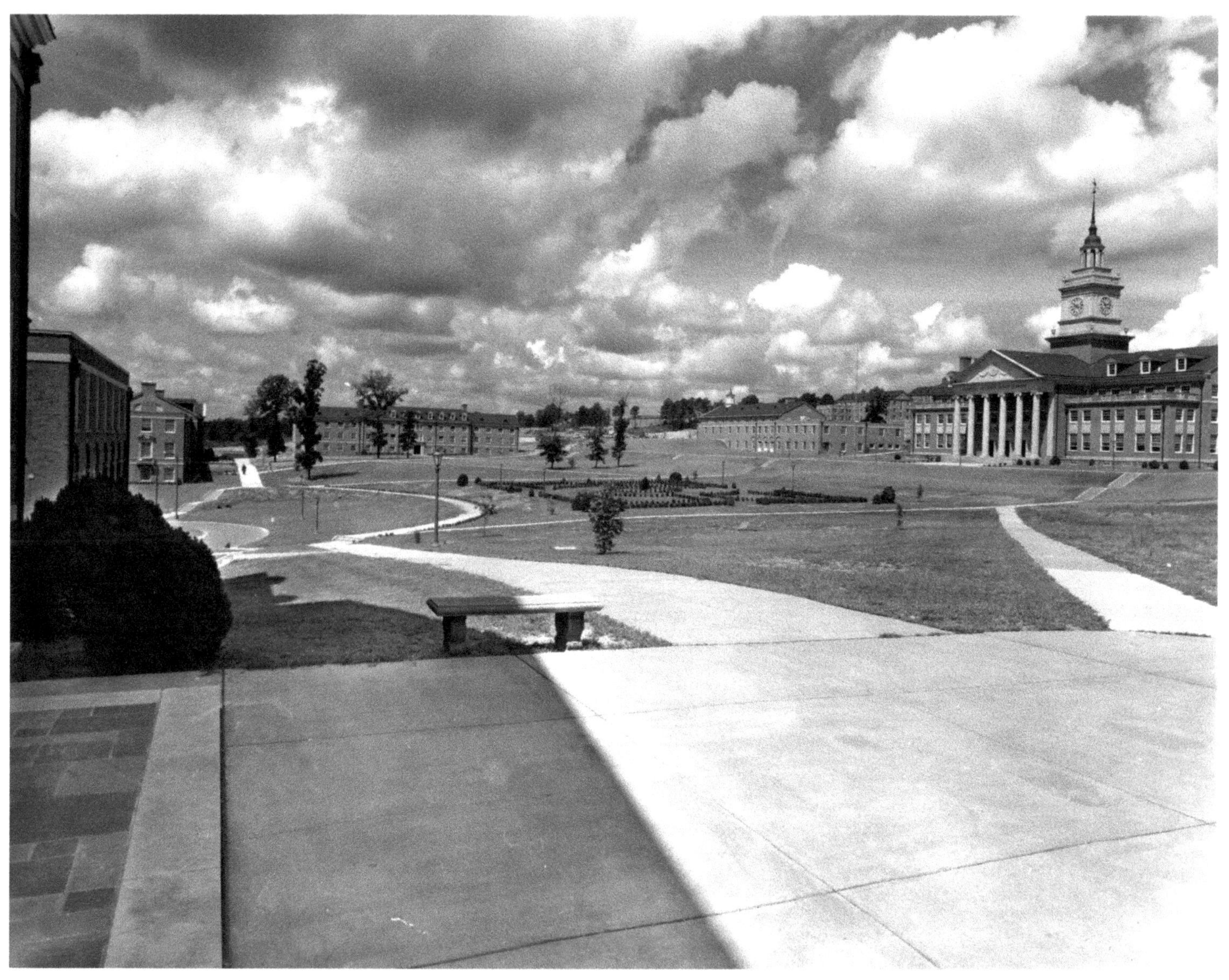

The campus of Howard College, later Samford University, on Lakeshore Drive as seen from the Biology building. Visible in this image are the men's dormitory, cafeteria building, and the library.

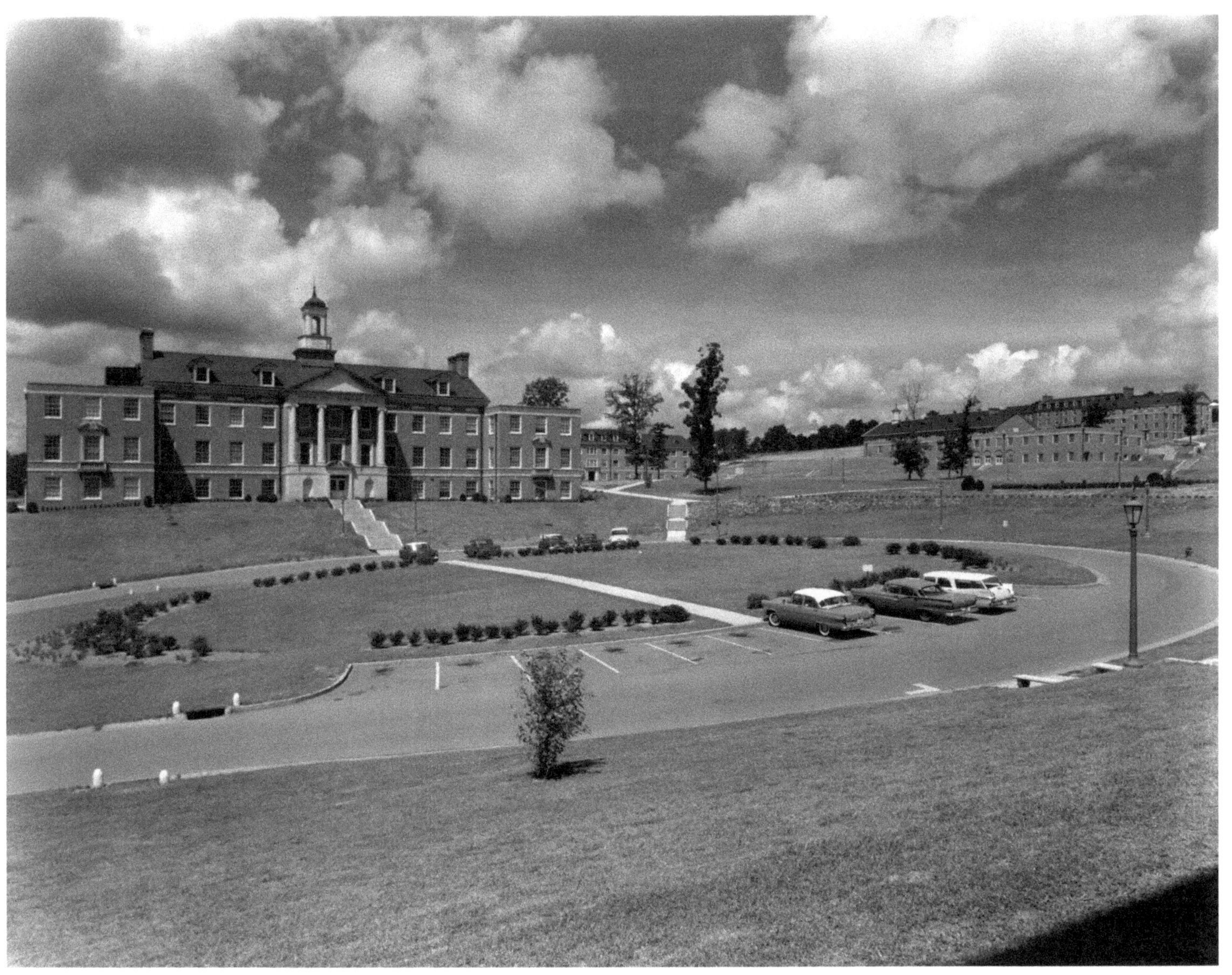

The campus of Howard College as seen from the pharmacy school. Visible is Samford Hall, the administration building, along with the men's dormitory, the cafeteria building, and the women's dormitory in the distance.

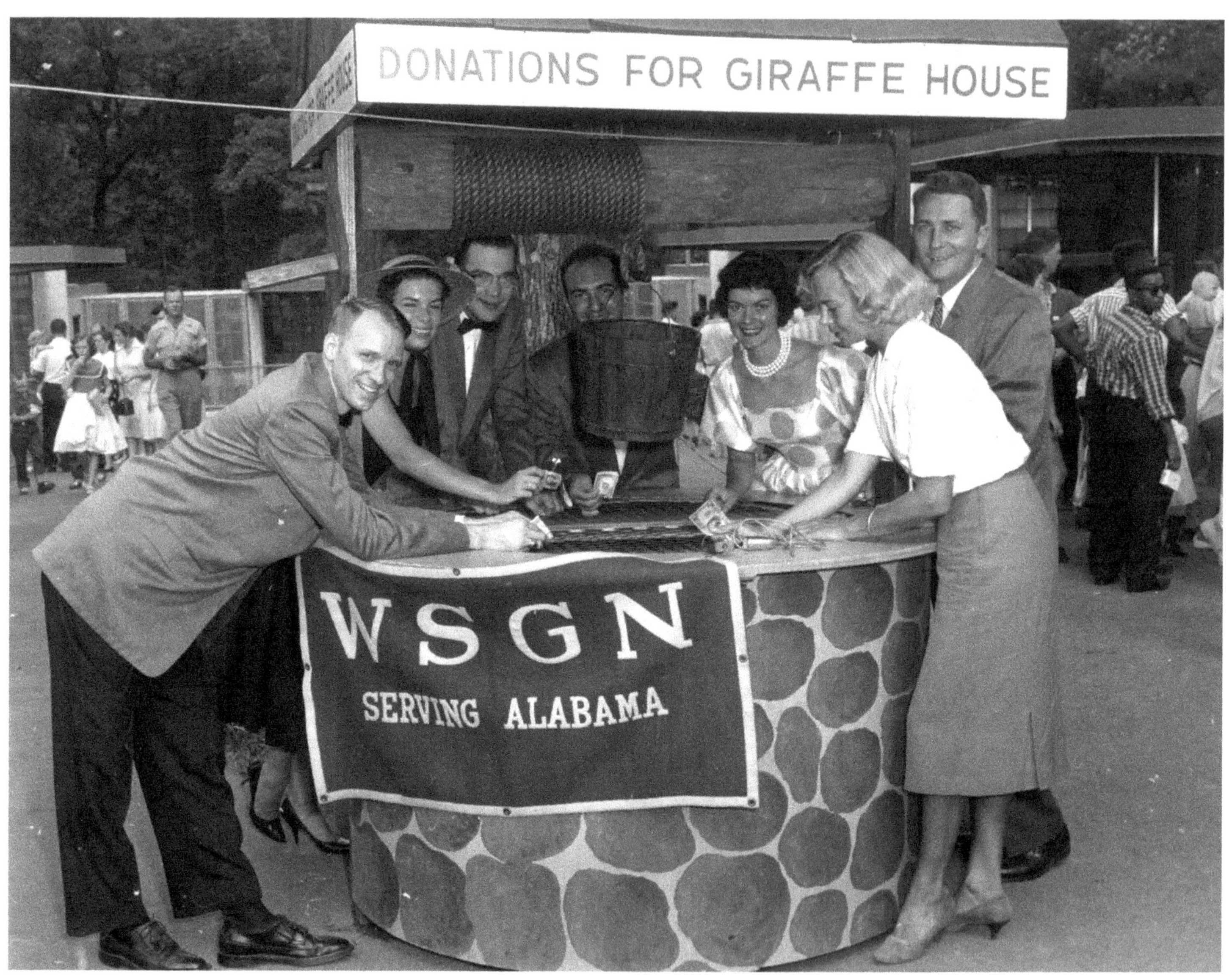

Bill Bolen, a radio announcer for WSGN, and other WSGN employees pitch in to raise donations for a new giraffe house at the Birmingham Zoo. The zoo opened in 1955 with Monkey Island as its first exhibit.

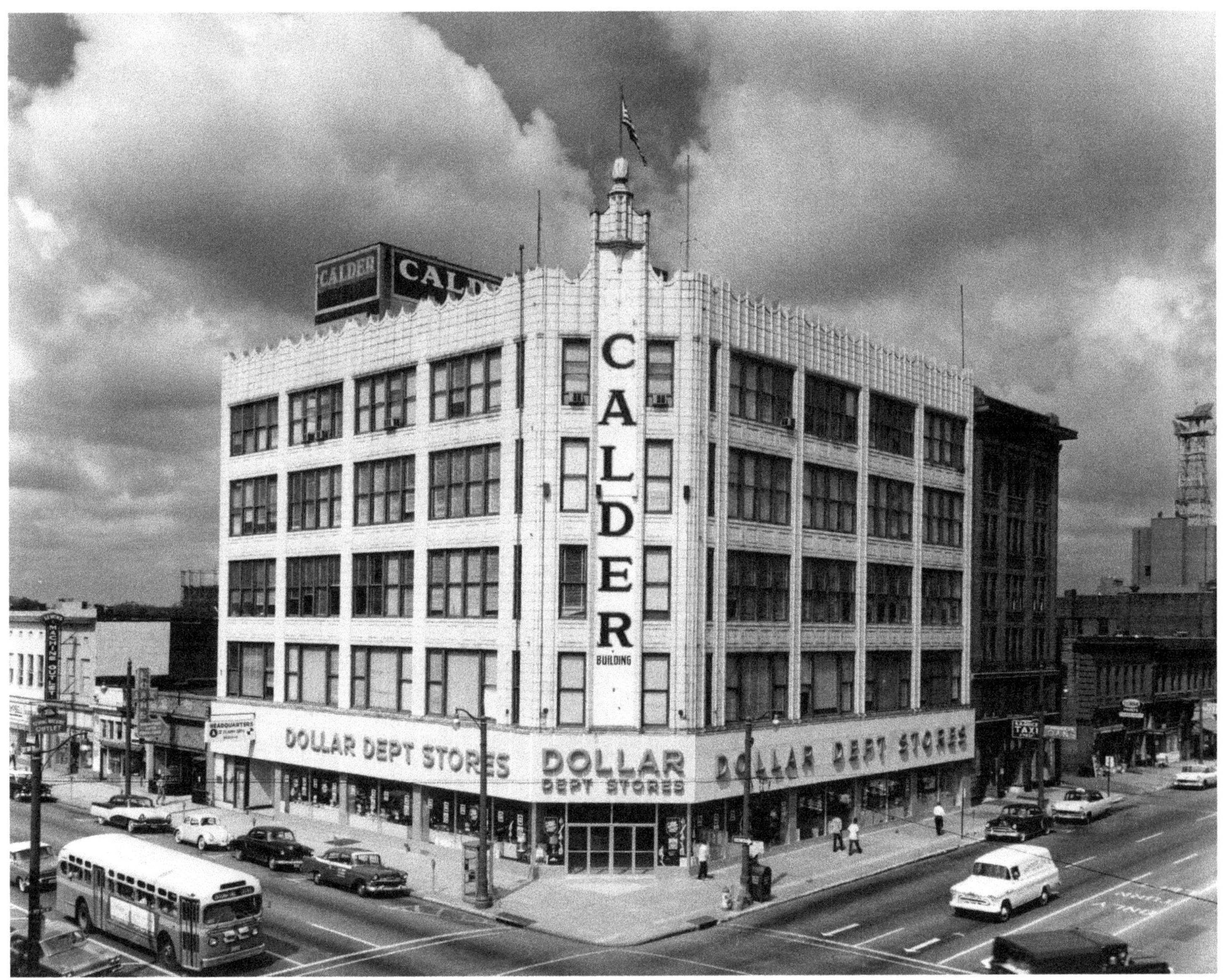

Dollar Department Stores in the Calder Building at the corner of 18th Street and 3rd Avenue North. Also in this area were the Pythian Temple building, the lodge for the Knights of Pythias, and the Rush Hotel, which catered to a black clientele.

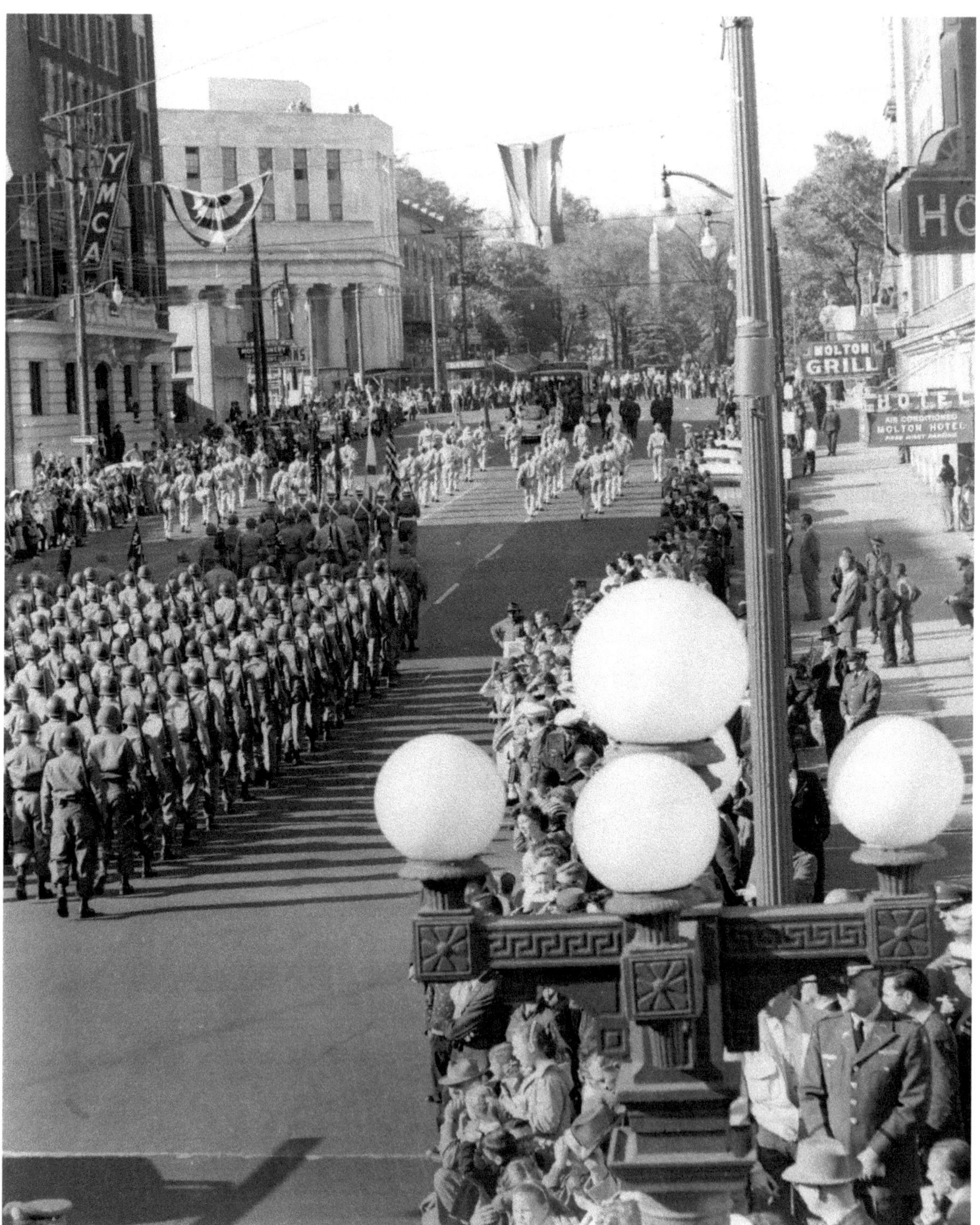

Birmingham celebrates local veterans with a parade. The 1959 Veteran's Day included an address by Vice Admiral Wallace M. Beakley, deputy chief of U.S. Naval Operations, and a colorful parade, complete with armed services units and elaborately decorated floats. Here the parade passes the Y.M.C.A. and the Molton Hotel.

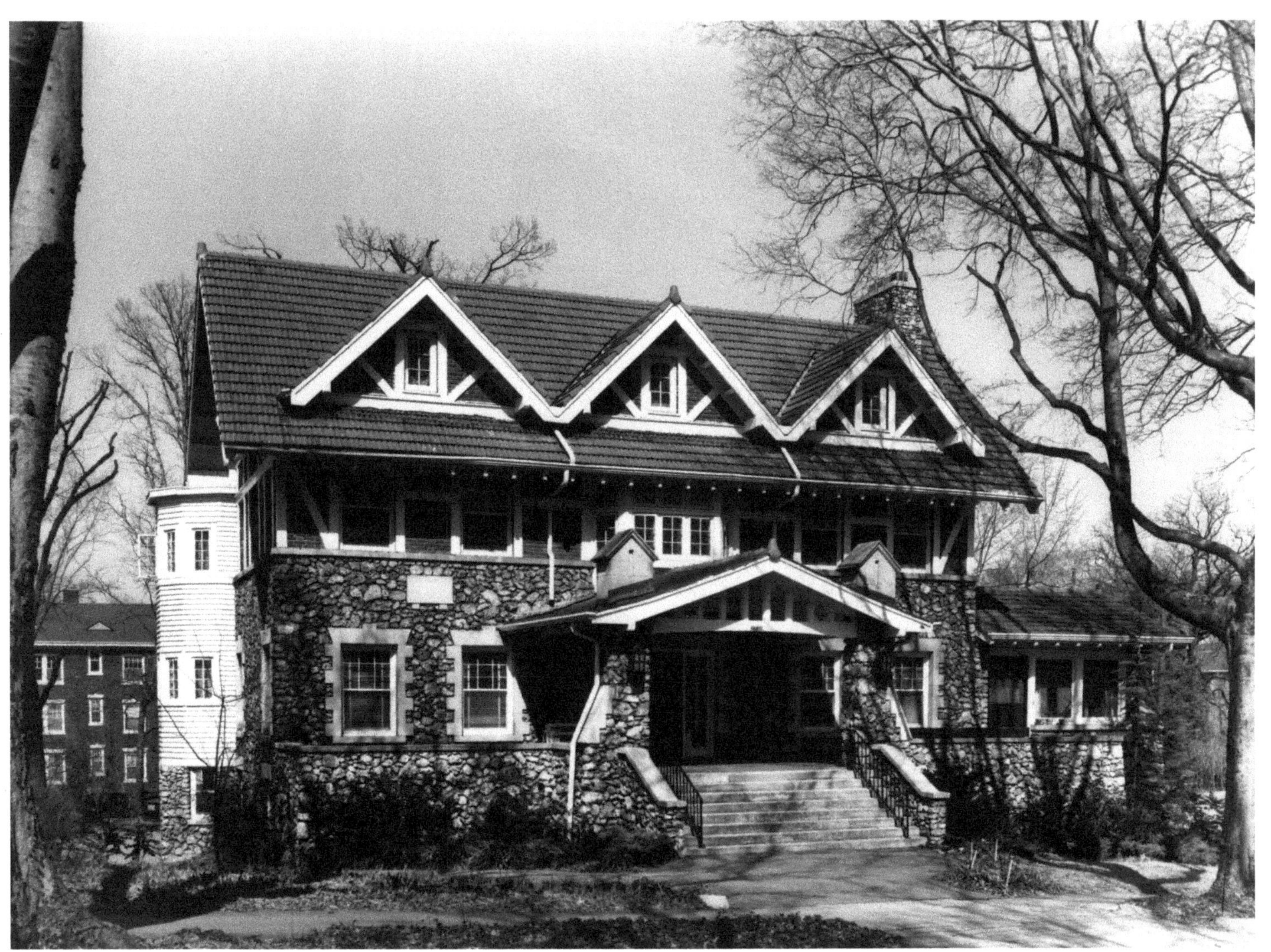

This building housed the Birmingham Teachers Club whose primary purpose was to provide aid to retired teachers of the Birmingham public schools who were in need of assistance. Housing accommodations, food, clothing, medical attention, and care were all part of the assistance the club supplied.

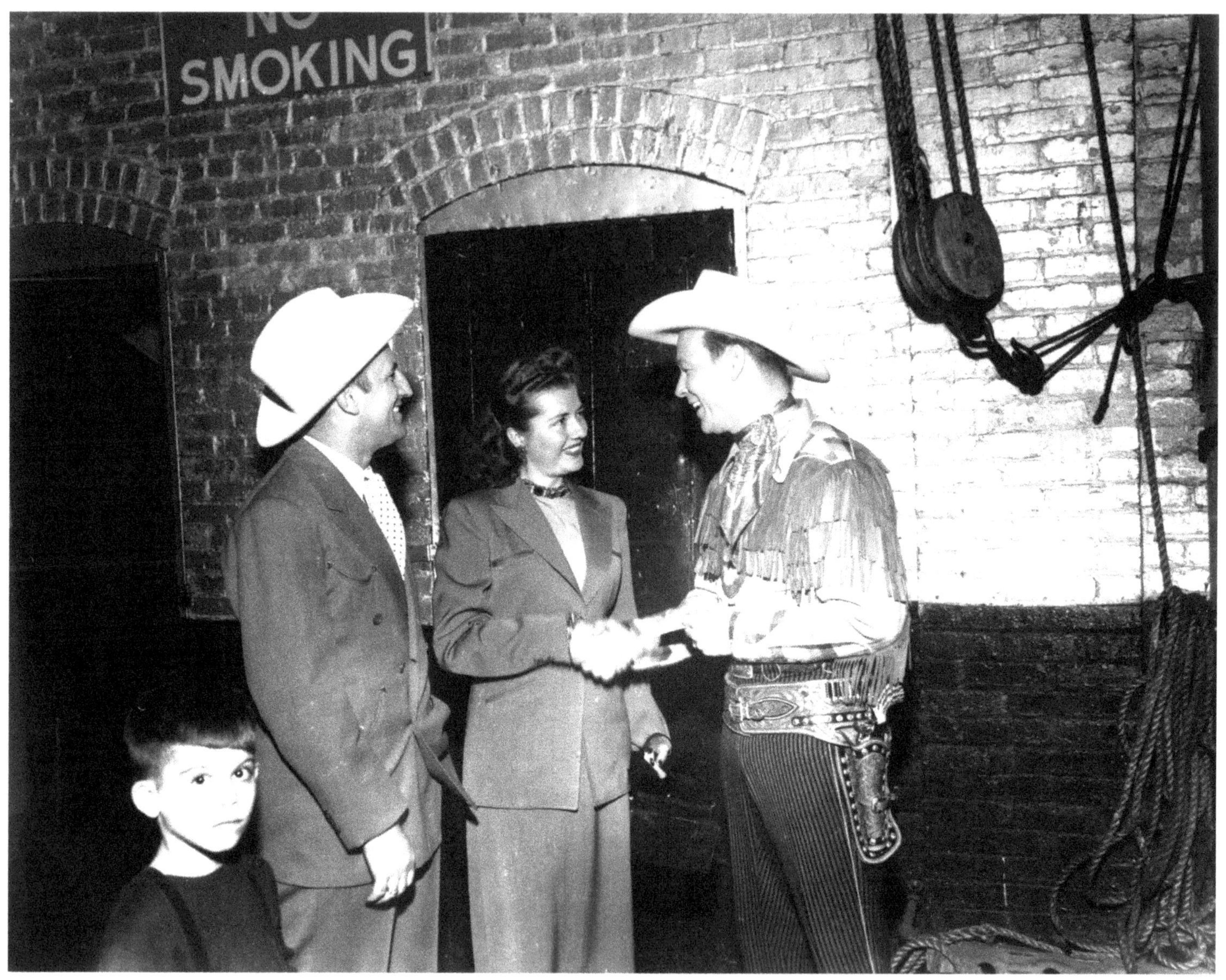

Hollywood's "King of the Cowboys" Roy Rogers visits backstage with Happy Hal Burns and fans.

A Line in the Sand

(1960–1969)

If the 1950s was harbinger of the changes to arrive in Birmingham, the 1960s were the chaotic storms that blew the conflict throughout the city. It is common knowledge that the 1960s were transformative for the majority of American cities. In Birmingham, what was reported was the scenes of violence, but the changes overall were more understated and complex and not all of them were racially driven.

Headlining the news were incidents like the confrontation at Kelly Ingram Park where police officers turned fire hoses on African-American protesters, some of whom were children and young teenagers. Birmingham had also gained the nickname Bombingham, given to the city because of the bombings that targeted prominent black homes, churches, and businesses. Sit-ins, parades, integration protests, and the jailing of Martin Luther King, Jr., were all widely reported and influential to the direction of the city during the decade. These racially motivated incidents and forcible integration led George C. Wallace, governor of Alabama during the 1960s, to proclaim that he would draw a "line in the sand" against integration, a sentiment shared by many constituents. Several photographs in this section highlight the dramatic protests.

Quoted in the *Birmingham Post-Herald,* one segregationist expressed the opinion of many: "Let the Negroes have Birmingham and see if the downtown bunch can survive." In 1960, Birmingham had a population of 340,887, which would drop by 11 percent by 1969 as white Americans in Birmingham and across the nation left inner-city neighborhoods for suburbia, in part at least as a reaction to a rising number of unpopular federal rulings.

Other changes during the decade drew less attention from the media. The production of coal, iron, and steel dropped as the emphasis on medical research, scientific experimentation, and academia rose. At the end of the 1960s, the construction of the University of Alabama at Birmingham heralded new beginnings. Movie theater construction enjoyed a boom. In 1965 alone, three theaters opened—one of which was "an ultra-modern indoor suburban movie house." McDonalds came to Birmingham in the early 1960s. Veteran's Day parades, outdoor concerts, the creation of the Birmingham Botanical Gardens, the construction of the Bank for Savings Building skyscraper, and the First National Bank–Southern Natural Gas skyscraper were all indicators of a changing city.

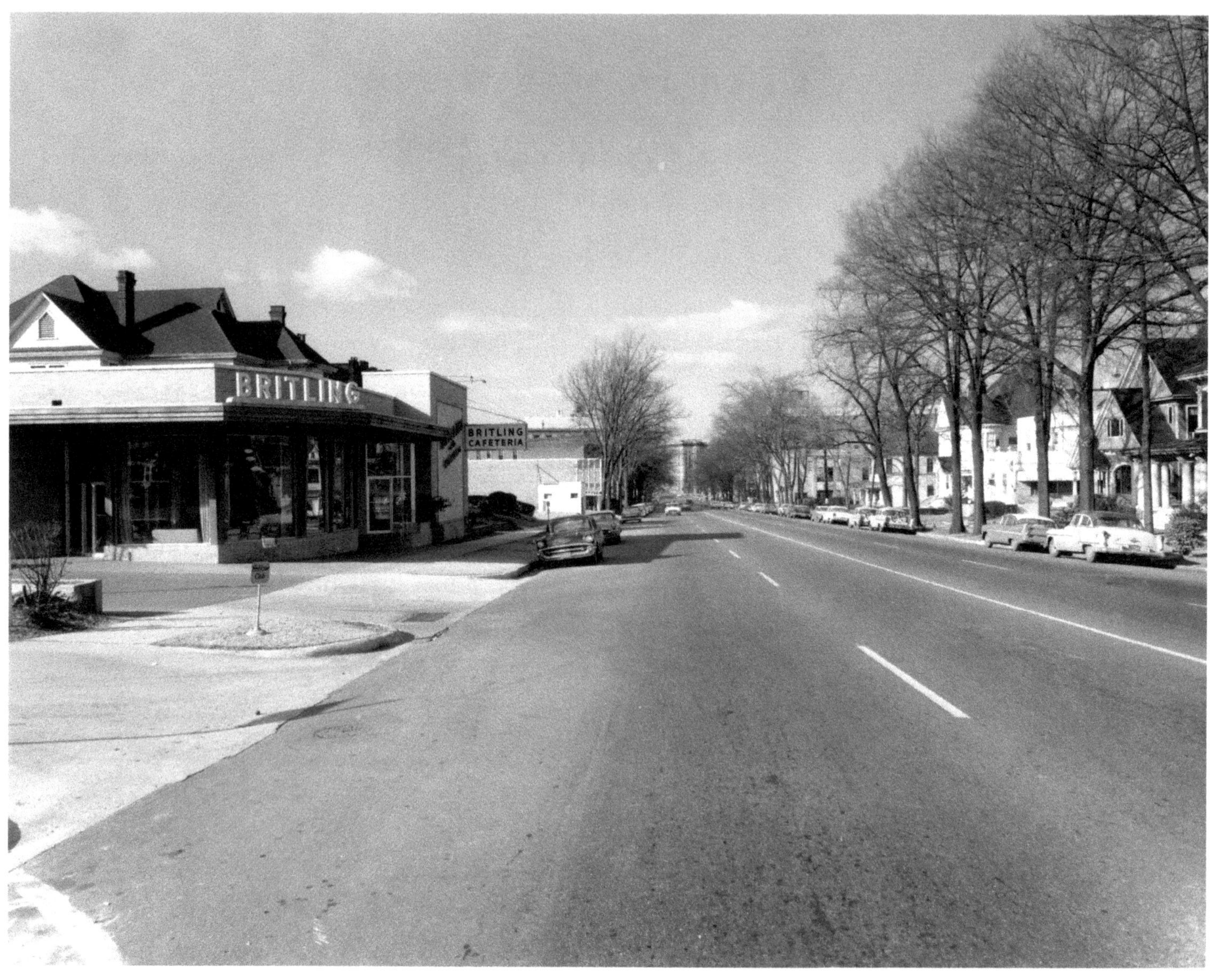

Facing westward toward 20th Street is this view of Highland Avenue. Britling Cafeteria named after the H. G. Wells novel *Mr. Britling Sees It Through* is visible along the street.

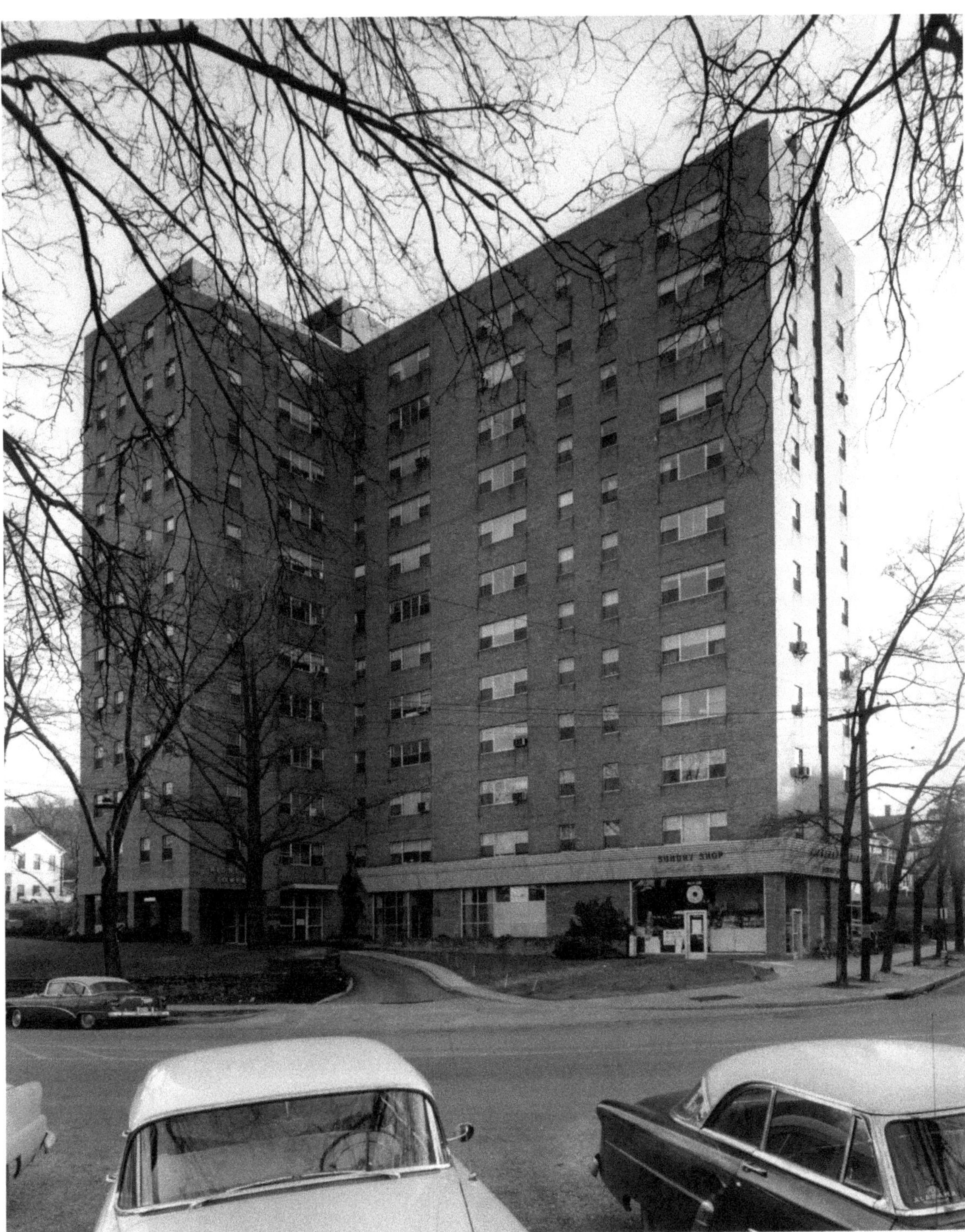

Highland Tower Apartments on Highland Avenue.

The Protective Life Insurance Company Building and the Comer Building flank 21st Street North.

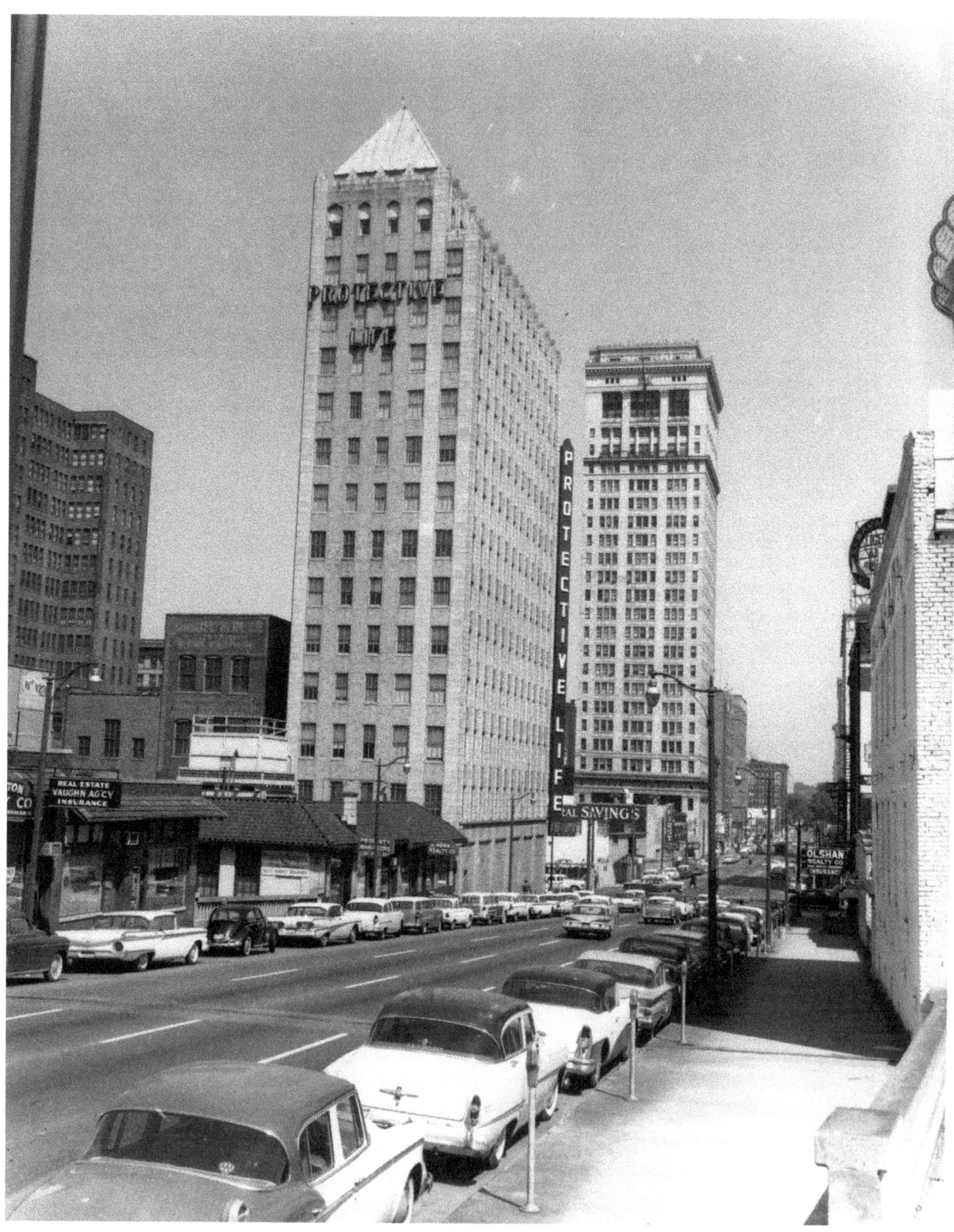

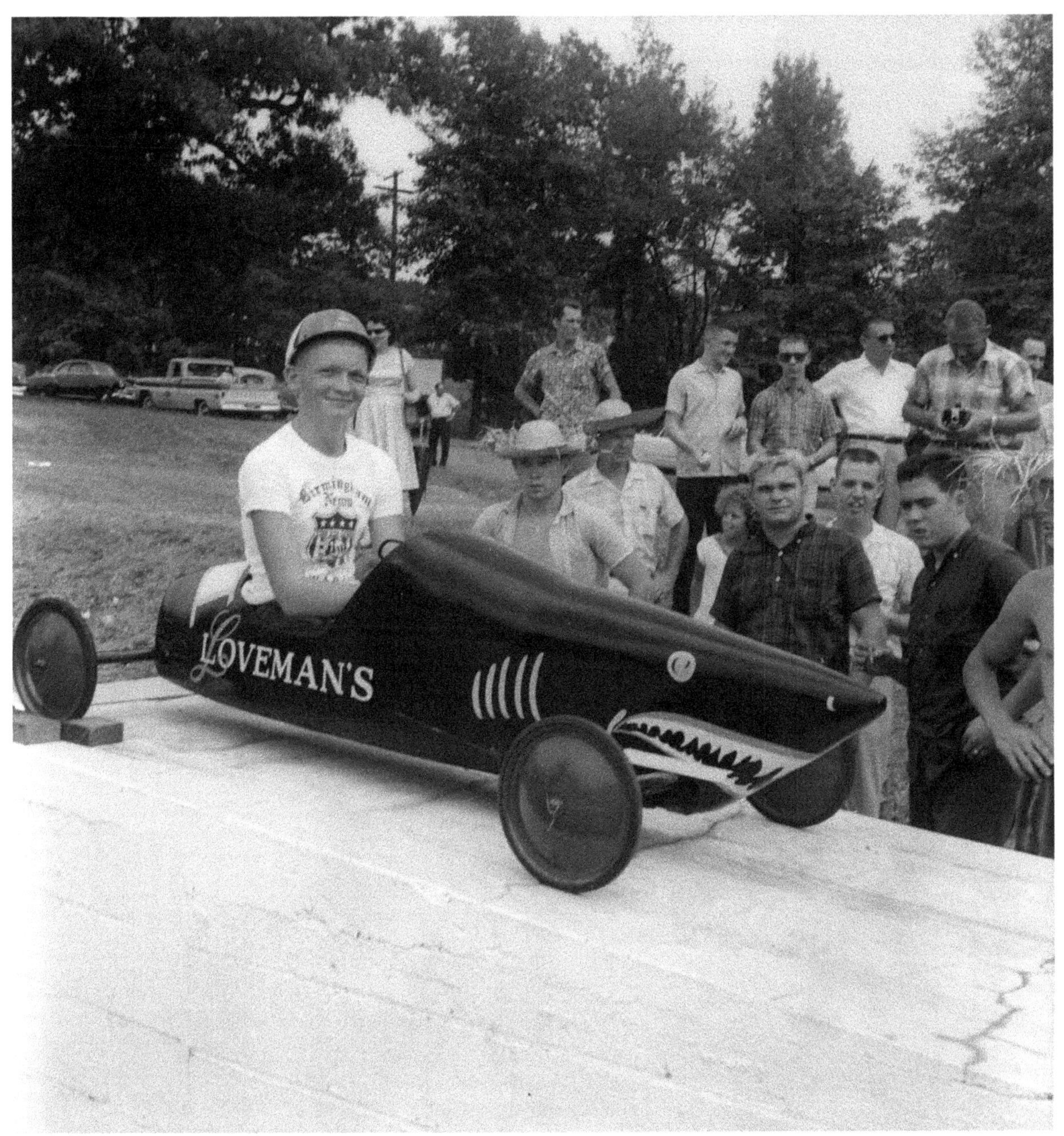

A proud driver shows off his shark-themed soap box car in Loveman's Soap Box Derby.

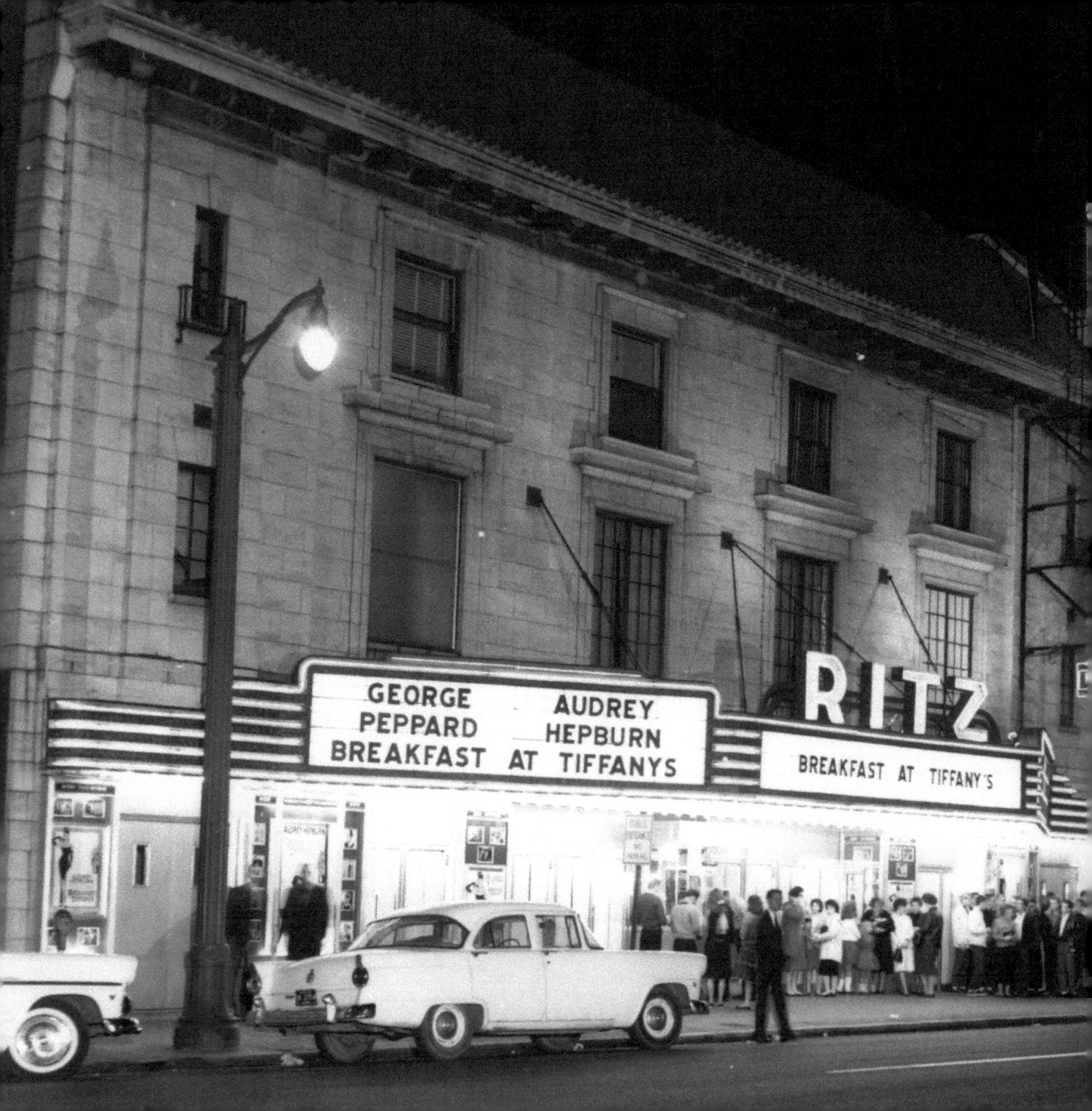

GEORGE AUDREY
PEPPARD HEPBURN
BREAKFAST AT TIFFANYS
RITZ
BREAKFAST AT TIFFANY'S

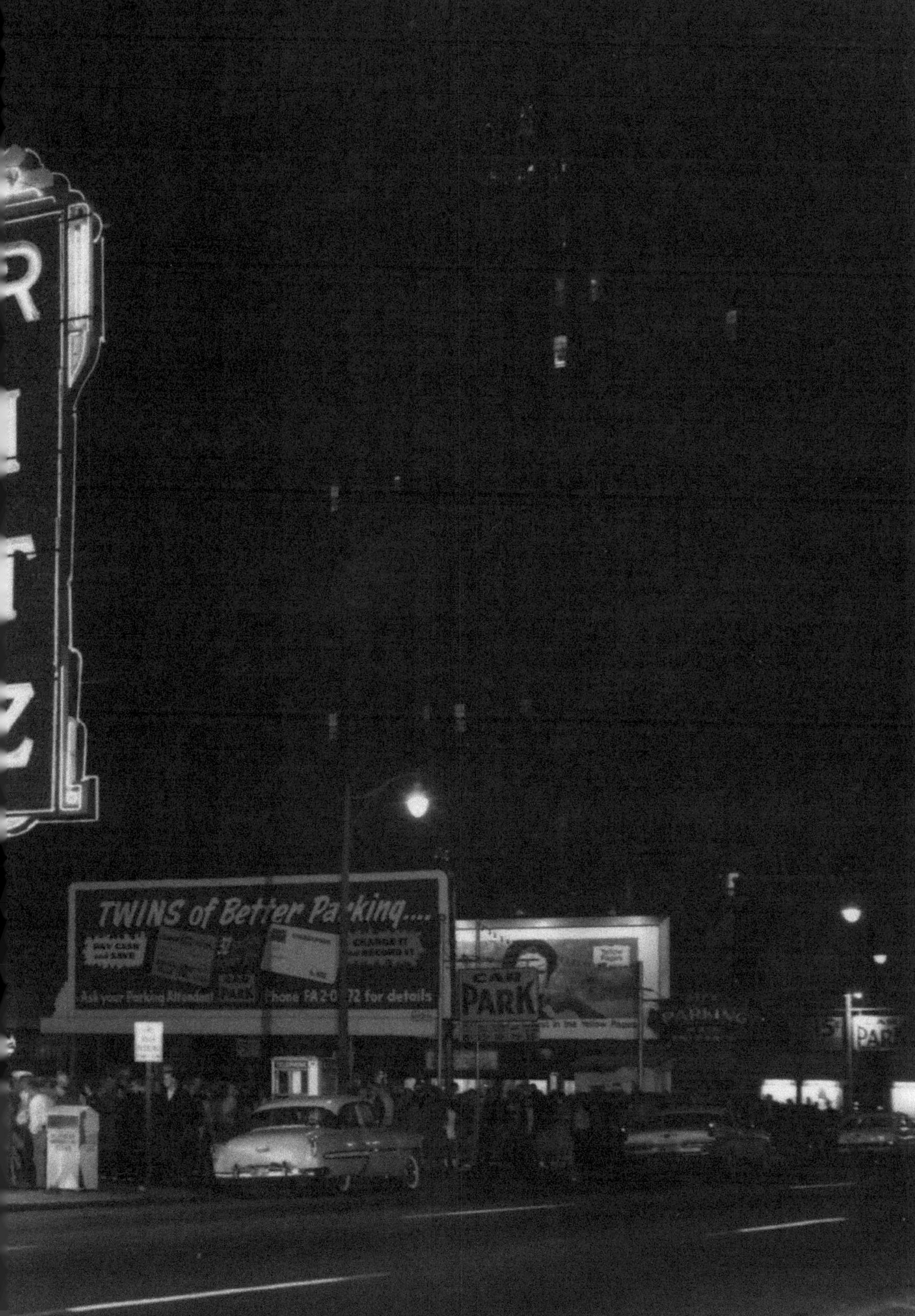

The Ritz Theater on 2nd Avenue North advertises *Breakfast at Tiffany's,* starring Audrey Hepburn, George Peppard, Buddy Ebsen, and the haunting melody "Moon River." In 1962, the Ritz became Alabama's first Cinerama theater, complete with three projectors to project film images on three large screens, giving the audience the effect of being in the movie.

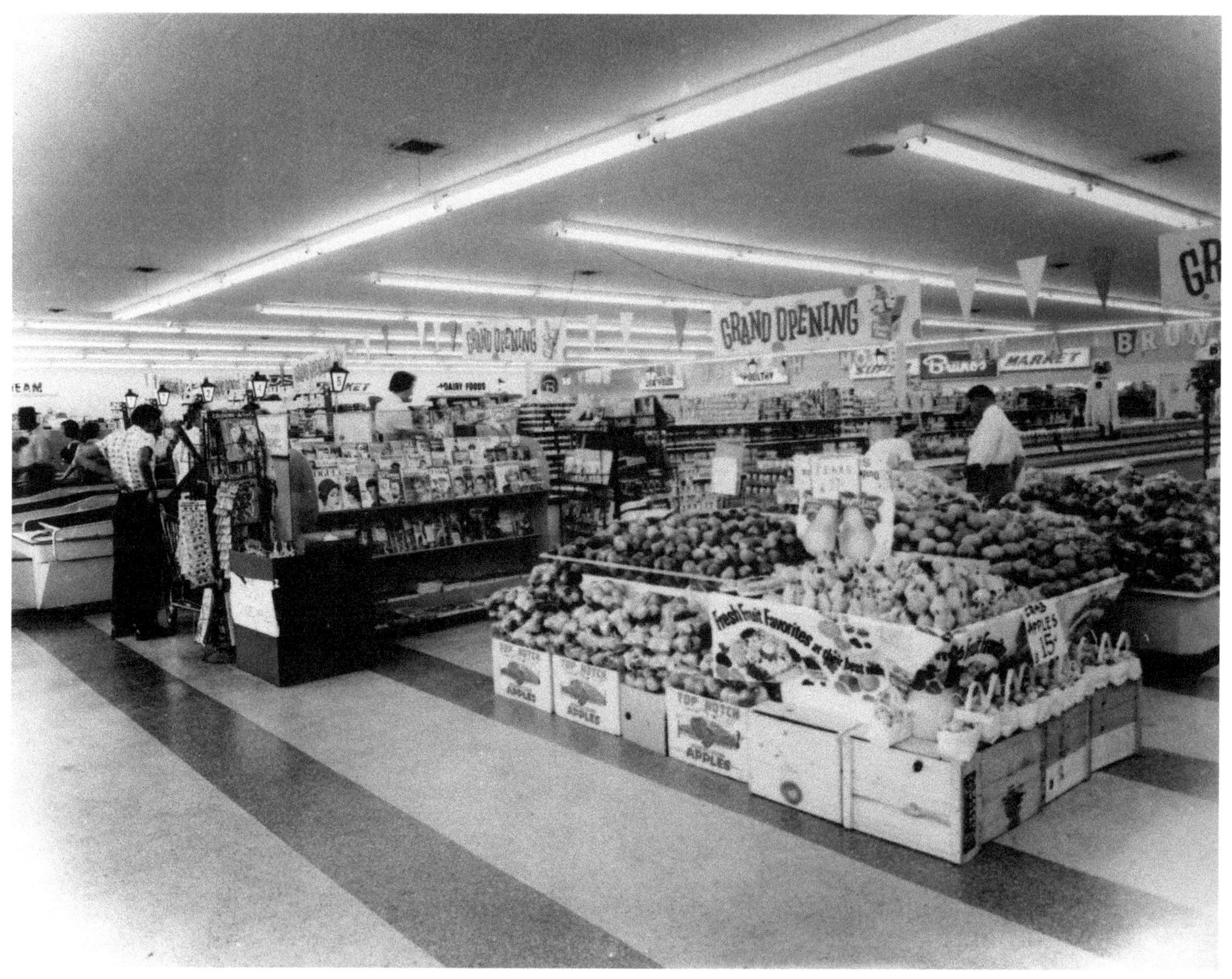

Liberty Supermarket in the Roebuck neighborhood prepares for its grand opening.

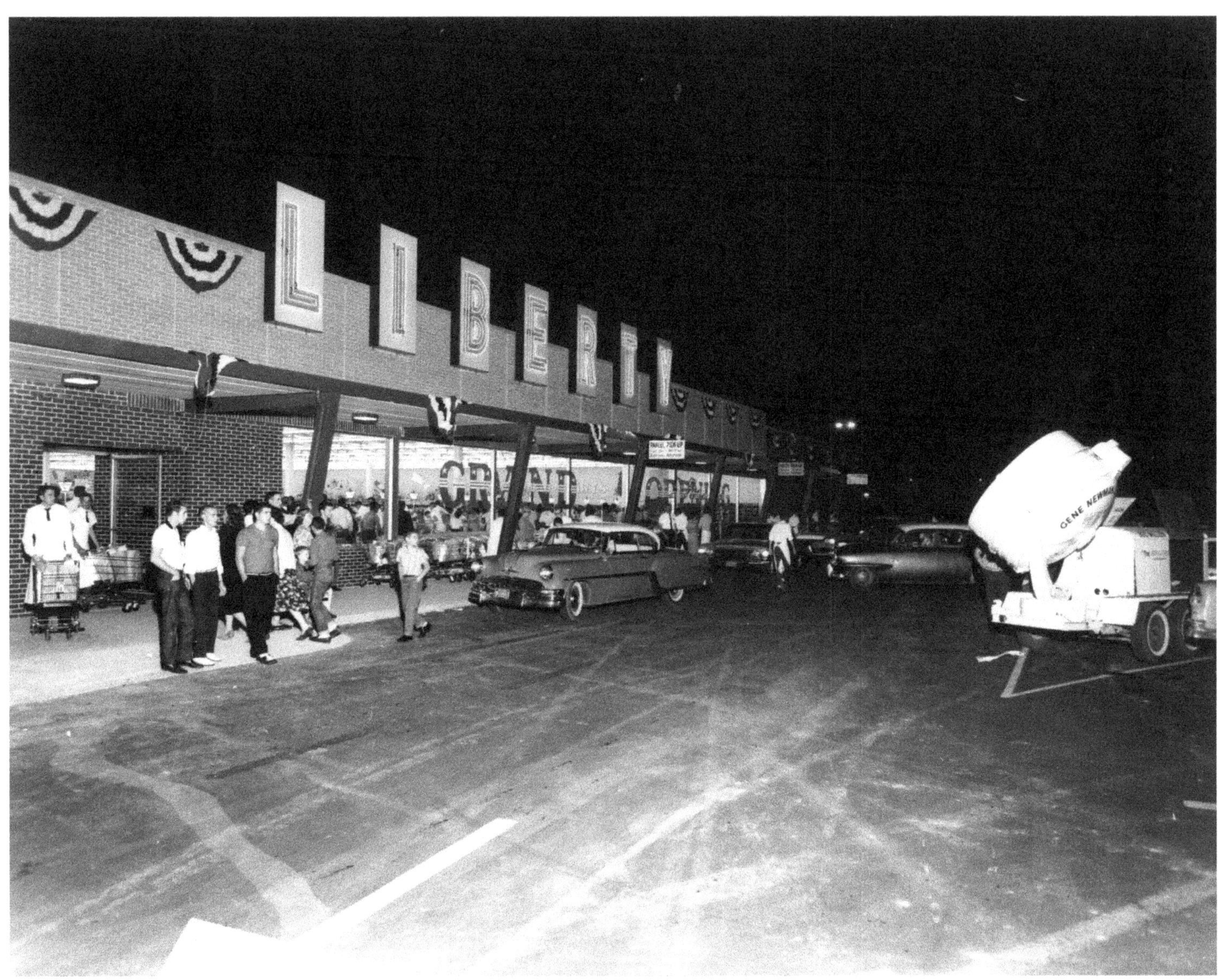

Shoppers visit Liberty Supermarket looking for grand opening bargains.

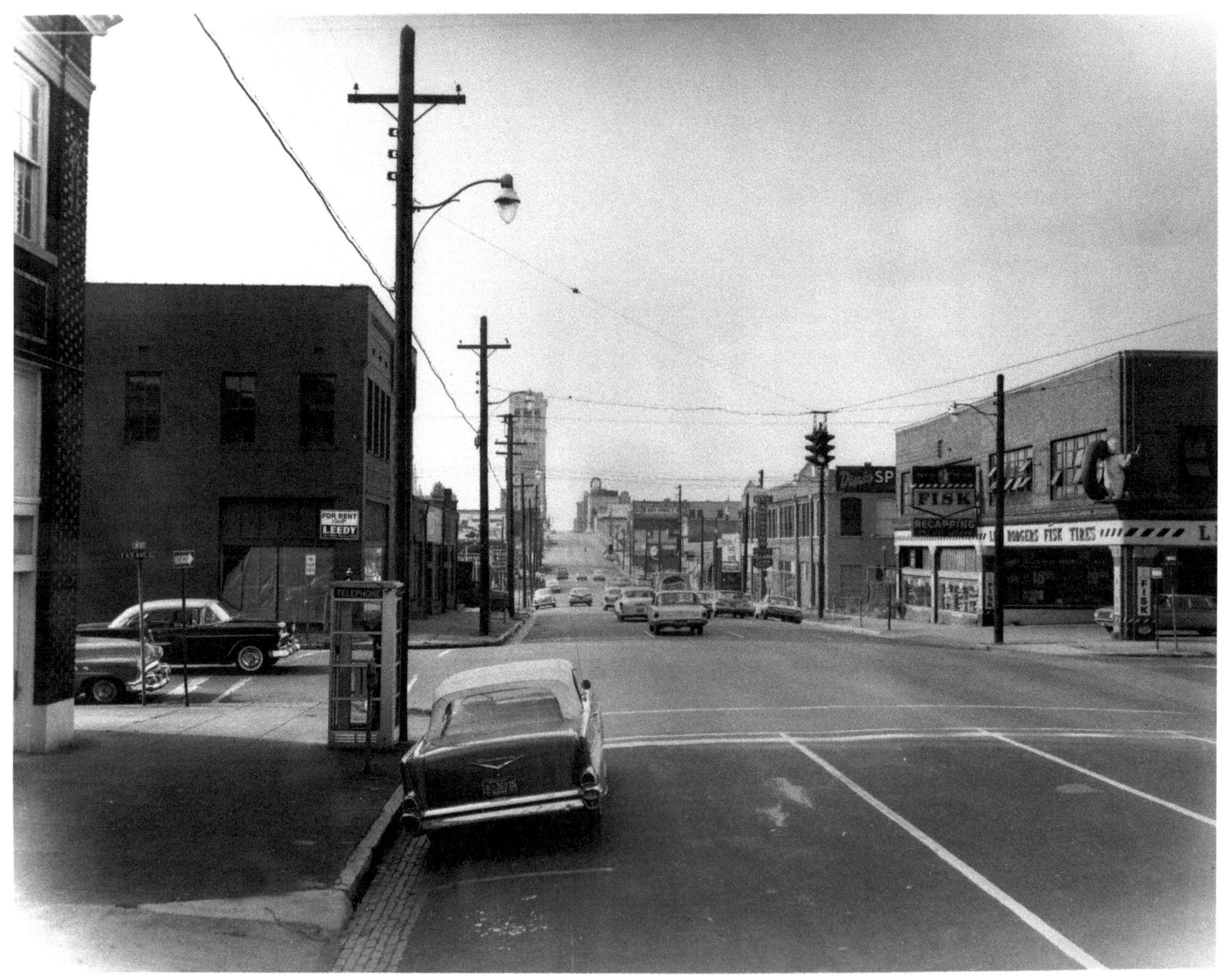

A north-facing shot of 21st Street South from 4th Avenue South. Rodgers Fisk Tires, and Dixie Sporting are visible.

The Watts Building during the 1960s.

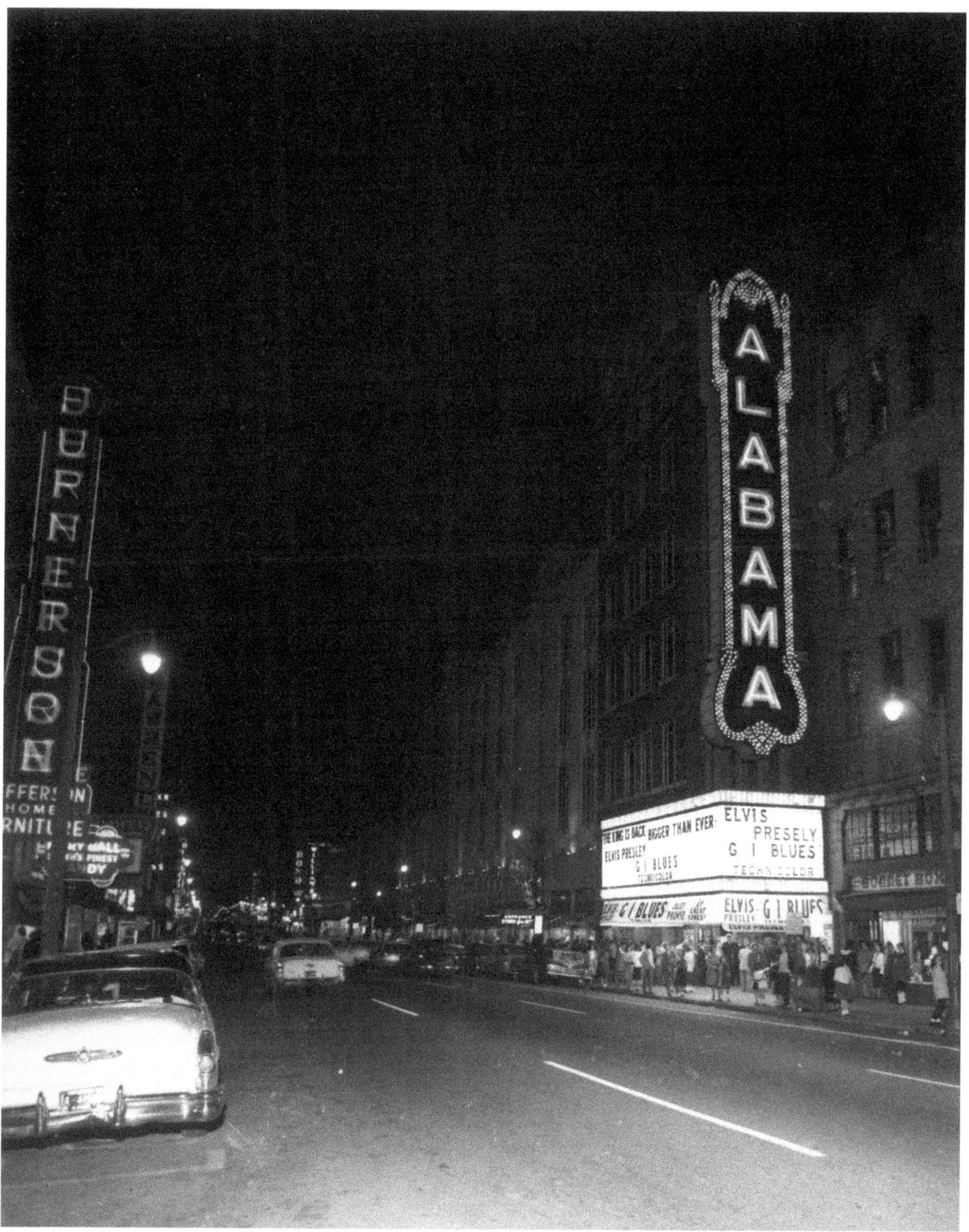

Elvis Presley's fifth film, *G.I. Blues,* is showing at the Alabama Theater.

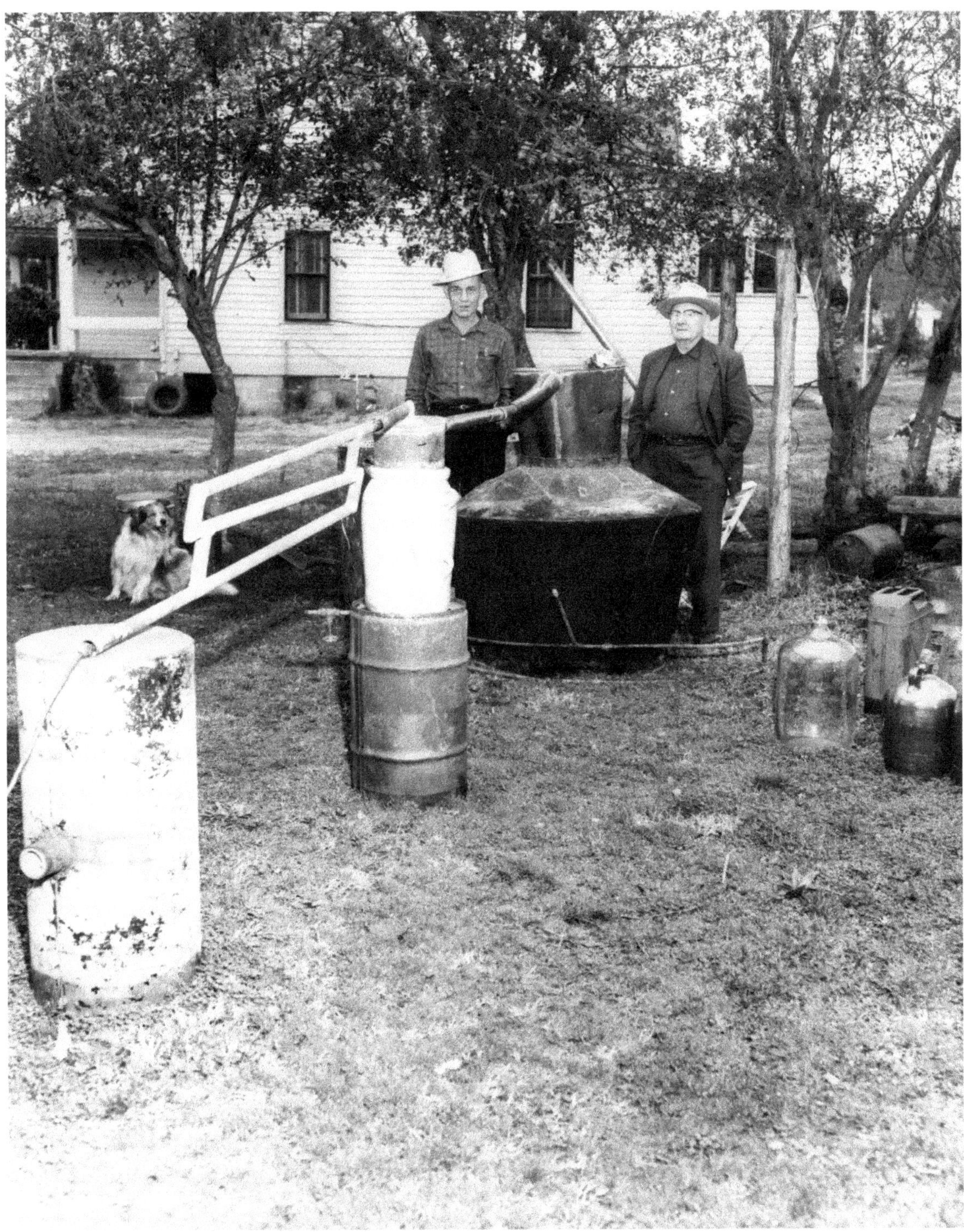

Two older gentlemen proudly display their enterprising business, which seems to focus on the production of moonshine.

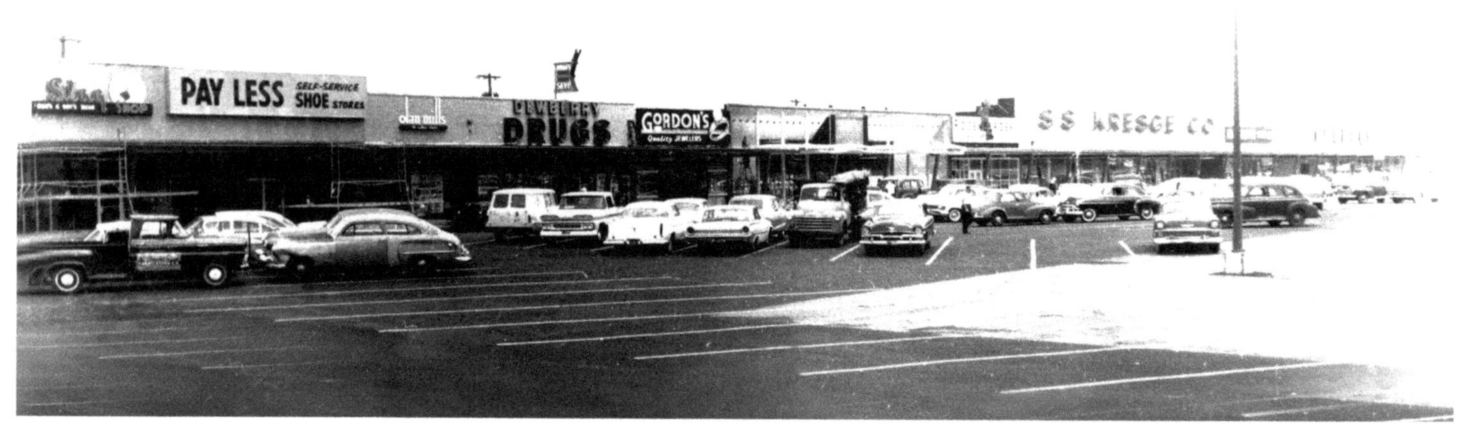

Pay Less shoe store, Dewberry drugstore, Gordon's quality jewelers, and S. S. Kresge Company were among the tenants of the Roebuck Shopping Center. The emergence of suburbia and suburban shopping centers was a significant change that would affect the economy of Birmingham.

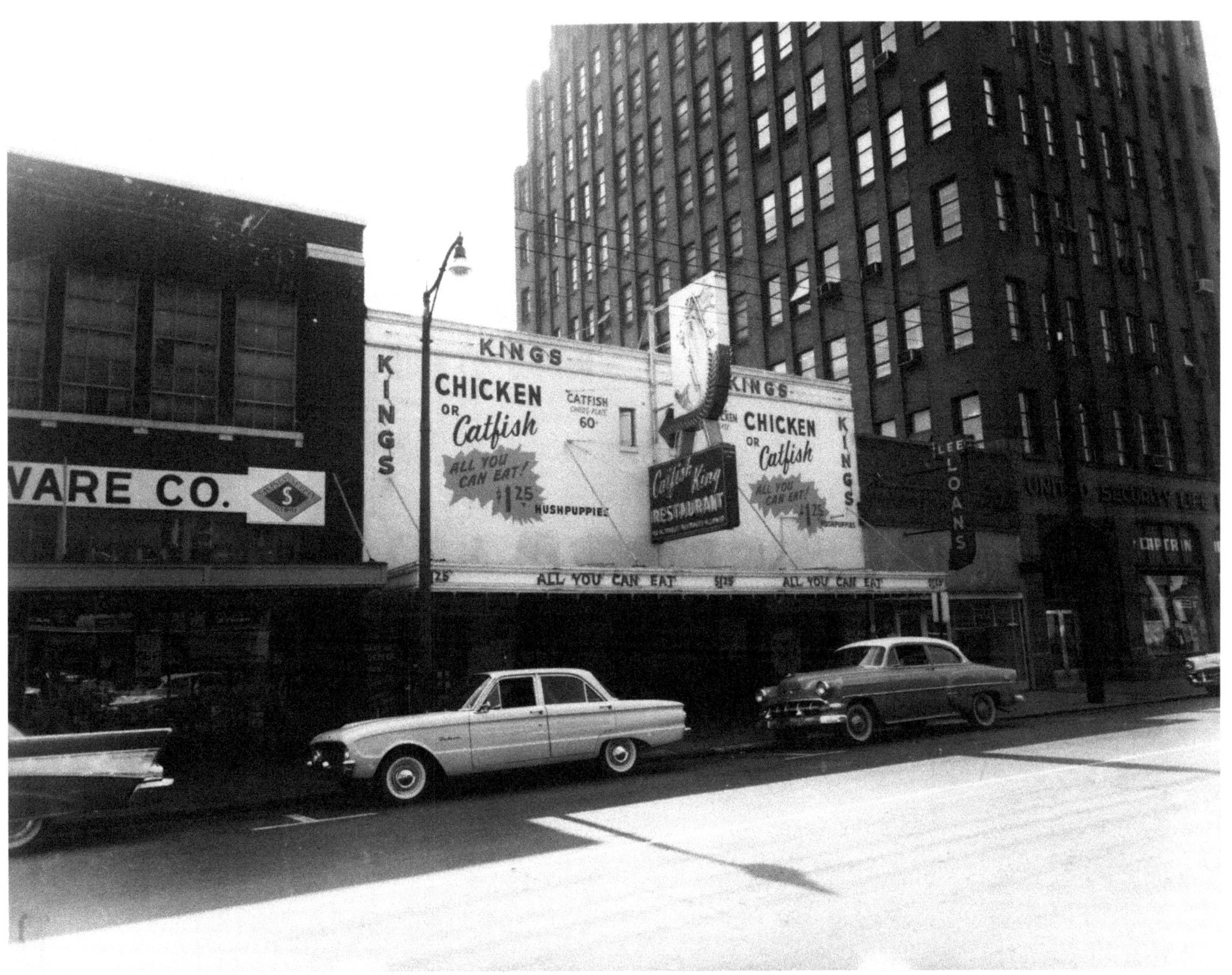

Advertising an all-you-can-eat menu for only $1.25, Kings Restaurant is open for business on Avenue E in Ensley next to the United Security Life Insurance Building, formerly the Ramsay-McCormack Building.

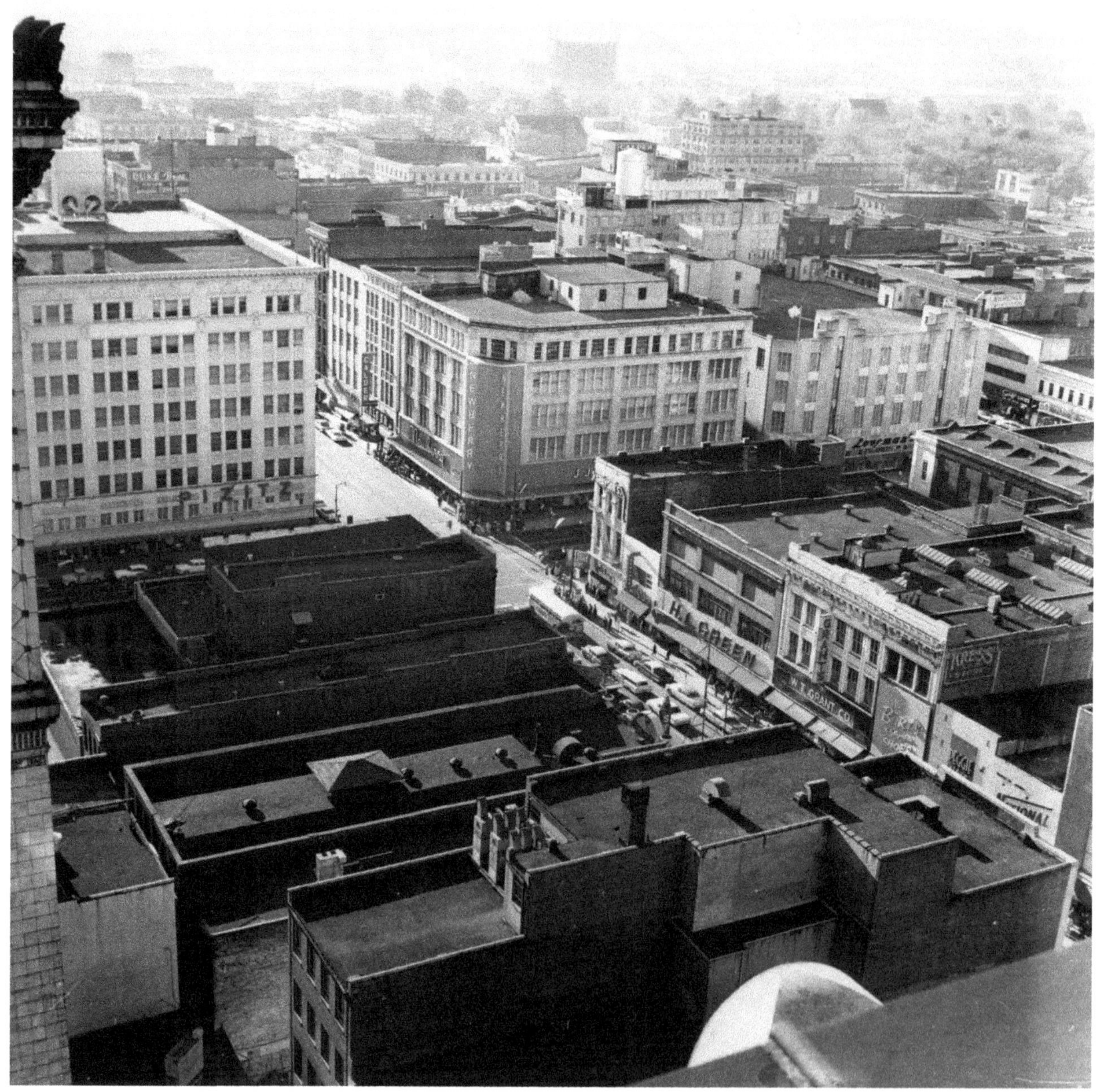

W. T. Grant Company, H. L. Green, and Newberry are all visible in this rooftop view of downtown.

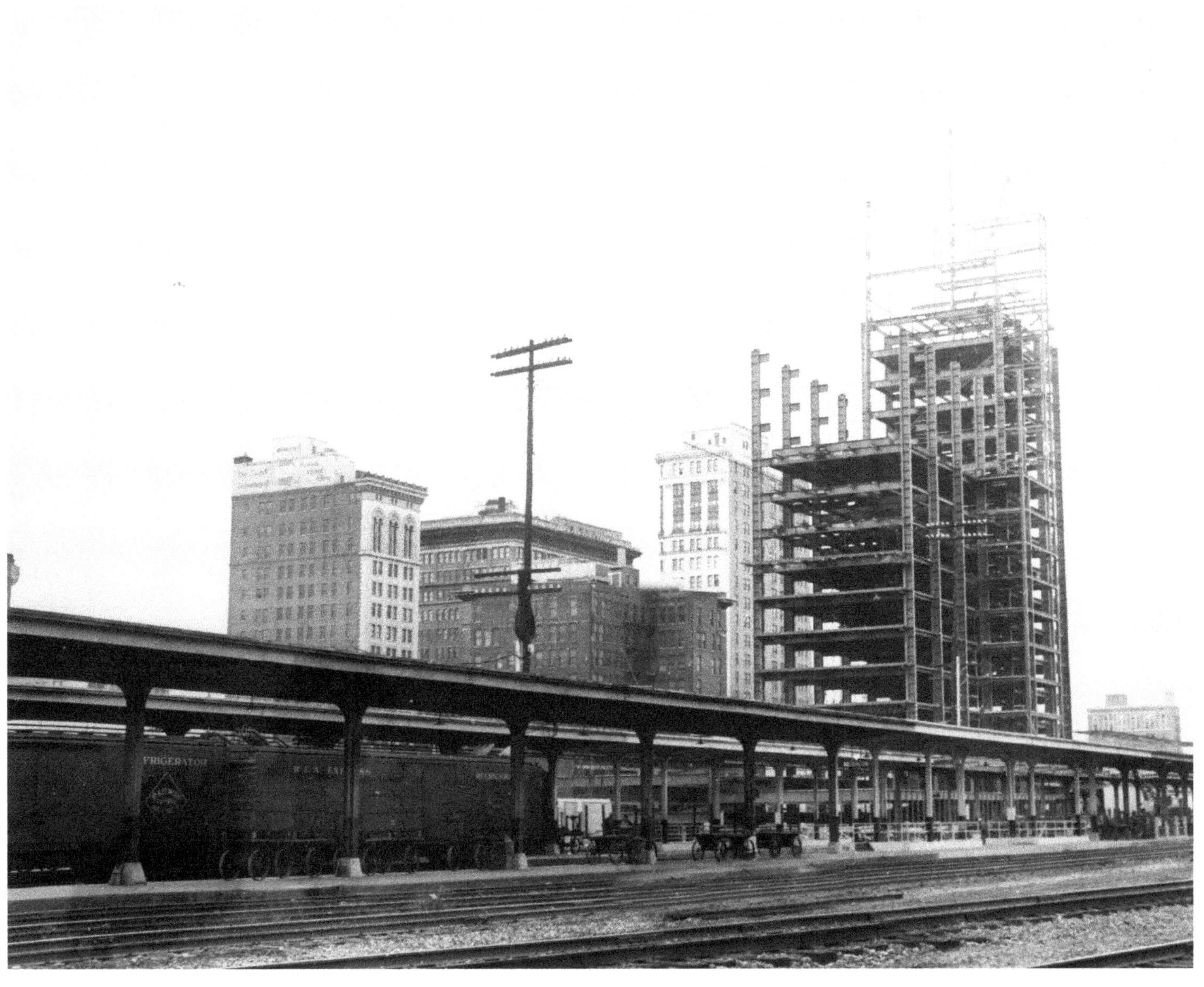

The Bank for Savings Building skyscraper slowly rises above Birmingham, in this view from the railroad tracks, to become one of the first major downtown construction projects undertaken after World War II.

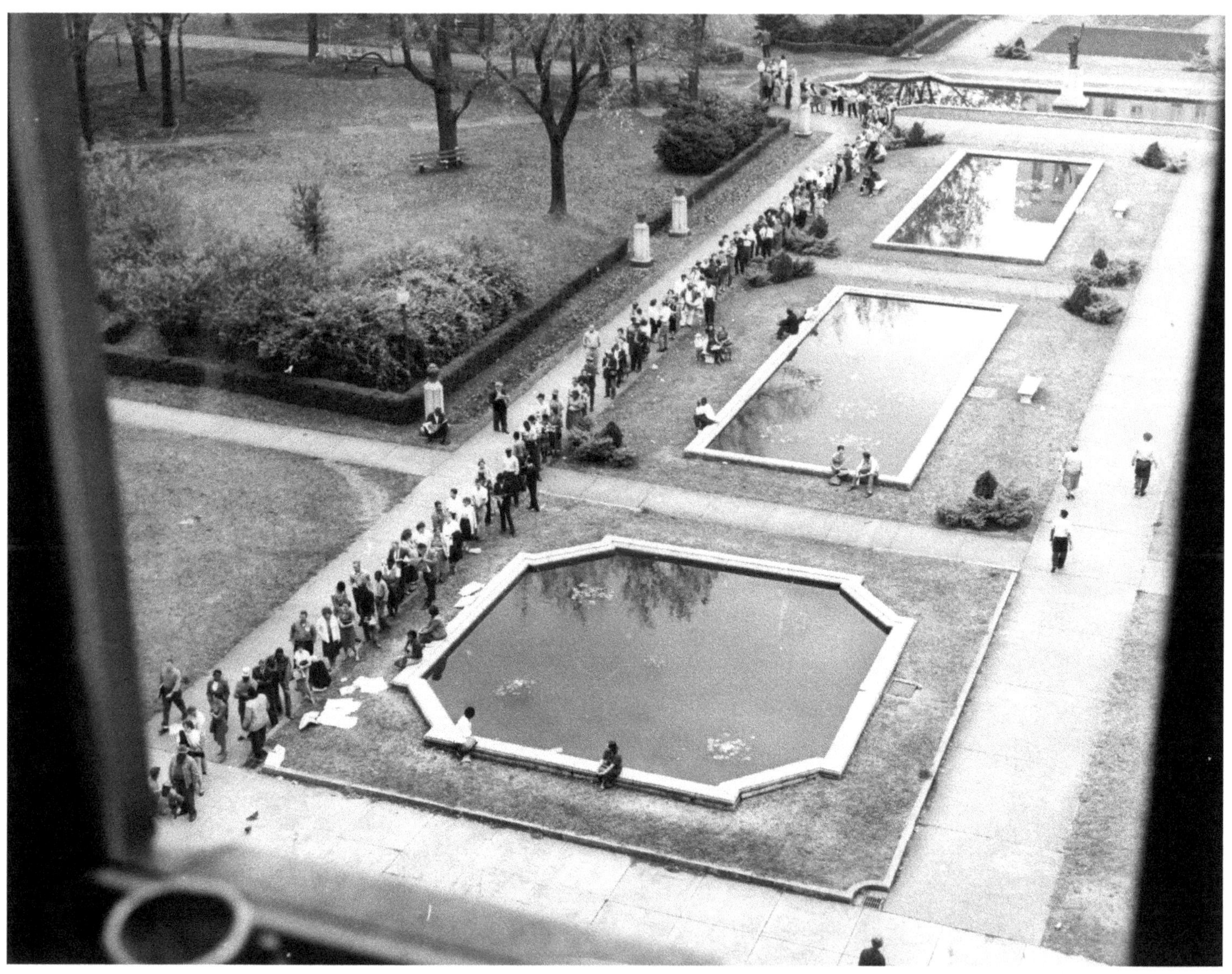

In the 1960s, a majority of citizens were required to purchase car tags on the same day. This requirement created massive lines and extremely long wait times. In this image, automobile owners stand in a particularly lengthy tag line at the Jefferson County Courthouse in Woodrow Wilson Park.

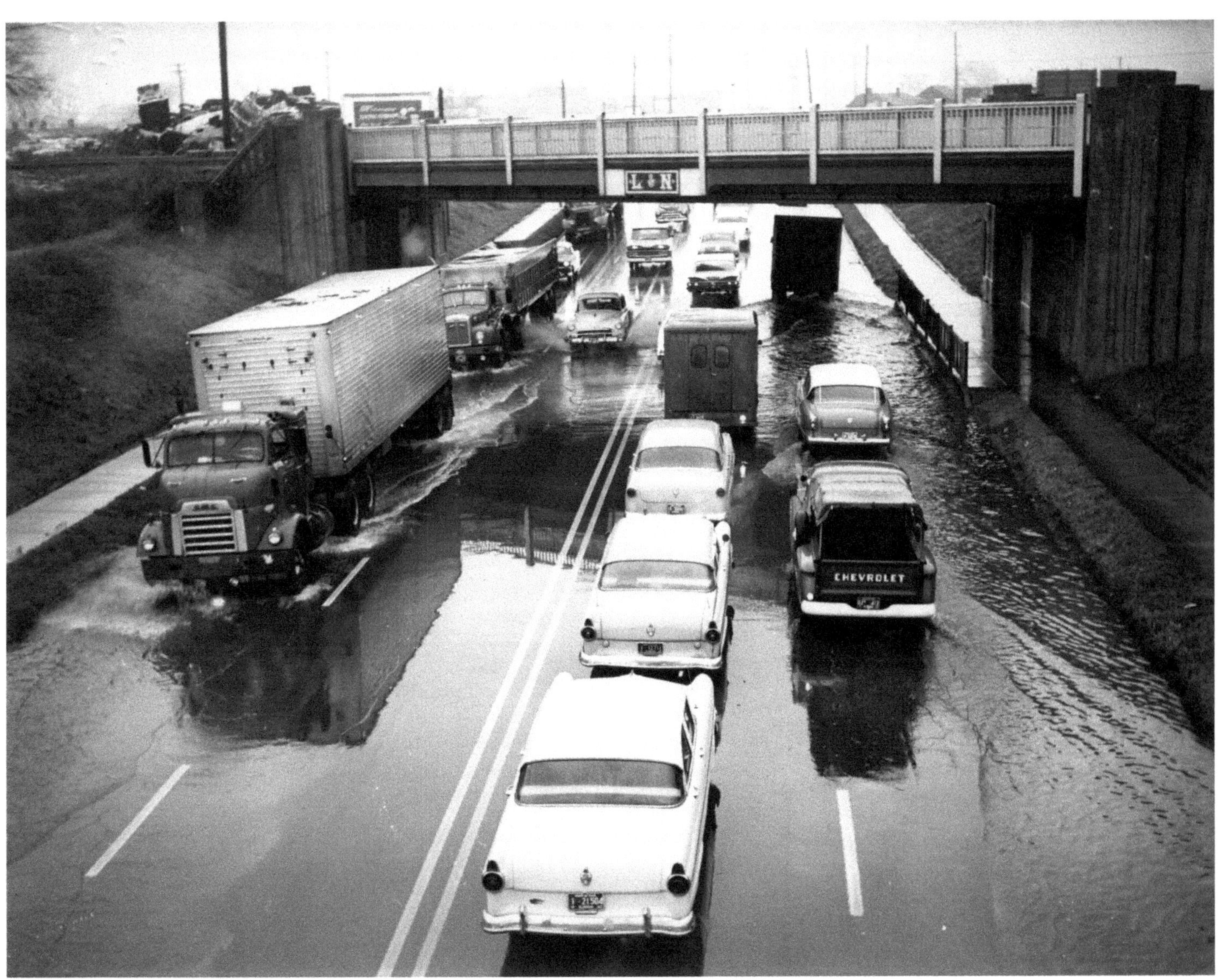

Motorists drive through a flooded street after a Birmingham downpour.

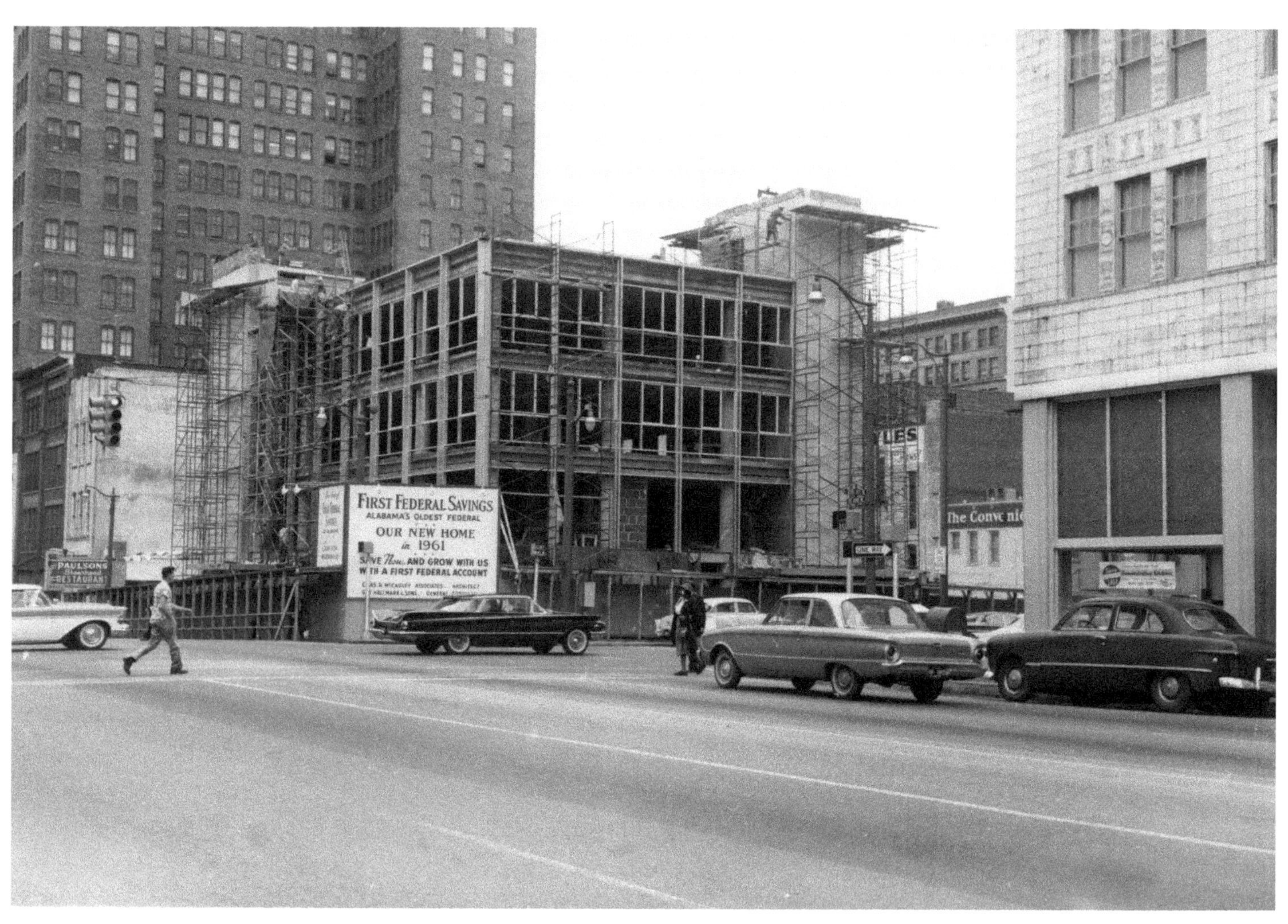

In 1961, workers construct the new home of First Federal Savings Bank.

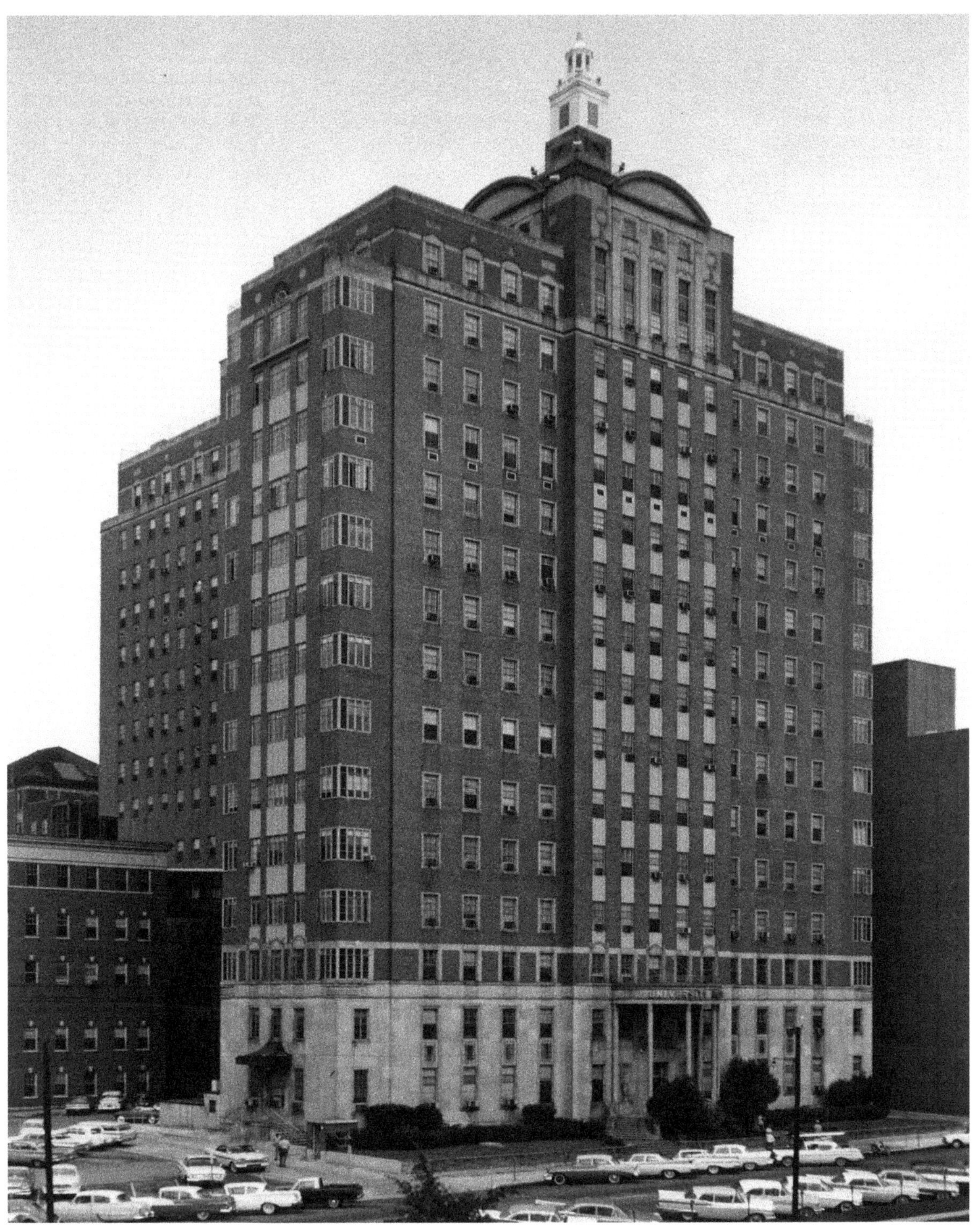

In May 1955, the Jefferson-Hillman Hospital was renamed the University of Alabama Hospital and Hillman Clinic, or as it was commonly called, University Hospital. Within University Hospital were a nursing program and other training opportunities for medical students. The opening of the hospital presaged the birth of the University of Alabama at Birmingham in the late 1960s.

This skyline view of Birmingham from Red Mountain shows the Medical Center complex at center and Ramsay High School in the foreground.

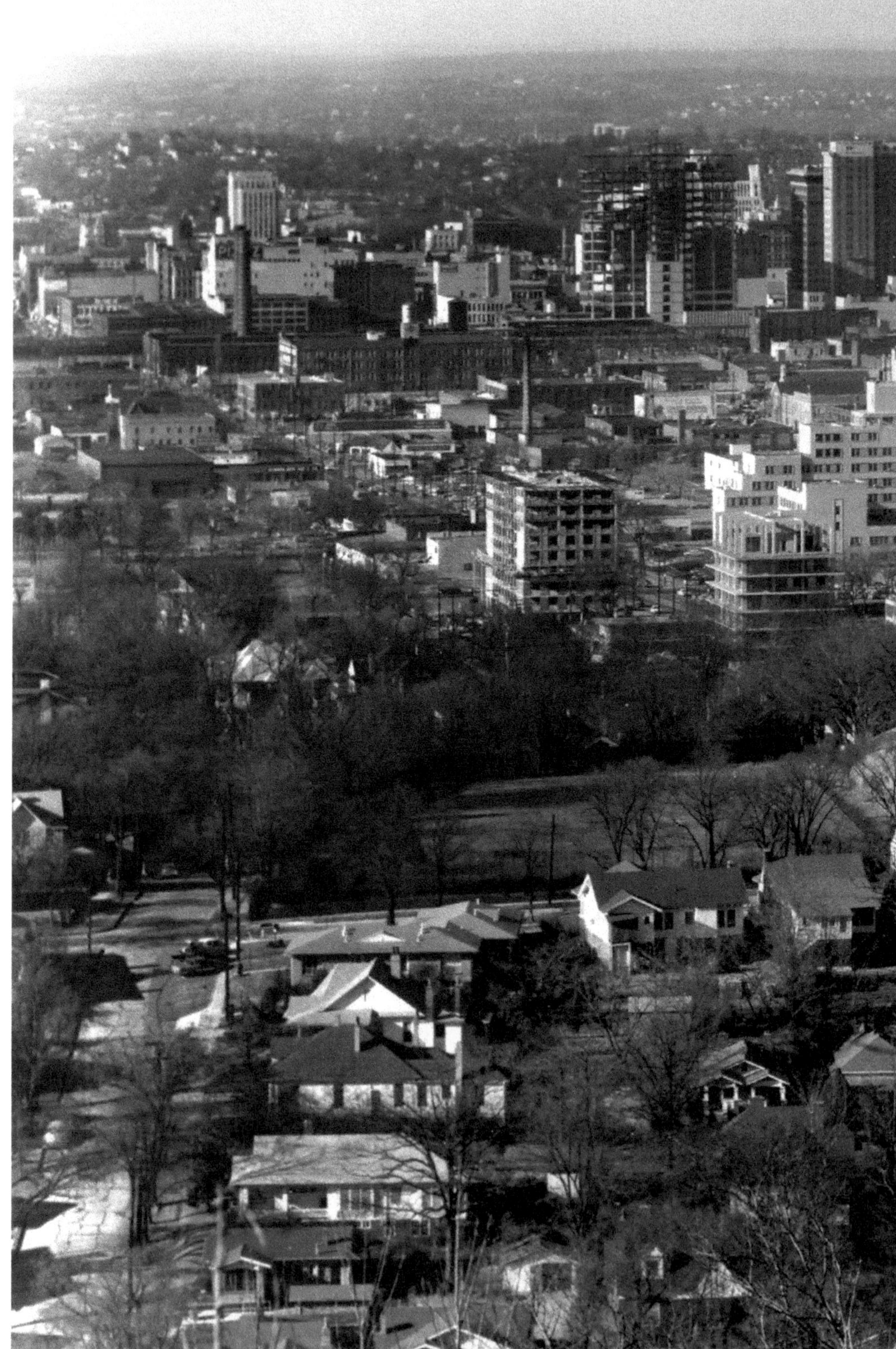

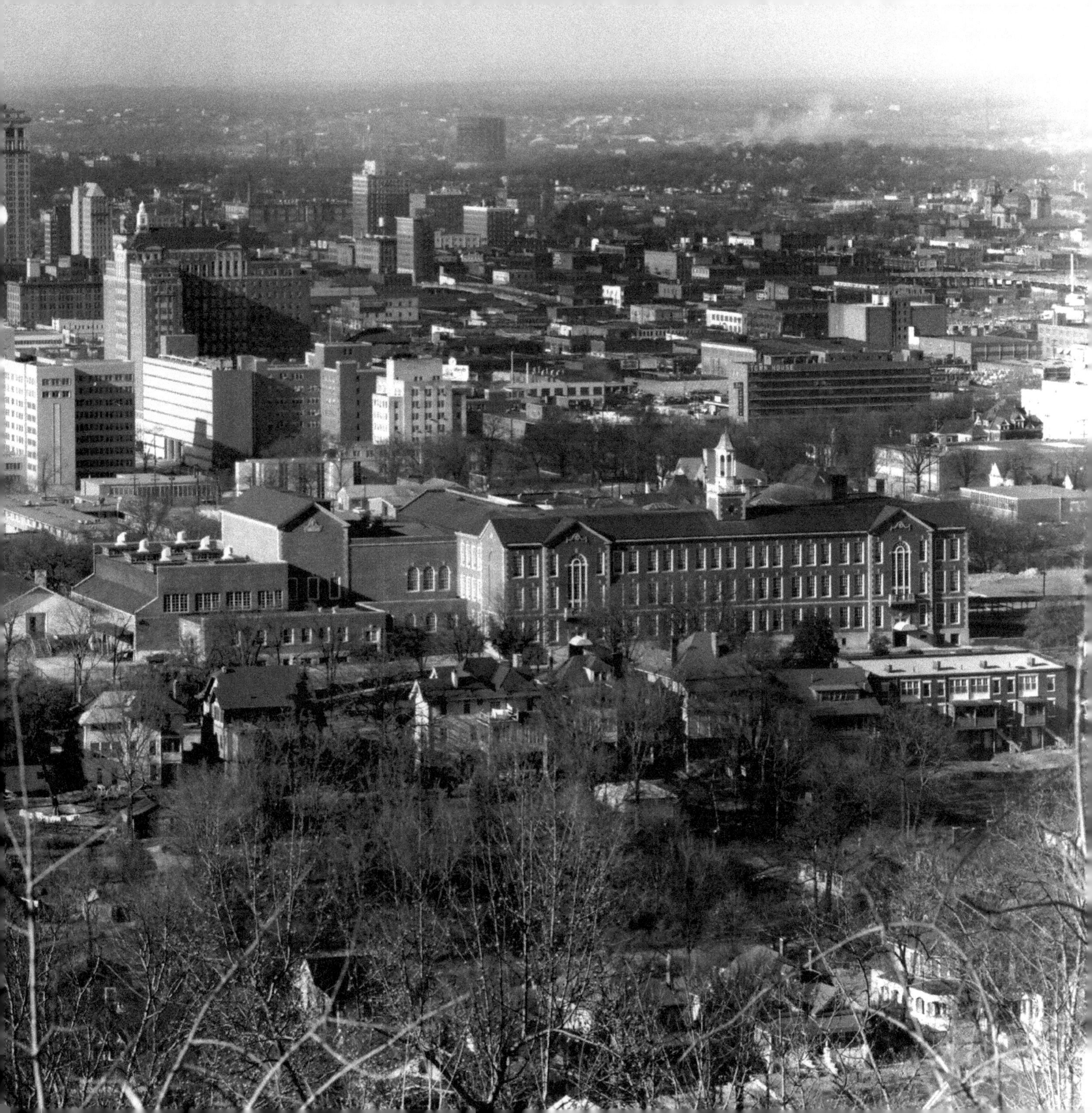

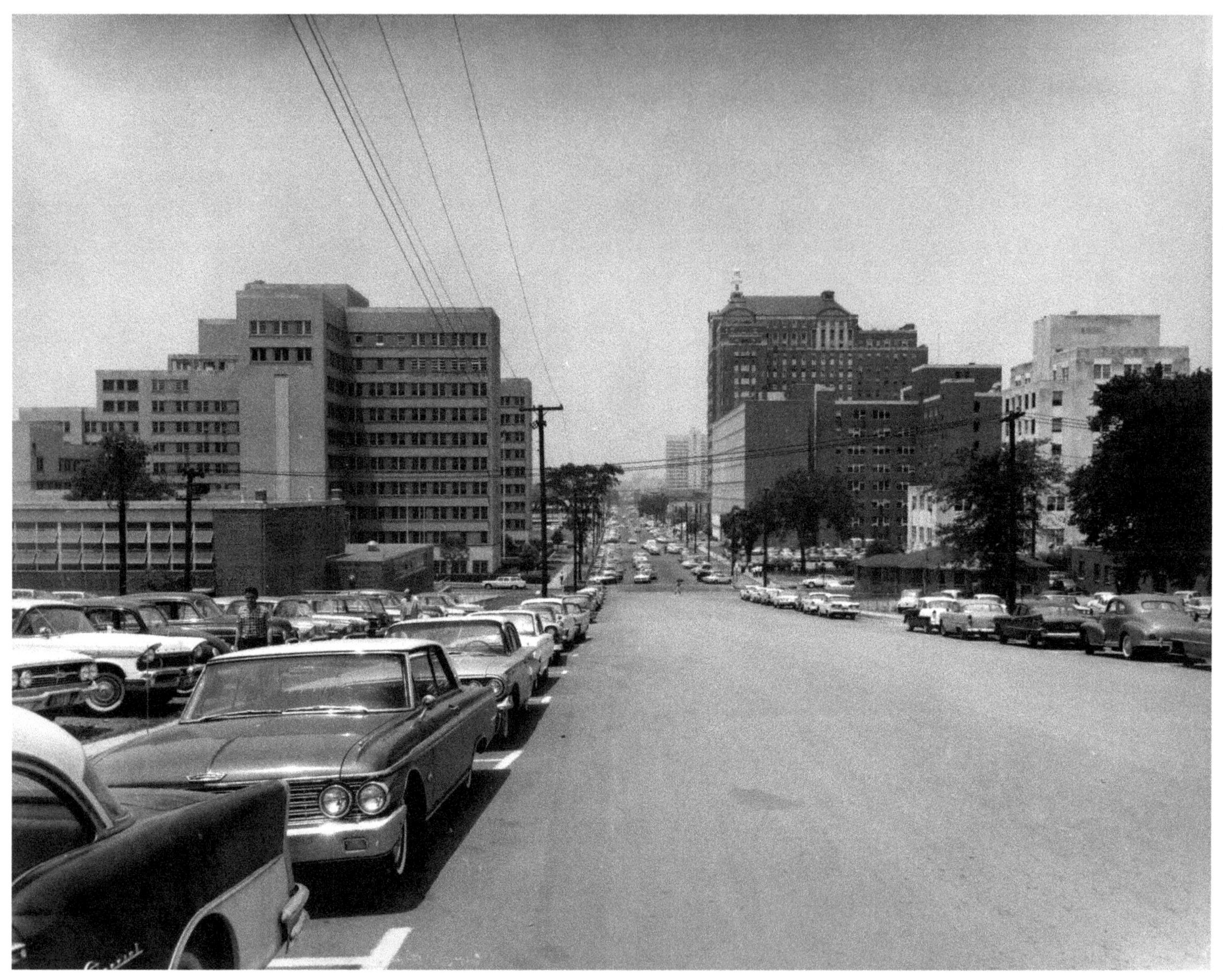

Veteran's Administration Hospital and University Hospital are shown here bordering 19th Street South.

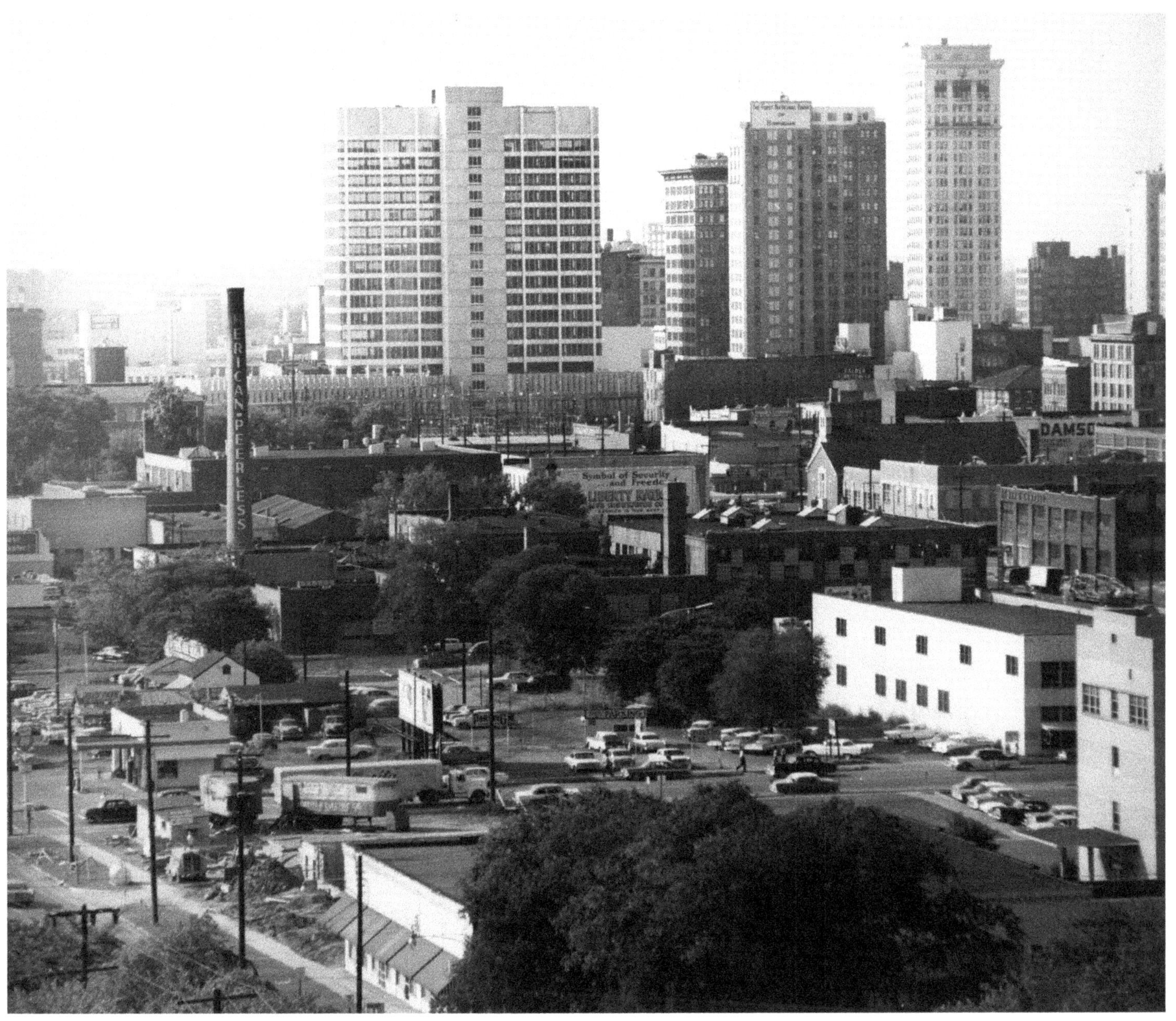

Downtown Birmingham as seen from the Medical Center. The First National Bank of Birmingham, Liberty National Life Insurance Company, and American Peerless are visible.

The newly completed Bank for Savings Building stands on Morris Avenue where Union Depot once stood, one of Birmingham's train stations. The Bank for Savings Building represented the beginning of a new period of growth and development in the city.

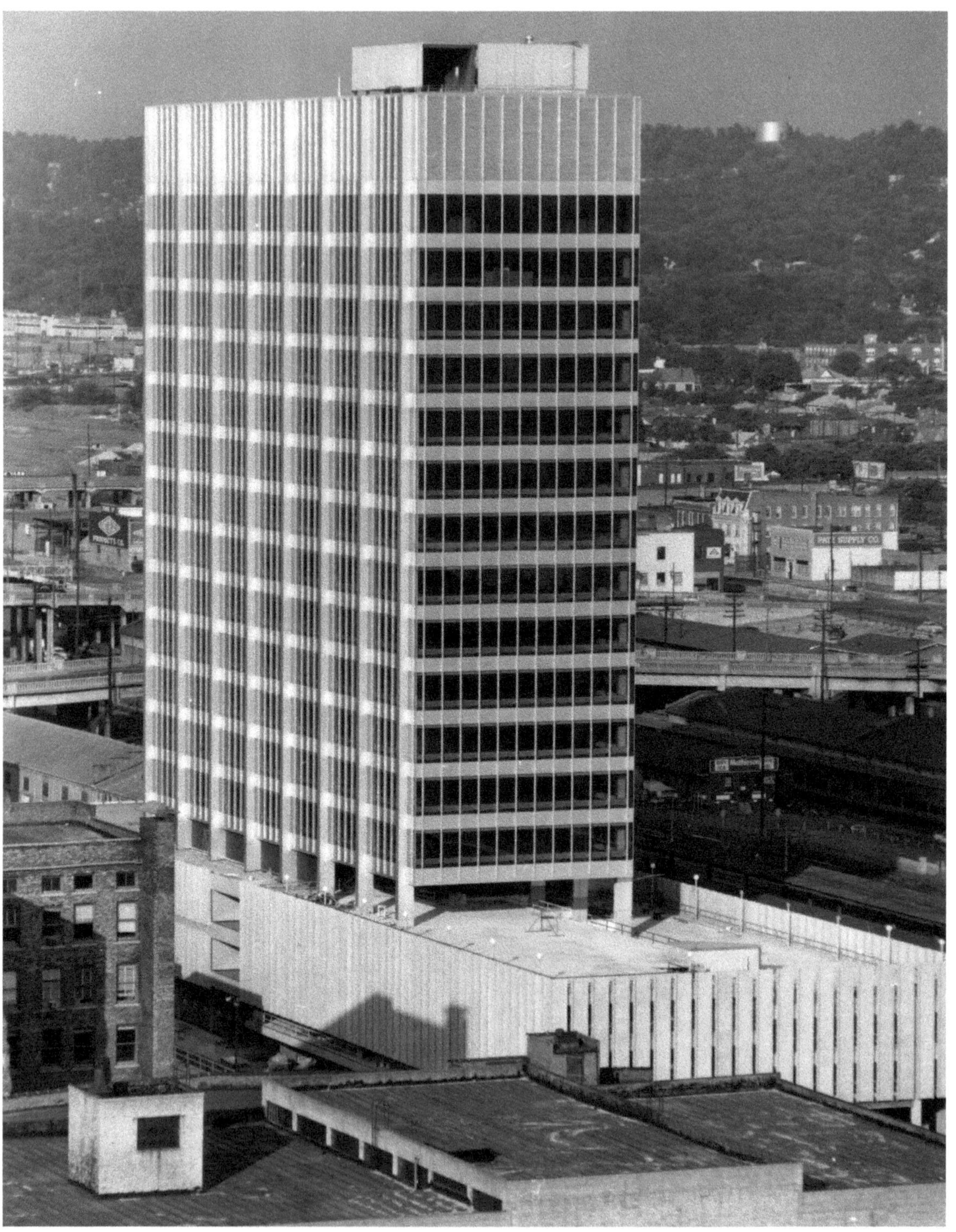

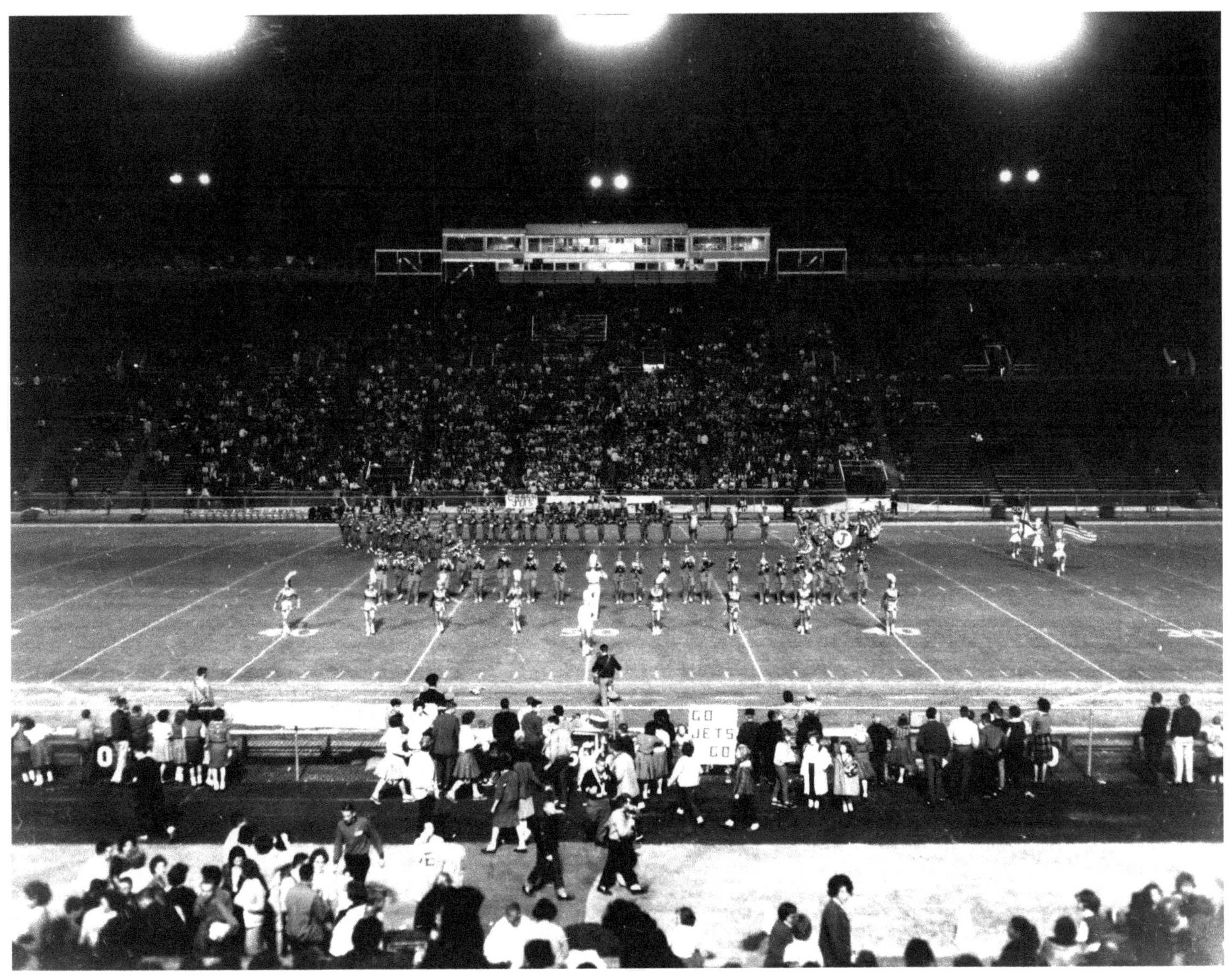

The Banks High School Jets battle the Woodlawn High School Colonels in this football game at Legion Field. The high school band is on the field for a performance at halftime.

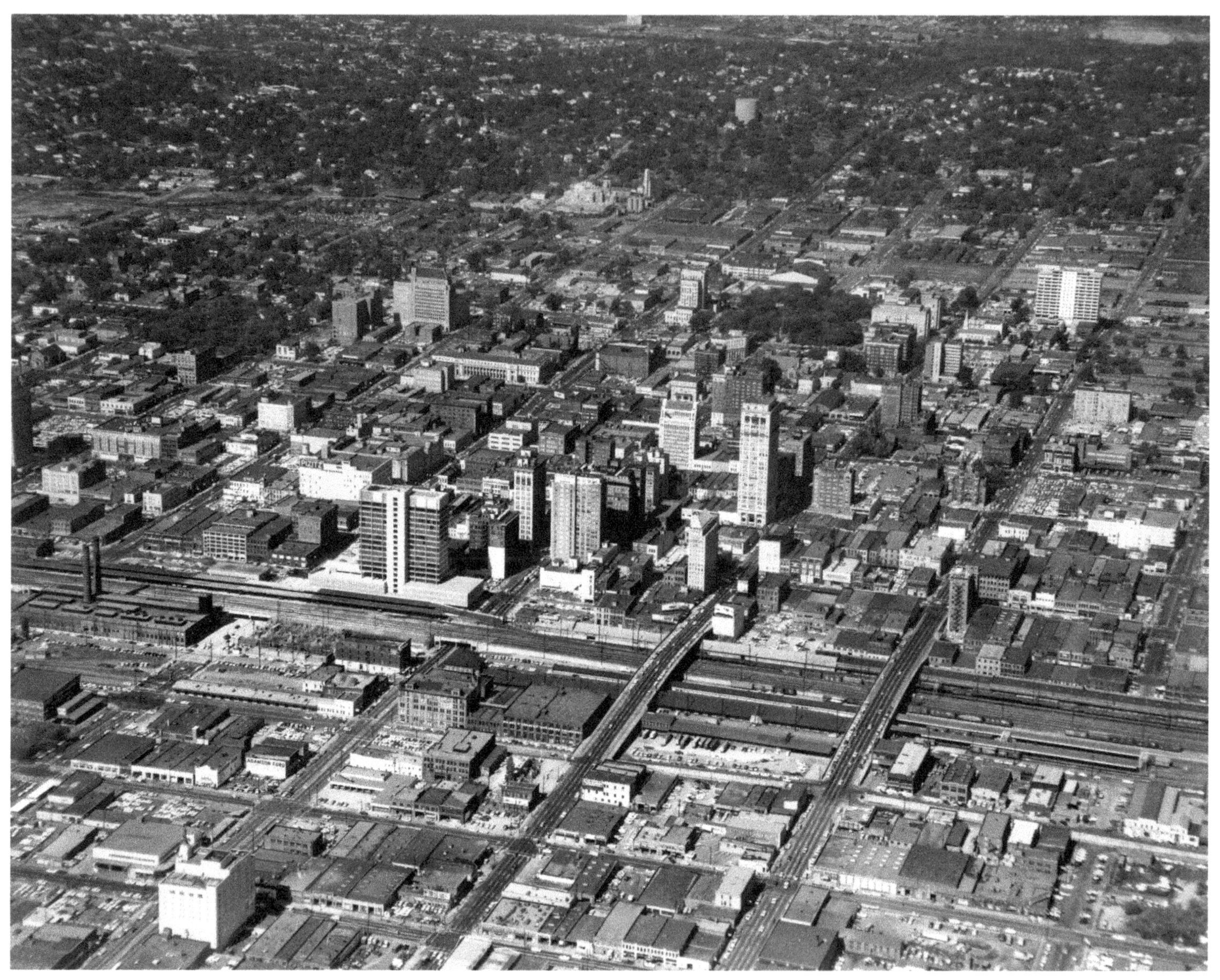

An aerial view of downtown as viewed from the south.

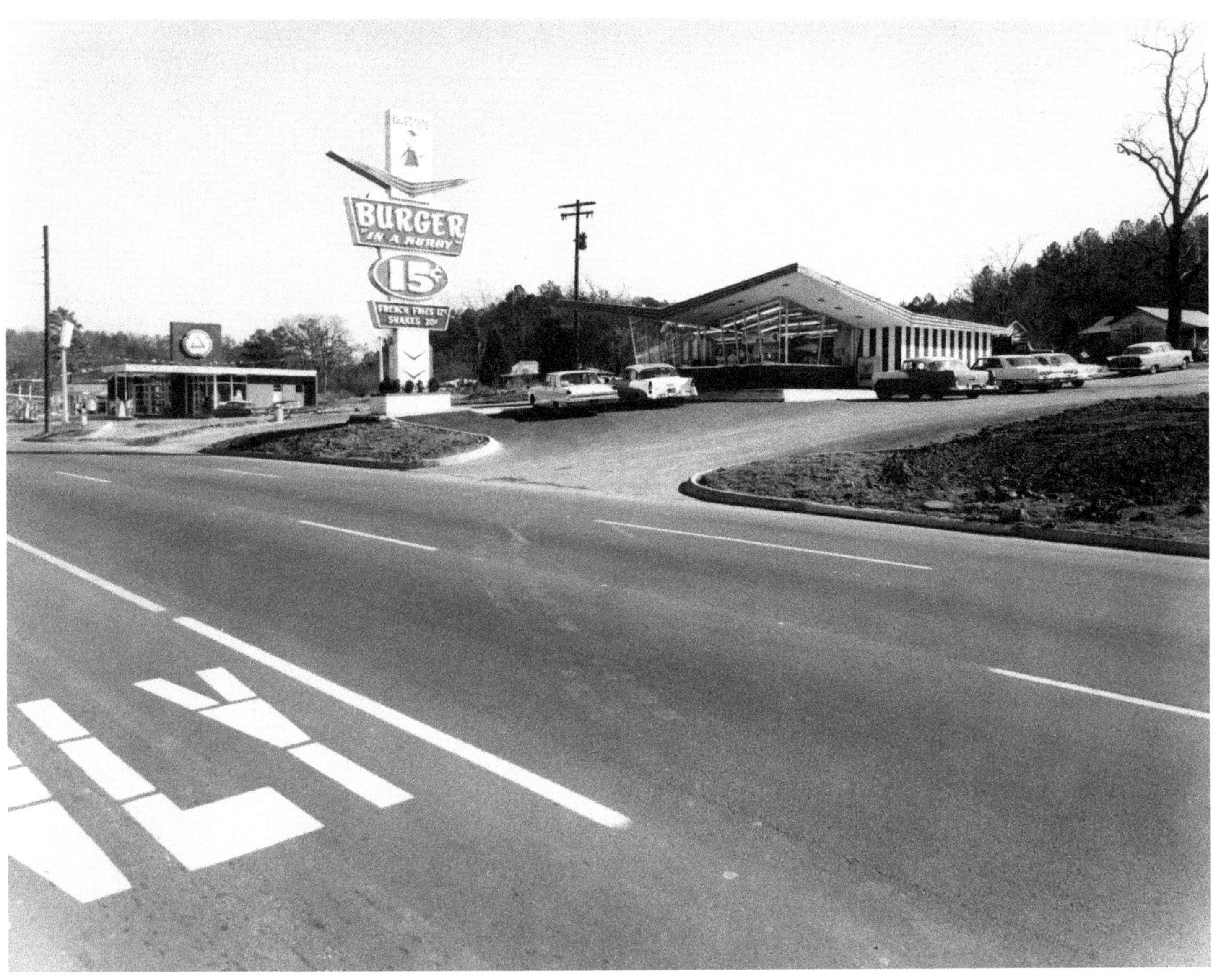

Mr. Good's Burger "In A Hurry" restaurant on 1st Ave North in Roebuck offered 15-cent hamburgers to hungry customers during the 1960s. French fries were 12 cents and shakes were 20 cents. In the golden age of fast food, the food was fast—and affordable.

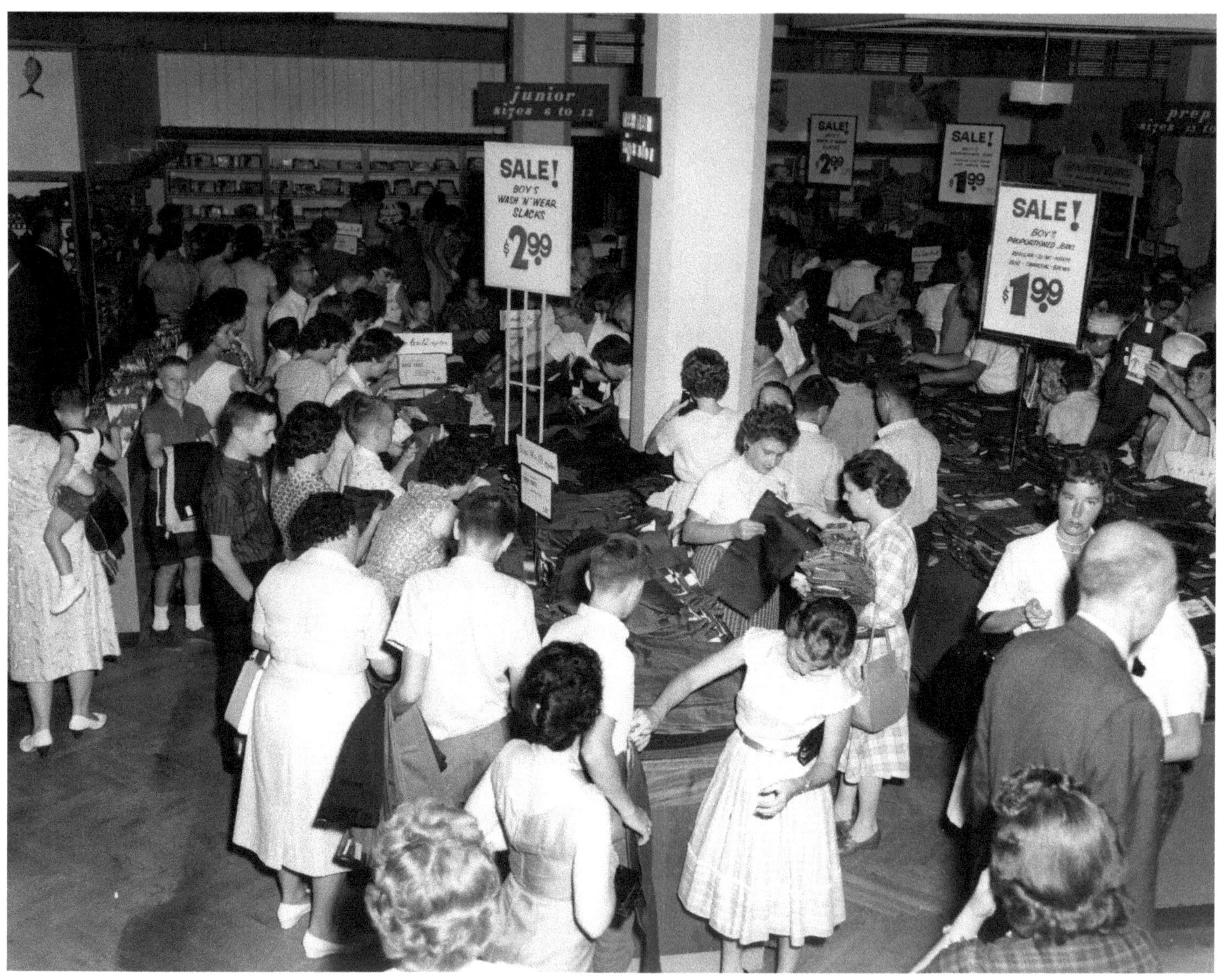

Customers take advantage of Loveman's sale on the first floor of the store, the day after Christmas, December 26, 1962.

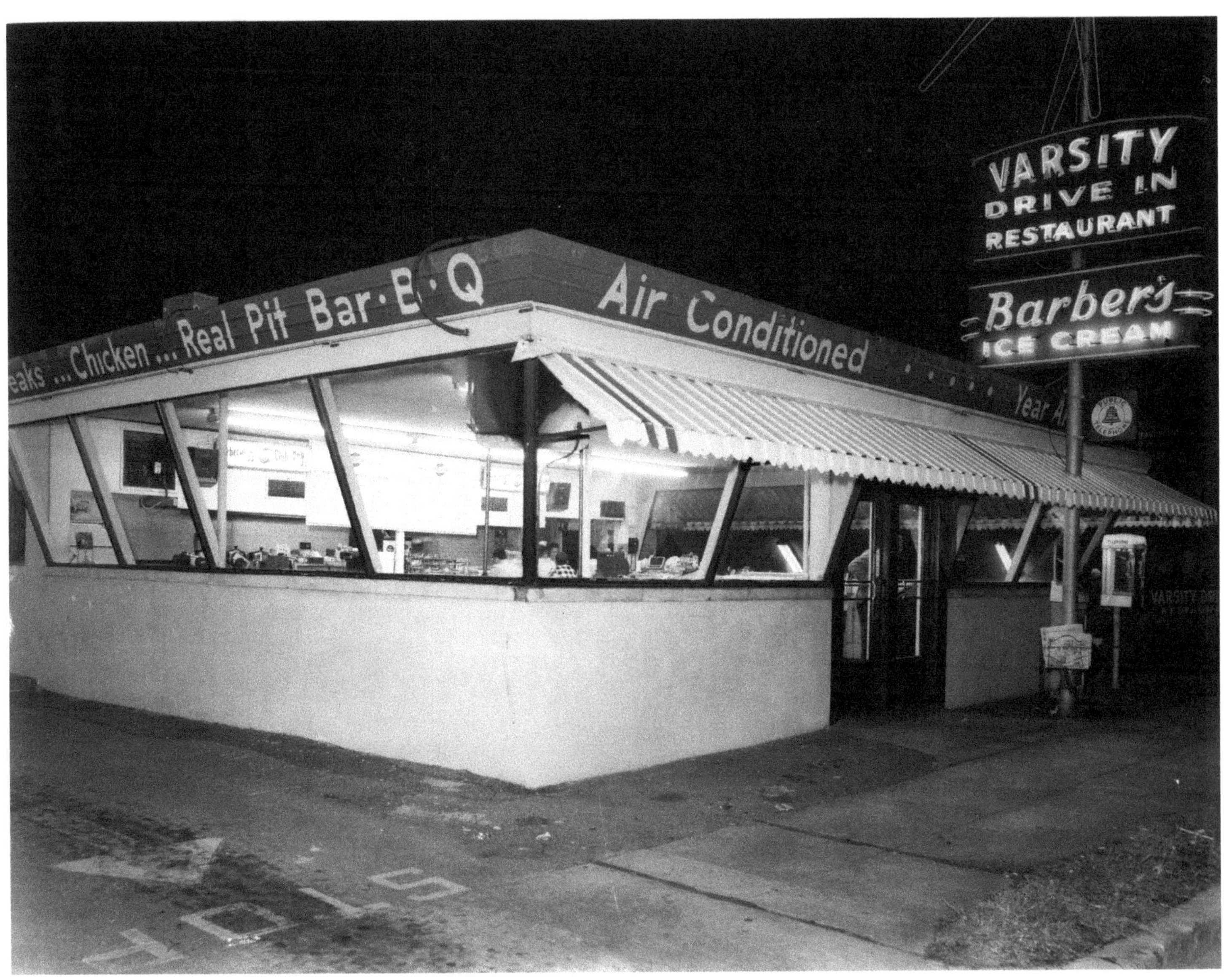

The Varsity Drive In Restaurant on 7th Avenue South was situated just down the road from the Medical Center.

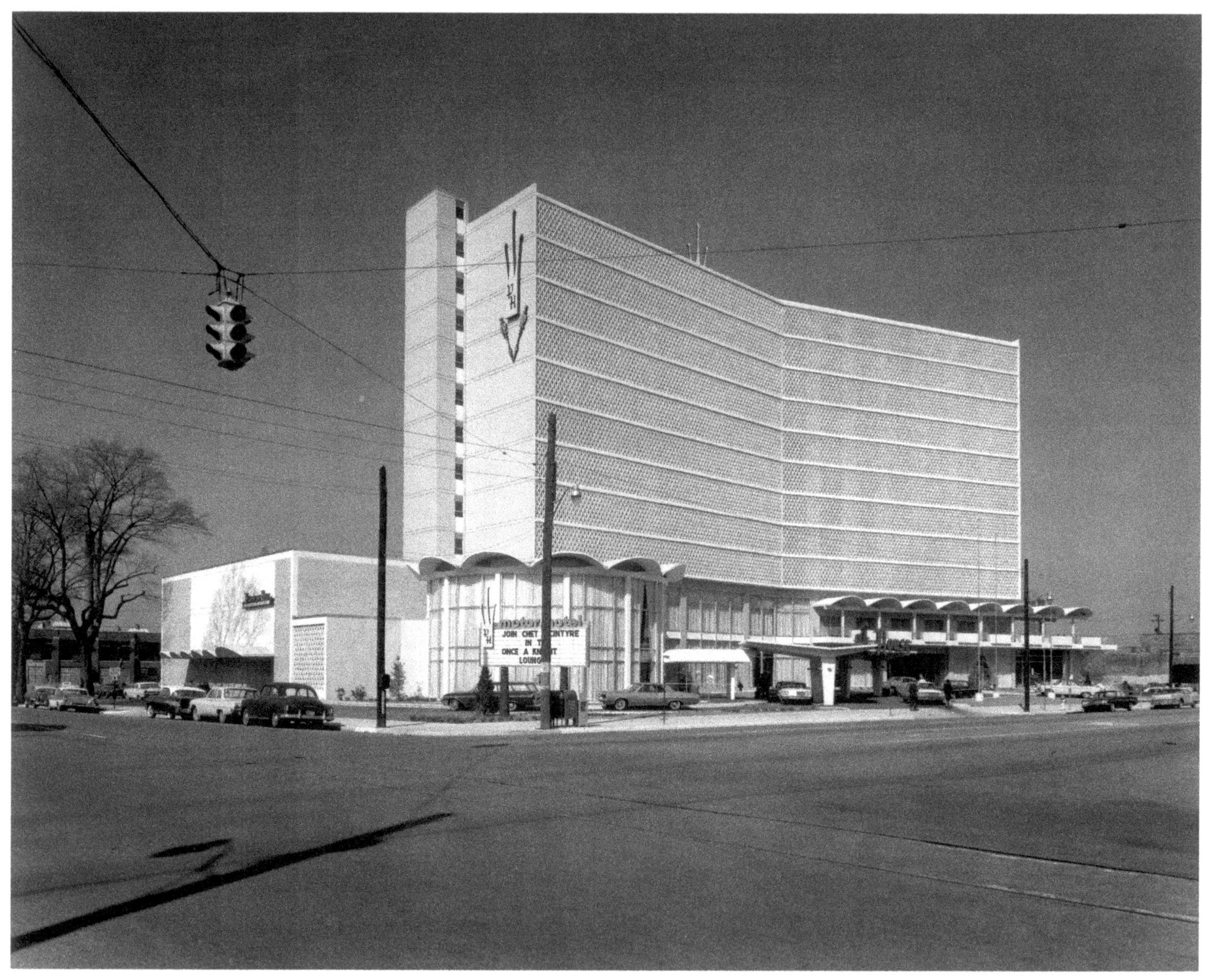

During the 1960s, downtown Birmingham offered plenty of hotels for visitors. The Parliament House Hotel on 20th Street South is an example of the many lodgings available to incoming visitors.

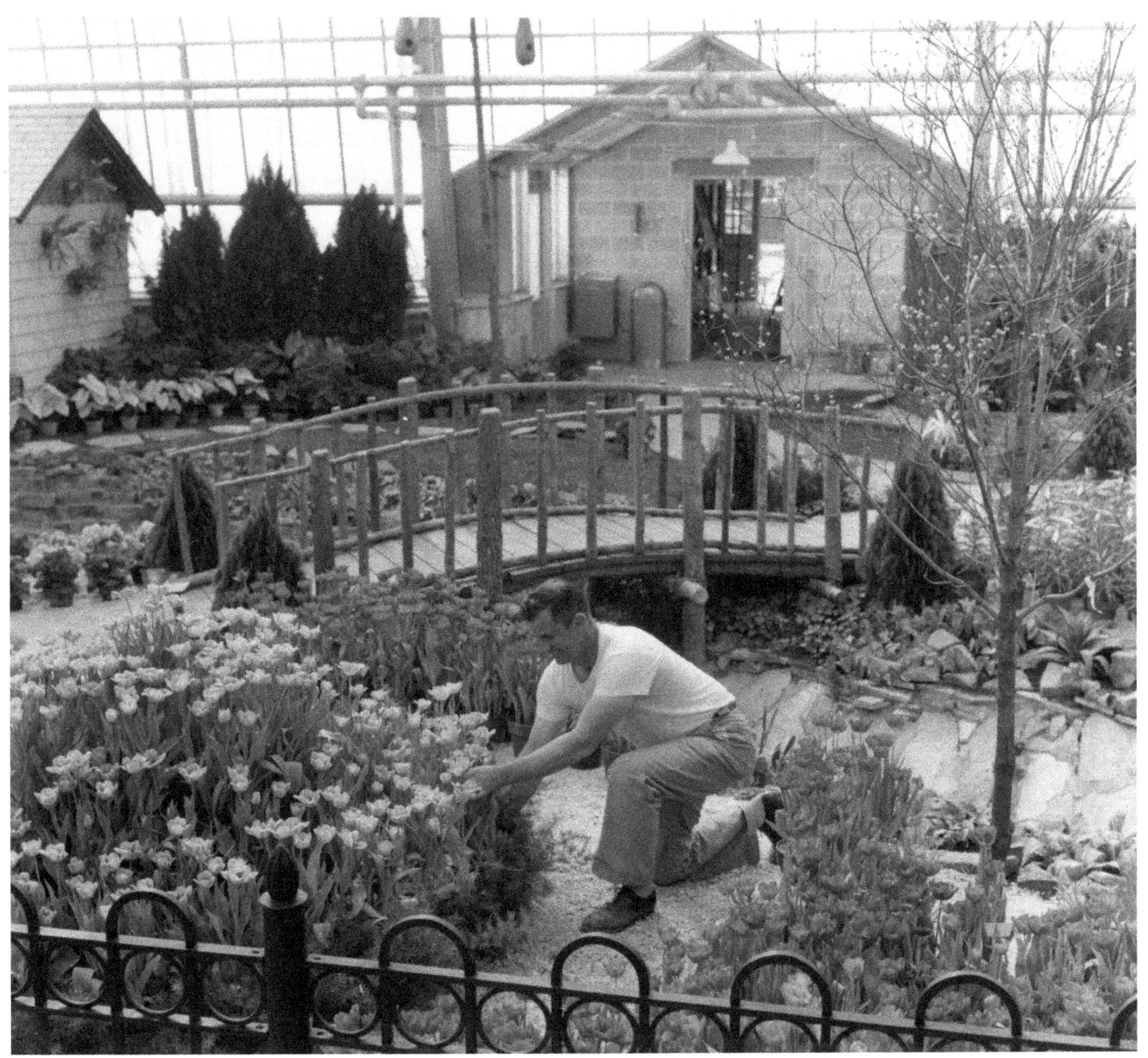

A horticulturist works with the tulips blooming at the Botanical Gardens, an attraction that opened in 1963.

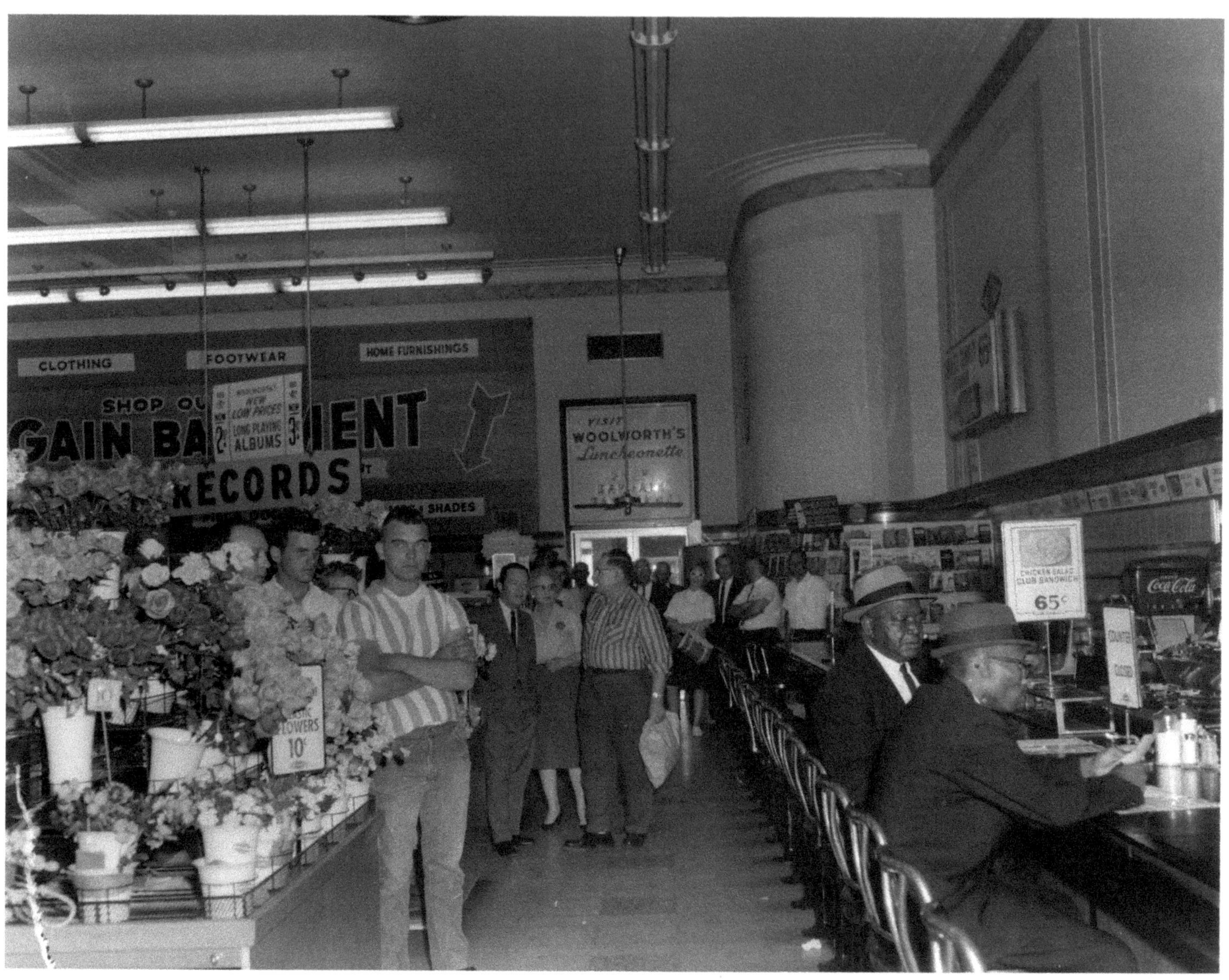

The motivating force behind the rising demand for integration came from the arrival of the Southern Christian Leadership Conference and Martin Luther King, Jr., whose brother, A. D. King, lived in Birmingham. Here a pair of protesters participate in a sit-in at a local lunch counter while other store patrons look on.

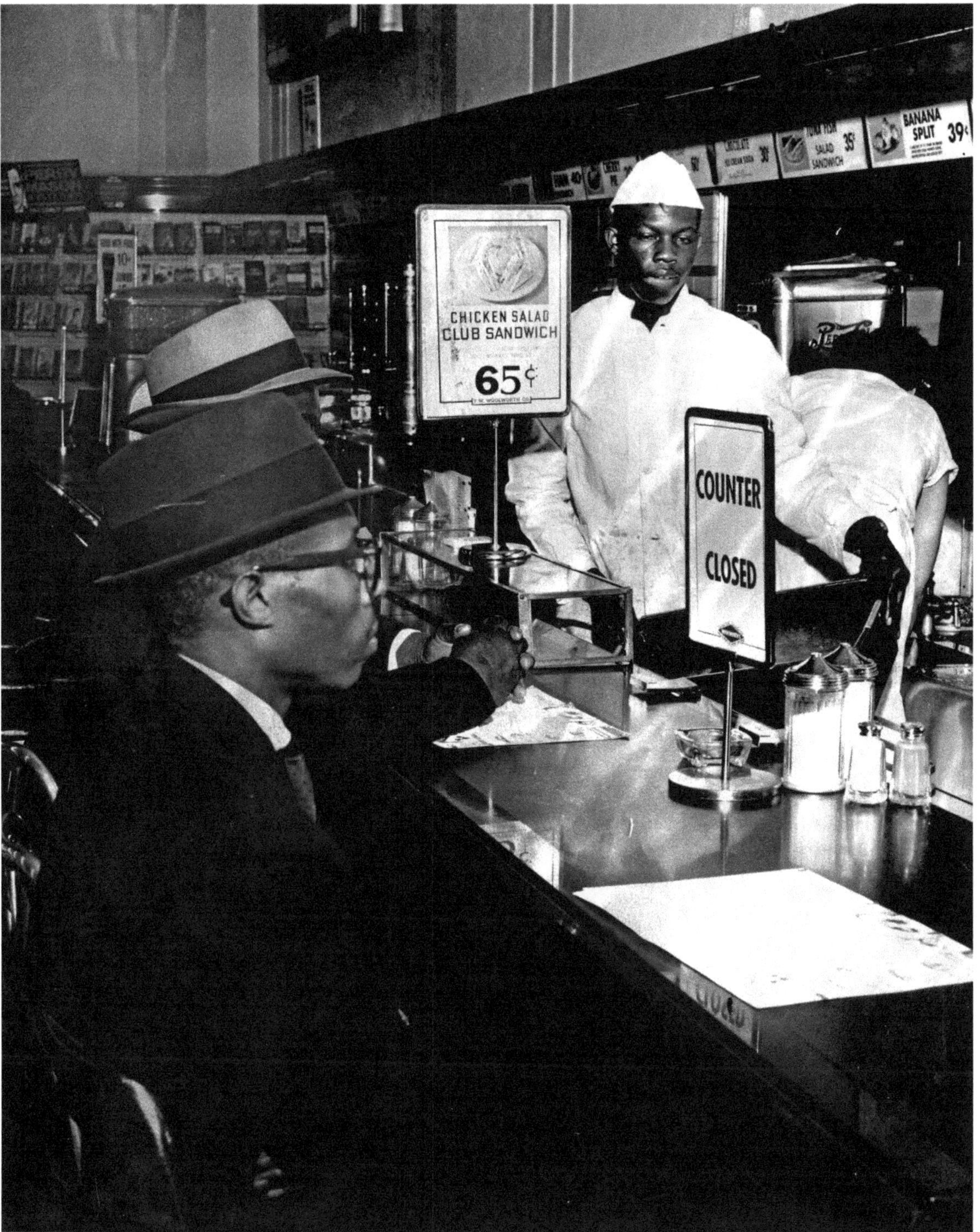

During the course of protests and racial unrest, more than 200 people were arrested for seeking service at segregated downtown lunch counters and for marching downtown with protest signs without parade permits.

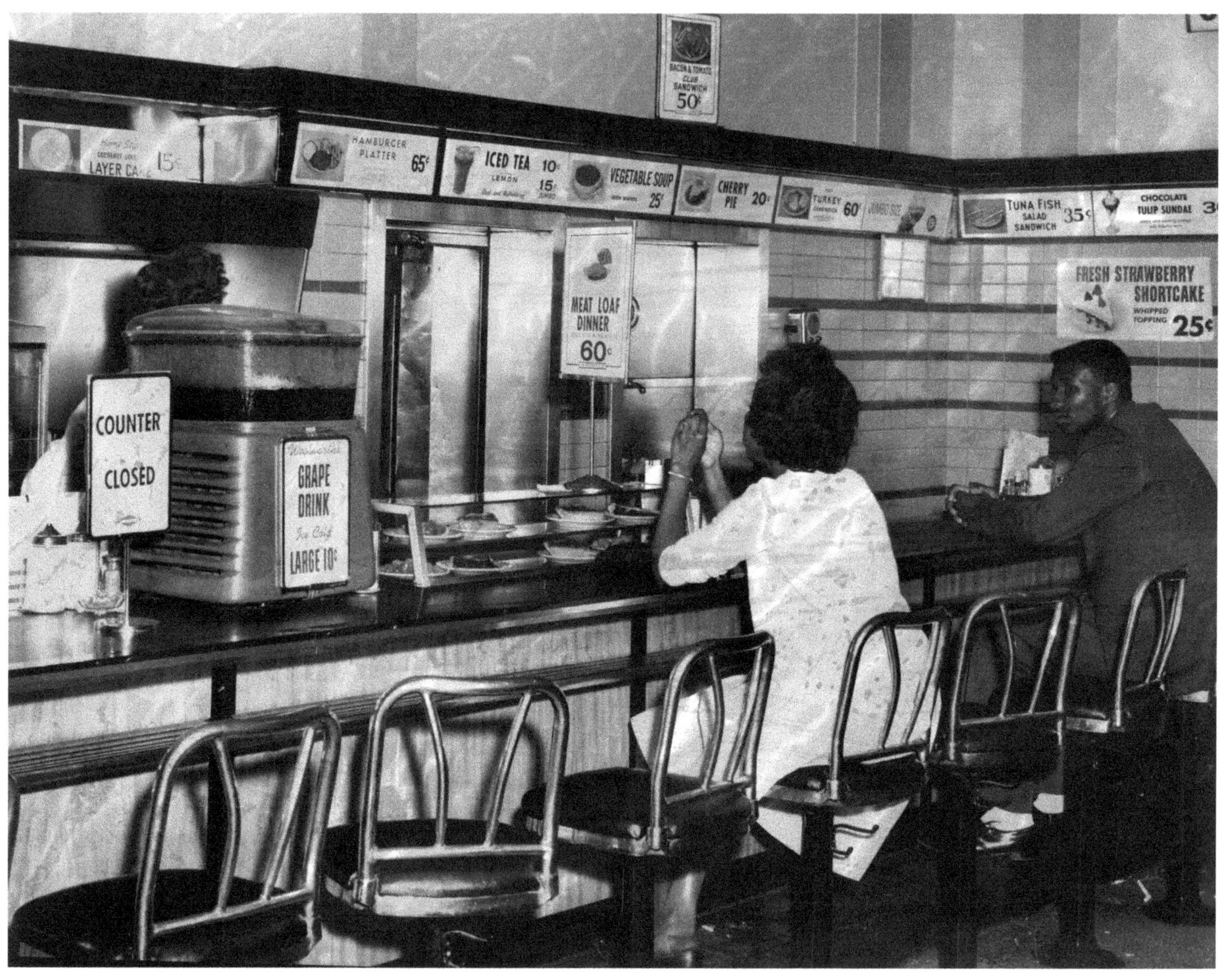

Two protesters take part in a sit-in. Along with desegregated downtown lunch counters, the Southern Christian Leadership Conference demanded the integration of restrooms, drinking fountains, employment of clerks in stores, and city government.

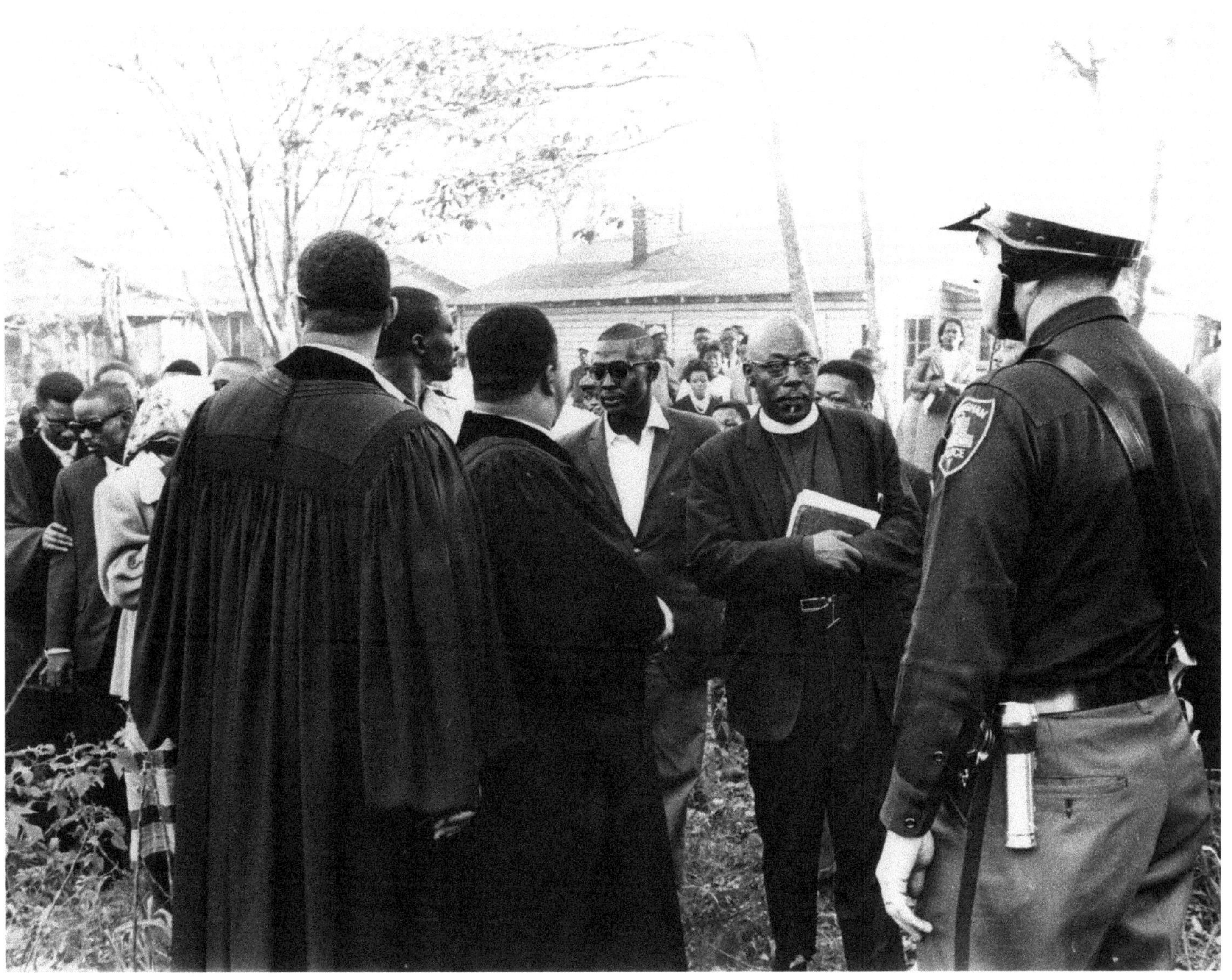

On Palm Sunday 1963, John Porter, N. H Smith, and A. D. King, brother of Martin Luther King, Jr., led protesters toward City Hall. They were put under arrest but were allowed to say a quick prayer before being taken away. In Kelly Ingram Park, there is a statue depicting the praying figures of the three ministers.

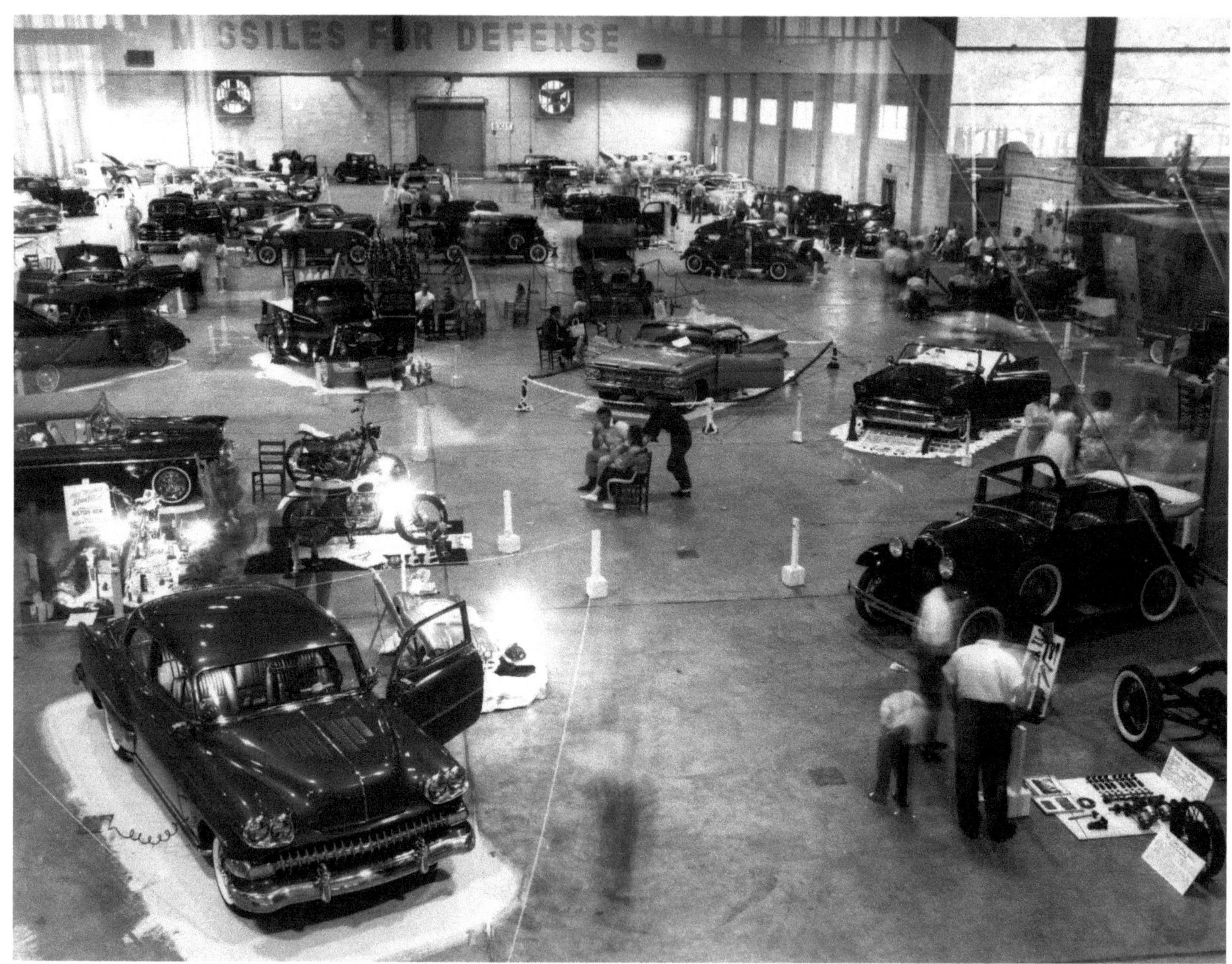

Rods and custom cars are on display at this show at the Alabama State Fairgrounds. In the background is evidence of the far-reaching tentacles of the cold war then being fought against the Soviet Union. The sign reads "Missiles for Defense." Fall-out shelters remained clearly labeled with yellow-and-black signage during the decade, during which the United States under President Kennedy failed in a bid to unseat Cuba's Castro and came close to unleashing nuclear war. Two decades later, President Reagan's tough stance against the Soviets would end the cold war, ultimately leading to the demise of communist rule in Russia and the former Soviet bloc.

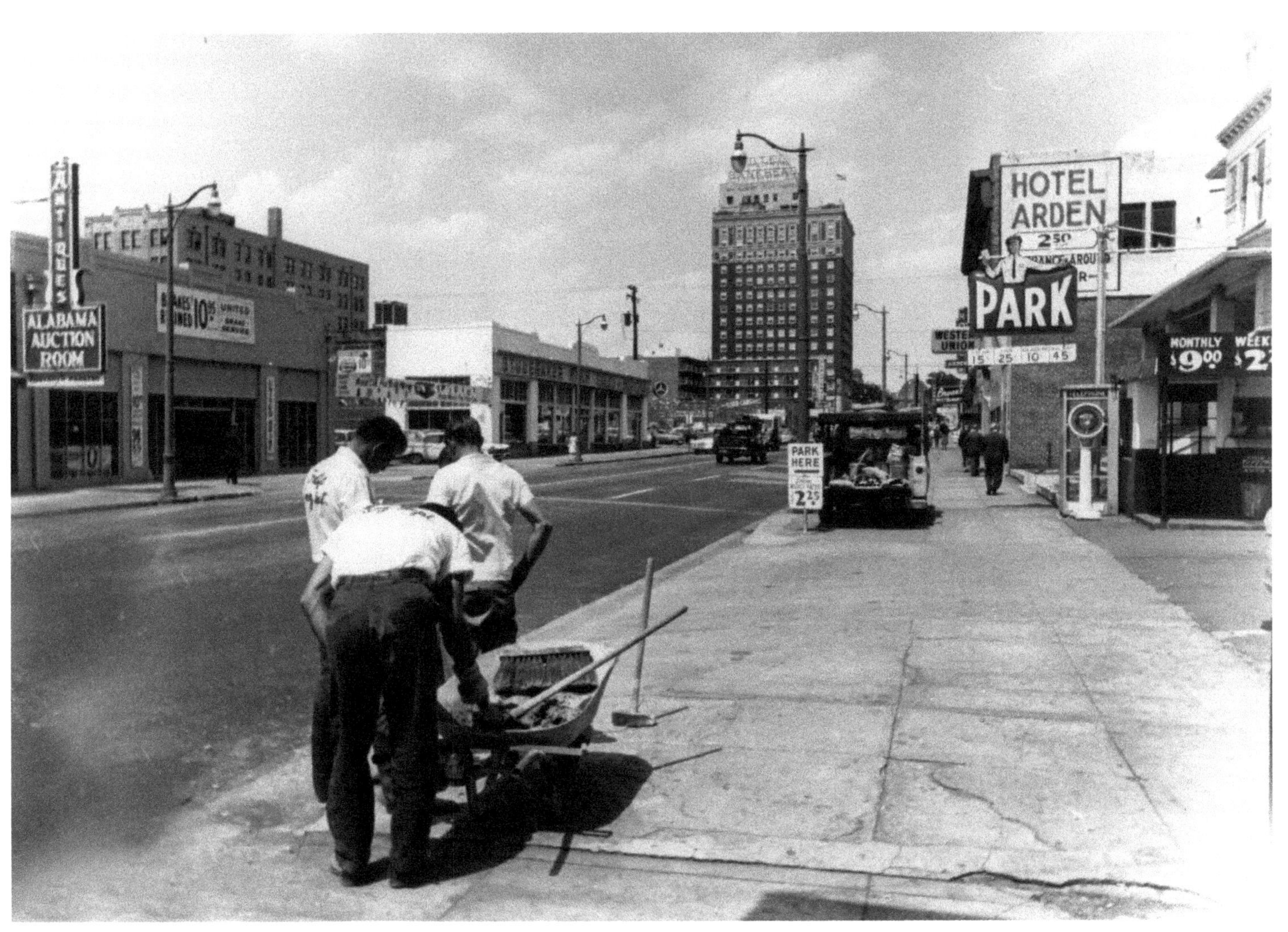

City workers install parking meters along 5th Avenue.

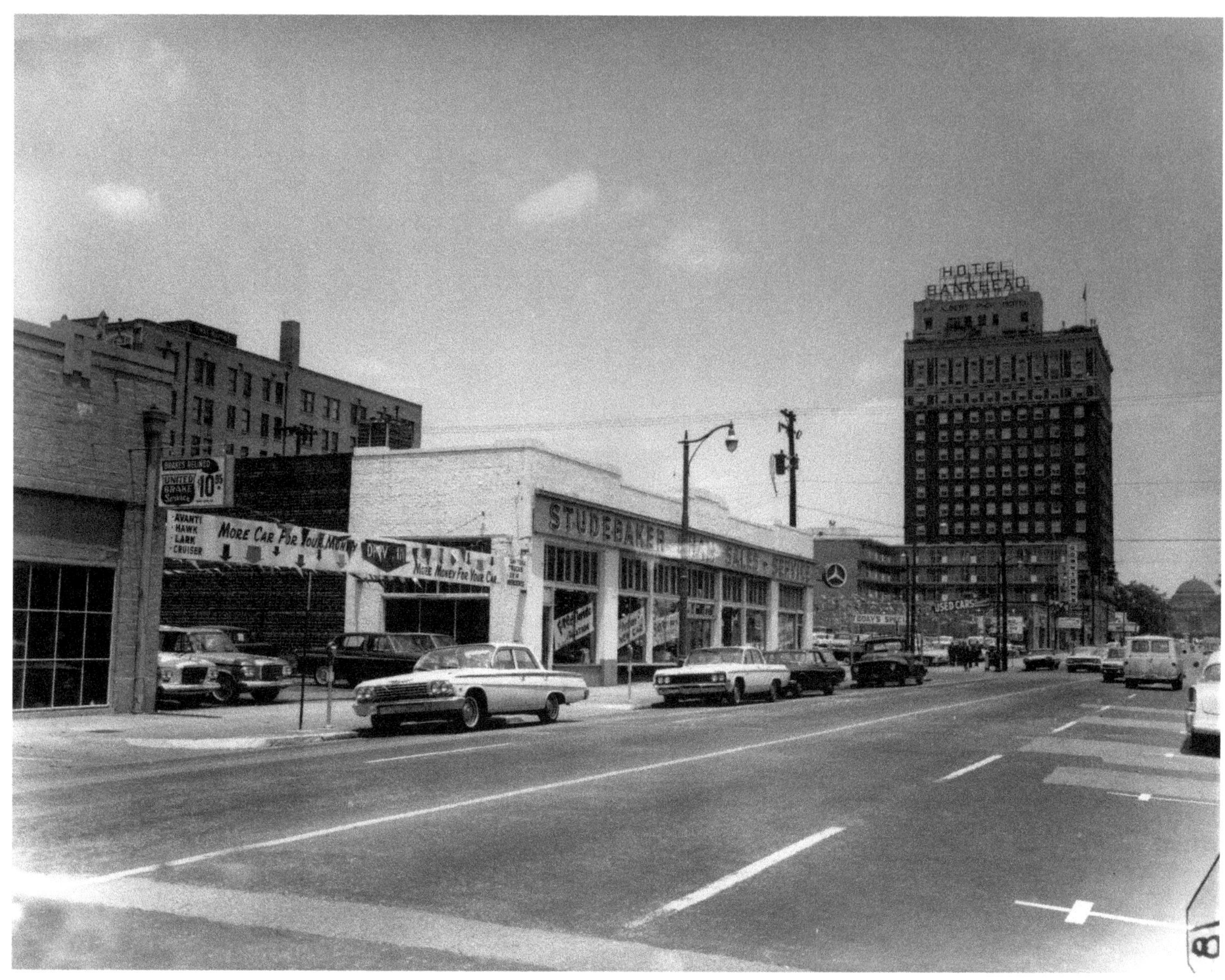

Studebaker of Birmingham Sales and Service on 5th Avenue North readys itself for business.

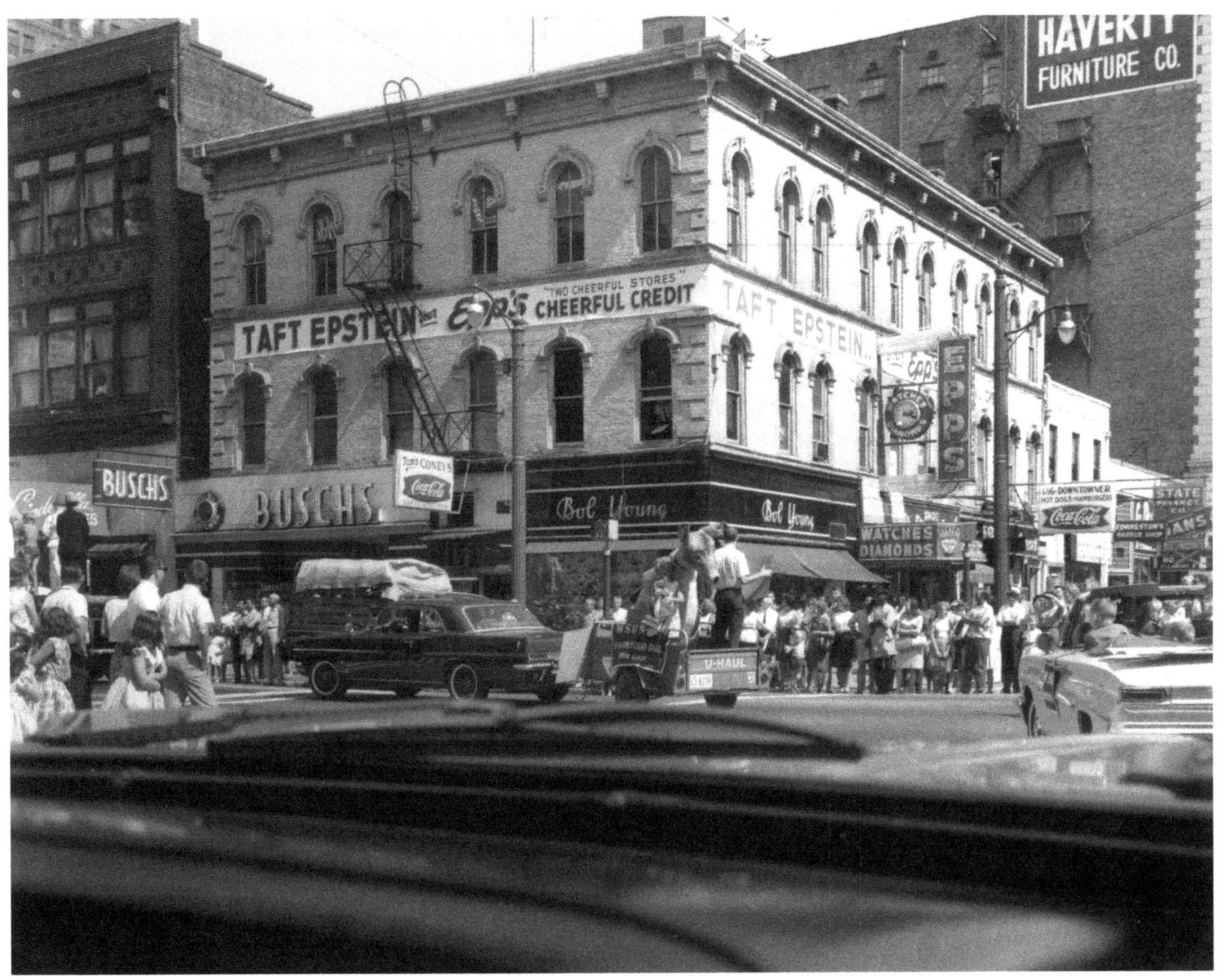

The WSGN Shriners Parade travels down 2nd Avenue North from 19th Street.

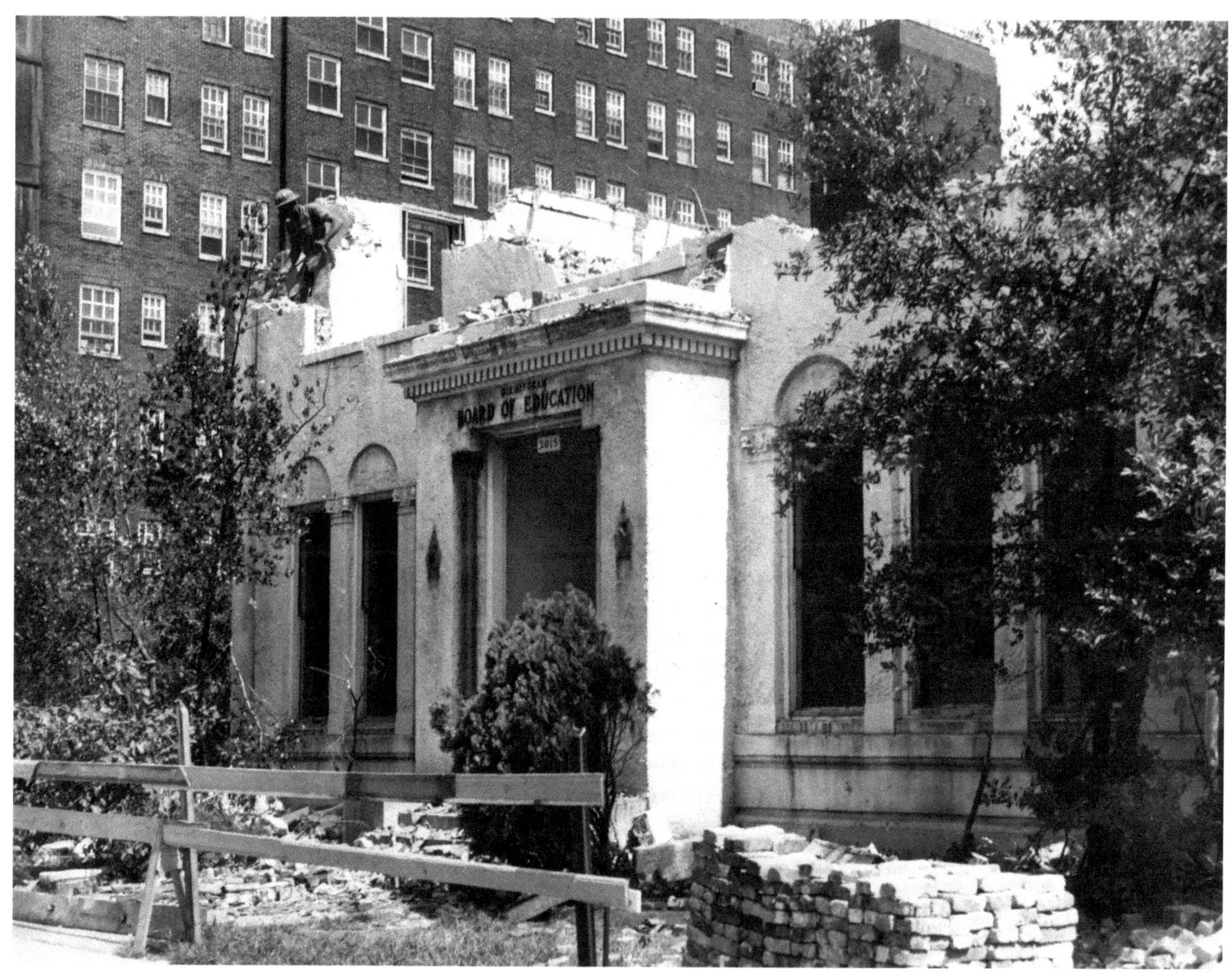

After 30 years of service, the Birmingham Board of Education building was demolished. During the flattening of the old stucco building and construction of the new building, the board conducted business from the 10th floor of City Hall.

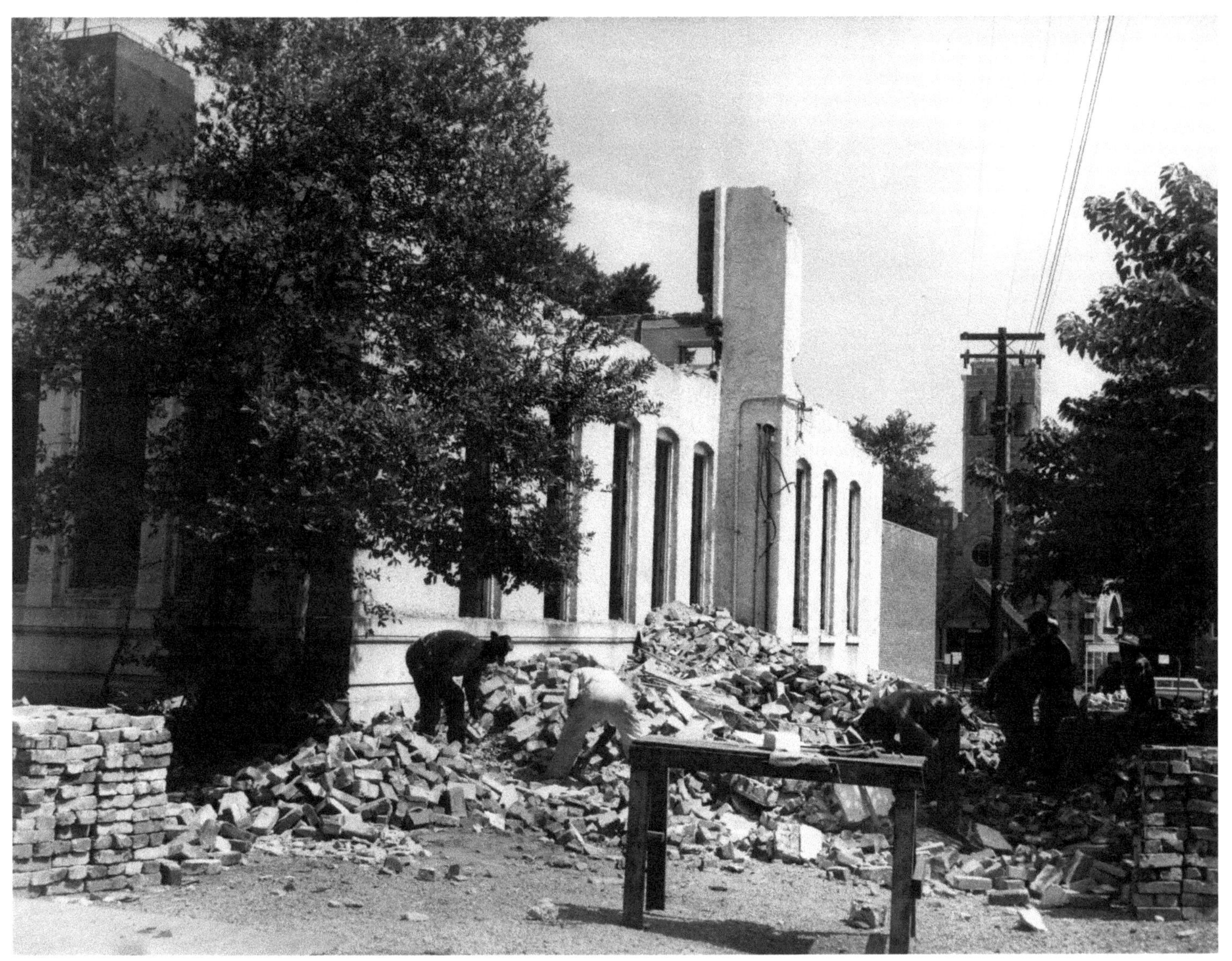

Men shift through the rubble of the demolished Board of Education building.

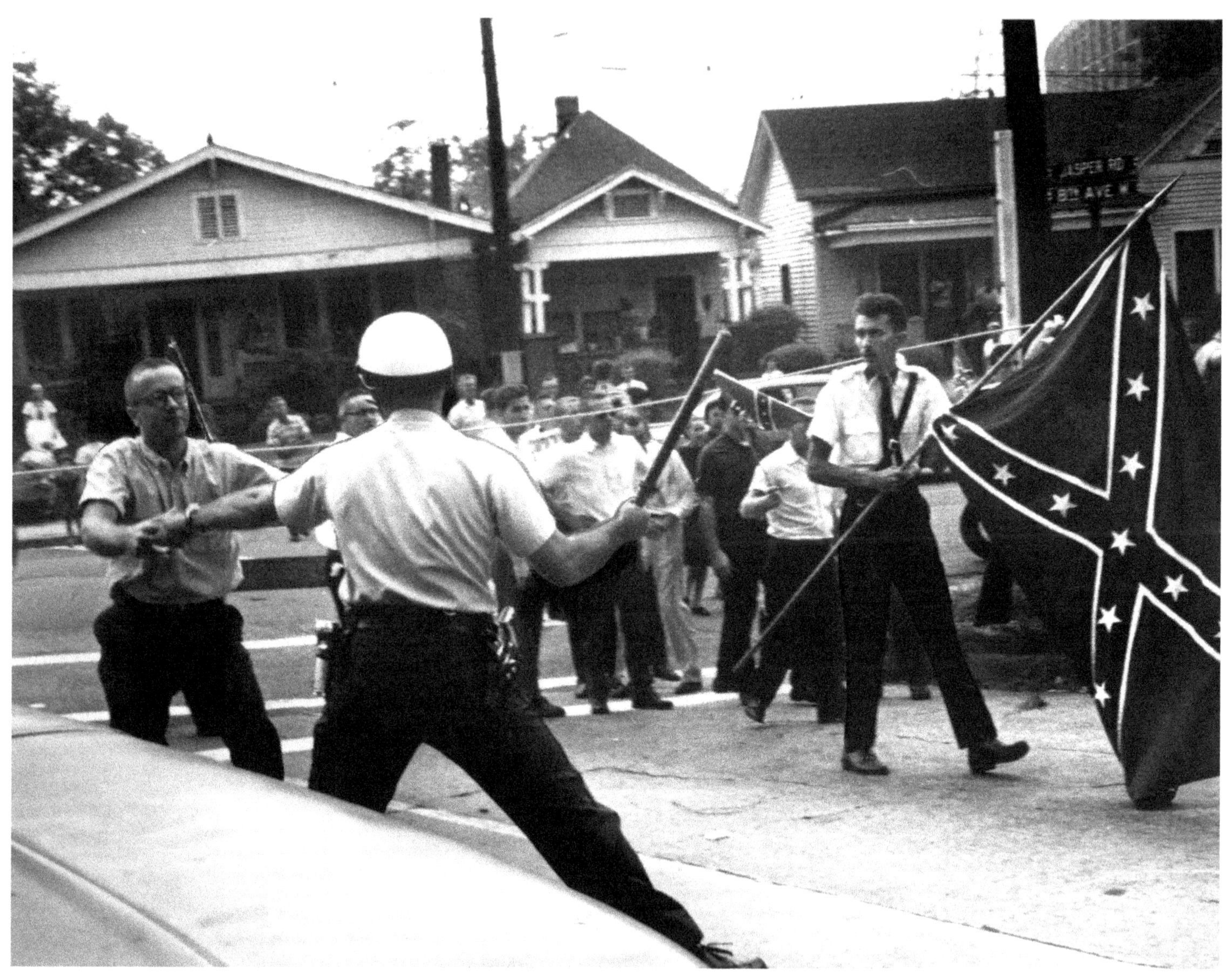

While National States Righter Jerry Dutton carries the Confederate flag along Jasper Road, a helmeted police officer forces back another demonstrator who broke through police lines at Graymont Elementary School.

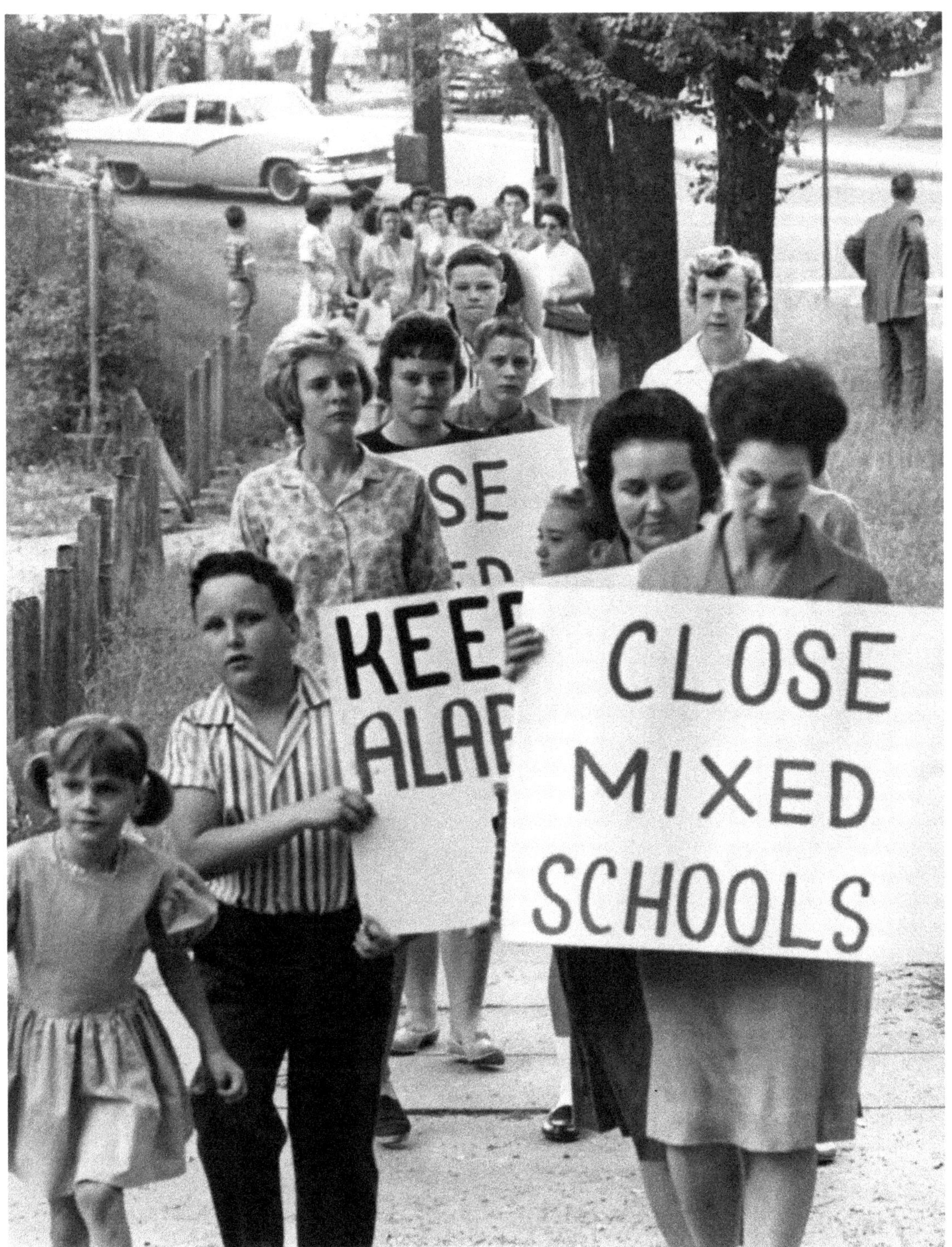

Concerned parents accompany children to school while carrying counter-protest signs.

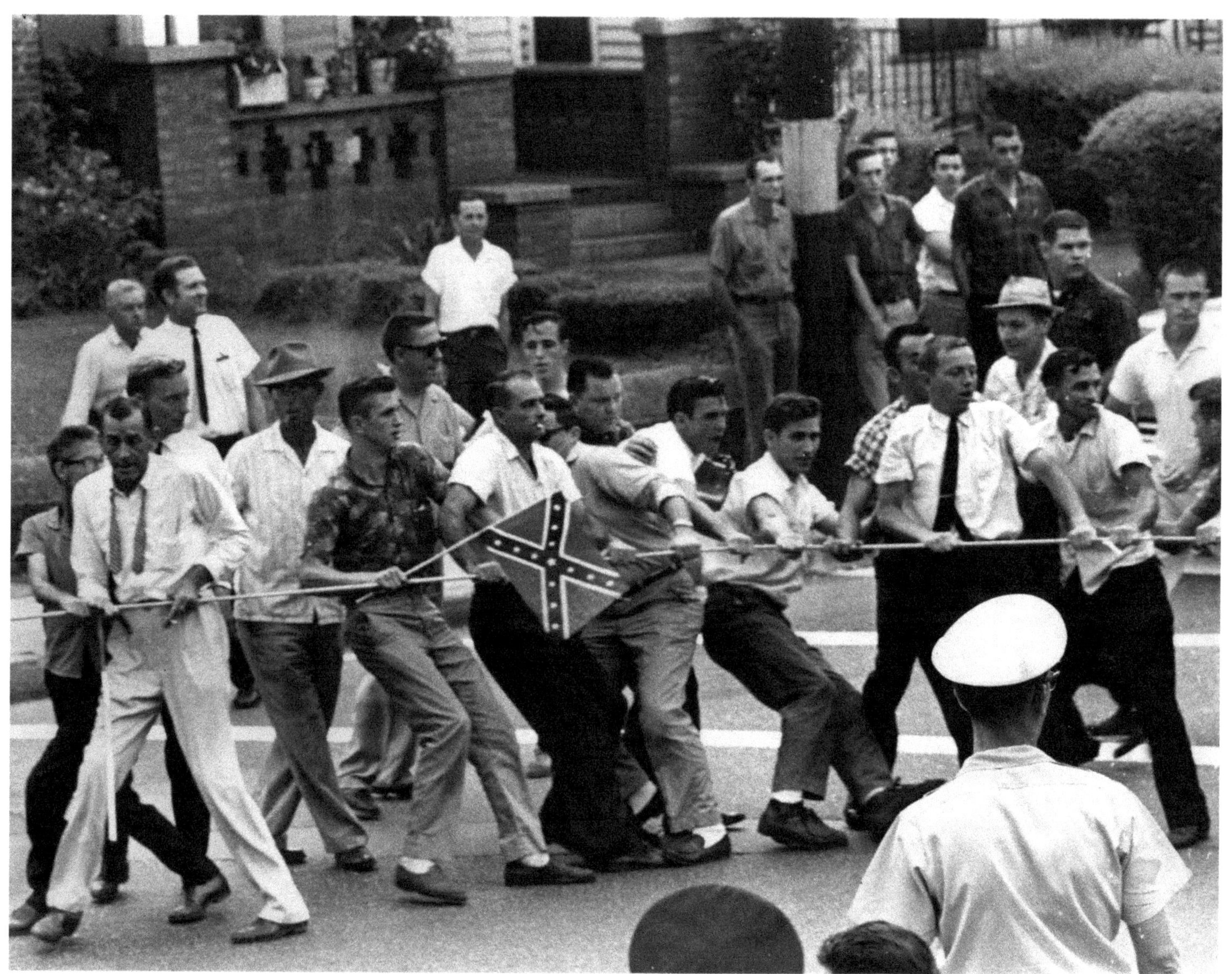

Demonstrators tear away a police rope barrier at Graymont Elementary School, while police pull the other end to restore the barrier. Many counter-protesters were not parents of students but members of the National States Rights Party, a white supremacist political party vehemently opposed to integration.

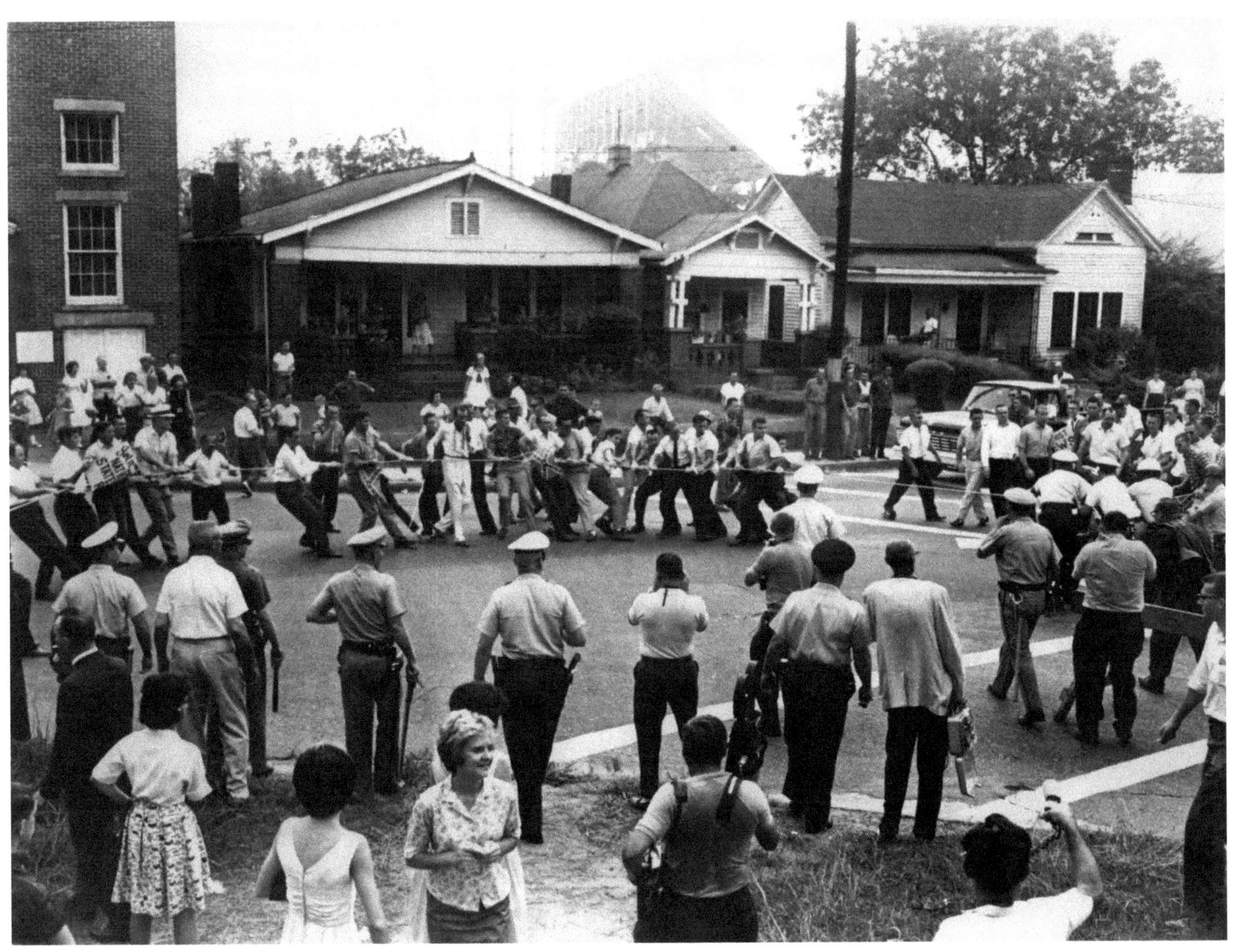

At Graymont Elementary School, the protests kept nearly 351 white students from registering. Ultimately, the school had to close for a few days because of the demonstrations.

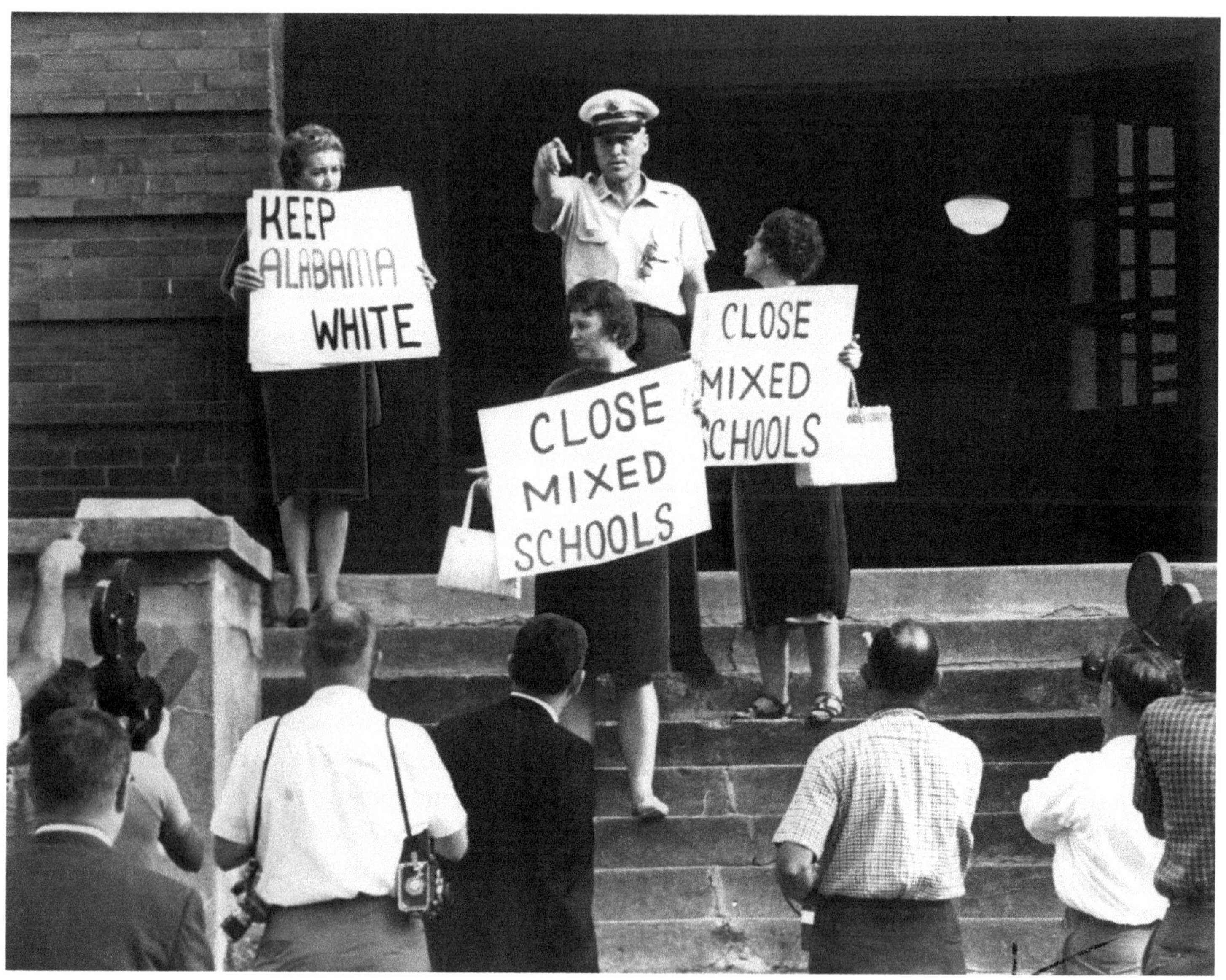

Counter-protesters demand maintenance of the status quo while standing on the front steps of Graymont Elementary School.

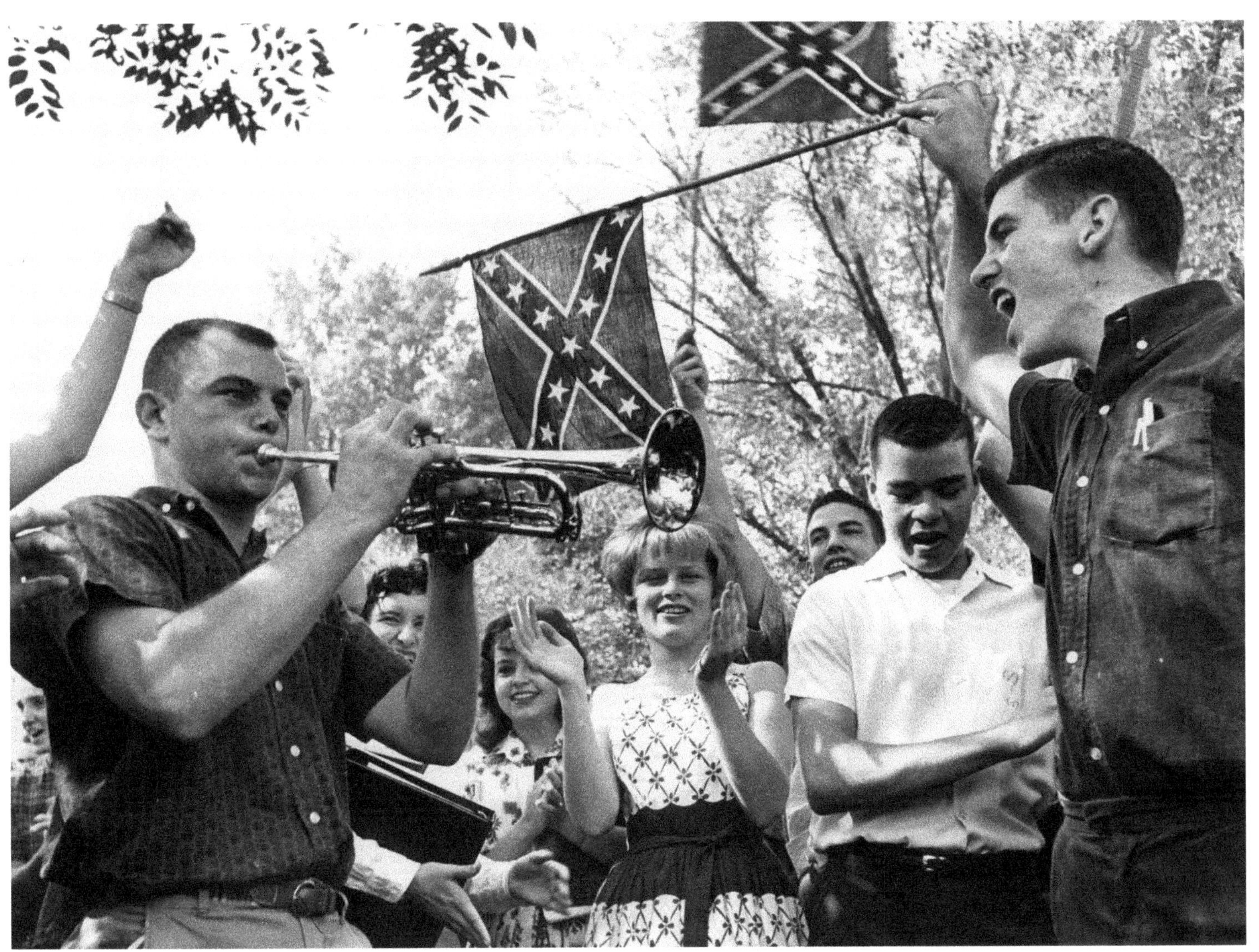

To show their opposition to integration, West End High School students sing "Dixie" while waving Confederate flags, symbolic of their white southern heritage. When they weren't singing, students chanted slogans. Counter-protests did not stop the admittance of two black students.

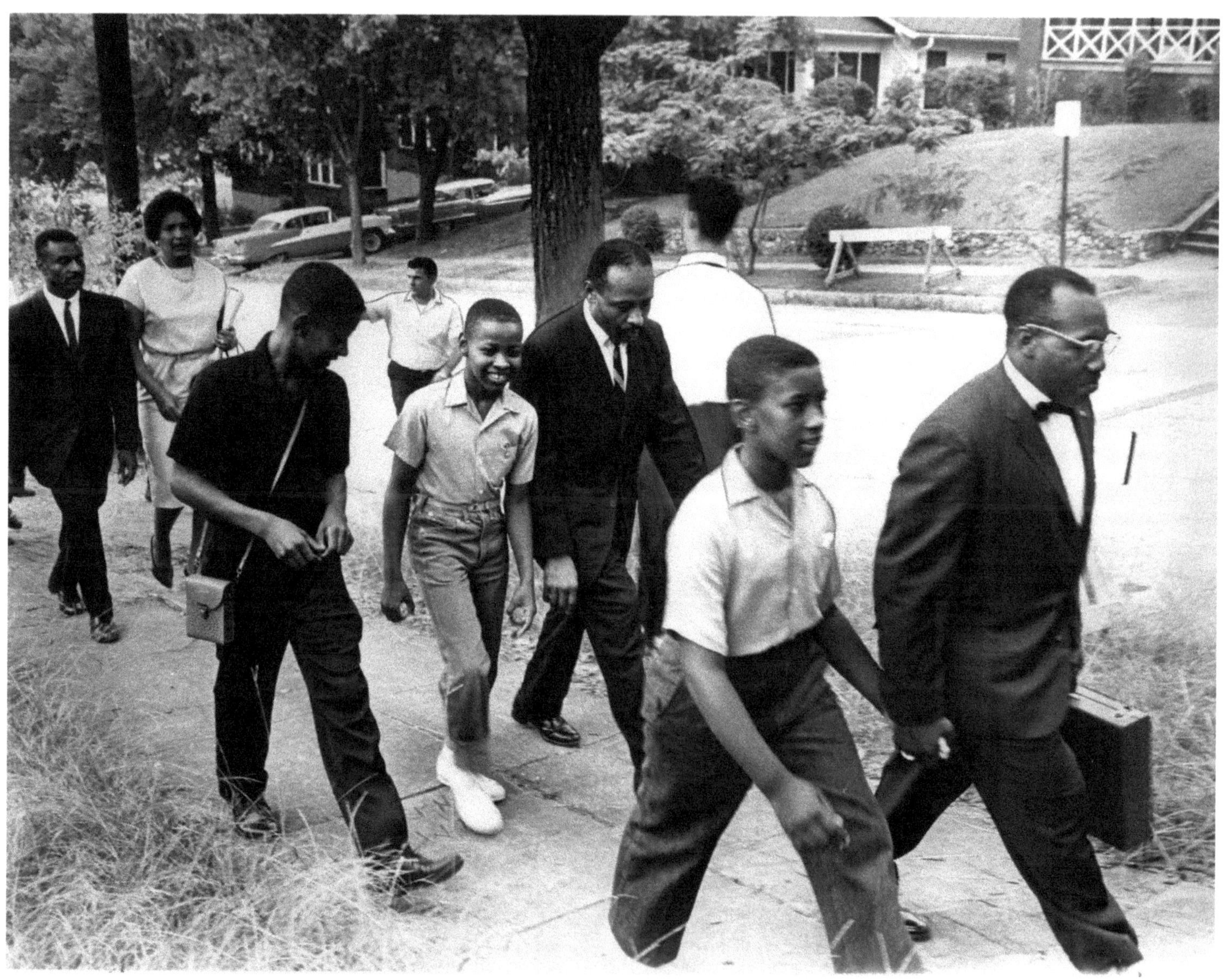

Floyd and Dwight Armstrong leave Graymont Elementary School after becoming the first blacks admitted to a white Birmingham public school. Accompanying them were their attorneys, father, and brother.

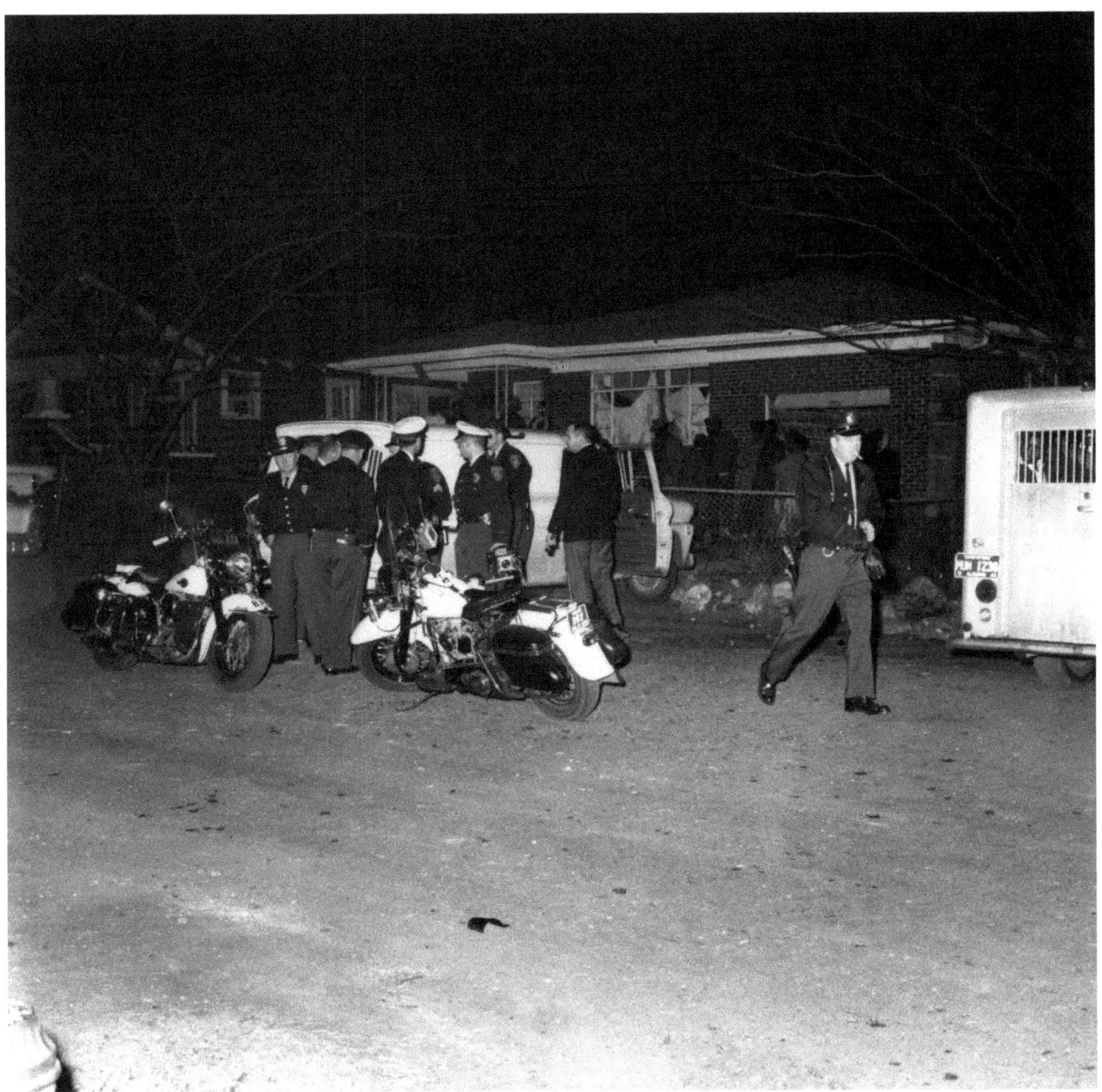

Police investigate a bombed house, possibly one of the four houses damaged when a dynamite bomb was tossed from a car in December 1963 in front of Bethel Baptist Church. According to police, the bomb did not have a specific target and as a result damaged four houses and the church, leaving a wide crater in the street.

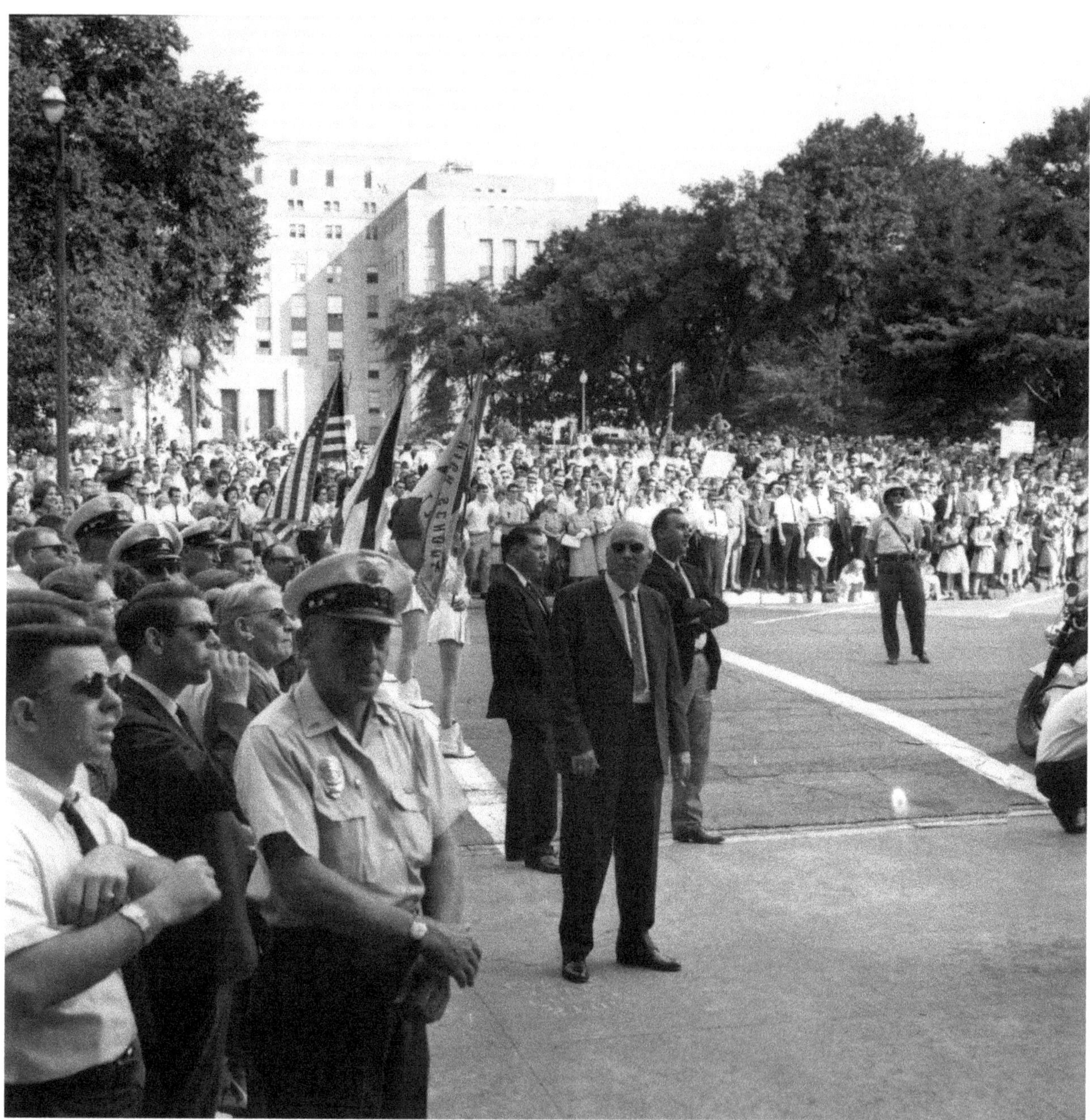

Two thousand five hundred Birmingham residents gather to hear Governor George Wallace, who was running for president on the Democratic ticket, speak from the steps of Birmingham City Hall during his first Alabama stop after Maryland's presidential primary. Wallace talked civil rights and his intense opposition to the Civil Rights bill. Lyndon Johnson would defeat Wallace to become the Democratic nominee in the 1964 election.

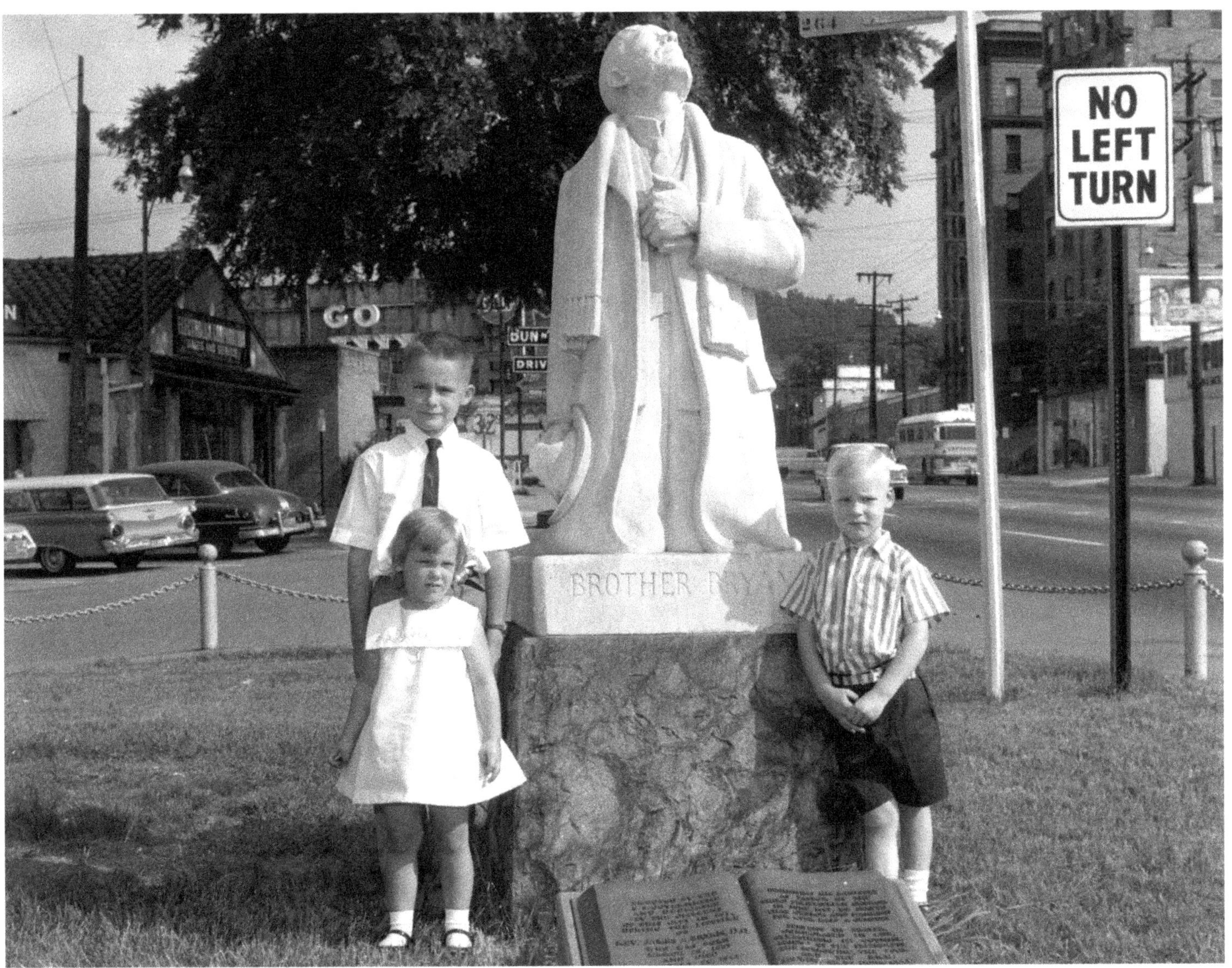

Birmingham's first official chaplain, Brother Bryan, was a generous man who freely gave to the downtrodden. George Bridges immortalized Brother Bryan with the creation of this statue in 1934. Twenty-three years after his death, Bryan's great-grandchildren visit the memorial at the corner of 10th Avenue and 20th Street.

A Shriner and child ring the bell for the USS *Alabama* in an attempt to raise money for the battleship, which had served the nation during World War II. The ship had been retired by the Navy from duty and in 1964 Alabamians helped bring "the gallant *Alabama*" home to Mobile Bay.

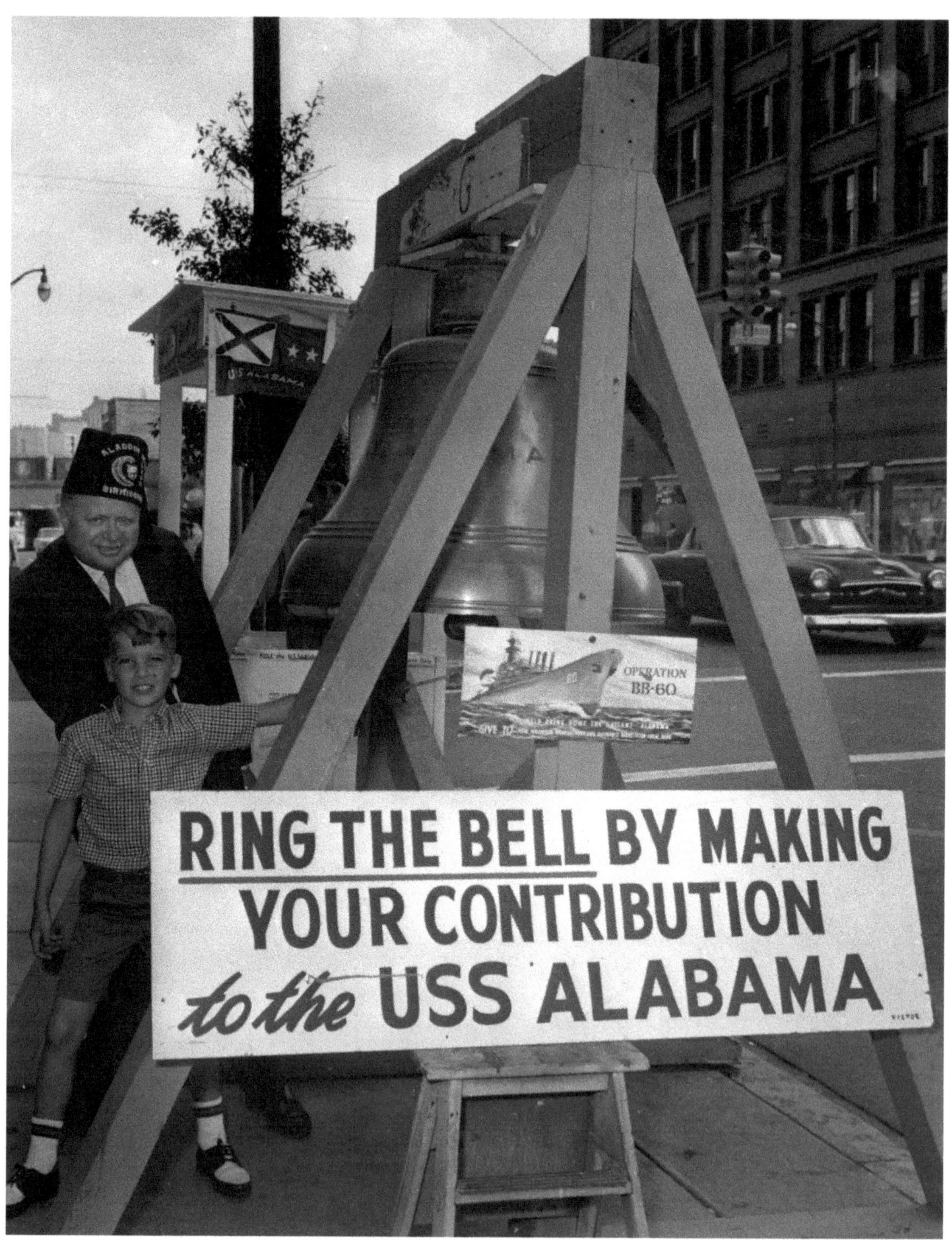

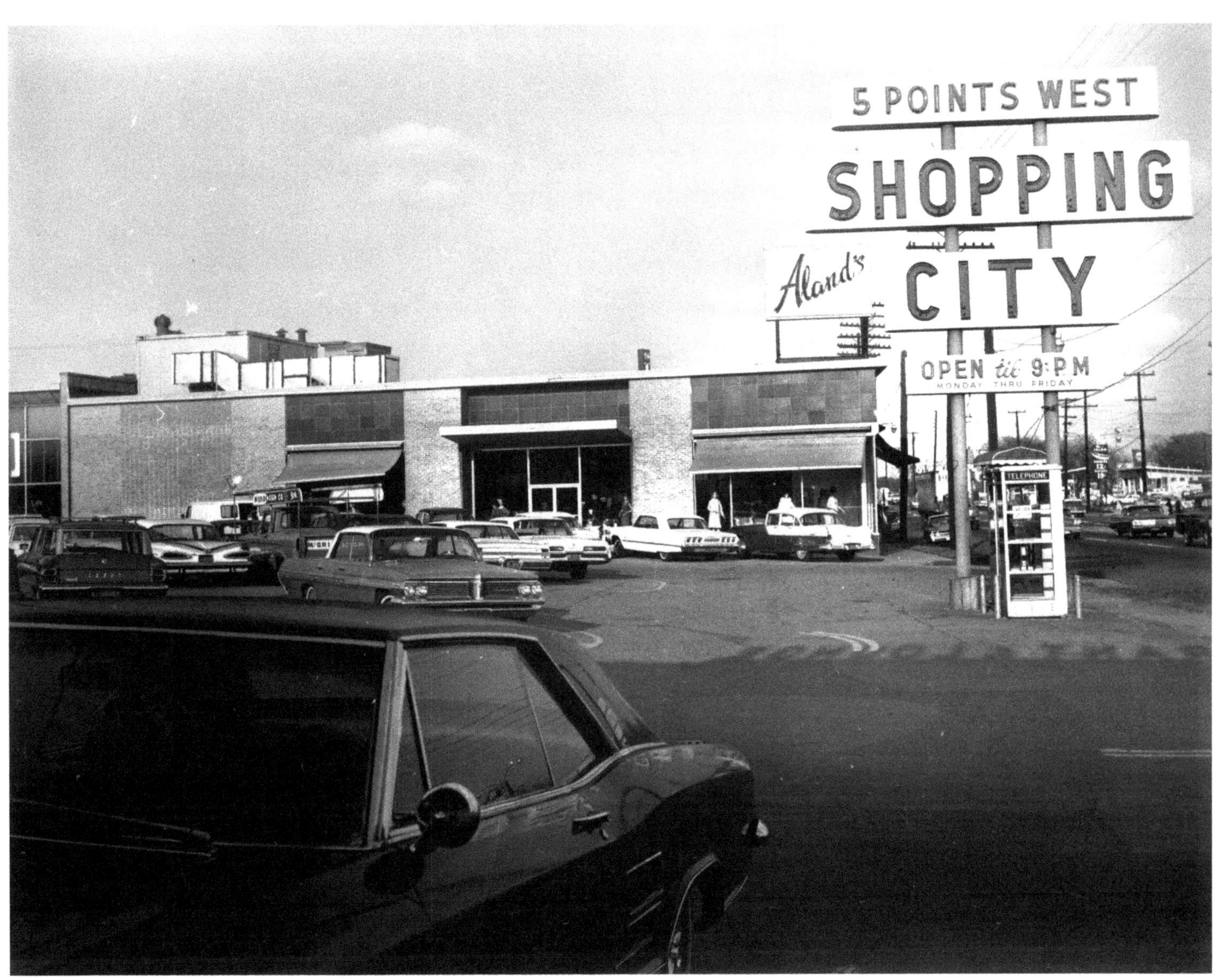

Aland's, a specialty clothing store, is open for business in 5 Points West Shopping City.

WATV's radio antenna tower stands atop the Thomas Jefferson Hotel.

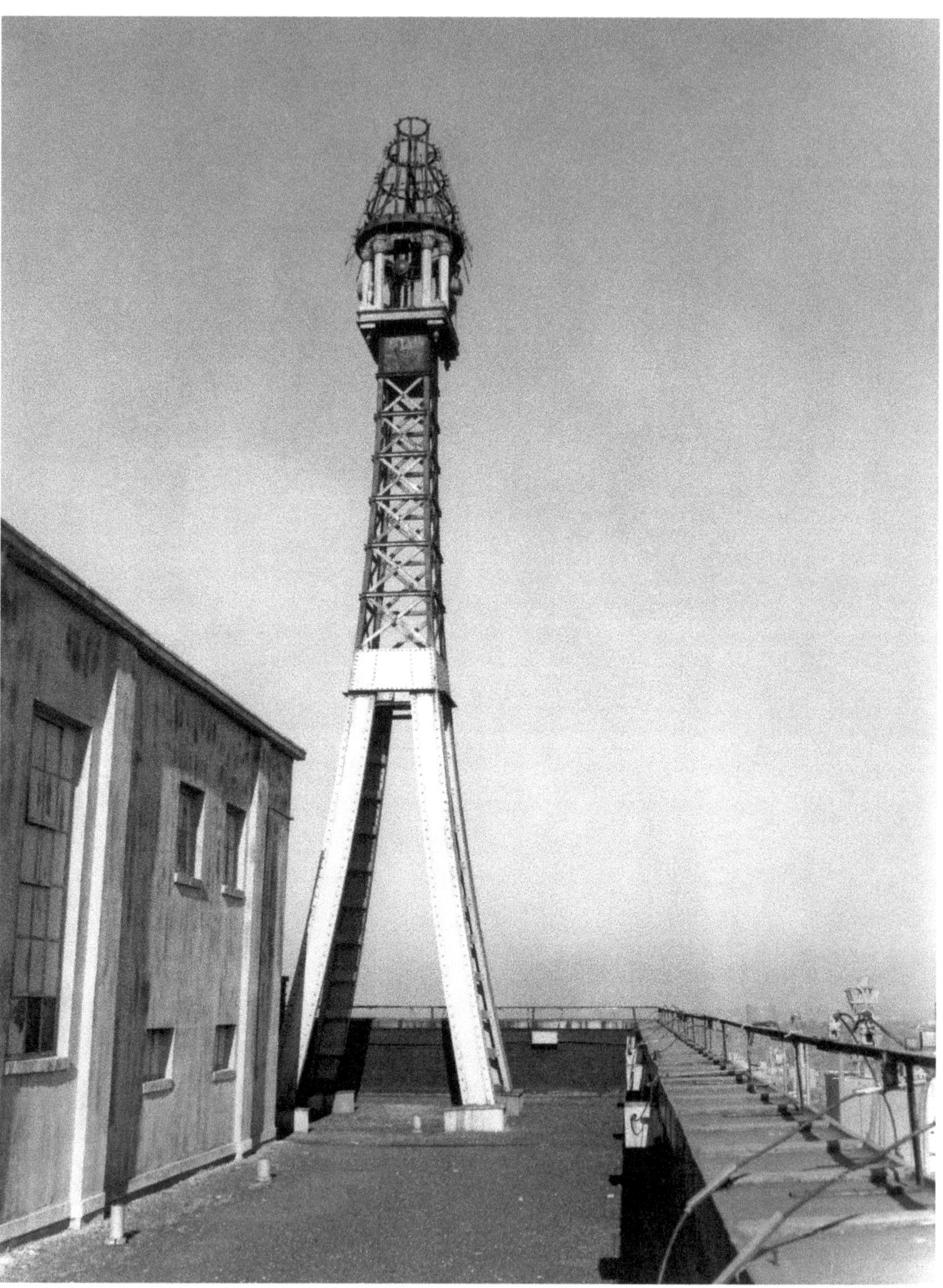

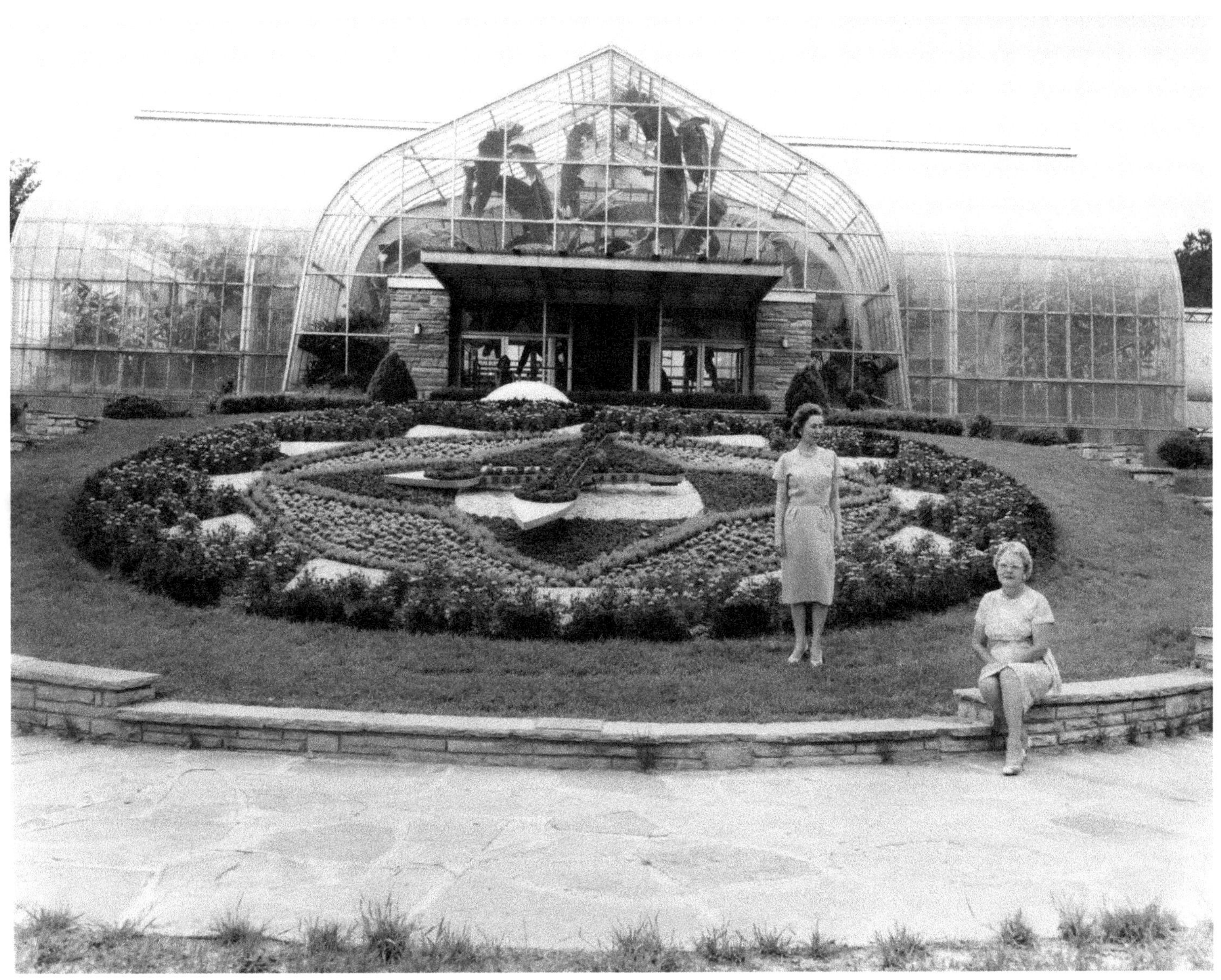

Two ladies enjoy the view outside the greenhouse at the Botanical Gardens.

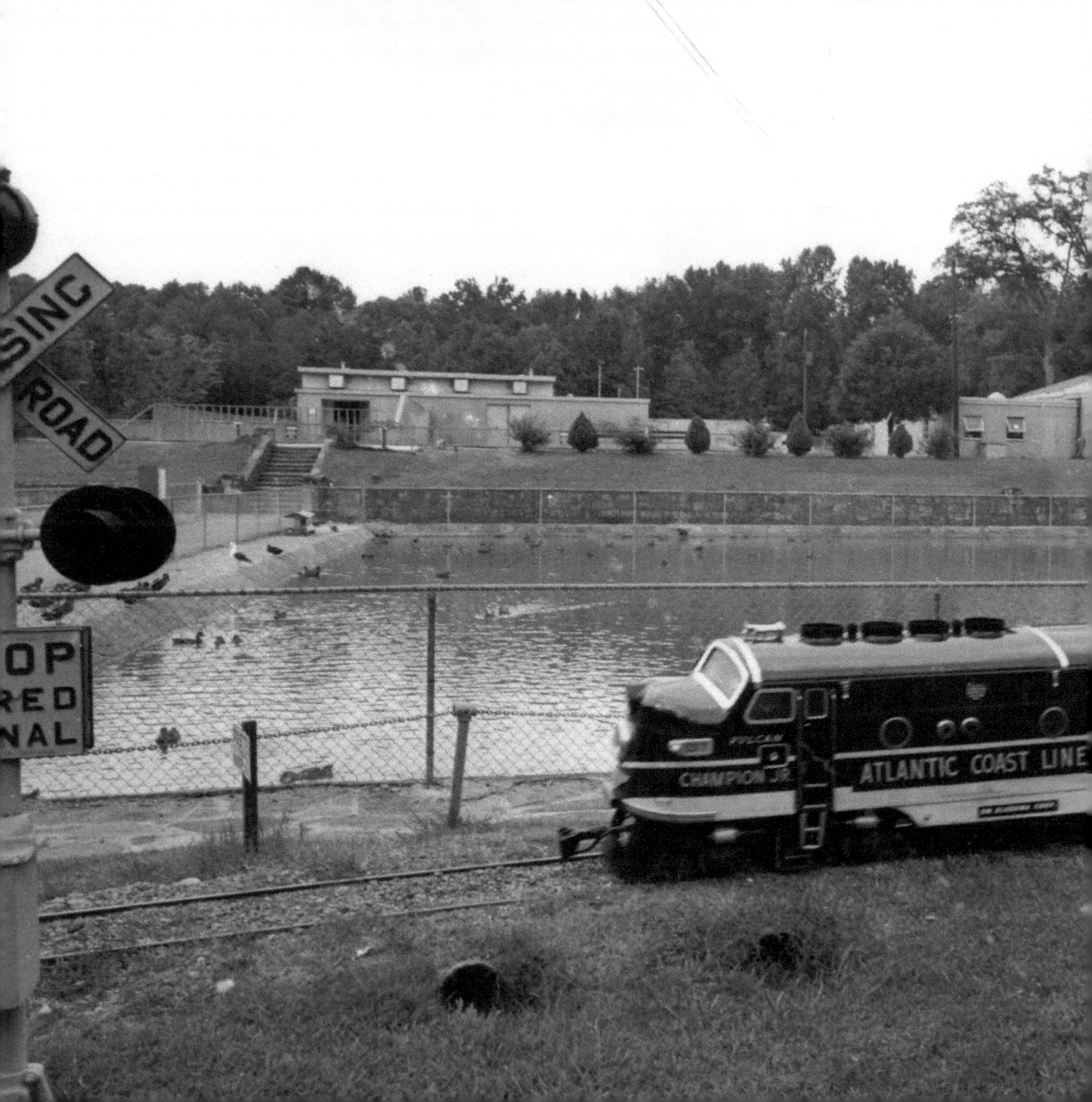
SING
ROAD
OP
RED
NAL
CHAMPION JR.
ATLANTIC COAST LINE

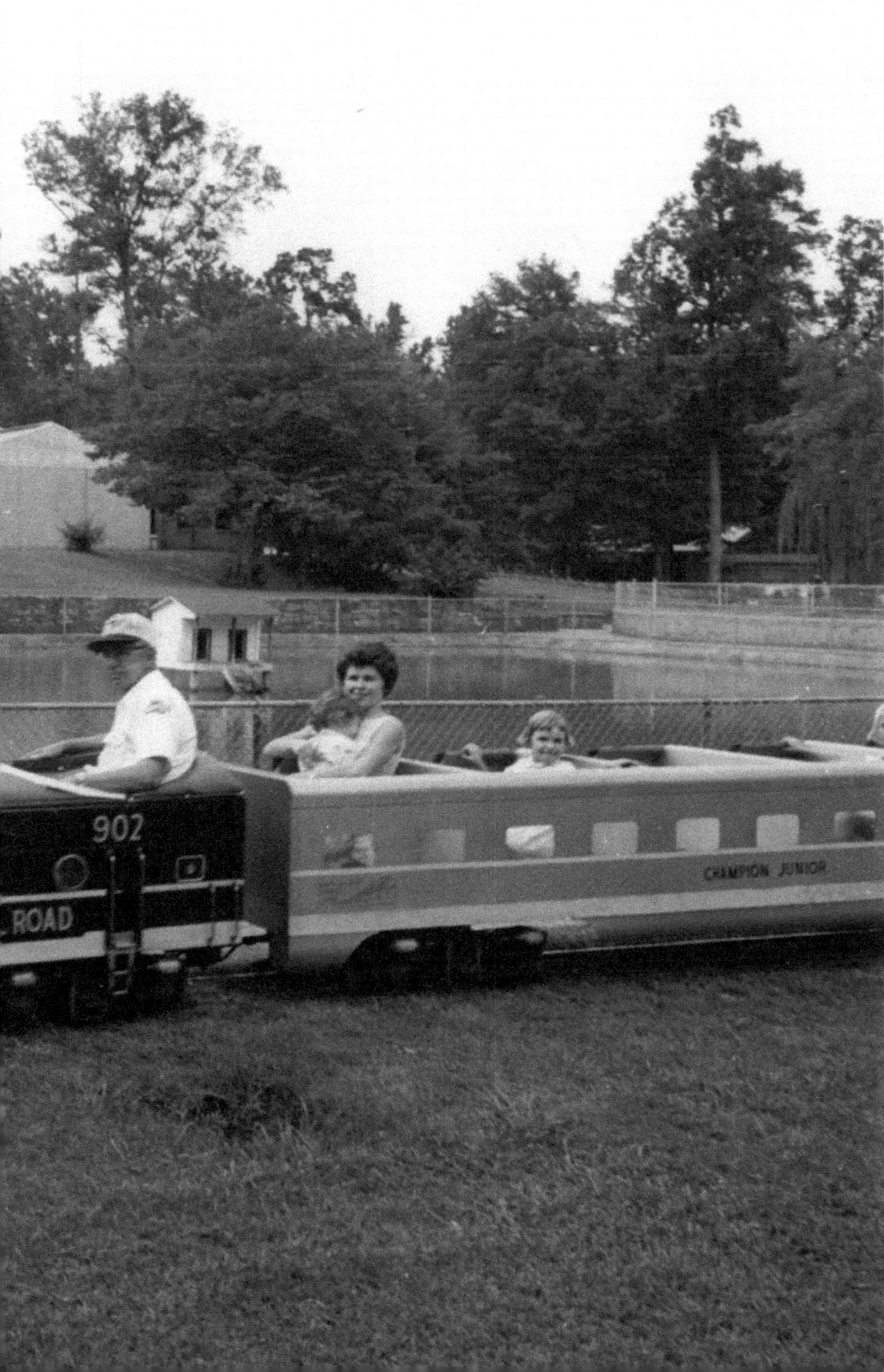

A miniature train gives zoo visitors a tour of the grounds and exhibits.

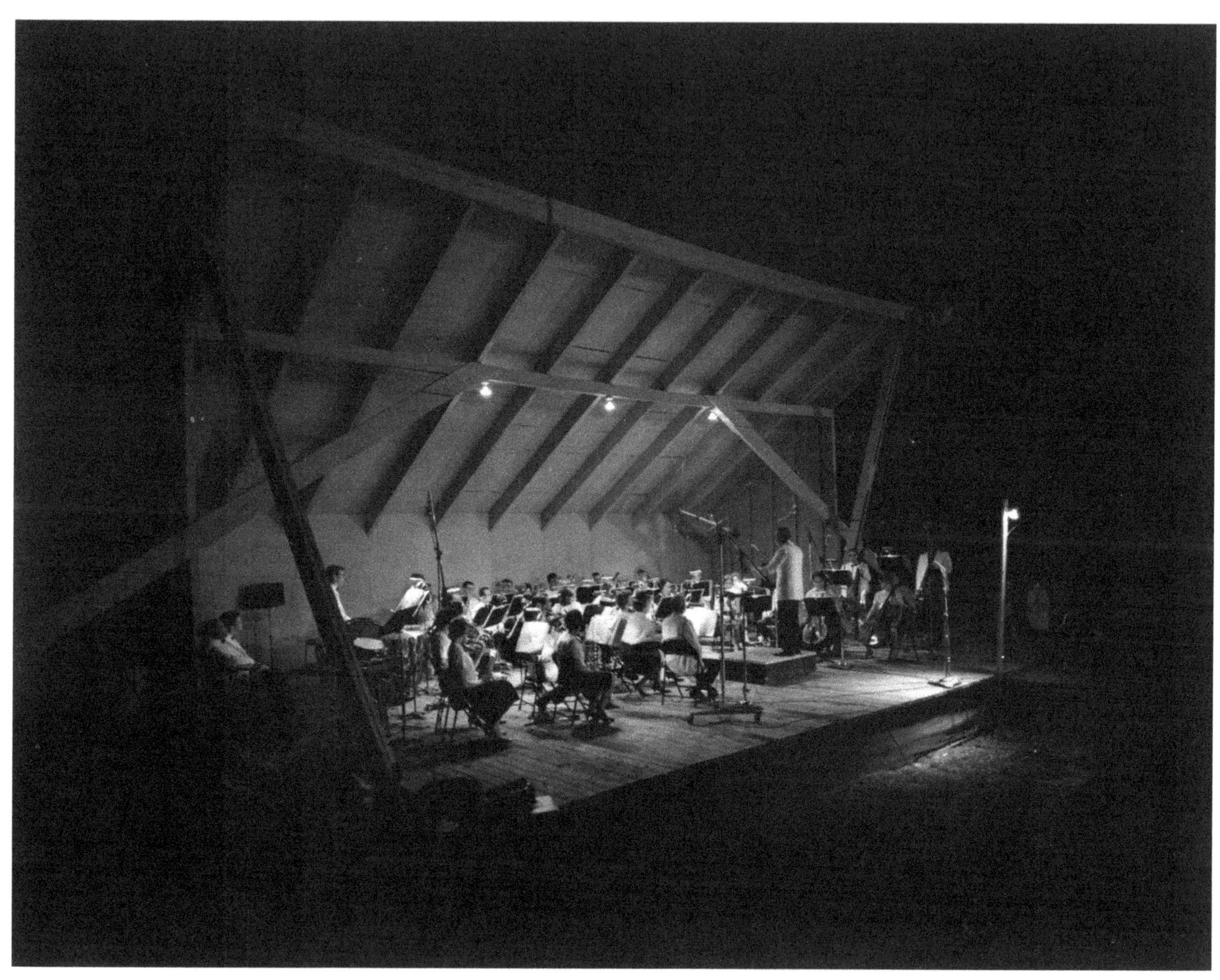

An outdoors concert is performed by the Birmingham Symphony.

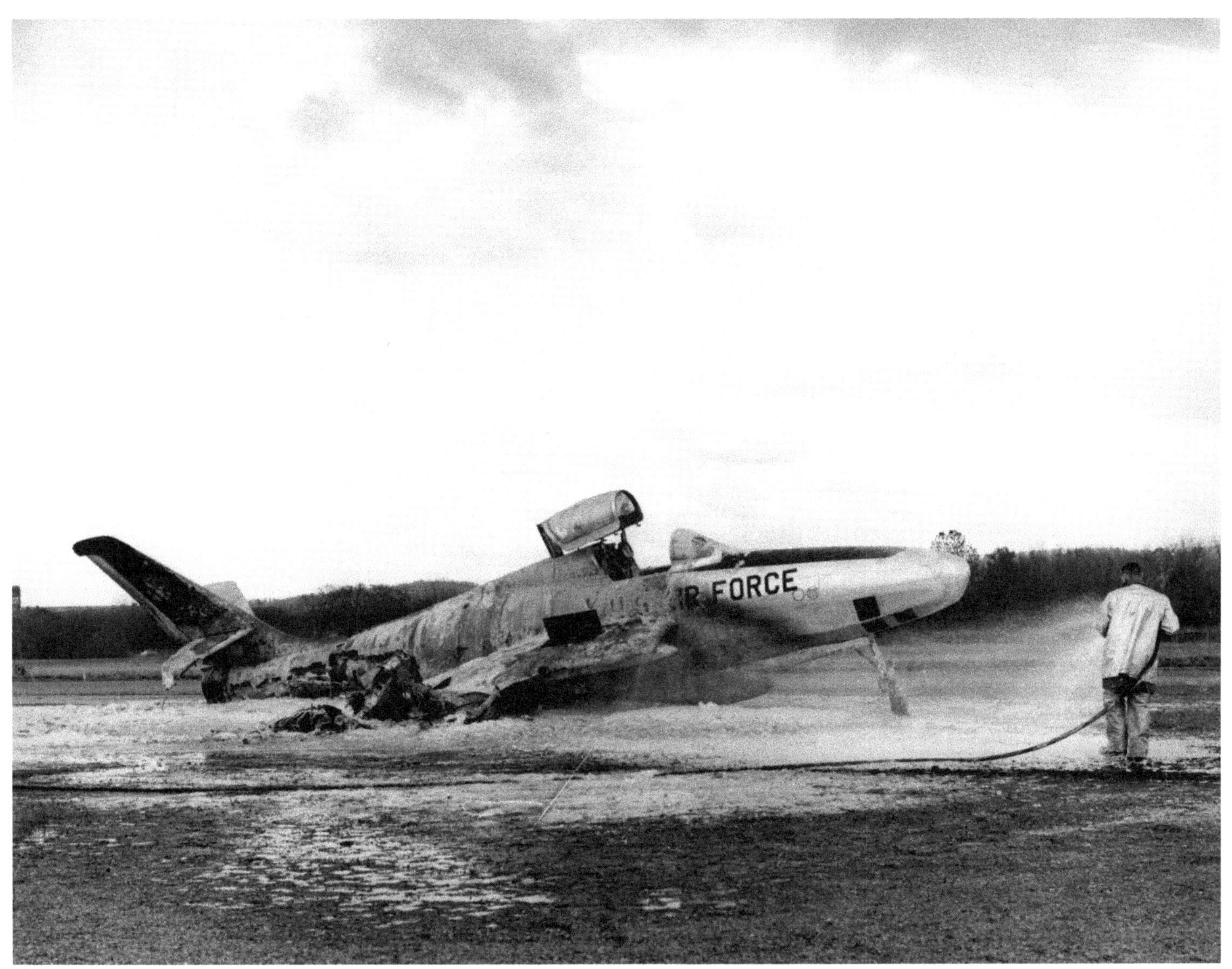

This RF-84F reconnaissance jet of the Alabama Air National Guard crashed into a runway barrier at Sumpter Smith Air National Guard Base. The air base is named for Walter Sumpter Smith, a veteran of both world wars who organized and served as commanding officer of the 106th Observation Squadron.

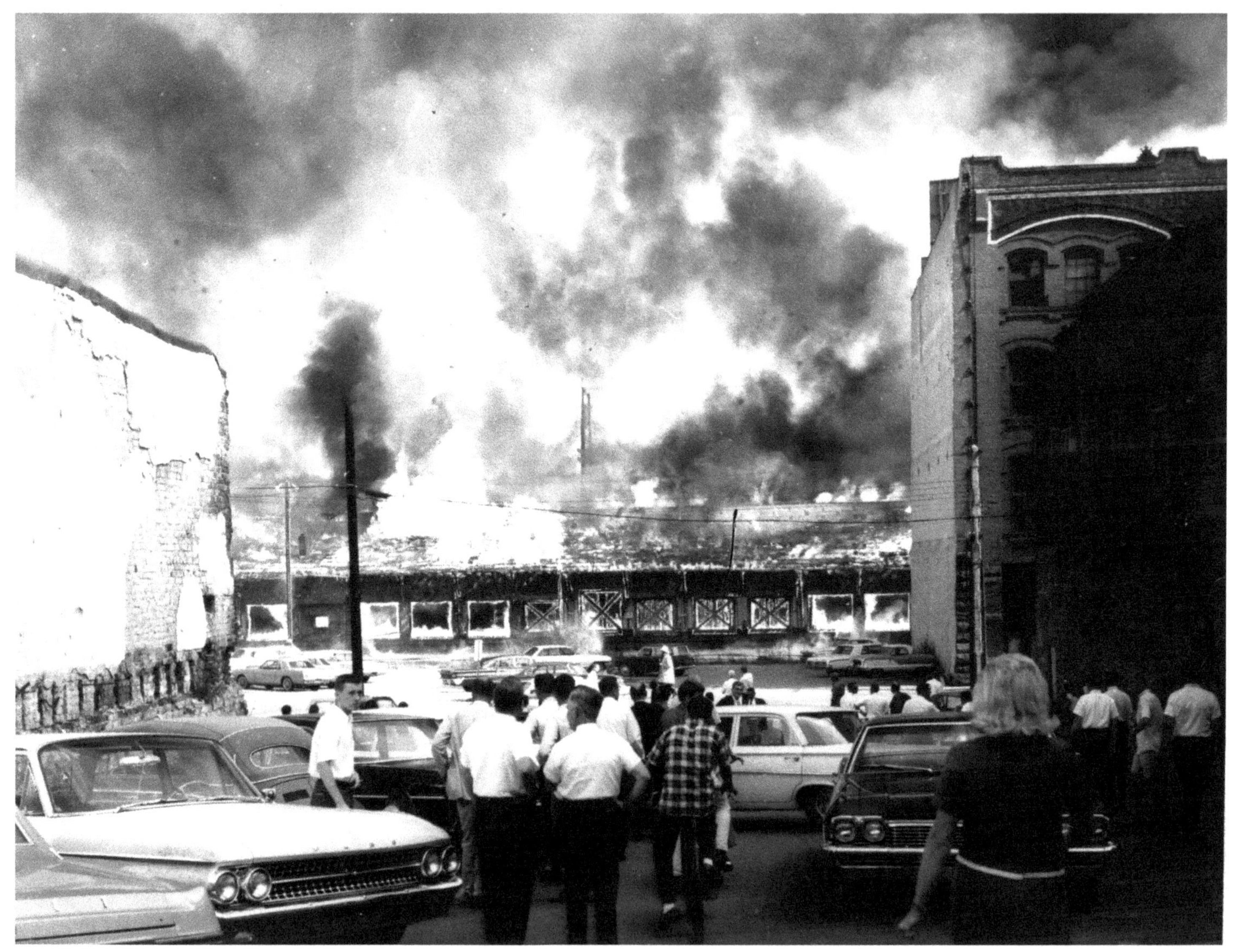

Stunned witnesses watch as fire destroys the L&N Warehouse on Morris Avenue. The blaze spread to two nearby empty buildings and leveled them before it could be contained.

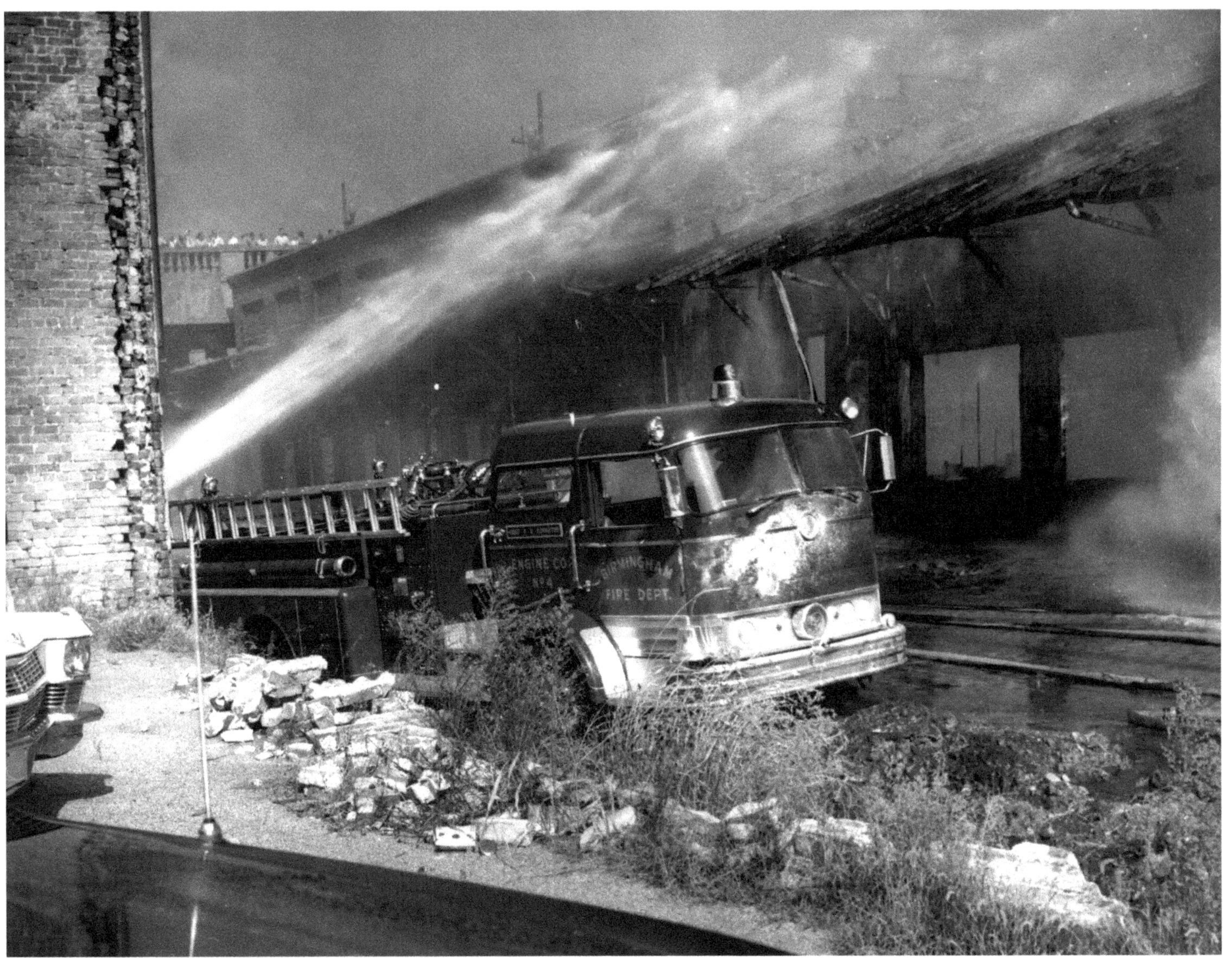

The Birmingham Fire Department rushes to put out the fire on Morris Avenue. Seventeen firemen were hospitalized after being overcome by heat and smoke, or sustaining other injuries. Fire department officials later declared that the fire at the L&N Warehouse was the work of an arsonist who had used gasoline to ignite the fire.

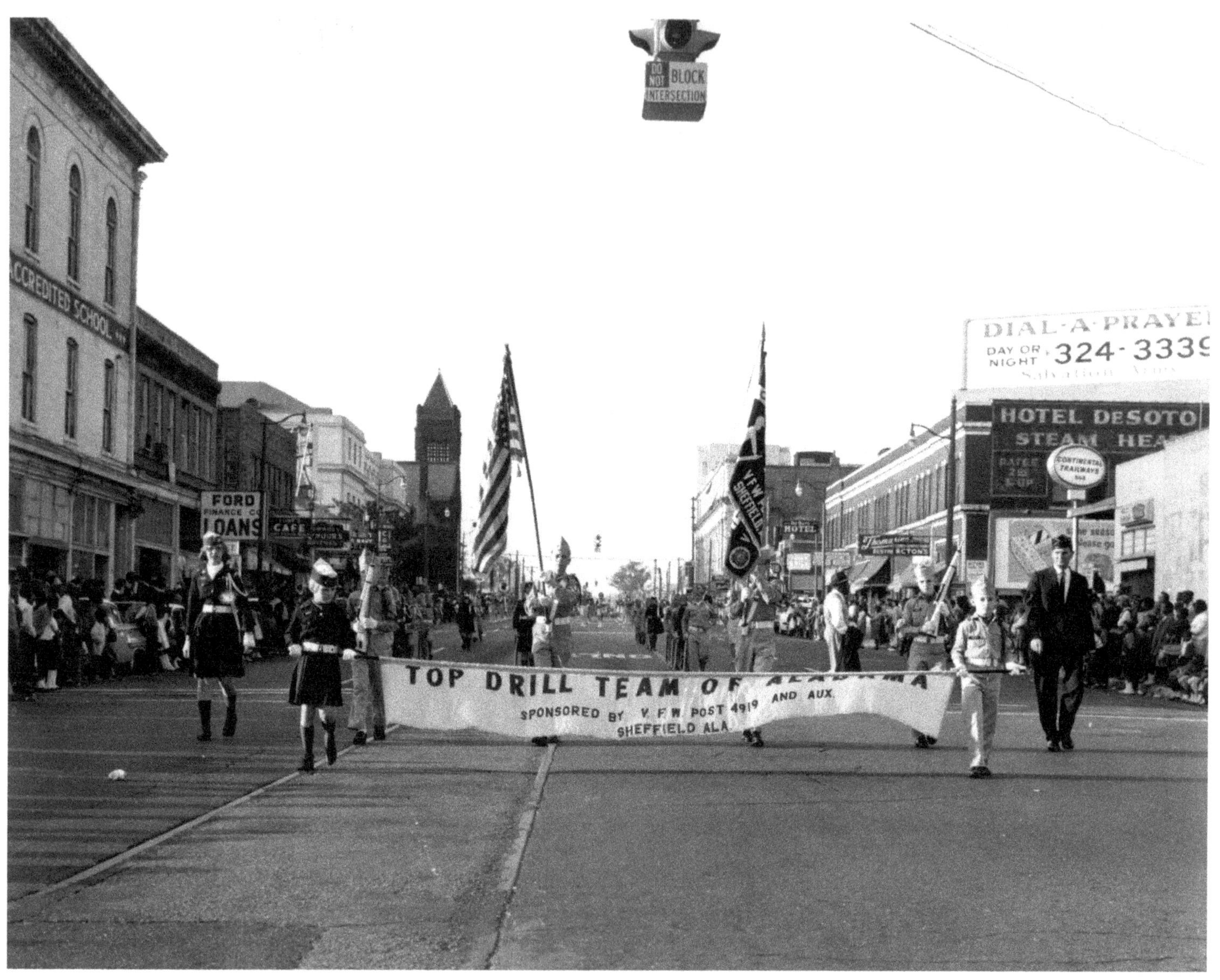

The top drill team of Alabama performs during the Veteran's Day Parade for 1964.

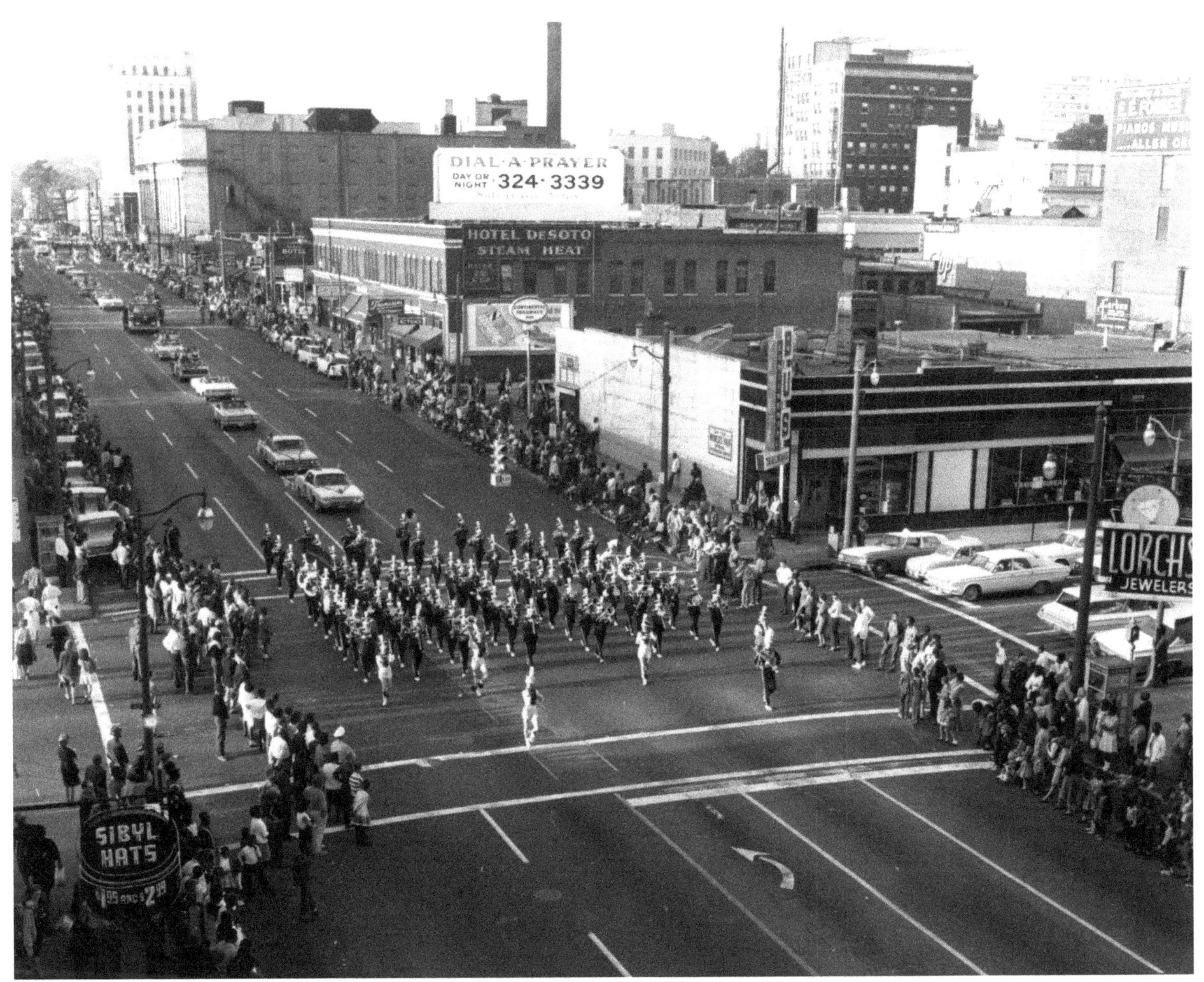

More bands performed during the Veteran's Day Parade in 1964 then ever before.

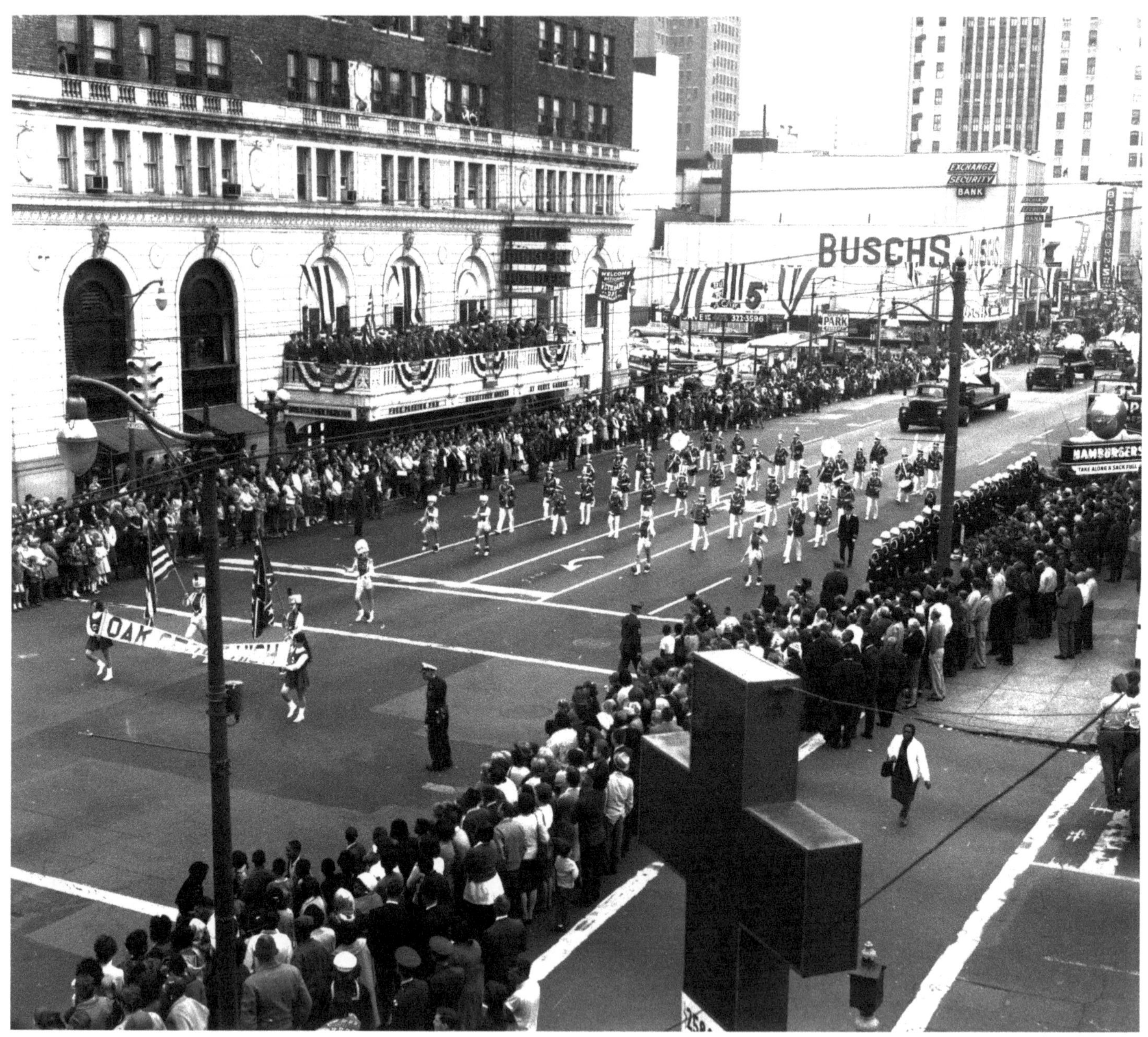

The Oak Grove High School band participates in the Veteran's Day Parade.

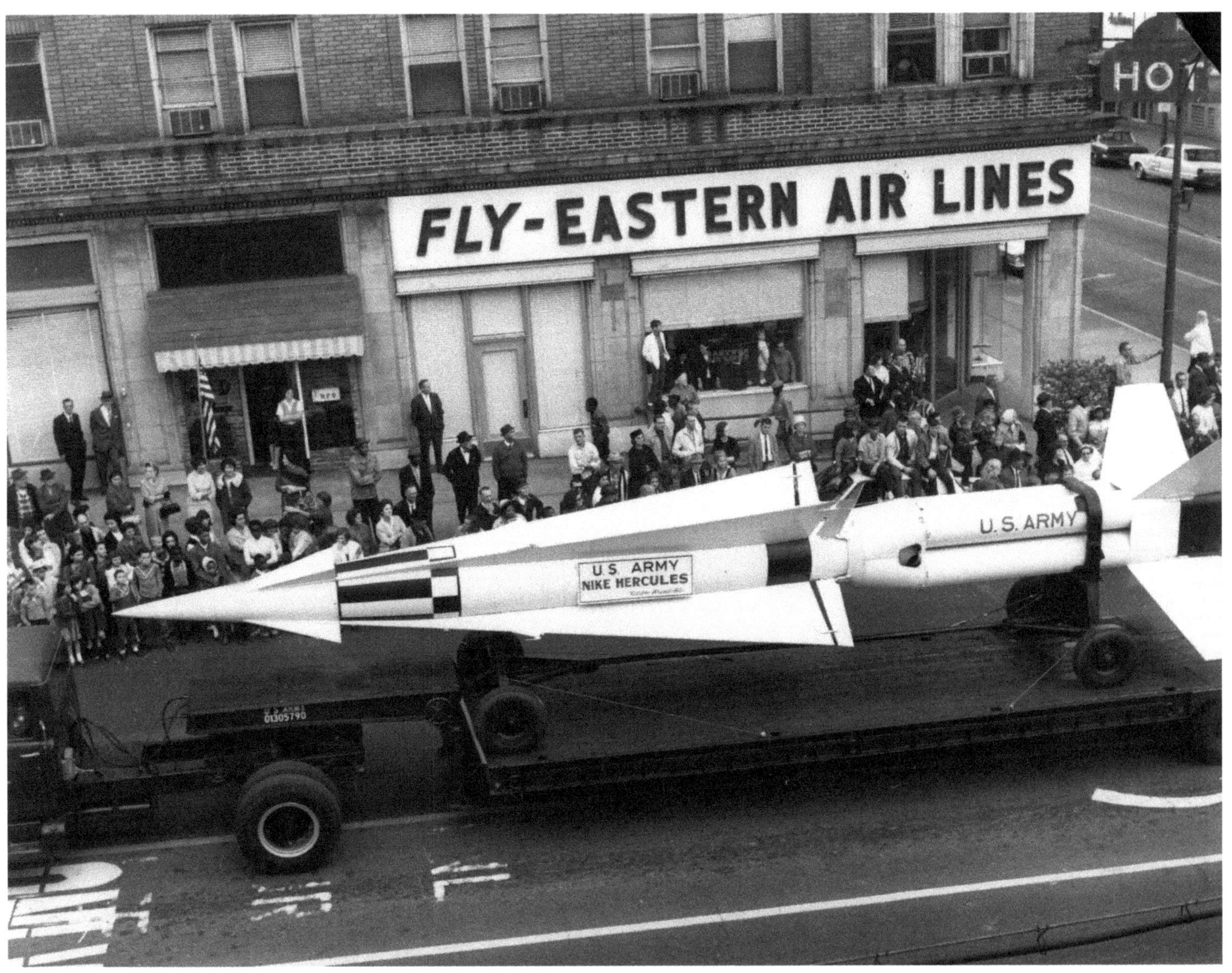

A Nike Hercules Missile was also part of the caravan in the Veteran's Day Parade. The surface-to-air missile was developed during the cold war in the fight against America's adversaries.

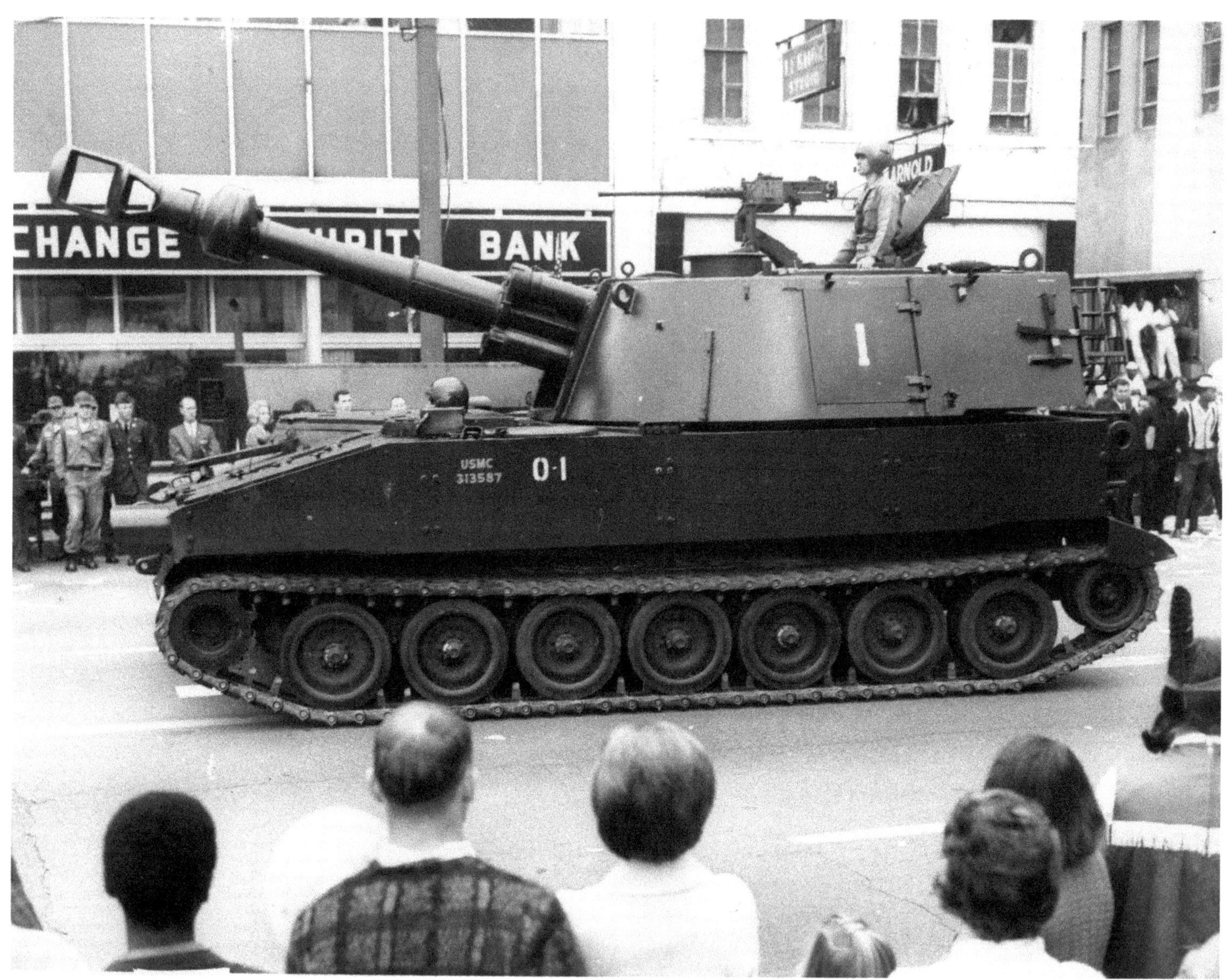

The Veteran's Day Parade also included this armed services tank.

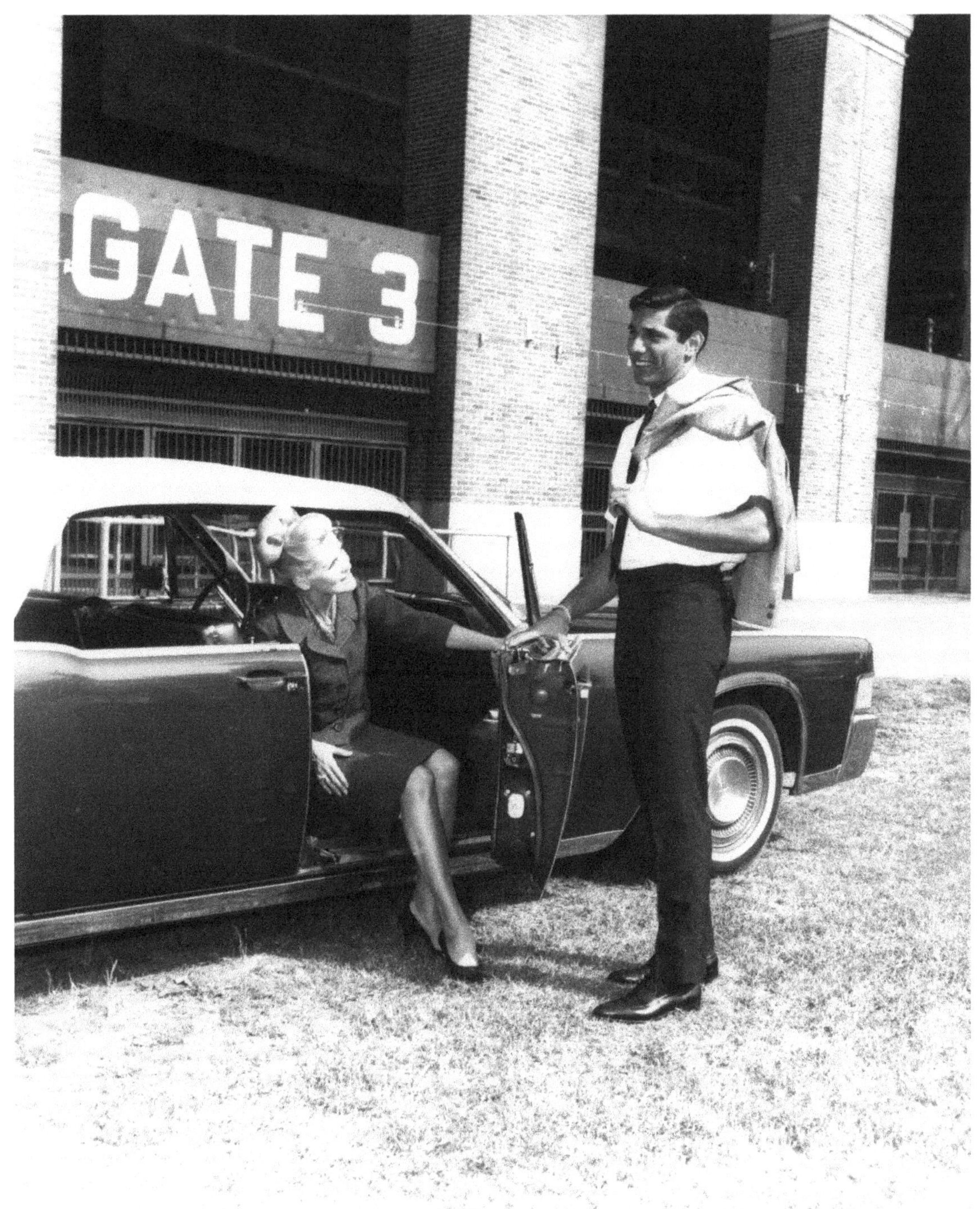

Former University of Alabama football player Joe Namath helps a friend out of the car at Legion Field. Namath was quarterback for the University of Alabama from 1962 until 1964 and went on to a stellar career in professional football with the New York Jets.

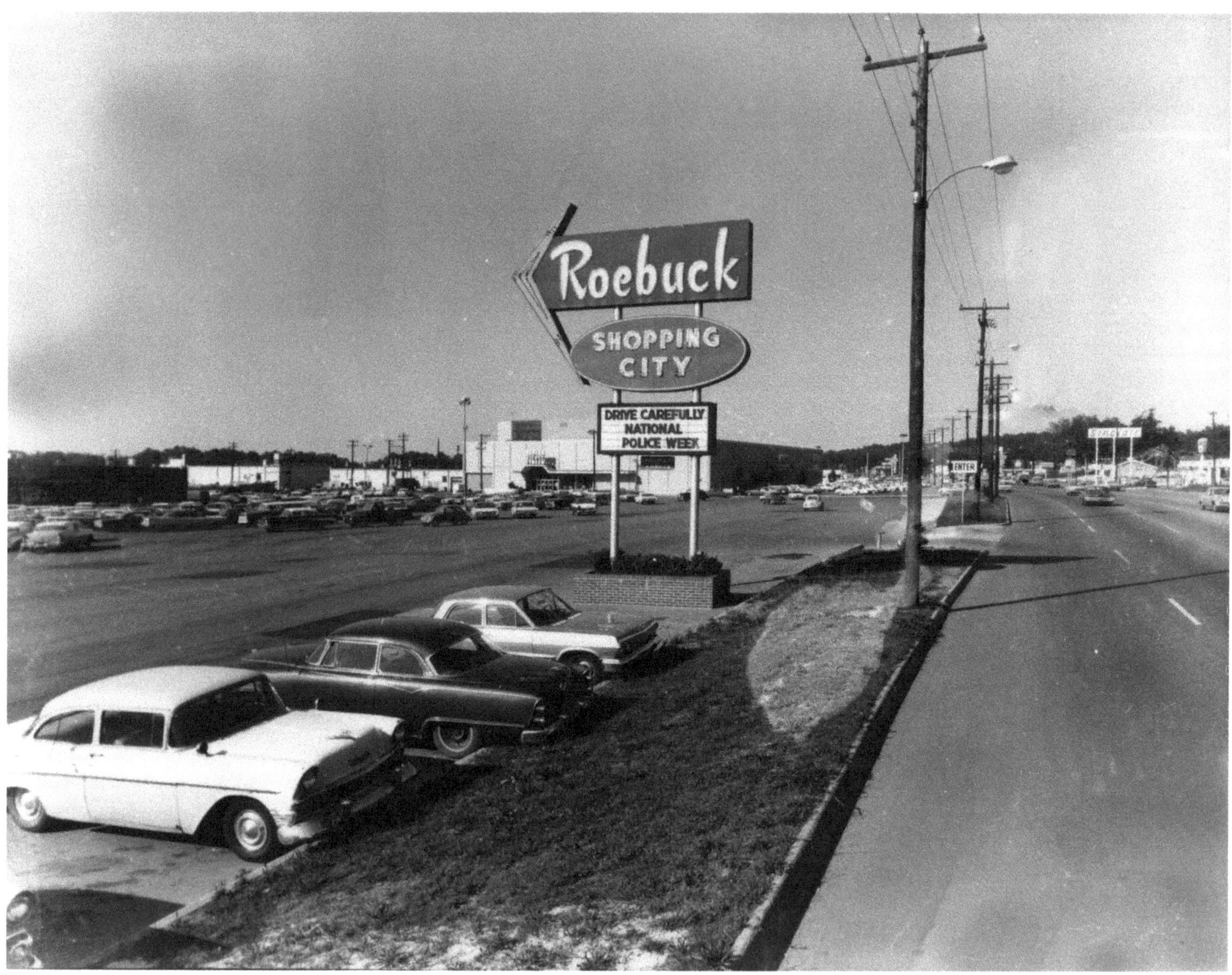

Roebuck Shopping City urges motorists to "drive carefully." Strip malls like this one were becoming a trend nationwide, favored by shoppers over stand-alone shops.

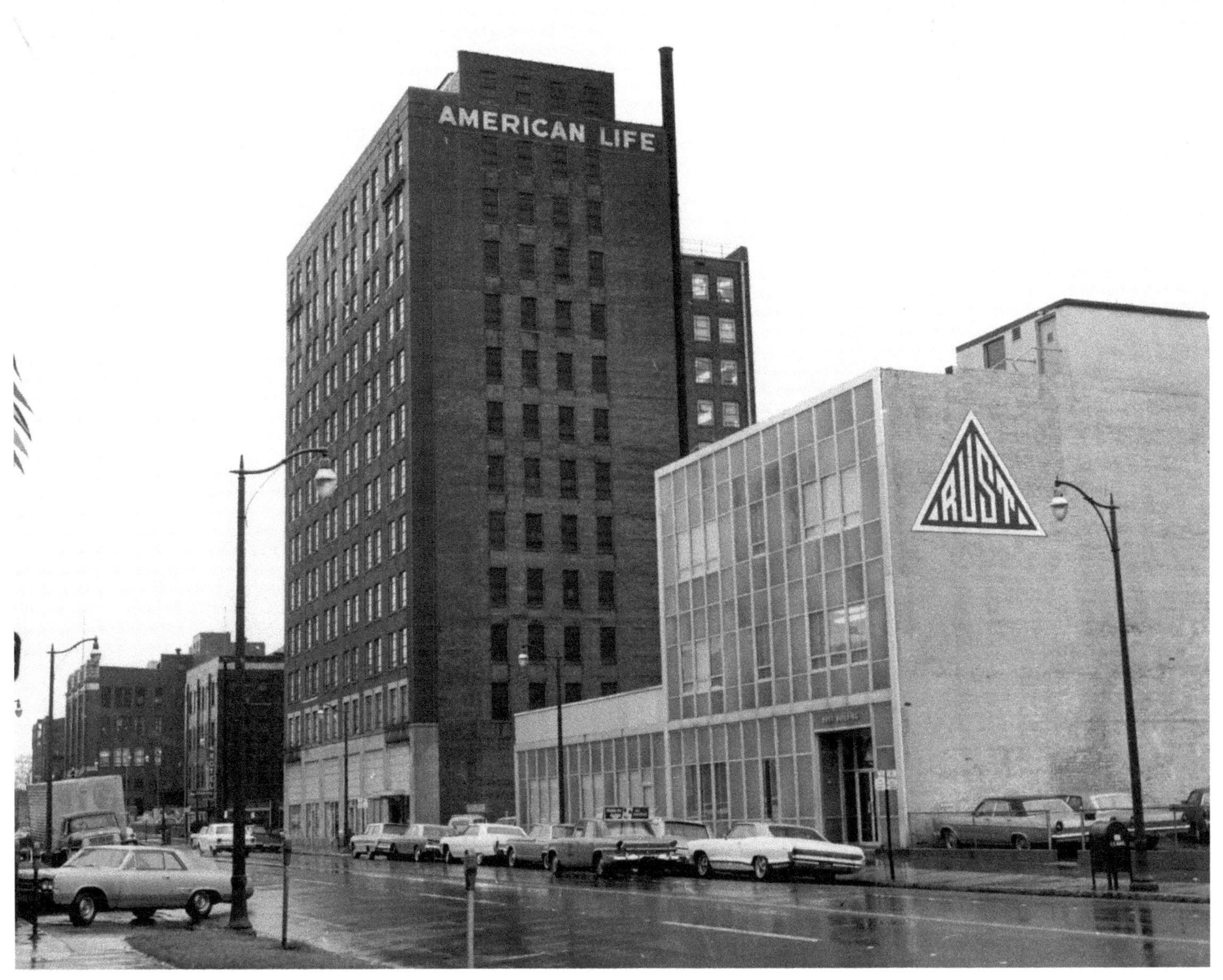

Located on 4th Avenue North, the American Life Building in the 1960s housed not only the American Life Insurance Company but also the United Mine Workers of America, an FBI office, Birmingham Baptist Association, and other tenants.

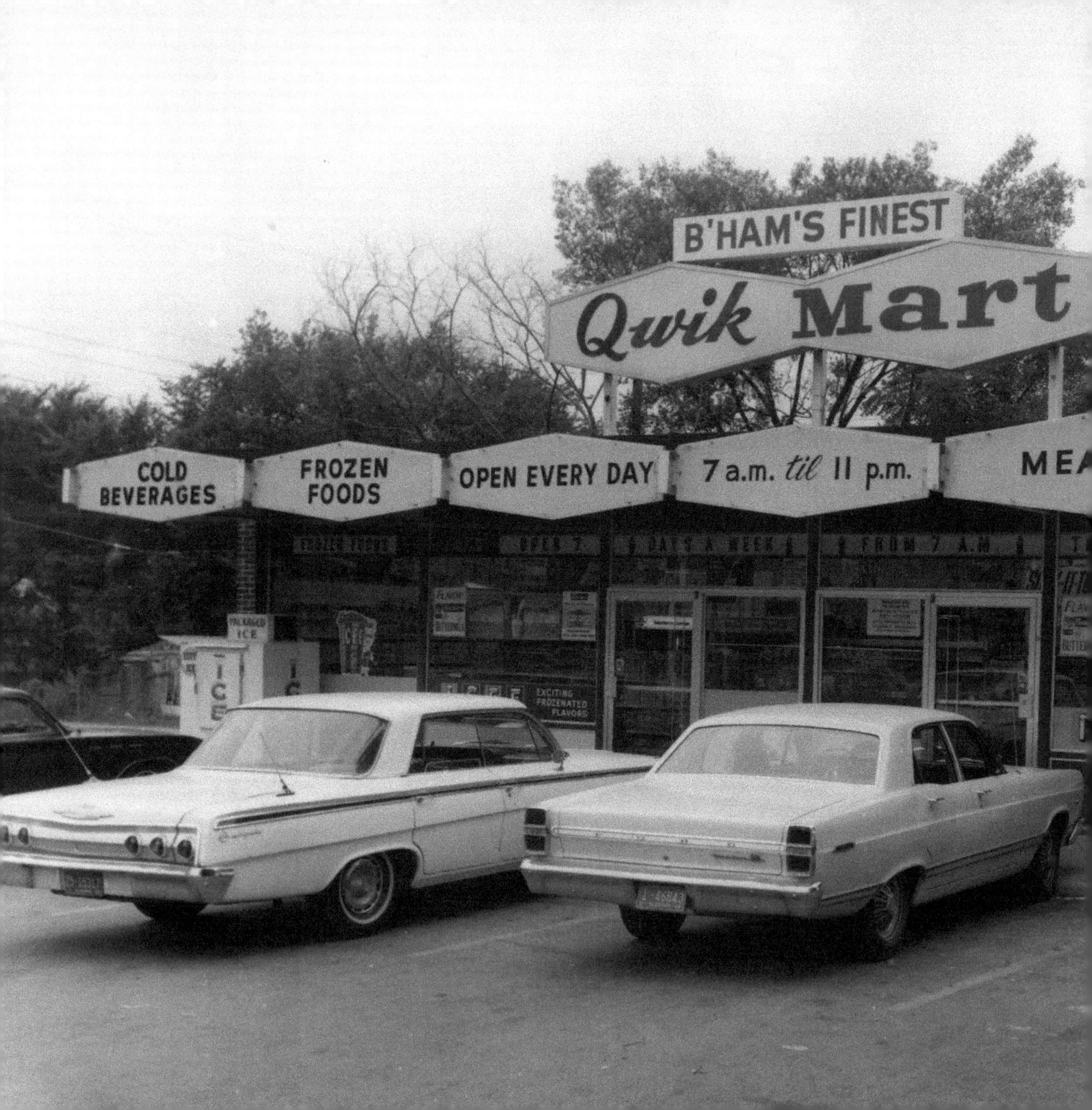

B'HAM'S FINEST
Qwik Mart
COLD BEVERAGES
FROZEN FOODS
OPEN EVERY DAY
7 a.m. til 11 p.m.
MEA
PACKAGED ICE
ICE
EXCITING FROZENATED FLAVORS

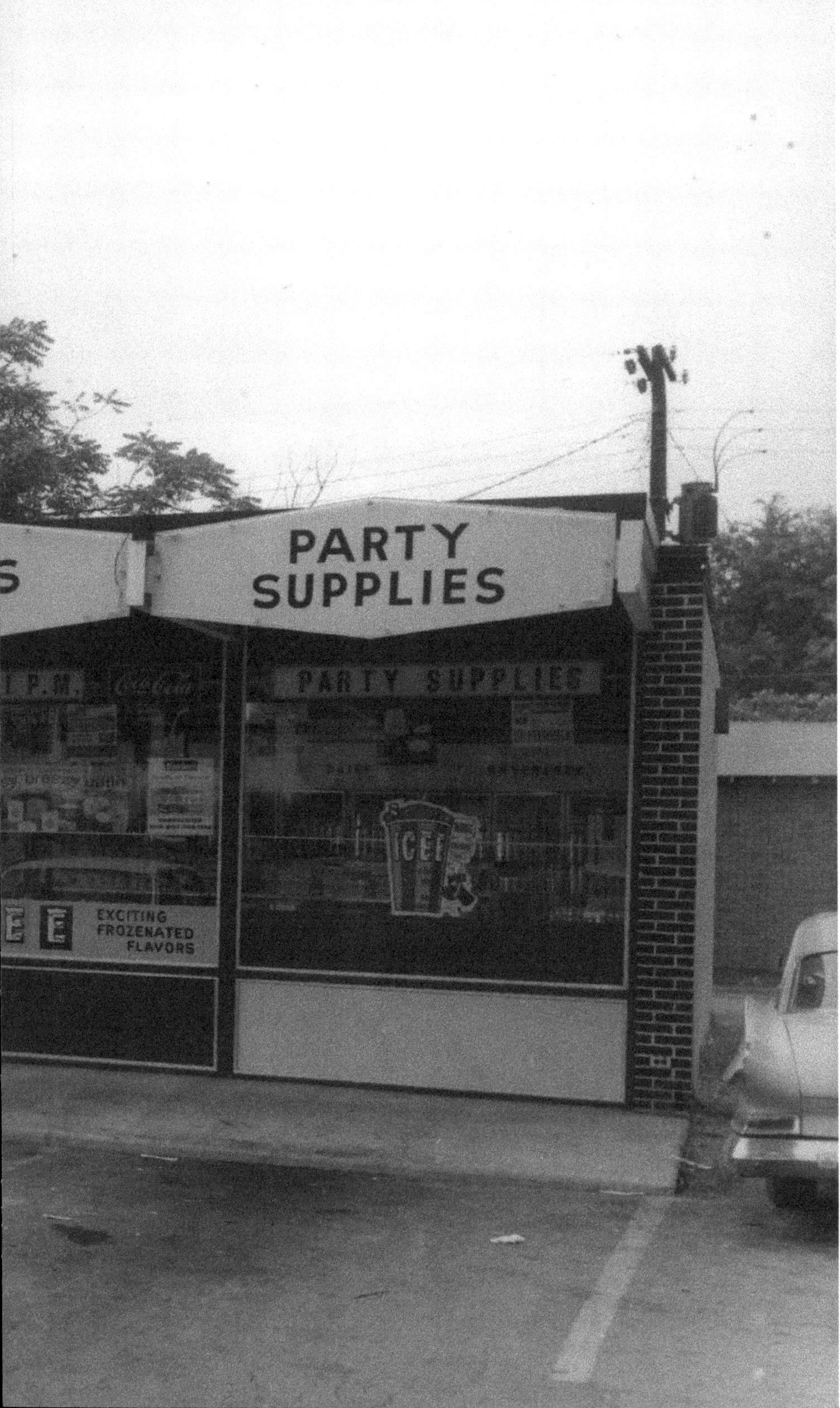

One of 26 Qwik Marts in Birmingham, this store advertises Barber's dairy products and Icees—a new kind of frozen slush treat invented in the early 1960s featuring "exciting frozenated flavors." With syrup and ice that remained mixed right down to the last slurp, Icees became widely popular.

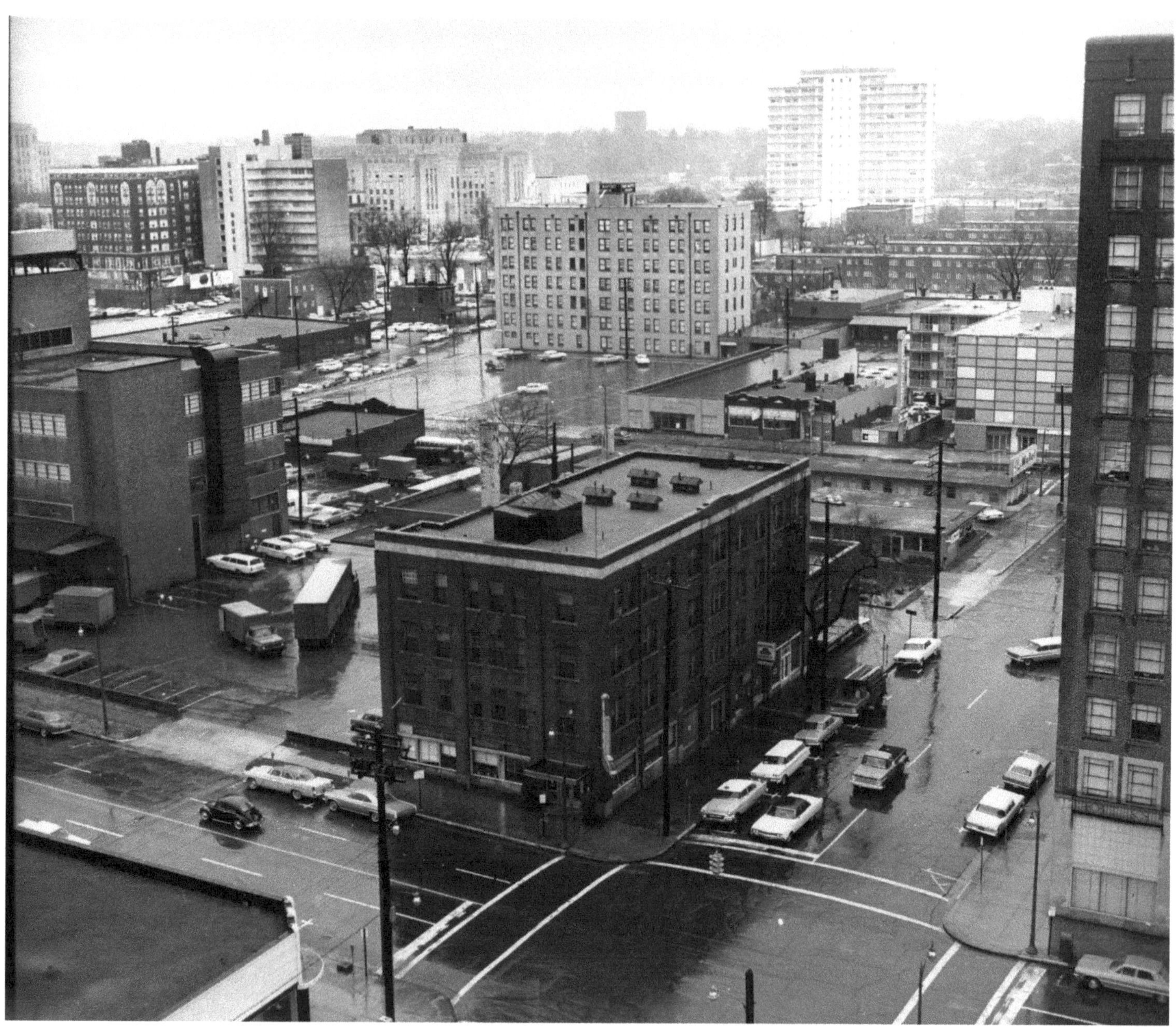

Cars and trucks drive past the American Life Building on a rain-soaked day.

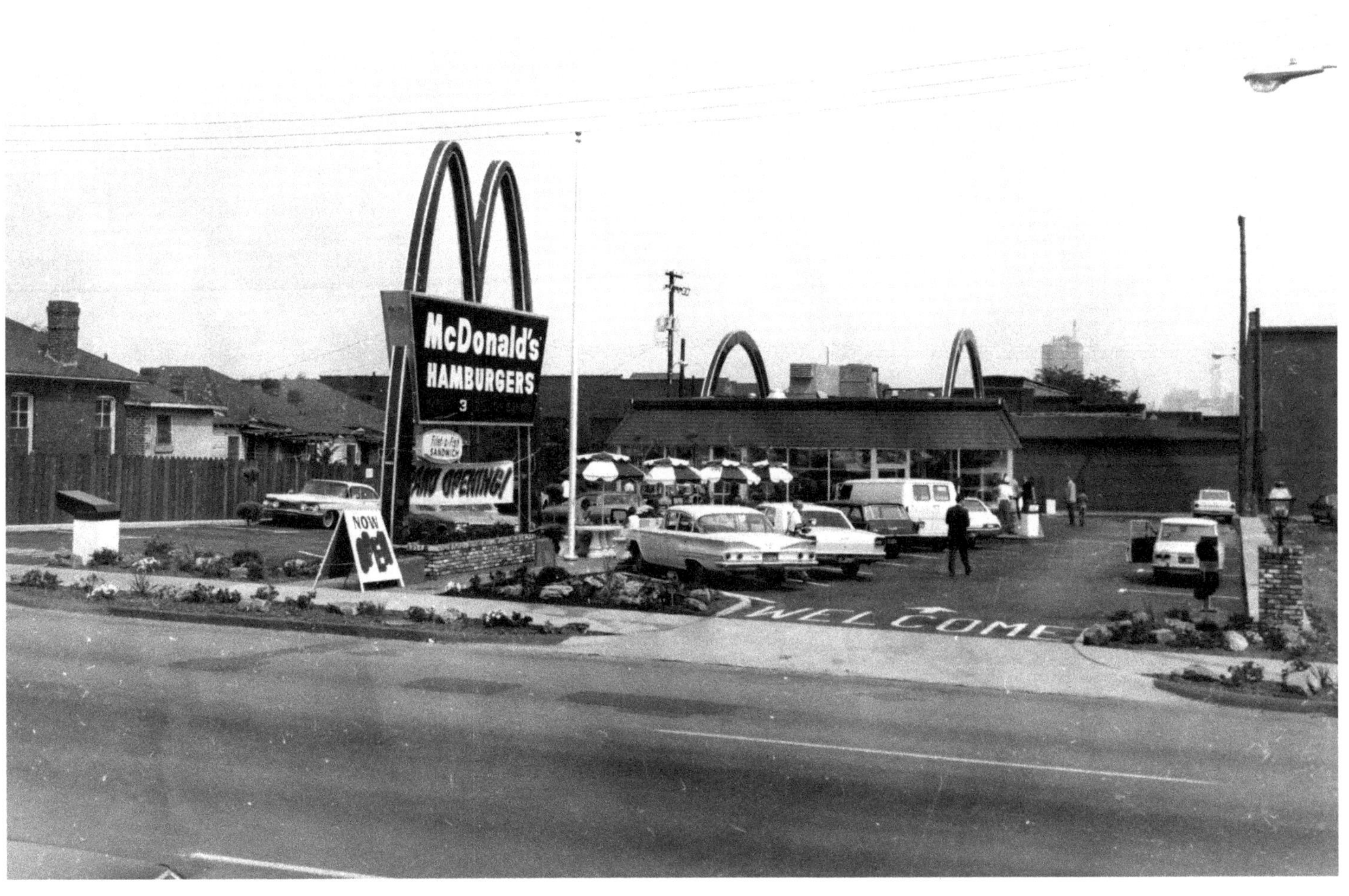

A McDonald's hamburgers restaurant celebrates its grand opening on 6th Avenue South near 18th Street. McDonald's had arrived in Birmingham six years before this photo was taken.

Located on 27th Street, the Claridge Manor had offered apartments to Birmingham residents since the mid-1920s.

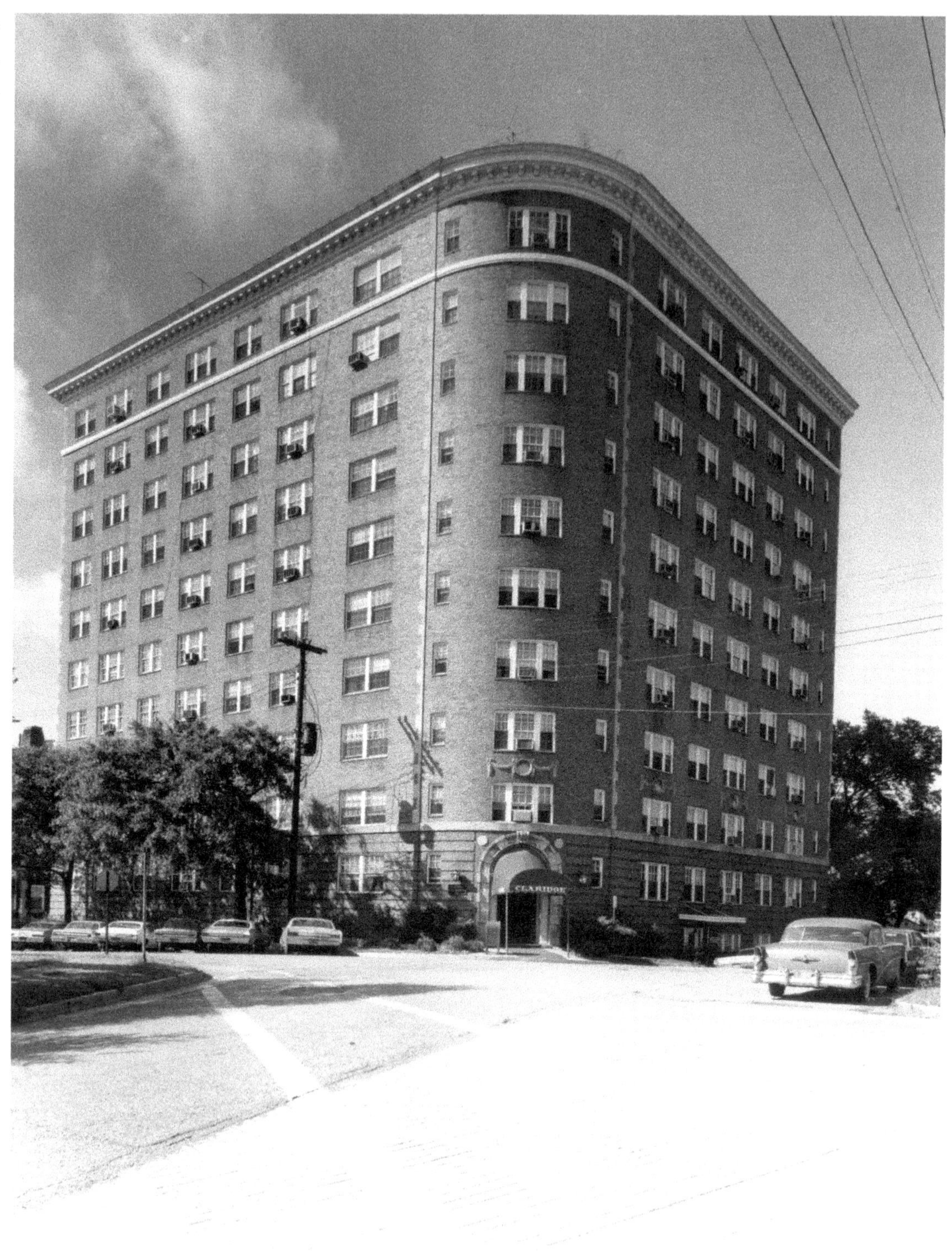

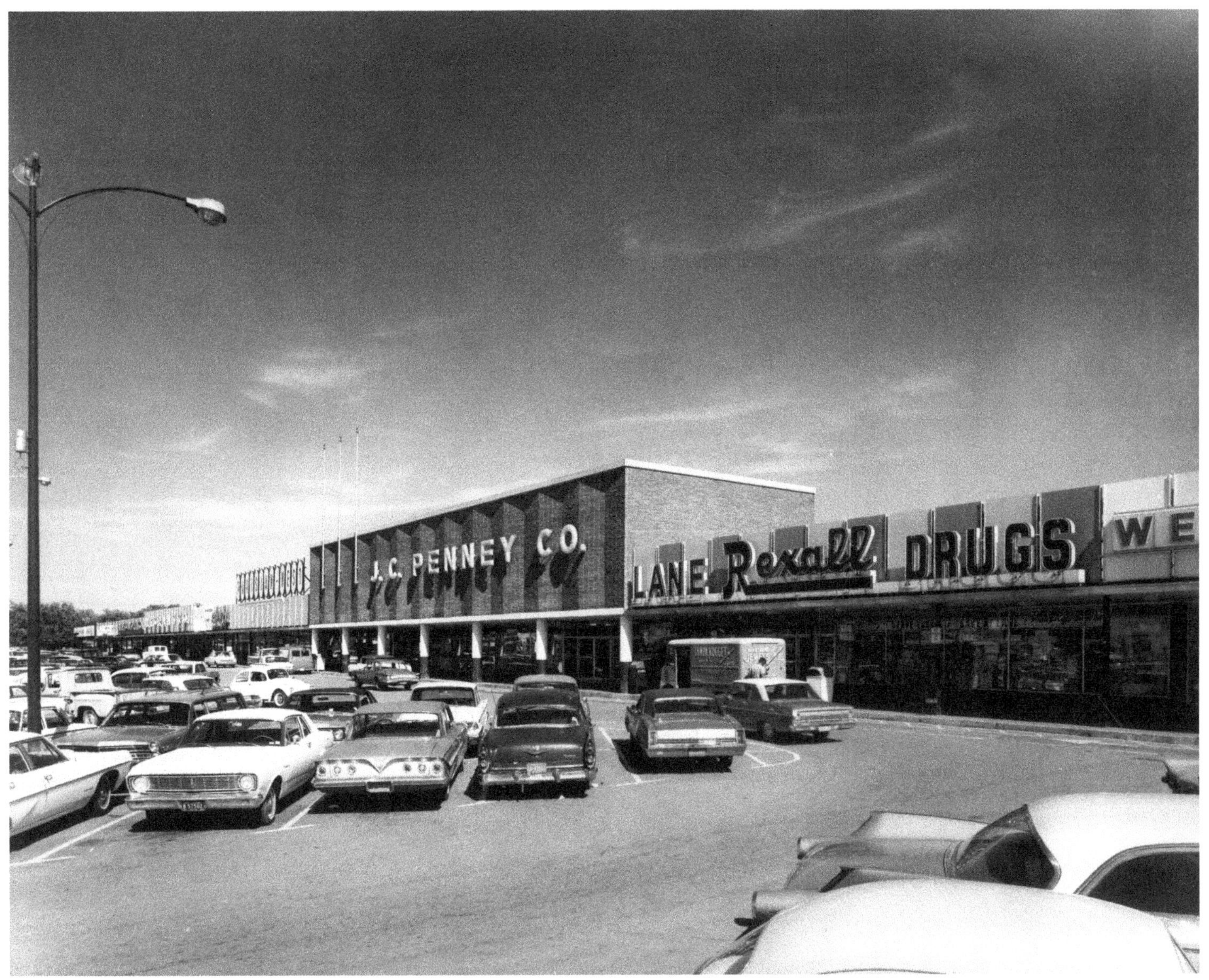

From the late-1950s onward, Five Points West Shopping City offered convenient shopping options for the residents of Ensley.

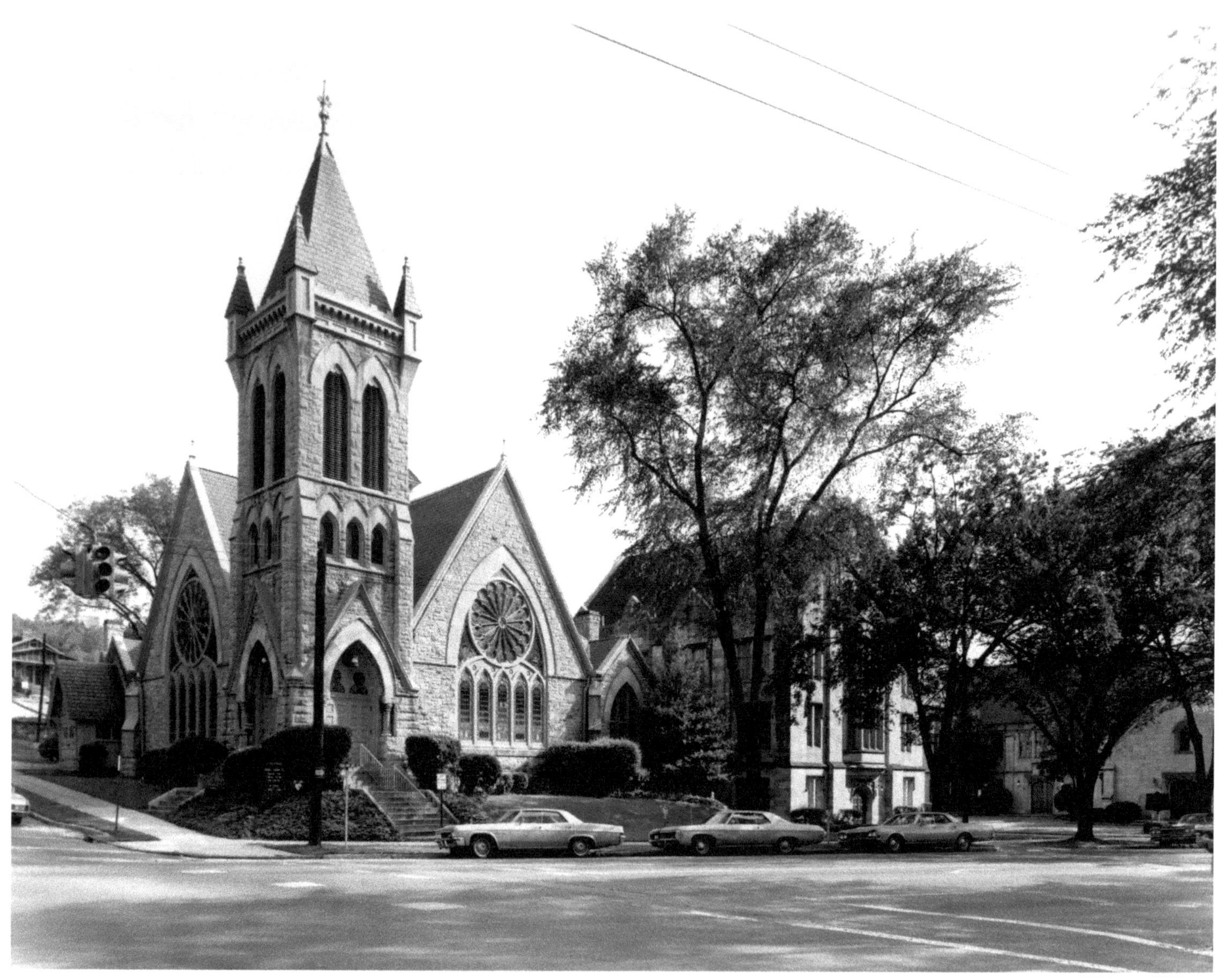

South Highlands Presbyterian Church stands on Highland Avenue. The church has served the historic Southside since its creation in 1888. One of its earliest efforts was to open a Sunday school for convicts at Pratt Mines Prison No. 2, where the state placed its convicts to mine coal.

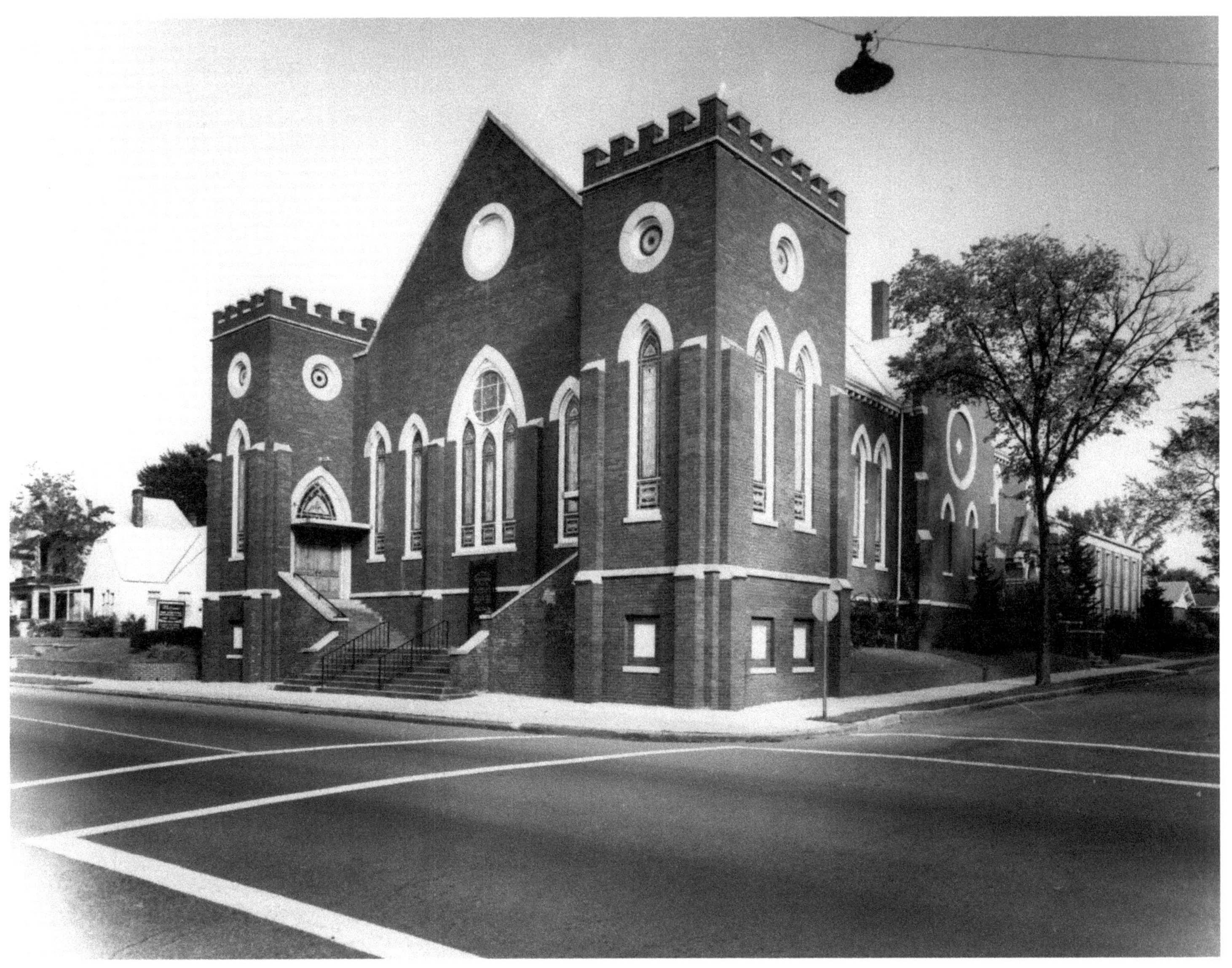

Ann Waldron, writer of mysteries and children's books and a native Alabamian, once attended Vine Street Presbyterian Church, located at 925 Cotton Avenue.

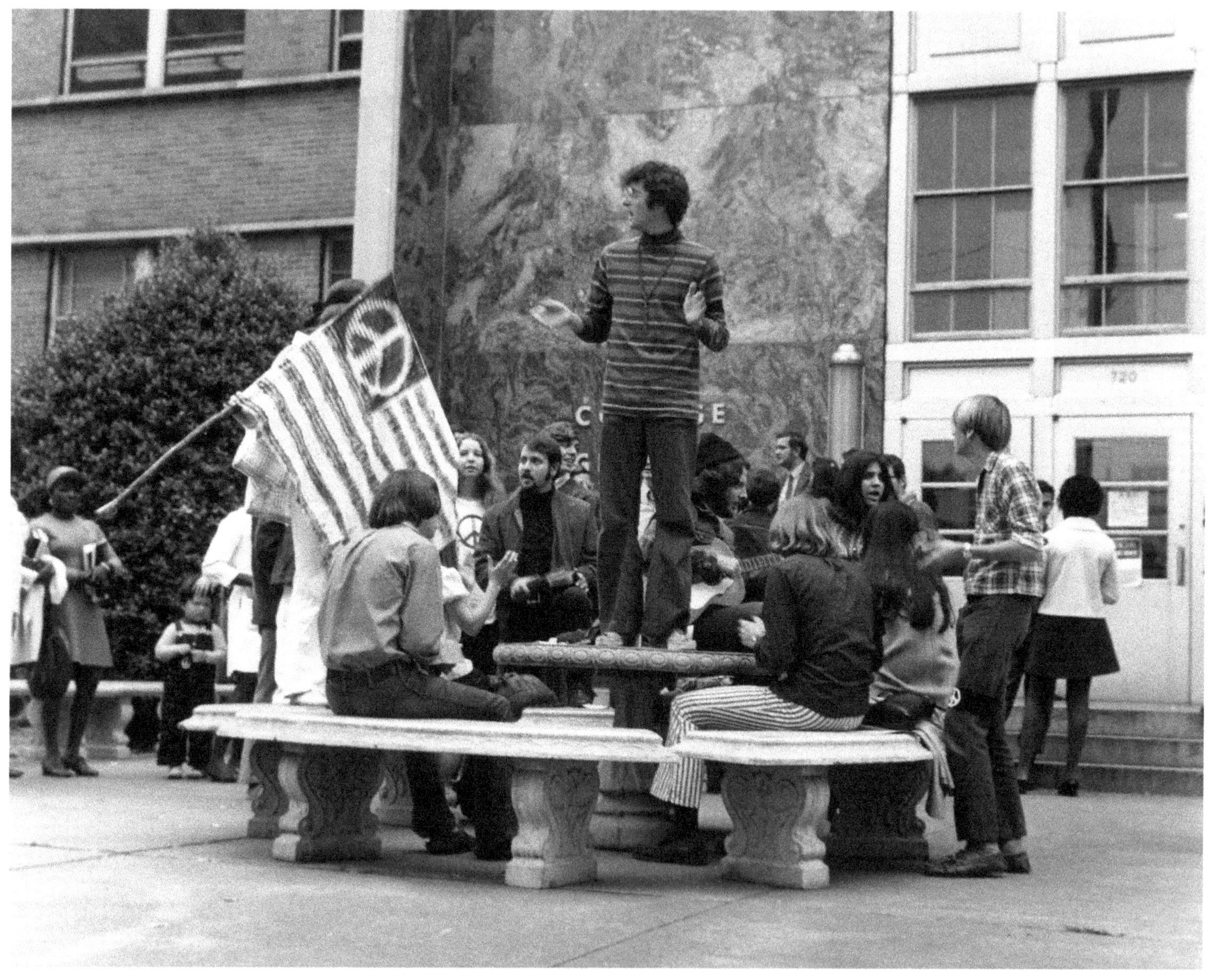

University of Alabama at Birmingham students gather to protest the Vietnam War after the violent events at Kent State. Four students were killed and nine were wounded by national guardsmen after riots broke out that included throwing bottles at police and burning the campus R.O.T.C. building.

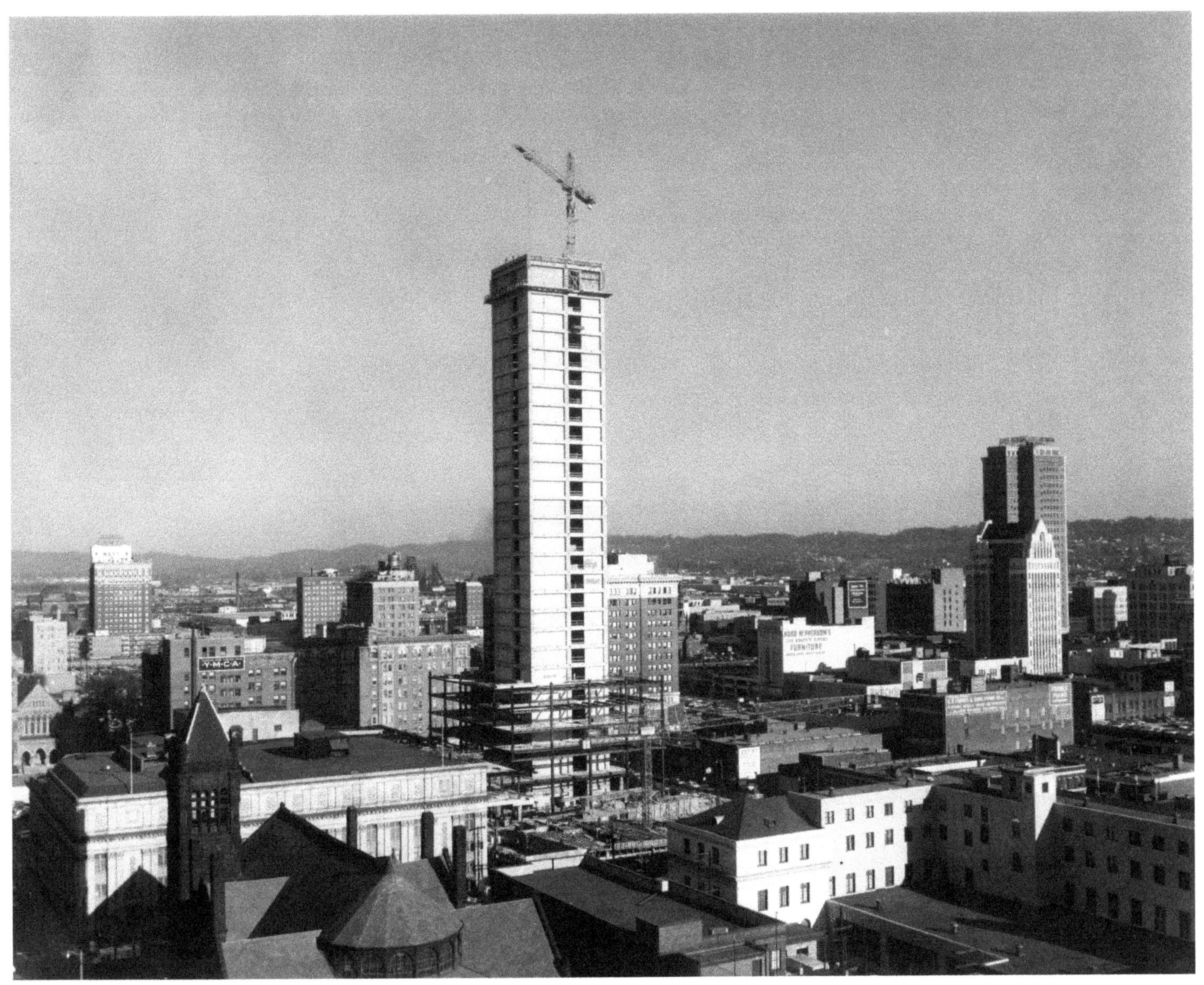

The construction of the First National Bank–Southern Natural Gas skyscraper is under way. The $19 million building would feature 2,700 windows of reflective insulating glass and 5,508 panes of glass along with a cafeteria with seating for 400 persons.

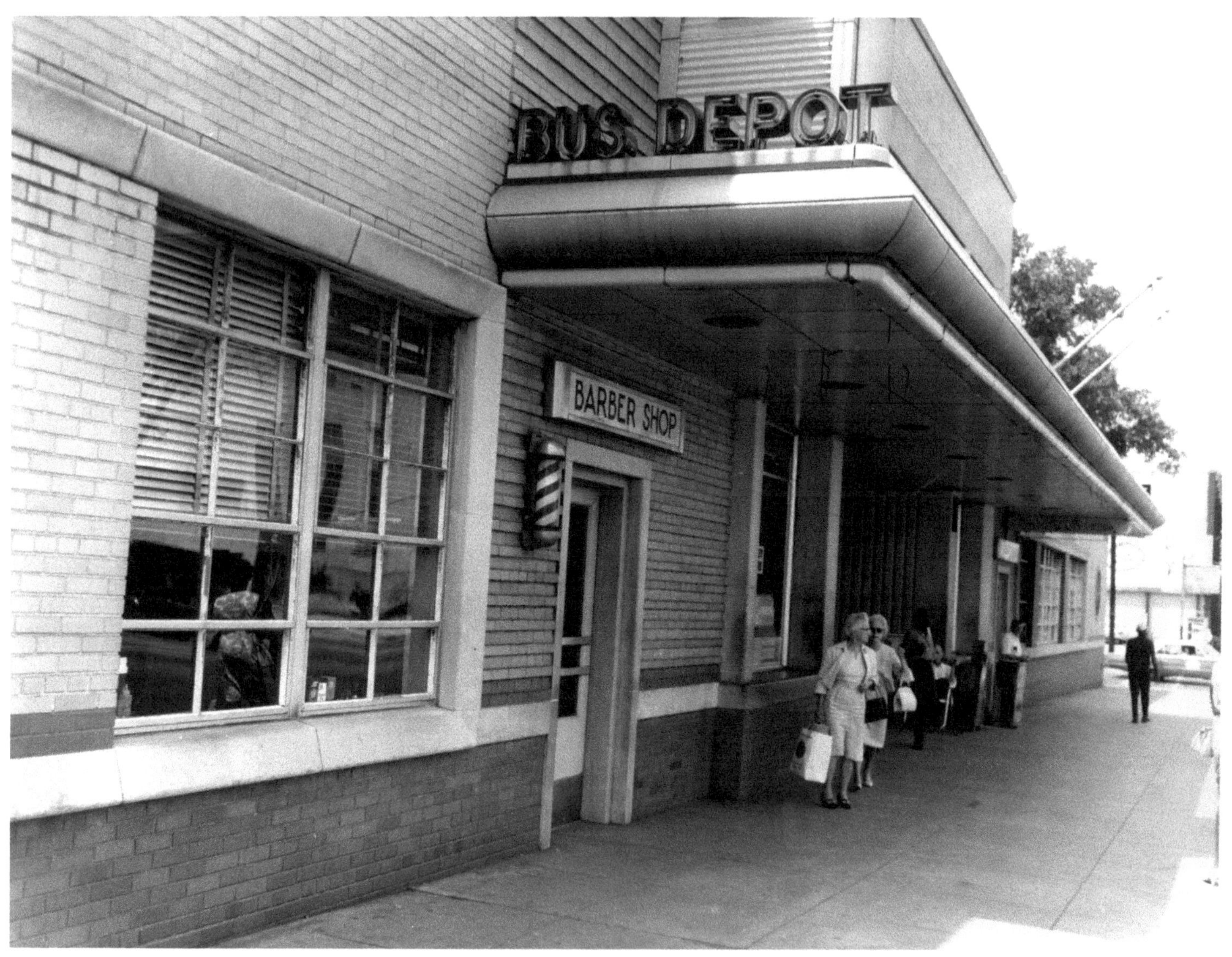

The Greyhound Bus Lines station also housed a barbershop for those needing a trim before setting out on their journey.

Operation New Birmingham

(1970–1979)

Although the 1960s had brought radical change to Birmingham, the subsequent rise of suburbia and suburban communities' refusal of annexation created a decline in the city's population and commerce that continued into the 1970s. Streets once flooded with shoppers were now desolate and falling into disrepair. In the 1970s, shops like Loveman's and Pizitz and movie theaters were closed or remodeled to serve the needs of a new demographic. Vacant and crumbling buildings were a common site. It seemed Birmingham and cities across the nation were dying.

To address the problem, city leaders created Operation New Birmingham, a program dedicated to changing the city's image. Construction of the Birmingham-Jefferson Civic Center Complex, the expansion of the Municipal Airport, the building of Red Mountain expressway, and the creation of the University of Alabama at Birmingham were all progressive changes aimed at keeping the city alive.

Changes in industry had a strong impact on the city during the 1970s. After the 1950 discovery of high-grade iron ore in Venezuela, the demand for Birmingham iron dropped. The decline of the iron industry underscored the need for a true diversification in Birmingham's economy. Though the Medical Center had always been a key component of the city, the establishment of UAB, Spain Rehabilitation Center, the Lister Hill Medical Library, and cancer research programs contributed to diversification, fostering a balance between the "heavy steel based blue-collar working force" and medical research, education professions, and many other "white-collar" occupations.

In 1979, Richard Arrington, Jr., became the first African-American mayor of Birmingham, only seventeen years after blacks protested for the right to sit at a lunch counter with whites. Amid accusations of corruption, Arrington would go on to win a fourth term as mayor, raking in two-thirds of the vote in a city then more than 60 percent African-American.

The history of Birmingham is complex and sometimes eccentric. Although it seems to be true of Birmingham that "hard times come here first and stay longest," the city and her people have found and will continue to find ways to pull together.

Dr. Joseph F. Volker, president of the University of Alabama at Birmingham (at left); Albert P. Brewer, governor of Alabama (center); and Dr. George W. Campbell, dean of the College of General Studies (right) participate in ground-breaking ceremonies for classroom and office buildings in January 1970.

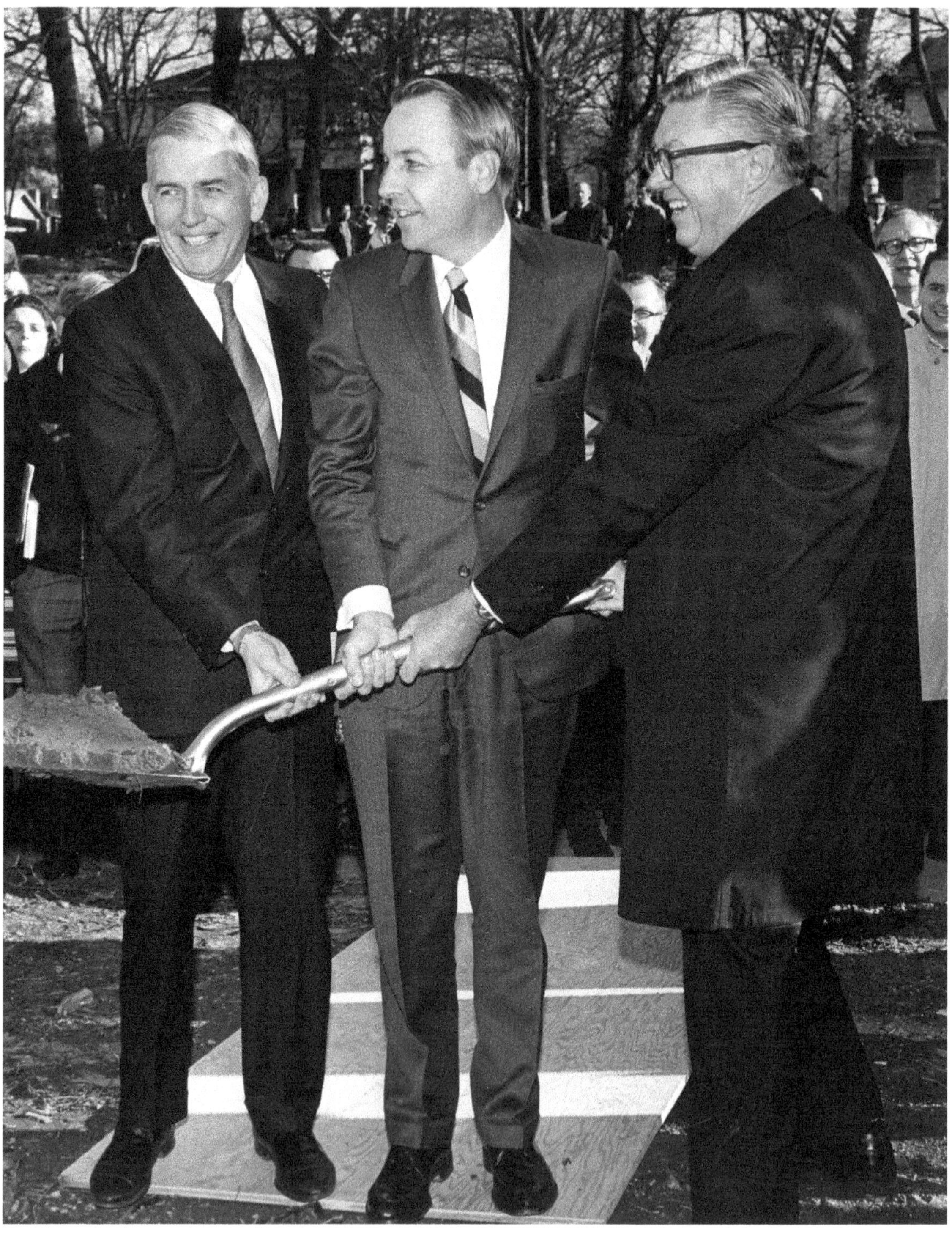

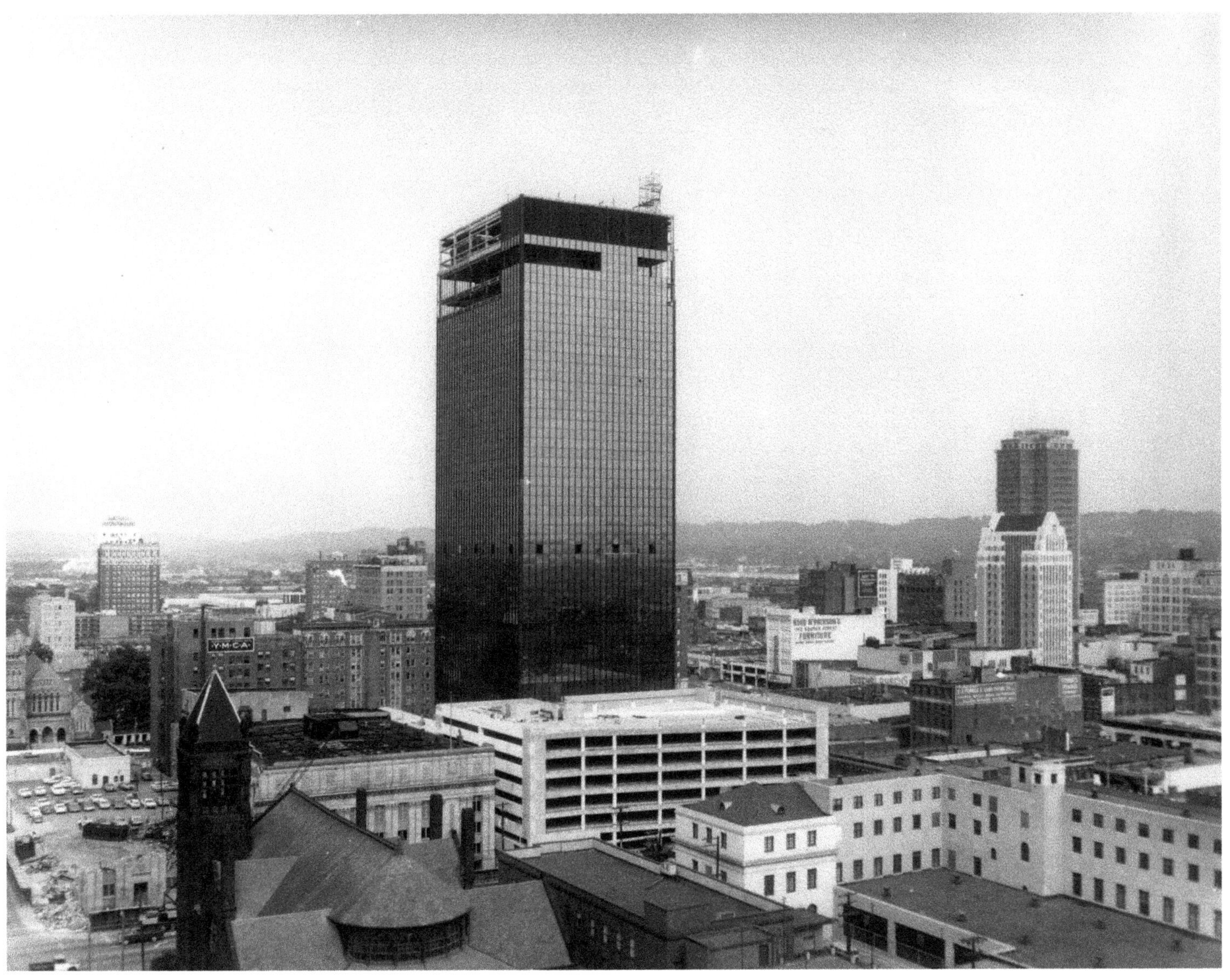

The 30-story office tower known as the First National–Southern Natural Building nears completion at the northwest corner of 5th Avenue North, between 19th and 20th streets. The building included a 390-car parking garage.

After an assassination attempt during a presidential campaign stop in Maryland in 1972 left him crippled, Governor George Wallace entered therapy at Spain Rehabilitation at the University of Alabama at Birmingham. The ability of a local facility to care for the governor points to the growth of the medical field in the Birmingham area.

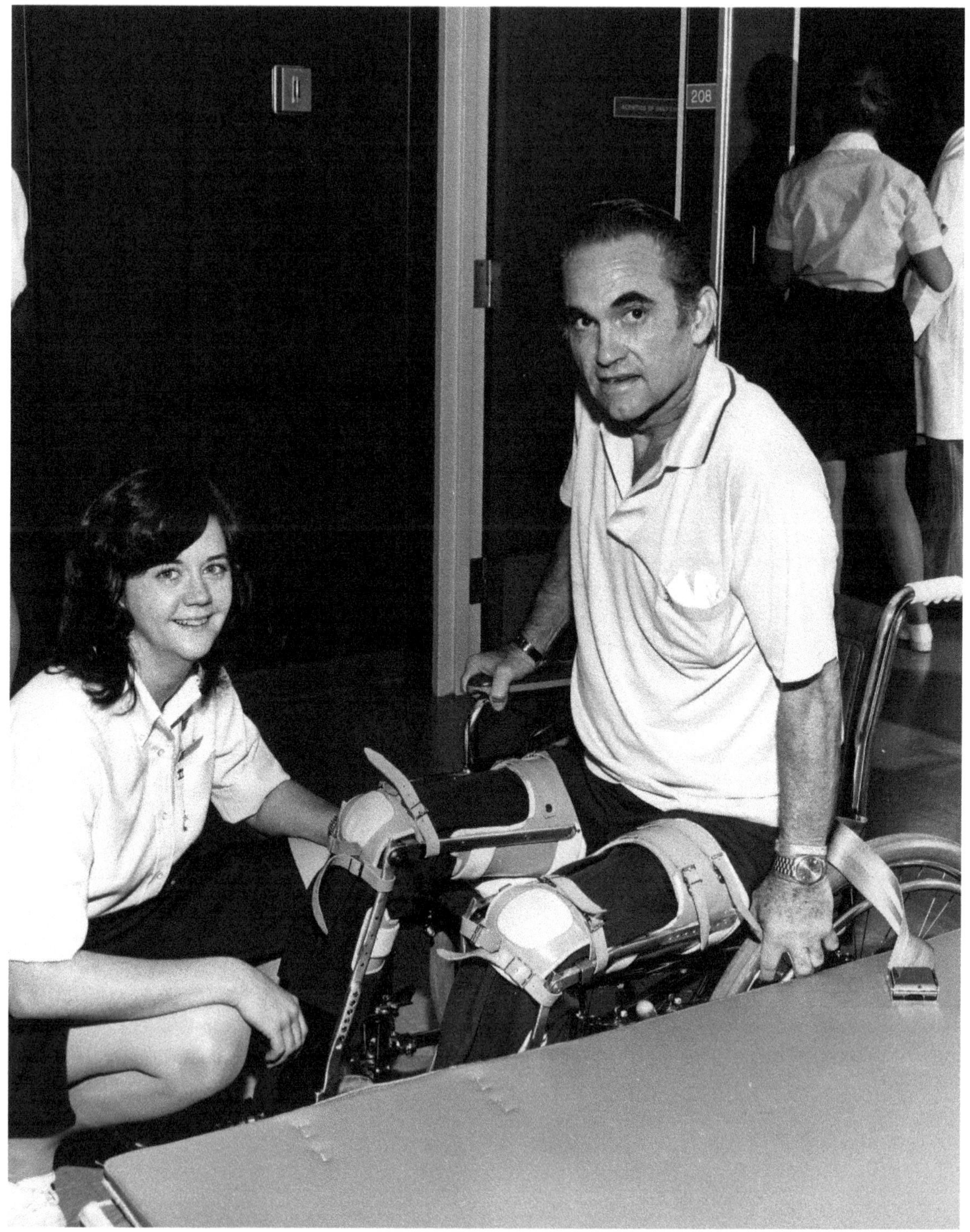

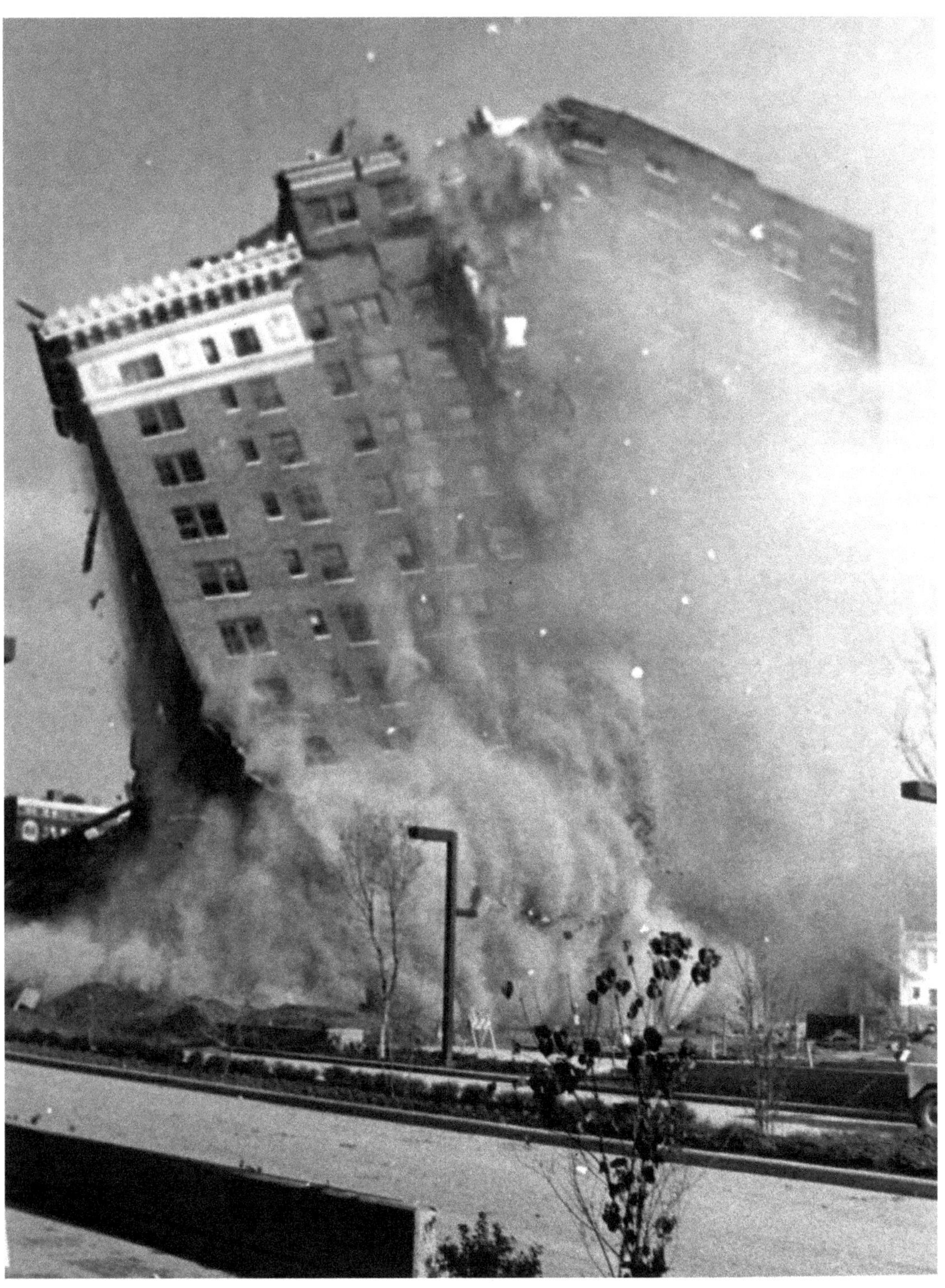

Great Southern Investment Corporation closed the Tutwiler Hotel in 1972 after promising to refurbish the venerable structure. The historic hotel once visited by prominent members of society was imploded in 1974, ending the Tutwiler's reign as Birmingham's premier hotel from the era of the grand hotels. Disregard for the nation's built history would give rise during the 1960s and 1970s to historic preservation groups devoted to saving historic structures from the wrecking ball.

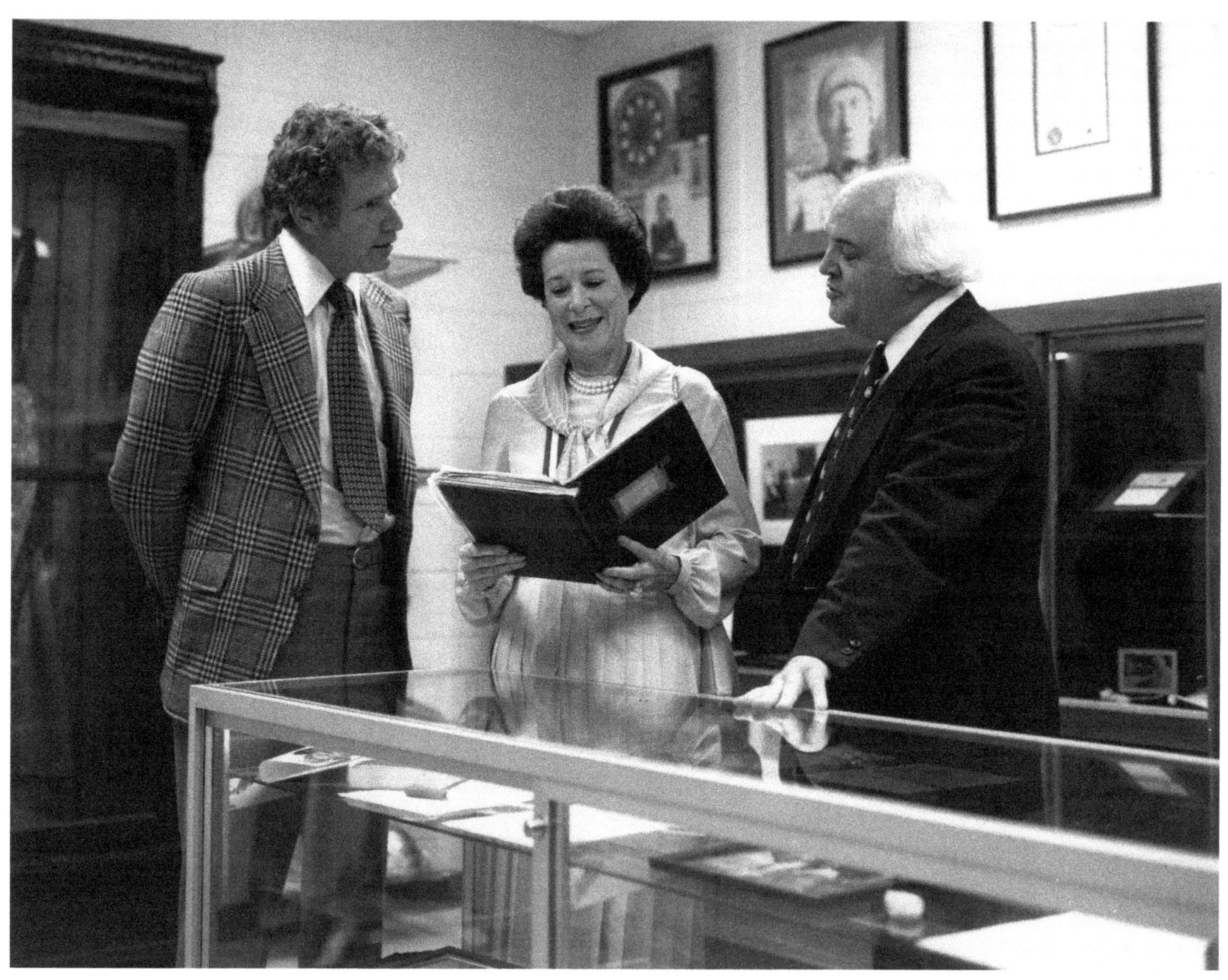

Actress Kitty Carlisle Hart (at center) and TV's *MASH* actor and Ramsay High School alumnus Wayne Rogers (left) view artifacts in the Town and Gown Theatre. Founded in 1950, the theater was owned and operated by James F. Hatcher (right) who also ran Summerfest and the Miss Alabama Pageant.

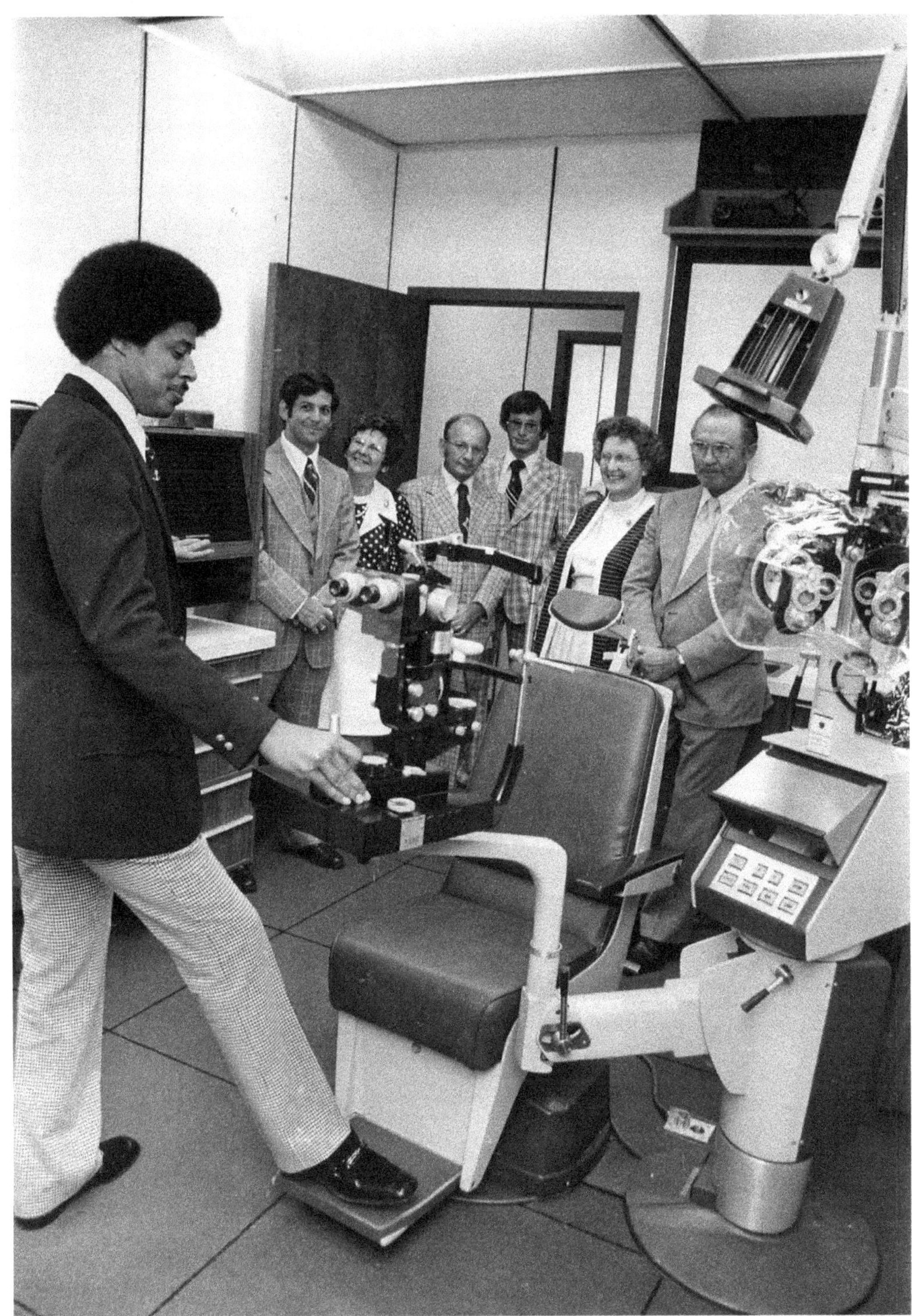

Student Terrence Ingraham demonstrates equipment at the dedication of the optometry building at the University of Alabama at Birmingham. He was the first African-American student to graduate from the optometry program.

Originally located between 20th and 21st Street and 6th Avenue South in 1910, Saint Elias Maronite Roman Catholic Church later moved to its current location on 8th Street and 9th Street South.

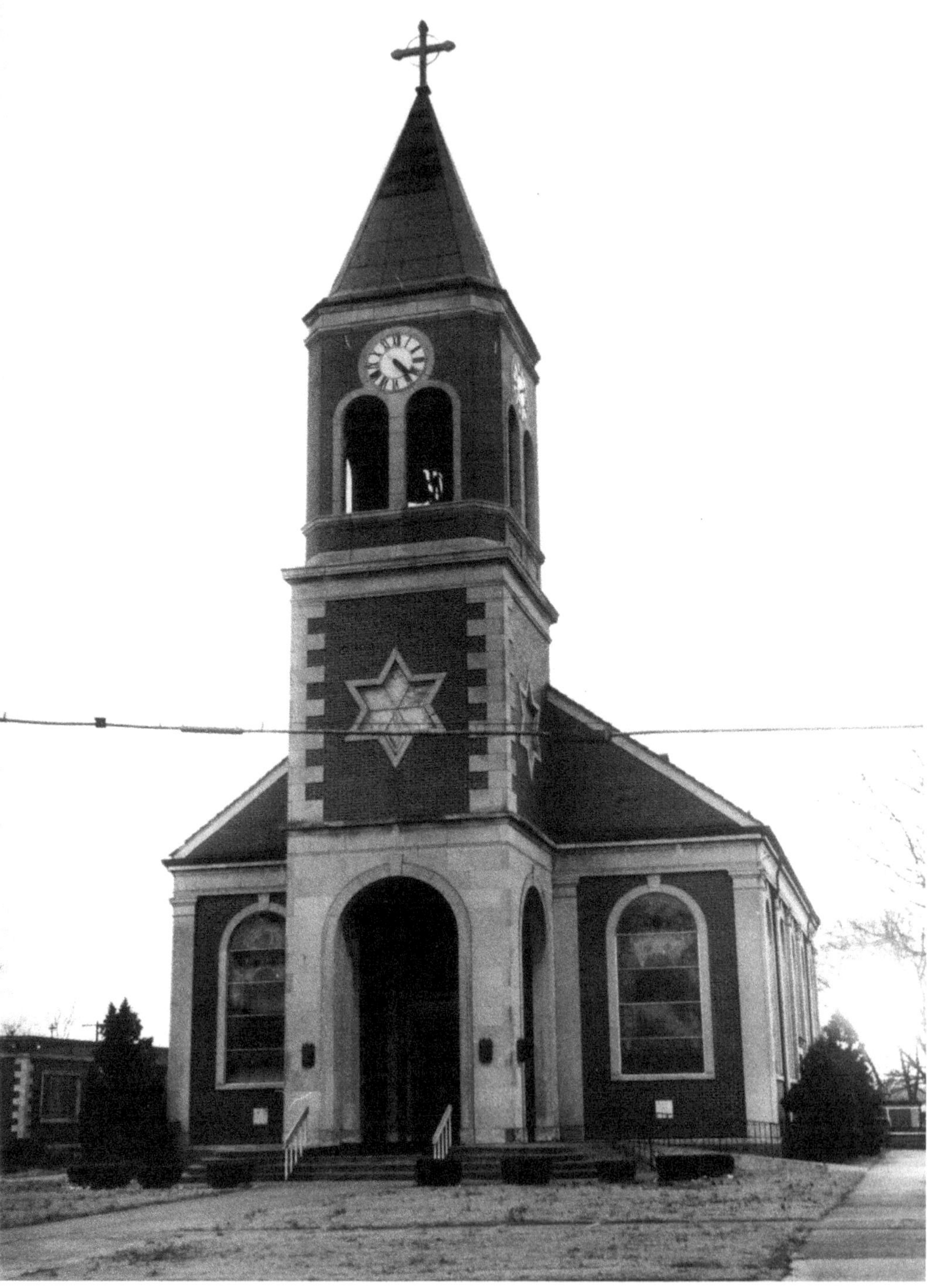

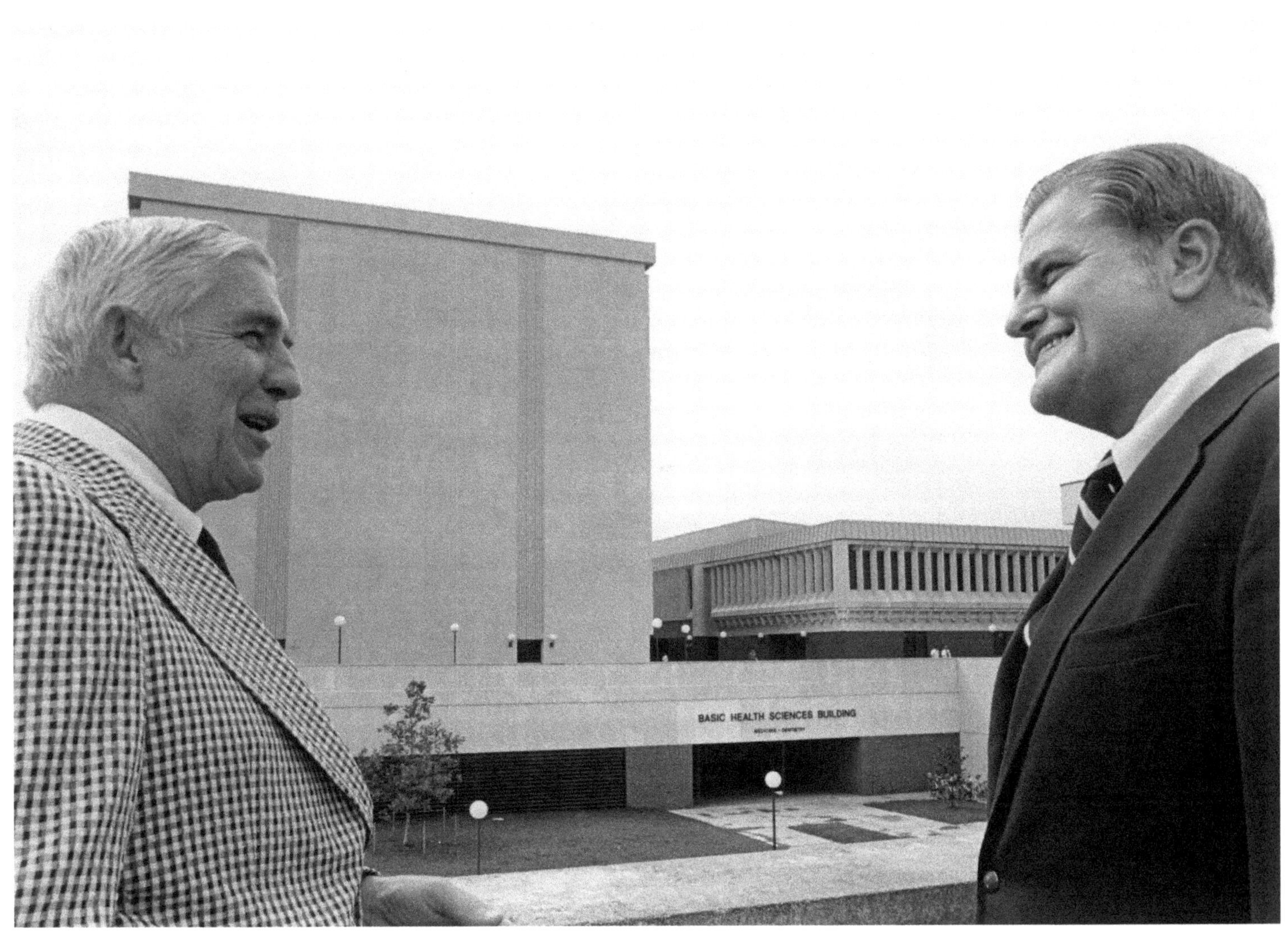

President S. Richardson Hill talks cordially with Chancellor Joseph Volker in 1977 in front of the Basic Health Science building on the campus of the University of Alabama at Birmingham. The building would be renamed Volker Hall to honor the first president of UAB.

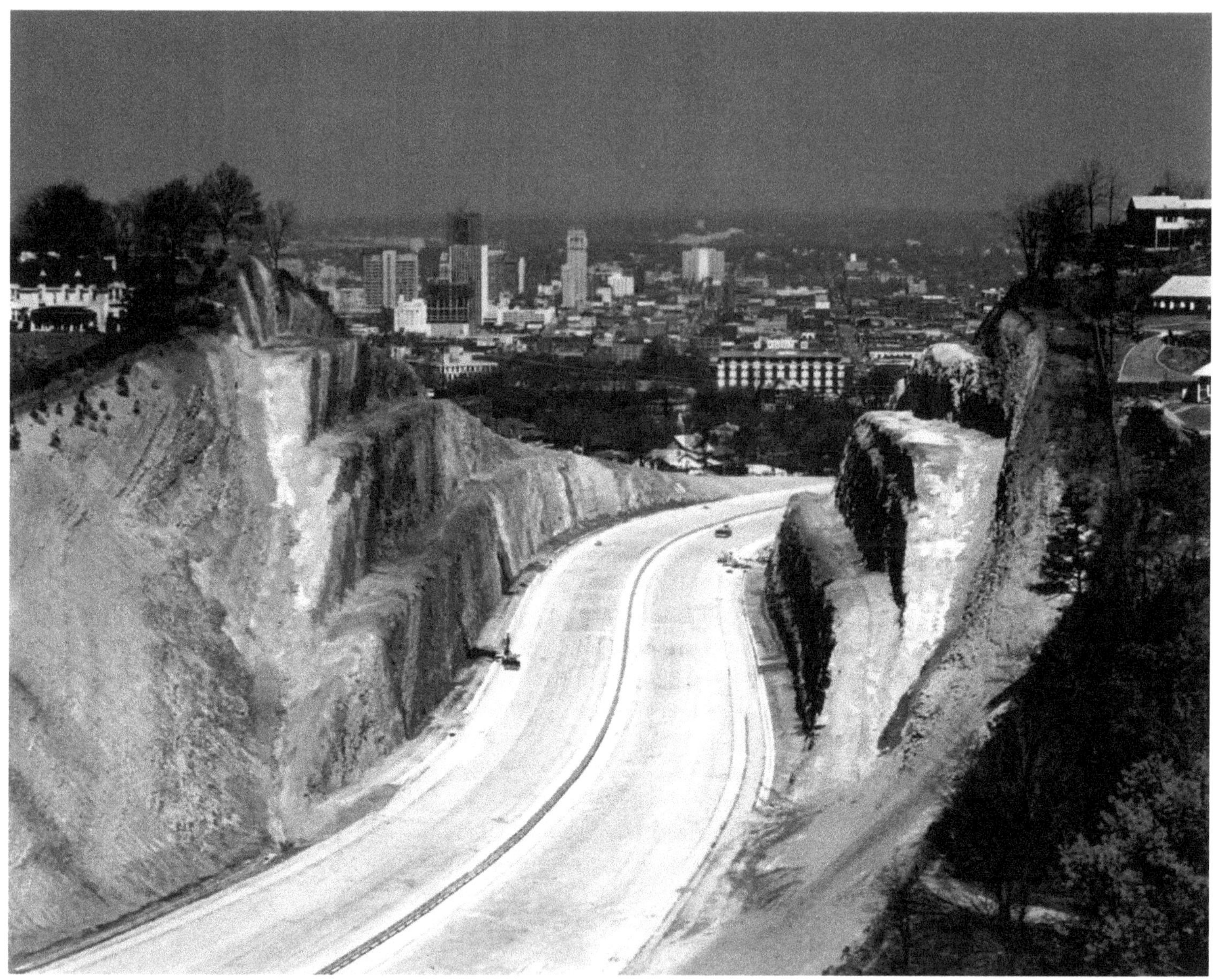

Elton B. Stephens Expressway, also known as Red Mountain Expressway, is shown under construction. The expressway would provide easy access to downtown or an alternative route to avoid downtown altogether. Ultimately, the route aided the rise of suburban neighborhoods.

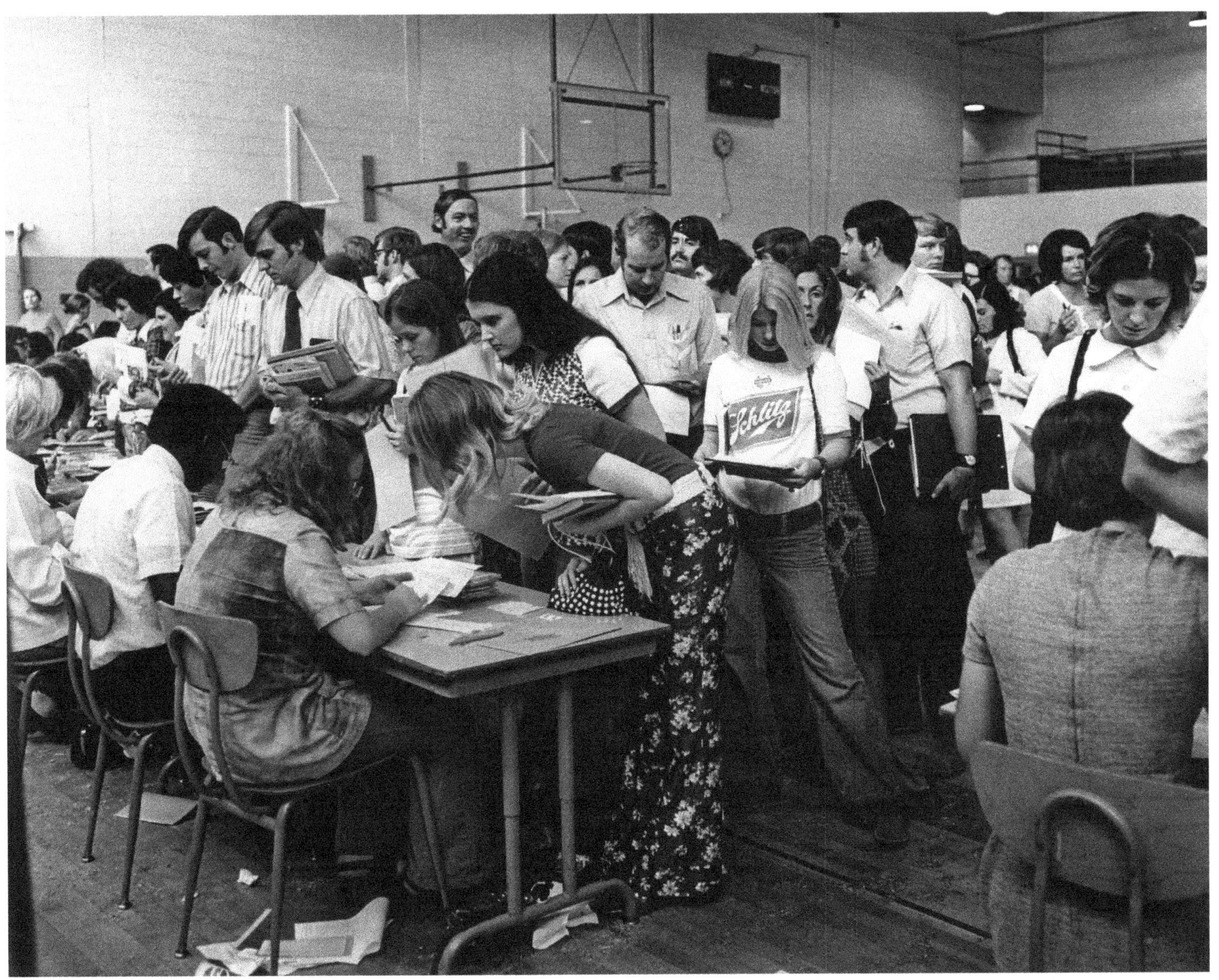

Here in the 1970s, eager students register for classes at the University of Alabama at Birmingham. With college classes now being offered in the city, many of the city's young people chose the local and fairly affordable UAB. The school also attracted a diverse population of students from elsewhere.

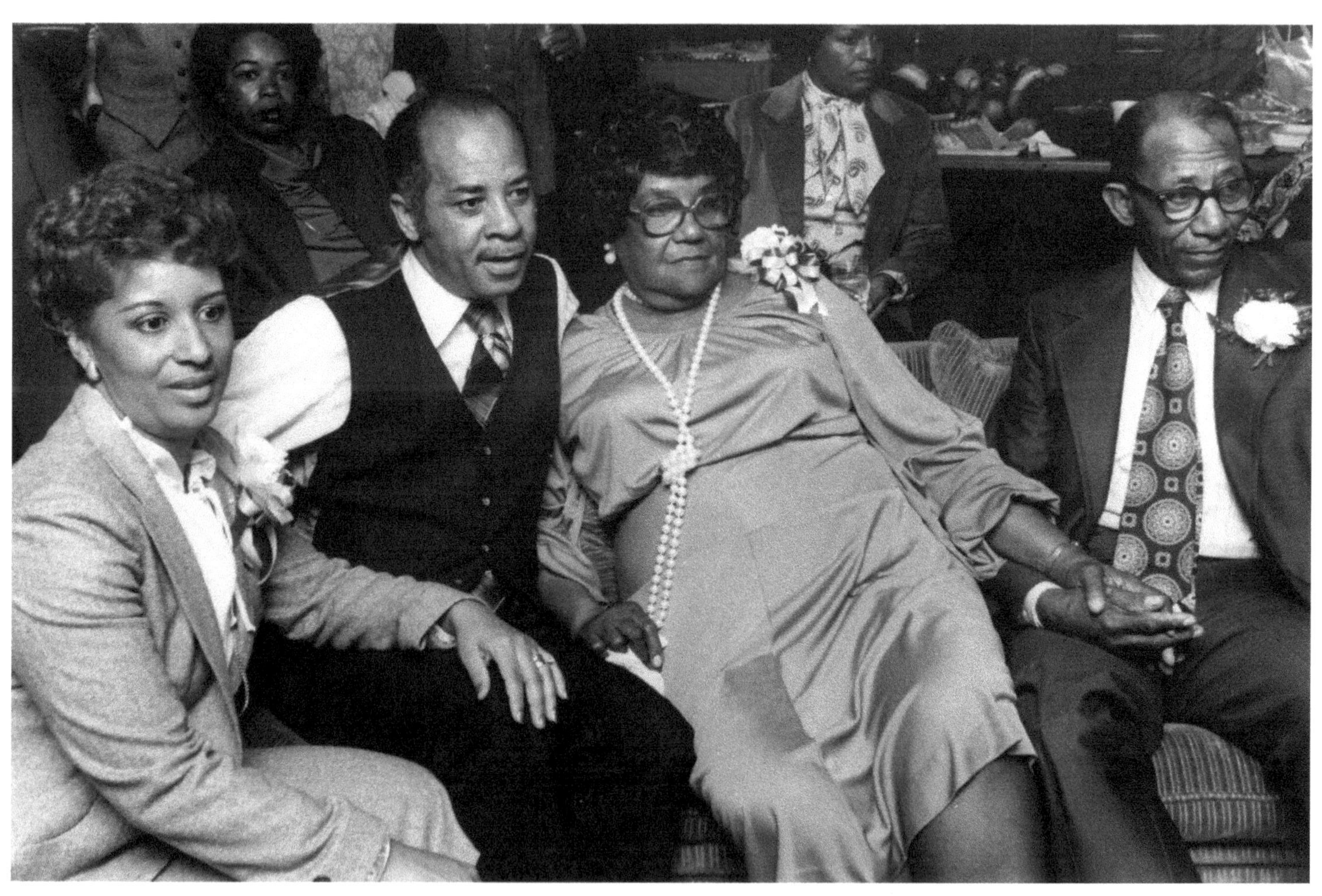

Richard Arrington, Mrs. Arrington, and his parents watch the election results in November 1979. Arrington, a former professor and administrator at Miles College, would win the election to become Birmingham's first African-American mayor.

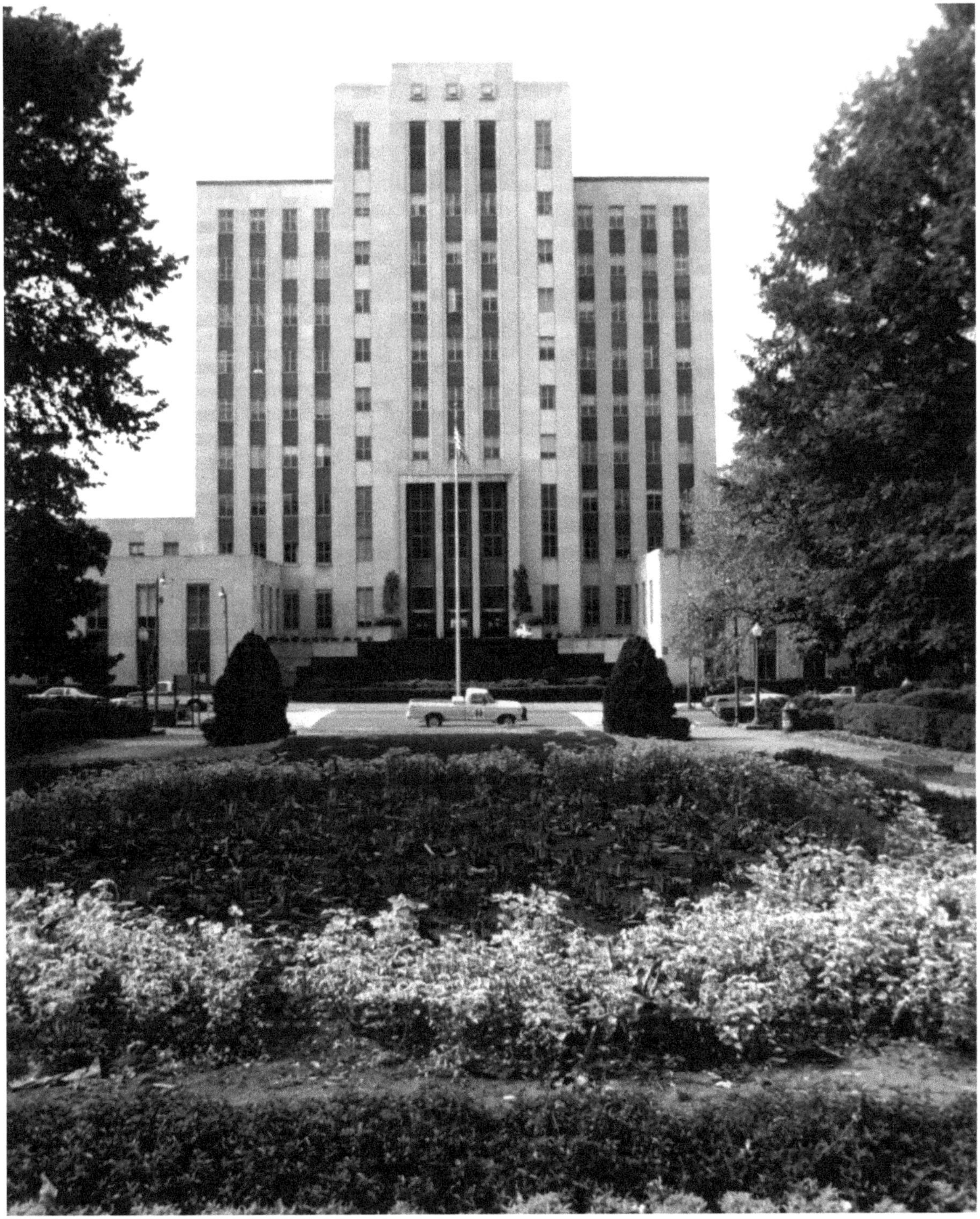

City Hall during the 1970s.

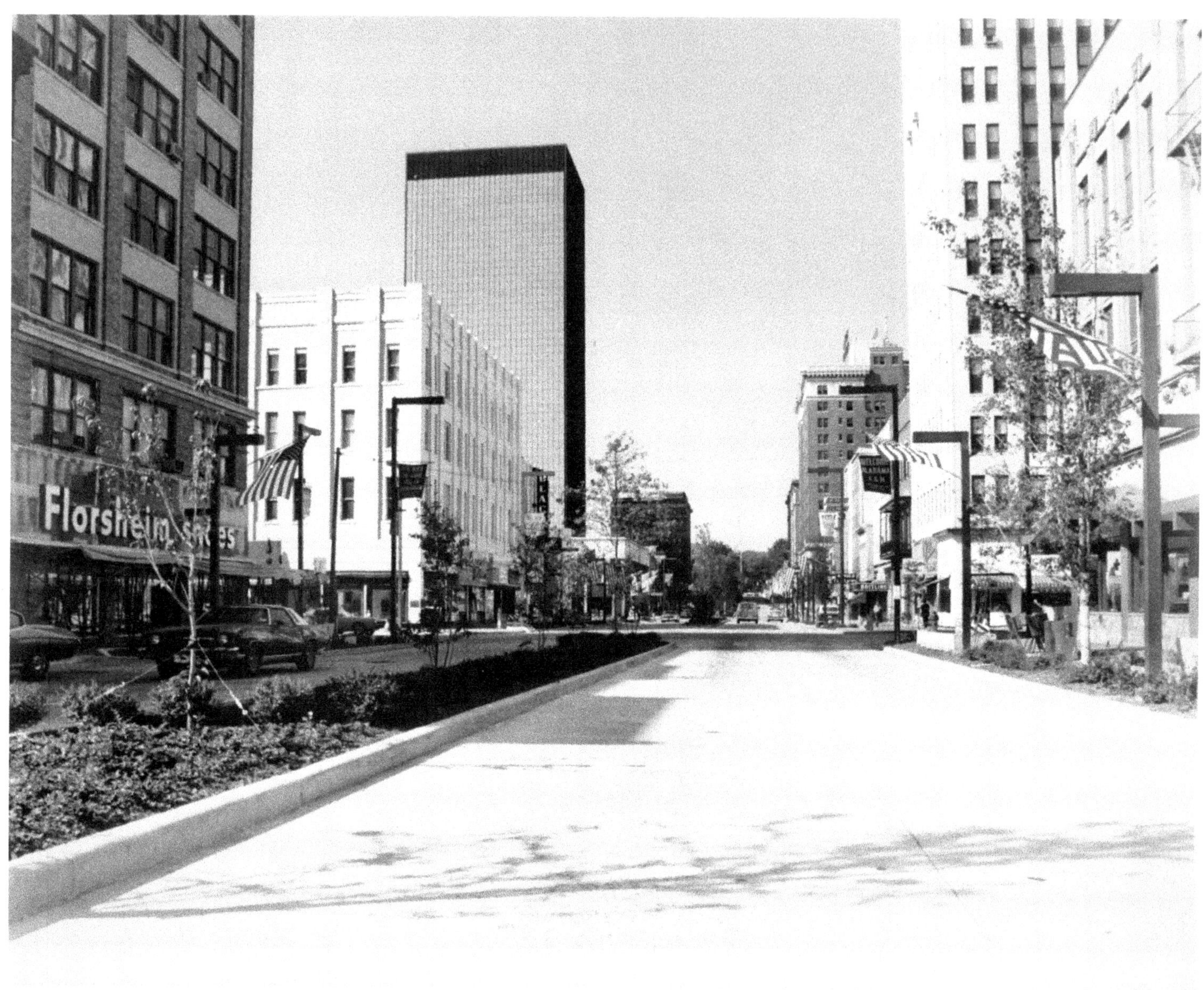

Once a busy street, 20th Street during the 1970s symbolized the dramatic change occurring in Birmingham. With the rise of new suburban neighborhoods made possible by better roads, and with new federal laws that included forced busing of students to poor-quality inner-city schools, many families chose to leave the city's older neighborhoods, a phenomenon taking place in cities across the nation. When customers departed, businesses followed.

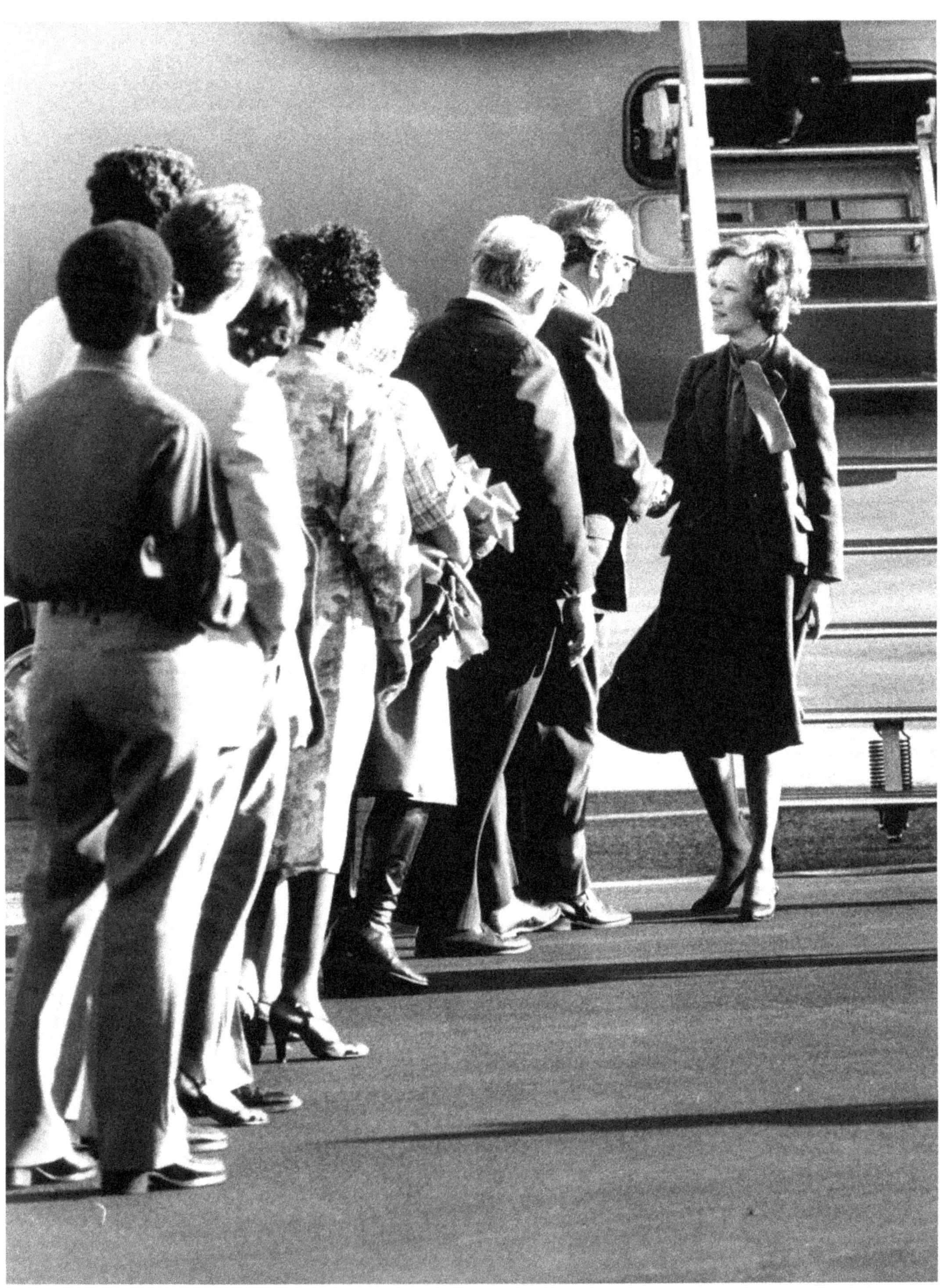

Mayor David Vann and others warmly greet First Lady Rosalyn Carter, who visited Birmingham as part of a campaign tour for her husband, President Jimmy Carter. She held a brief news conference, attended a reception, and spoke at a $100-a-plate fund-raising dinner for Carter's reelection campaign during her five-hour visit to Birmingham on October 8, 1979. Carter's "malaise"-stricken economy and inept handling of the Iranian hostage crisis would help bring Ronald Reagan to the White House in a 1980 landslide election.

Notes on the Photographs

These notes, listed by page number, attempt to include all aspects known of the photographs. Each of the photographs is identified by the page number, photograph's title or description, photographer and collection, archive, and call or box number when applicable. Although every attempt was made to collect all data, in some cases complete data may have been unavailable due to the age and condition of some of the photographs and records.

ii **Panorama with Vulcan**
UAB Archives, University of Alabama at Birmingham
A93-05P-0103
8

vi **A View from Red Mountain**
Birmingham, Ala. Public Library Archives
Cat. # 820.14.16

x **City Hall**
Birmingham, Ala. Public Library Archives
Cat. # 98.5800 A

2 **Ready for Take-off at the Municipal Airport**
Birmingham, Ala. Public Library Archives
Cat. # 98.6761

3 **The Tutwiler Hotel**
Birmingham, Ala. Public Library Archives
Cat. # 98.6758

4 **Eddie Rickenbacker**
Birmingham, Ala. Public Library Archives
Cat. # 98.6160

5 **Sealtest Dairy Delivery Truck**
Birmingham, Ala. Public Library Archives
Cat. # 820.11.43

6 **First Methodist Church**
Birmingham, Ala. Public Library Archives
Cat. # 820.12.38

7 **LaDame Cleaners and the Gilbert Hotel**
Birmingham, Ala. Public Library Archives
Cat. # 820.12.17

8 **The Watts Building**
Birmingham, Ala. Public Library Archives
Cat. # 820.11.26

9 **Businesses on 3rd Avenue North**
Birmingham, Ala. Public Library Archives
Cat. # 820.11.1

10 **Latest Models at Kirksey Motors**
Birmingham, Ala. Public Library Archives
Cat. # 98.6830B

11 **Loveman Joseph & Loeb Delivery Trucks**
Birmingham, Ala. Public Library Archives
Cat. # 98.6799A

12 **Fashion Show at the Tutwiler**
Birmingham, Ala. Public Library Archives
Cat. # 98.6968B

13 **Greyhound Bus Station**
Birmingham, Ala. Public Library Archives
Cat. # 820.11.27

14 **First Avenue North, Early 1950s**
Birmingham, Ala. Public Library Archives
Cat. # 98.7056A

15 **Shriners on Parade**
Birmingham, Ala. Public Library Archives
Cat. # 98.7082

16 **Sloss Furnaces**
Birmingham, Ala. Public Library Archives
Cat. # 98.7126

17 **The 1951 Miss Alabama Pageant**
Birmingham, Ala. Public Library Archives
Cat. # 98.7345B

18 **Miss America Yolanda Betbeze**
Birmingham, Ala. Public Library Archives
Cat. # 98.6479C

19 **Eastern Air Lines Ticket Window**
Birmingham, Ala. Public Library Archives
Cat. # 98.7613

20 **Highland Avenue Shopping Center**
Birmingham, Ala. Public Library Archives
Cat. # 98.6750B

21 **Happy Hal Burns at WBRC**
Birmingham, Ala. Public Library Archives
Cat. # 98.6700C

22 **View from the Martin Building**
Birmingham, Ala. Public Library Archives
Cat. # 820.12.13

23 **The Crippled Children's Clinic**
Birmingham, Ala. Public Library Archives
Cat. # 820.11.18

24 **Miss Alabama Jeanne Moody at the Terminal Station**
Birmingham, Ala. Public Library Archives
Cat. # 98.8024C

25 **Panorama from Red Mountain**
Birmingham, Ala. Public Library Archives
Cat. # 98.9962A

26 **Bird's-eye View**
Birmingham, Ala. Public Library Archives
Cat. # 98.8164A

27 Butler Manufacturing Employees on Diesel
Birmingham, Ala. Public Library Archives
Cat. # 98.8157

28 First Presbyterian Church
Birmingham, Ala. Public Library Archives
Cat. # 820.15.19

29 Pizitz Department Store Decorated for Christmas
Birmingham, Ala. Public Library Archives
Cat. # 98.8549B

30 Miss Alabama 1952, Gwen Harmon
Birmingham, Ala. Public Library Archives
Cat. # 98.8312A

31 Harmon at Terminal Station Bound for Atlantic City
Birmingham, Ala. Public Library Archives
Cat. # 98.8312F

32 Epp's Jewelry Grand Opening
Birmingham, Ala. Public Library Archives
Cat. # 98.8725B

33 Shaver Pontiac Used Cars Showroom
Birmingham, Ala. Public Library Archives
Cat. # 98.8631A

34 Title Guarantee and Trust Building
Birmingham, Ala. Public Library Archives
Cat. # 820.11.47

35 "Happy Wilson" and the "Golden River Boys"
Birmingham, Ala. Public Library Archives
Cat. # 98.8924

36 Birmingham Symphony Performance
Birmingham, Ala. Public Library Archives
Cat. # 98.8856B

37 U.S. Steel Smokestacks
Birmingham, Ala. Public Library Archives
Cat. # 98.9000b

38 U.S. Steel Housing in Ensley
Birmingham, Ala. Public Library Archives
Cat. # 98.9000A

39 Loveman, Joseph & Loeb Annex
Birmingham, Ala. Public Library Archives
Cat. # 820.11.32

40 Krystal Hamburgers
Birmingham, Ala. Public Library Archives
Cat. # 98.9184A

41 Traffice on 1st Avenue North
Birmingham, Ala. Public Library Archives
Cat. # NoAR#(First Avenue North)

42 Alabama Theater 3-D Attraction
Birmingham, Ala. Public Library Archives
Cat. # 98.8928A

43 Alabama Theater 3-D Attraction no. 2
Birmingham, Ala. Public Library Archives
Cat. # 98.9183

44 George Ward's Vestavia
Birmingham, Ala. Public Library Archives
Cat. # 98.9320

45 Dance Hosted by Coca-Cola
Birmingham, Ala. Public Library Archives
Cat. # 98.9369

46 The Scene at Jim Burke Buick
Birmingham, Ala. Public Library Archives
Cat. # 98.9384A

47 Shopping for a New Used Car
Birmingham, Ala. Public Library Archives
Cat. # 98.9384B

48 English Village at Mountain Brook, 1954
Birmingham, Ala. Public Library Archives
Cat. # 98.9544

49 Aerial View of Government Buildings
Birmingham, Ala. Public Library Archives
Cat. # 98.9880D

50 Confederate Memorial Day at Loveman's
Birmingham, Ala. Public Library Archives
Cat. # 98.9834

51 Eastern Air Lines Stewardess
Birmingham, Ala. Public Library Archives
Cat. # 98.9932A

52 Ruhama Baptist Church
Birmingham, Ala. Public Library Archives
Cat. # 820.15.25

53 WABT News
Birmingham, Ala. Public Library Archives
Cat. # 98.10232

54 Ford Thunderbird at Loveman's
Birmingham, Ala. Public Library Archives
Cat. # 820.15.49

55 Robert Smith's "The Club"
Birmingham, Ala. Public Library Archives
Cat. # 98.10333A

56 New Citizens Being Sworn In
Birmingham, Ala. Public Library Archives
Cat. # 98.10327

57 White Christmas in Birmingham
Birmingham, Ala. Public Library Archives
Cat. # 98.10389A

58 Symphony Rehearsal
Birmingham, Ala. Public Library Archives
Cat. # 820.11.20

59 West End Methodist Church After Services
Birmingham, Ala. Public Library Archives
Cat. # 820.11.46

60 The McKesson & Robbins Building
Birmingham, Ala. Public Library Archives
Cat. # 820.11.31

61 The Tutwiler Air-Conditioned
Birmingham, Ala. Public Library Archives
Cat. # 98.10836

62 Pit Fire Charcoal at Pizitz
Birmingham, Ala. Public Library Archives
Cat. # 98.10969

63 Fess Parker as Disney's Davy Crockett
Birmingham, Ala. Public Library Archives
Cat. # 98.10917

64 The American Life Insurance Company Building
Birmingham, Ala. Public Library Archives
Cat. # 98.10835A

65 Jefferson County Courthouse
Birmingham, Ala. Public Library Archives
Cat. # 98.13439

67 Shell Oil Soap Box Derby
Birmingham, Ala. Public Library Archives
Cat. # 98.14001A

68 Alabama Gas Corporation
Birmingham, Ala. Public Library Archives
Cat. # 98.13603A

69 Elephant at Birmingham Zoo
Birmingham, Ala. Public Library Archives
Cat. # 98.14315A

70 **Radio Celebrity Duke Rumore on WSGN**
Birmingham, Ala. Public Library Archives
Cat. # 98.15046

71 **Empire Hotel and the Hotel District**
Birmingham, Ala. Public Library Archives
Cat. # 98.15298

72 **Kirksey Motors on Parade**
Birmingham, Ala. Public Library Archives
Cat. # 98.14319A

73 **Kirksey Motors on Parade no. 2**
Birmingham, Ala. Public Library Archives
Cat. # 98.14319C

74 **Proliferation of Parking Lots**
Birmingham, Ala. Public Library Archives
Cat. # 98.18869

75 **Bobby Darin and DJ Jim Lucas at WSGN**
Birmingham, Ala. Public Library Archives
Cat. # 98.15274

76 **Ramshackle Housing**
Birmingham, Ala. Public Library Archives
Cat. # 98.15377B

77 **Alabama Theater Concessions**
Birmingham, Ala. Public Library Archives
Cat. # 98.15503

78 **Parade of Cars at the Fairground Raceway**
Birmingham, Ala. Public Library Archives
Cat. # 98.15499

79 **The Scene on 20th Street**
Birmingham, Ala. Public Library Archives
Cat. # 98.15825A

80 **A Queue to See Birmingham Native Lili Gentle**
Birmingham, Ala. Public Library Archives
Cat. # 98.15872

82 **Football Benefit at Legion Field**
Birmingham, Ala. Public Library Archives
Cat. # 98.17035A

83 **Rumore's Record Rack**
Birmingham, Ala. Public Library Archives
Cat. # 98.16002

84 **WBRC and Other Businesses**
Birmingham, Ala. Public Library Archives
Cat. # 98.15191

85 **Betty Furness at the Tutwiler**
Birmingham, Ala. Public Library Archives
Cat. # 98.18142

86 **Delta Air Lines Plane Crash**
Birmingham, Ala. Public Library Archives
Cat. # 98.18105A

87 **Shoppers at a Local Grocery**
Birmingham, Ala. Public Library Archives
Cat. # 98.18931

88 **Sledding a Slope**
Birmingham, Ala. Public Library Archives
Cat. # NoAR#SnowDay

89 **Youngsters on Thick Ice**
Birmingham, Ala. Public Library Archives
Cat. # NoAR#SnowDay2

90 **The Alabama Theater Air-Conditioned**
Birmingham, Ala. Public Library Archives
Cat. # 98.18733

91 **Rolling in the Aisle at the Alabama**
Birmingham, Ala. Public Library Archives
Cat. # 98.18714

92 **Tommy Charles WSGN Promotion**
Birmingham, Ala. Public Library Archives
Cat. # 98.19035

93 **Fashion Show at Woodlawn High School**
Birmingham, Ala. Public Library Archives
Cat. # 98.19525

94 **The Stars and Stripes over City Hall**
Birmingham, Ala. Public Library Archives
Cat. # 820.12.53

95 **Skyline View from the Essex House**
Birmingham, Ala. Public Library Archives
Cat. # 820.12.19

96 **L&N Ticket Office**
Birmingham, Ala. Public Library Archives
Cat. # 820.12.20

97 **Downtown at Night**
Birmingham, Ala. Public Library Archives
Cat. # 820.15.39

98 **Campus of Howard College**
Birmingham, Ala. Public Library Archives
Cat. # 820.12.41

99 **Campus of Howard College no. 2**
Birmingham, Ala. Public Library Archives
Cat. # 820.12.42

100 **Campaign for a Giraffe House**
Birmingham, Ala. Public Library Archives
Cat. # 98.19983A

101 **Calder Building Businesses**
Birmingham, Ala. Public Library Archives
Cat. # 820.13.47A

102 **Veteran's Day Parade, 1959**
Birmingham, Ala. Public Library Archives
Cat. # 820.15.63

103 **The Birmingham Teachers Club**
Birmingham, Ala. Public Library Archives
Cat. # 239.3.4.2.6

104 **Roy Rogers and Happy Hal Burns**
Birmingham, Ala. Public Library Archives
Cat. # 98.7508

106 **Britling Cafe on Highland Avenue**
Birmingham, Ala. Public Library Archives
Cat. # 820.14.11

107 **Highland Tower Apartments**
Birmingham, Ala. Public Library Archives
Cat. # 820.14.12

108 **The Protective Life Insurance Company**
Birmingham, Ala. Public Library Archives
Cat. # 98.20621B

109 **Loveman's Soap Box Derby Contestant**
Birmingham, Ala. Public Library Archives
Cat. # 98.20813A

111 **The Ritz Theater**
Birmingham, Ala. Public Library Archives
Cat. # 98.20728

112 **Liberty Supermarket Grand Opening**
Birmingham, Ala. Public Library Archives
Cat. # 98.20972B

113 **Liberty Supermarket Grand Opening no. 2**
Birmingham, Ala. Public Library Archives
Cat. # 98.20972C

114 **Twenty-first Street South**
Birmingham, Ala. Public Library Archives
Cat. # 98.21857B

115 **The Watts Building, 1960s**
Birmingham, Ala. Public Library Archives
Cat. # 820.14.32

116 **Elvis Feature Attraction at the Alabama Theater**
Birmingham, Ala. Public Library Archives
Cat. # 98.21227a

117 **Moonshiners**
Birmingham, Ala. Public Library Archives
Cat. # 854.585.1

118 **Roebuck Shopping Center**
Birmingham, Ala. Public Library Archives
Cat. # 854.719.1

119 **Kings Restaurant**
Birmingham, Ala. Public Library Archives
Cat. # 98.21885B

120 **Rooftop View of Downtown**
Birmingham, Ala. Public Library Archives
Cat. # 854.828.1A

121 **Bank for Savings Construction**
Birmingham, Ala. Public Library Archives
Cat. # 854.828.1B

122 **Gridlocked for Government Metaling**
Birmingham, Ala. Public Library Archives
Cat. # 854.832.1

123 **Rainy Day Street**
Birmingham, Ala. Public Library Archives
Cat. # 854.873.2

124 **First Federal Savings Construction**
Birmingham, Ala. Public Library Archives
Cat. # NoAR#FirstFederalSavingsBldgA

125 **The University Hospital**
UAB Archives, University of Alabama at Birmingham
A94-02P-0104
4

126 **Skyline View from Red Mountain**
Birmingham, Ala. Public Library Archives
Cat. # 820.12.48

128 **Hospitals on 19th Street South**
Birmingham, Ala. Public Library Archives
Cat. # 820.12.35

129 **Downtown Birmingham**
Birmingham, Ala. Public Library Archives
Cat. # 854.917.1A

130 **Bank for Savings Building Completed**
Birmingham, Ala. Public Library Archives
Cat. # 854.917.1B

131 **High School Football Game at Legion Field**
Birmingham, Ala. Public Library Archives
Cat. # 98.22794

132 **Aerial View of Downtown, 1960s**
Birmingham, Ala. Public Library Archives
Cat. # 820.12.5

133 **Mr. Good's Burger "In A Hurry"**
Birmingham, Ala. Public Library Archives
Cat. # 820.13.15

134 **Loveman's After Christmas Sale**
Birmingham, Ala. Public Library Archives
Cat. # 820.13.53

135 **Varsity Drive In Restaurant**
Birmingham, Ala. Public Library Archives
Cat. # 820.13.46

136 **The Parliament House Hotel**
Birmingham, Ala. Public Library Archives
Cat. # 820.14.9

137 **Scene at the Botanical Gardens**
Birmingham, Ala. Public Library Archives
Cat. # NoAR#BotanicalGardensMan

138 **Lunch Counter Sit-in**
Birmingham, Ala. Public Library Archives
Cat. # 827.1.1.6.11

139 **Lunch Counter Sit-in no. 2**
Birmingham, Ala. Public Library Archives
Cat. # 827.1.75

140 **Lunch Counter Sit-in no. 3**
Birmingham, Ala. Public Library Archives
Cat. # 827.1.78

141 **Protesters on Palm Sunday**
Birmingham, Ala. Public Library Archives
Cat. # 827.1.71

142 **State Fairgrounds Custom Auto Show**
Birmingham, Ala. Public Library Archives
Cat. # 98.23120

143 **Installation of Parking Meters**
Birmingham, Ala. Public Library Archives
Cat. # 854.948.1

144 **Studebaker Sales and Service**
Birmingham, Ala. Public Library Archives
Cat. # 98.23223B

145 **WSGN Shriners Parade**
Birmingham, Ala. Public Library Archives
Cat. # 98.233208

146 **Demolition of Board of Education Building**
Birmingham, Ala. Public Library Archives
Cat. # 854.973.1A

147 **Demolition of Board of Education Building no. 2**
Birmingham, Ala. Public Library Archives
Cat. # 854.973.1B

148 **Counter-protesters at Graymont School**
Birmingham, Ala. Public Library Archives
Cat. # 827.2.54

149 **Counter-protest March**
Birmingham, Ala. Public Library Archives
Cat. # 827.2.50

150 **Demonstrators at Police Line**
Birmingham, Ala. Public Library Archives
Cat. # 827.2.43

151 **Protest Line at Graymont School**
Birmingham, Ala. Public Library Archives
Cat. # 827.2.37

152 **Counter-protesters with Signs**
Birmingham, Ala. Public Library Archives
Cat. # 827.2.51

153 **High School Students in Counter Protest**
Birmingham, Ala. Public Library Archives
Cat. # 827.2.21

154 **First Blacks Admitted to White School**
Birmingham, Ala. Public Library Archives
Cat. # 827.2.49

155 **Bombing Investigation**
Birmingham, Ala. Public Library Archives
Cat. # 827.1.1.8.31

156 **Citizens Assembled for Wallace Speech**
Birmingham, Ala. Public Library Archives
Cat. # 827.1.1.10.53

157 **Brother Bryan Memorial**
Birmingham, Ala. Public Library Archives
Cat. # NoAR#BroBryan

158 **Campaign to Save the USS Alabama**
Birmingham, Ala. Public Library Archives
Cat. # 854.1070.1

159 **Aland's Clothing at 5 Points West**
Birmingham, Ala. Public Library Archives
Cat. # 854.1084

160 **WATV Antenna Tower**
Birmingham, Ala. Public Library Archives
Cat. # 820.14.14

161 **A Visit to the Botanical Gardens**
Birmingham, Ala. Public Library Archives
Cat. # 820.14.4

163 **Zoo's Miniature Train**
Birmingham, Ala. Public Library Archives
Cat. # 854.1122.1

164 **Outdoor Symphony Concert**
Birmingham, Ala. Public Library Archives
Cat. # 854.1120.1

165 **Alabama Air National Guard RF-84F Crash Scene**
Birmingham, Ala. Public Library Archives
Cat. # 854.1126.1

166 **Arson Fire at the L&N Warehouse**
Birmingham, Ala. Public Library Archives
Cat. # 854.1123.1A

167 **Arson Fire at the L&N Warehouse no. 2**
Birmingham, Ala. Public Library Archives
Cat. # 854.1123.1B

168 **Top Drill Team in Veteran's Day Parade, 1964**
Birmingham, Ala. Public Library Archives
Cat. # 854.1086.1A

169 **Band in Veteran's Day Parade**
Birmingham, Ala. Public Library Archives
Cat. # 854.1086.1B

170 **Oak Grove High School Band in Parade**
Birmingham, Ala. Public Library Archives
Cat. # 854.1130.1

171 **Hercules Missile in Parade**
Birmingham, Ala. Public Library Archives
Cat. # 854.1130.2

172 **Armed Forces Tank in Parade**
Birmingham, Ala. Public Library Archives
Cat. # 854.1130.3

173 **Joe Namath at Legion Field**
Birmingham, Ala. Public Library Archives
Cat. # 98.24478

174 **Scene at Roebuck Shopping City**
Birmingham, Ala. Public Library Archives
Cat. # 854.1091.3

175 **The American Life Building, 1960s**
Birmingham, Ala. Public Library Archives
Cat. # NoAR#American Life Bldg 4 Ave A

177 **Qwik Mart Treats**
Birmingham, Ala. Public Library Archives
Cat. # 820.15.60

178 **Rainy Day Downtown**
Birmingham, Ala. Public Library Archives
Cat. # NoAR#American Life Bldg 4 Ave B

179 **McDonald's Grand Opening**
Birmingham, Ala. Public Library Archives
Cat. # 820.13.45

180 **Claridge Manor Apartments**
Birmingham, Ala. Public Library Archives
Cat. # 820.12.39

181 **Five Points Shopping at Ensley**
Birmingham, Ala. Public Library Archives
Cat. # 820.12.29

182 **South Highlands Presbyterian Church**
Birmingham, Ala. Public Library Archives
Cat. # 820.14.7

183 **Vine Street Presbyterian Church**
Birmingham, Ala. Public Library Archives
Cat. # NoAR#VineSt155

184 **University Student Protest**
UAB Archives, University of Alabama at Birmingham
A93-12P-1024
5

185 **First National Bank–Southern Natural Gas Building Rising**
Birmingham, Ala. Public Library Archives
Cat. # 820.14.19

186 **Scene at Bus Depot**
Birmingham, Ala. Public Library Archives
Cat. # 820.15.4

188 **Ground-breaking for Classroom**
UAB Archives, University of Alabama at Birmingham
A90-01-0366
3

189 **First National–Southern Natural Building Completed**
Birmingham, Ala. Public Library Archives
Cat. # NoAR#Beck (1st National Bank Southern NaturalBuilding)

190 **Governor Wallace in Wheelchair**
UAB Archives, University of Alabama at Birmingham
A93-05P-0905
2

191 **Implosion of the Tutwiler Hotel**
Birmingham, Ala. Public Library Archives
Cat. # 31.65

192 **Kitty Carlisle at the Town and Gown Theatre**
UAB Archives, University of Alabama at Birmingham
A94-04P-0167
7

193 **Scene at Dedication of UAB Optometry Building**
UAB Archives, University of Alabama at Birmingham
A93-05P-1505
9

194 **Saint Elias Roman Catholic Church**
Birmingham, Ala. Public Library Archives
Cat. # NoAR#StElias

195 **UAB's President Hill and Chancellor Volker, 1977**
UAB Archives, University of Alabama at Birmingham
A93-04-1053
6

196 **Red Mountain Expressway Construction**
Birmingham, Ala. Public Library Archives
Cat. # 1556.29.69

197 **UAB Registration**
UAB Archives, University of Alabama at Birmingham
A93-05P-2070
1

198 **Mayoral Election Results, 1979**
Birmingham, Ala. Public Library Archives
Cat. # NoAR#Richard Arrington

199 **City Hall, 1970s**
Birmingham, Ala. Public Library Archives
Cat. # 1556.24.03

200 **Twentieth Street During the 1970s**
Birmingham, Ala. Public Library Archives
Cat. # 1556.34.81+

201 **Rosalyn Carter in Birmingham**
Birmingham, Ala. Public Library Archives
Cat. # NoAR#Rosalyn Carter

HISTORIC PHOTOS OF BIRMINGHAM IN THE 50s, 60s, AND 70s

Between 1950 and 1979, Birmingham, Alabama, experienced some of the most dramatic growth and change in its history. Booming suburbs, desegregation, the fall of steel and the rise of medical and educational research, a new emphasis on the fine arts, and other changes imparted to Birmingham a radical new look over that thirty-year period.

Historic Photos of Birmingham in the 50s, 60s, and 70s highlights the changes that took place through pictures of busy shoppers, amusing advertising ploys, eager audiences, cultural achievements, towering buildings, influential citizens, new institutions, famous actors, and violent protests and demonstrations.

Nearly 200 photographs, vividly reproduced in black-and-white with captions and introductions, give a clear idea of what the Birmingham landscape and environment was like during these years. This look back is the perfect reminiscence for those who remember the era and an ideal resource for those new to the city who may not.

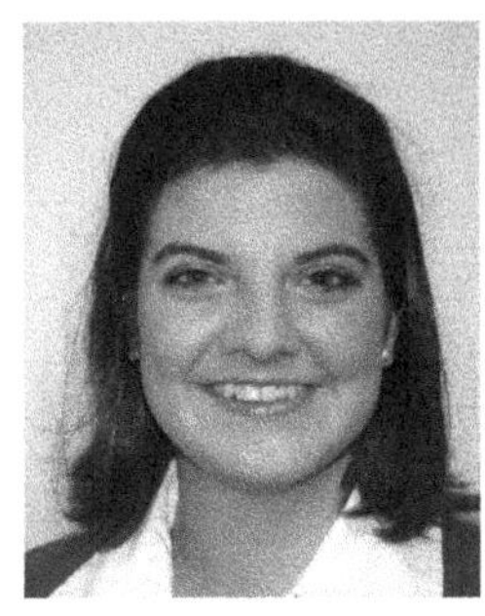

Though born in northwest, rural Tennessee, Jessica L. Barton grew up in Birmingham, Alabama, and has come to consider the city home. An alumna of both Samford University and the University of Alabama, she holds a bachelor of arts degree in history and a masters in library and information studies. She enjoys all things history related, genealogy research, good books, and writing. Currently, Barton is the assistant archivist at Birmingham Public Library Department of Archives and Manuscripts.

WWW.TURNERPUBLISHING.COM

www.ingramcontent.com/pod-product-compliance
Lightning Source LLC
LaVergne TN
LVHW060608110826
845154LV00003B/57

* 9 7 8 1 6 8 4 4 2 1 2 9 9 *